No Place Like Home

WEIMAR AND NOW: GERMAN CULTURAL CRITICISM

Edward Dimendberg, Martin Jay, and Anton Kaes, General Editors

No Place Like Home

Locations of Heimat in German Cinema

JOHANNES VON MOLTKE

University of California Press

BERKELEY   LOS ANGELES   LONDON

The publisher gratefully acknowledges the generous contribution to this book provided by the University of Michigan Department of Germanic Languages and Literatures, the Program in Film and Video Studies, and the Office of the Vice President for Research.

Portions of chapter 1 appeared earlier in different form in Johannes von Moltke, "Evergreens: The Heimat Genre," in *The German Cinema Book*, ed. Tim Bergfelder, Erica Carter, and Deniz Göktürk (London: BFI, 2002), 18–28. Portions of chapter 6 draw on material first published in Johannes von Moltke, "Trapped in America: The Americanization of the *Trapp-Familie*," *German Studies Review* 19.3 (1996): 455–78.

University of California Press
Berkeley and Los Angeles, California

University of California Press, Ltd.
London, England

© 2005 by The Regents of the University of California

Library of Congress Cataloging-in-Publication Data

Von Moltke, Johannes, 1966–
   No place like home : locations of Heimat in German cinema / Johannes von Moltke.
      p.   cm. — (Weimar and now ; 36)
   Includes bibliographical references and index.
   ISBN 0-520-24410-9 (cloth : alk. paper) — ISBN 0-520-24411-7 (pbk. : alk. paper)
      1. Heimatfilme—History and criticism. 2. Motion pictures—Germany—History.   I. Title. II. Series.

PN1995.9.H4V66   2005
791.43'6552—dc22   2004023017

Manufactured in Canada

14   13   12   11   10   09   08   07   06   05
10   9   8   7   6   5   4   3   2   1

Printed on Ecobook 50 containing a minimum 50% post-consumer waste, processed chlorine free. The balance contains virgin pulp, including 25% Forest Stewardship Council Certified for no old growth tree cutting, processed either TCF or ECF. The sheet is acid-free and meets the minimum requirements of ANSI/NISO Z39.48–1992 (R 1997) (Permanence of Paper).

Für Kerstin

Contents

Illustrations

Acknowledgments

Like the many ideas of home that it explores, this book is the result of a long journey. And like the idea of Heimat that it ultimately endorses, this study is merely the crystallization of many intersecting networks that have carried it along. The paths I have traveled have led back and forth across the Atlantic, in and out of different institutional contexts, and through various disciplines. Most importantly, they have been peopled by innumerable guides and fellow travelers who have sustained me over the many years I have spent working on this project. It is a pleasure to finally acknowledge them all and thank them for their support.

This study has some of its roots in the Graduate Program in Literature at Duke University and a few more at the Universität Hildesheim, where I taught my first seminar on the *Heimatfilm*. But it really took shape at the University of Michigan, where an ingrained commitment to interdisciplinary work provided nurturing ground for my exploration of German popular cinema. Both of my home departments—the Program in Film and Video Studies and the Department of Germanic Languages and Literatures—are models of disciplinary coherence and interdisciplinary openness. I thank Gaylyn Studlar and Frederick Amrine for fostering this climate, for their collegiality, and for their unflinching support of this project. I also value the exchanges I have had about the book's topic with colleagues in both units— among them particularly Kerstin Barndt, Ed Dimendberg, Geoff Eley, Julia Hell, Abé Mark Nornes, Helmut Puff, and Scott Spector.

The manuscript could not have been completed without substantial material support in the form of grants, fellowships, and leaves. A Summer Fellowship and Grant from the University of Michigan's Rackham School of Graduate Studies provided an unencumbered writing period in the early stages. A one-year fellowship at the Berlin Program for Advanced German and European Studies allowed me to complete my archival research; the biweekly, highly interdisciplinary colloquia provided a welcome forum for intellectual exchange and helped fuel my writing. The manuscript was completed during a Junior Leave from the University of Michigan. At Michigan, I also thank Rackham and the Office of the Vice President for Research for their fellowship and publication support. For their permission to incorporate in revised version material originally published elsewhere, I thank the editors of *German Studies Review* and the British Film Institute.

I am deeply grateful for the patient assistance I received in various libraries and archives over the years. Rosemarie van der Zee helped me with screenings and copies of production materials even as the Stiftung deutsche Kinemathek was packing up its collection to move to Potsdamer Platz; at the Bundesarchiv-Filmarchiv, Wolfgang Schmidt, Cornelia Okrug, and Ute Klawitter filled screening and research requests for a number of years running; and at the Deutsches Filminstitut–DIF in Frankfurt, Rüdiger Koschnitzky shared his expert knowledge. Andreas Mardersteig, grandson of Peter Ostermayr, kindly opened the vaults of his grandfather's archive, which he maintains in Munich. At the University of Michigan, Phil Hallman indulged even the most far-fetched requests for adding unsubtitled Heimat films to the collection he so brilliantly maintains for the Film/Video Program.

As the manuscript took shape, it began to travel with me. A number of invitations to present my work helped me to focus my arguments and provided stimulating feedback. I am grateful for these opportunities, and thank the organizers and audiences at Harvard University, Deutsches Haus at New York University, Washington University in St. Louis, the Ruhr-Universität Bochum, and the Zentrum für interdisziplinäre Frauen- und Geschlechterforschung at the Technische Universität Berlin. I also remember very fondly the Third Popular European Cinemas Conference (PEC 3) at Warwick, which provided a wonderful context to explore some of the ideas for this project in its early stages. Both at the Universität Hildesheim and the University of Michigan, I had the opportunity to teach seminars on the *Heimatfilm.* I am grateful to the students in both of these classes: alternating between exasperation and enthusiasm, their reactions and contributions went a long way toward convincing me of the continuing relevance of this project. I also owe a particular debt of gratitude to the group of colleagues who come together at the biannual German Film Institute. During the years I have spent working on the question of Heimat, I have come to think of the Institute as a crucial node in the networks in which I move—one of my intellectual "homes," defined, in this instance, by the dedication of its directors Tony Kaes and Eric Rentschler and the indefatigable Gerd Gemünden, by the intensity of the seminar debates, and by the intellectual generosity of its participants. I feel privileged to be working in a field that fosters collegial exchange in such an exemplary way.

This project would not have gotten off the ground without the early support of Geoff Eley, Julia Hell, Fredric Jameson, and Eric Rentschler. It would not have seen the light of day without Rick Rentschler's unflagging support at every step of the way. I value his insightful criticism, have benefited more than once from his encyclopedic knowledge, and am deeply grateful for his encouragement and endorsement at crucial moments. At Michigan, Julia Hell has played an equally vital role as mentor, colleague, and friend. Her enthusiasm for unraveling cultural, theoretical, and historical genealogies through careful analysis is contagious, and I can only hope that some of it carries over from our many conversations and emails into the pages of this book.

Many other friends and colleagues have helped me to formulate and, just as importantly, organize my arguments. I am grateful to Hans-Otto Hügel for spirited conversations in Hildesheim and Berlin as well as for the occasional flea market find by this expert collector. On two different occasions, Dorothee Wierling and Ulrike Weckel sat through *Rosen blühen auf dem Heidegrab* with me and generously shared their historians' perspectives on this horrific *Heimatfilm;* the conversation with Ulrike in particular is ongoing, and I am deeply indebted to her for suggestions and advice. For their comments and criticism at various stages of the book, I also thank Barton Byg, Erica Carter, Gerd Gemünden, Heide Fehrenbach, Noah Isenberg, Tony Kaes, Wolfgang Kaschuba, Lutz Koepnick, Tom Levin, Steven Lowry, Bob Moeller, Dorothea von Moltke, Ralf Schenk, Cliff Simms, and Jackie Vansant (who went far beyond the call of duty to provide me with valuable feedback at a crucial juncture). Both of the readers for the University of California Press offered eminently useful responses that helped to give the manuscript its final shape. At the Press, I am also deeply indebted to Mary Francis for her support of this project, to Jan Spauschus for her careful editing, and to the editors of Weimar and Now for including the book in their important series. My thanks to Paul Dobryden for preparing the index.

Finally, this project has been sustained in myriad material and emotional ways by close friends and family. We would not have managed our year in Berlin with a newborn had it not been for Marion Ebeling and Stefan Bruns, who indulged my work on this book even during some of our many shared vacations. Stefanie Brummer and Jörg Frieß have likewise been a real Berlin lifeline, providing everything from late-night rescues to regular supplies of videos to augment my corpus of films. With their hands on the pulse of

German cinema, they creatively applied the concept of Heimat to the films they came across, often challenging me to rethink my categories. Eggo Müller remains an inspiration in more ways than he knows; I can only hope to emulate his sharp analytical mind, and I treasure his friendship. Ulrike von Moltke's and Konrad von Moltke's unconditional support of my pursuits has always been profoundly enabling.

Even when I was battling deadlines and awaiting reports, Joris had the good-natured confidence that the book would eventually see the light of day. He likes being right, and I'm happy to prove here that he was. Lena's good cheer has likewise been an inspiration ever since she came into the picture. My dearest travel companion on this journey remains Kerstin Barndt. She has moved (with) me through all of this book's many phases, though I know it has often tried her patience. I thank her for her love and support, and for always challenging me to continue reinventing the meanings of home.

Introduction

Locating Heimat

> One would like to dispel the embarrassingly sweet tones that
> are associated with the word *Heimat* and that call forth a rather
> disturbing series of concepts. But they are stubborn, keep close
> to our heels, demand their effect.
>
> JEAN AMÉRY

NO PLACE LIKE HOME

"Repeat after me: there's no place like home . . ." Having just learned that
she already possesses what she has been looking for, Dorothy clicks together
the heels of her ruby slippers and dreamily chants the most famous line
from *The Wizard of Oz* (1939), a film full of memorable sound bites. As the
resolution of the film's dramatic structure, which takes Dorothy away from
home, through Oz, and back again, the words "there's no place like home"
contain the ideological message of the film. They condense its central concern with the meaning of home into a neat, iterable formula. Judy Garland's
delivery of these lines, however, might give us pause. While intended to
drive home the meaning of the phrase for Dorothy, Garland's trancelike repetition of the magic words as she drifts out of Oz and into consciousness has
an unsettling effect. The more often she mumbles the phrase, the more it
turns into a performative device that gets her home but does not tell us anything about home—at least nothing quite as tidy as the famous phrase suggests. For if we pause to consider the meaning of these words in the context
of the narrative they ostensibly resolve (let alone in the historical context
surrounding the film), Dorothy's incantation is remarkably ambivalent.
What does it mean for Dorothy—or Glinda, or the cinema—to insist that
"there's no place like home"?

At first glance, it seems that Dorothy is telling us that no place can rival
the one we call home: this is the place for which she yearns at the end of her
adventures in the land of Oz. At the beginning of the film, Dorothy wants
nothing more than to leave home and its stifling, black-and-white existence
for a place somewhere over the rainbow, "someplace where there isn't any
trouble." In the end, however, she can imagine nothing more comforting

1

than the prospect of return. Home, in this reading, is everything that her adventures have taught her to miss, and *The Wizard of Oz* is a lesson in the values of home, learned on a circular journey through everything that home is not. This is the overt ideological project of the film, summed up in what Salman Rushdie has described, in his wonderful monograph on *The Wizard of Oz*, as the "conservative little homily" at the "cloying ending" of the film.[1] Just before making the final transition back to Kansas, Dorothy spells out her lesson. Asked "What did you learn?" she replies, half in tears: "I think that it wasn't enough just to want to see Uncle Henry and Auntie Em. And it's that if I ever go looking for my heart's desire again, I won't look any further than my own backyard. Because if it isn't there, I never really lost it to begin with. Is that right?"

But as Rushdie reminds us, the notion that there is no place like home is "the least convincing idea in the film."[2] Or perhaps one should say that Dorothy's conservative self-criticism represents the least convincing reading of the spell she is about to cast. For her famous lines accumulate further layers of meaning in the context of the film's diegesis, and this is what makes them so memorable. We only need to take Dorothy's spell at face value to discover how it undermines its own normative design. Contrary to the literal meaning of the phrase, the narration and the famous color scheme of the film provide abundant evidence for the fact that there *is* a place "like" home; as the (dream) site of Dorothy's adventures, Oz is the Technicolor double of the ostensibly unparalleled place called home. For all its yellow-brick roads and red poppies, the expanse of Oz is as vast as the Kansas plains, and the country is peopled by doubles of Dorothy's closest acquaintances, from Miss-Gulch-turned-Wicked-Witch-of-the-West to the farmhand-turned-cowardly-lion. This doubling, or splitting, of home into Kansas as a "negative" (real) place of departure and Oz as its "positive" (fantasized, dreamed) likeness undermines Dorothy's desire to establish home as a singular point of origin and return.

In this respect, *The Wizard of Oz* evokes Sigmund Freud's blurring of the dividing line between home and its other in his famous essay "The Uncanny." Freud's definition of *das Unheimliche* as "that class of the frightening which leads back to what is known of old and long familiar" provides a veritable map to Dorothy's travels from Kansas to Oz and back again.[3] Just as Freud insists that the uncanny always builds on what is known, close by, *heimlich* or *heimatlich*, so does Oz repeat and rework fragments of Dorothy's daily existence in Kansas as material for her colorful dream. When Dorothy steps out of the safety of her house into the uncertain world of Oz, she is evidently scared; the new surroundings are manifestly *unheimlich.* While this permits us to see Oz as Dorothy's dream work of displacement (a reading authorized retroactively by the film's ending), the doubling of Oz for home also suggests that home is ontologically unstable. "Home" and "away," *heimlich* and *unheimlich,* can be more difficult to distinguish than we might have thought. At second glance, then, Dorothy's lines have some unsettling implications. Her belated realization that there is "no place like home" also suggests that home is an unstable concept to begin with, that its ostensible singularity is all too easily reproduced, that it is nothing but an illusion, or (in the most literal-minded reading of the phrase) that it exists only as "no place"—a utopia. What if there really is no clearly defined, unique, and bounded "place like home"? The doubling of Kansas and Oz, of reality and dream world, of *heimlich* and *unheimlich* undermines the ontological connotations of home and forces us to entertain the possibility that any place like home is ultimately a matter of (cinematic) representation. As one of the first films to use the new Technicolor process, *The Wizard of Oz* leads us from the reality of Kansas in black and white through a Technicolor spectacle, inviting us, too, to leave our everyday existence for a more colorful version of home in the cinema. If the metaphorical doubling of the spaces and people that could anchor any feeling of belonging makes home a difficult place to ascertain, if there *is* no place like home, then we might do best to look for it at the movies.

In this book I look at figurations of home in German cinema. I locate those figurations in the images and narratives of the *Heimatfilm,* a genre that for almost a century has circled obsessively around the questions of home and away, tradition and change, belonging and difference inscribed in the German term *Heimat.*[4] Whether we gauge a genre's importance in terms of its popularity, its longevity, or what it can tell us about the specificity of a "national cinema," the *Heimatfilm* deserves pride of place as a persistent presence since the early days of cinema. "If there ever was a real genre that owes its existence to German film history," writes one critic, "it was and is the '*Heimatfilm.*'"[5] Thomas Elsaesser even sees it as "Germany's only indigenous and historically most enduring genre."[6] With its roots in the *Heimatliteratur* of the late nineteenth century, the *Heimatfilm* weathered the sea changes and realignments of German (film) history in the twentieth. It endured by offering variations on the idea that there is "no place like home" in every one of the different cultural and political contexts in which it flourished—from the Wilhelmine Empire to the Weimar Republic; from the Nazi era and the rubble years after World War II to the founding of the Federal Republic in the West and the German Democratic Republic in the East; from the student movement in the late 1960s to the years since unification in 1990. In this book I ask, What have been the defining features of each of these moments in the history of the genre? And how has the *Heimatfilm* negotiated the ever-present threat to the stability of home that Dorothy dreamily articulates at the moment of her return?

NO PLACE LIKE HEIMAT

"My dear friends, allow me to say a few words before I take leave of you . . ."[7] In a rare introspective moment late in the spectacle-driven plot of *Grün ist die Heide* (1951), we are treated to another "conservative little homily" about the value of home, spelled out every bit as explicitly as Dorothy's lesson in *The Wizard of Oz*. This, too, occurs at a moment of imminent departure. Up until this point, we have followed the former landowner Lüder Lüdersen and his daughter, Helga, through the Gevacolor landscapes of the Lüneburg Heath, a picturesque area in Germany's sparsely populated northern plains. Driven from their estate in the eastern region of Pomerania after the war, father and daughter have come to perceive this remote province of the (recently constituted) Federal Republic as their second home (*zweite Heimat*). But the tranquility of that space and the Lüdersens' sense of belonging are profoundly troubled by the father's compulsion to poach in the local woods—a habit that functions as a manifest symptom of his underlying sense of homelessness and displacement. Faced with the consequent prospect of expulsion from the community whose laws he has transgressed, Lüdersen stands up at a lavishly staged local folk festival to deliver his farewell speech.

This address to the locals is representative in several ways, as Lüdersen speaks "not for myself alone, but for the many others who have found a second home here among you"—specifically, we are asked to infer, for the countless displaced Silesians who have flocked to the festival in their traditional dress, or *Trachten*. Lüdersen's speech is representative, furthermore, in its association of Heimat with self-identity and of a second Heimat with a recovered sense of self: "When I was in the forest here, often I felt as if I were at home again. The natural beauty comforted me and made me forget what I have lost. I was close to losing myself. But through the goodwill and understanding you have shown me, I have found myself again." Heimat, Lüdersen impresses on his listeners, is the place beyond alienation and displacement, a space where the unity of the self mirrors the unity of nature.

Lüdersen's speech is representative, too, for the way it articulates a generic logic. Imploring the locals not to be "too hard on the people who have fled to you," Lüdersen locates the lesson of Heimat in the experience of homelessness: "Whoever has not been compelled to leave his home cannot know what it means to be without one [*heimatlos*]." Like most Heimat films, *Grün ist die Heide* clearly locates its notion of Heimat in a binary construction whose second term the films of the genre variously define as exile, as "the foreign" (*die Fremde*), as rootlessness, displacement, or, as in this case, simply as homelessness. In their celebration of Heimat, the films regularly rely on such oppositions in order to stabilize a hierarchy of values and a moral universe that defines Heimat by expelling its various others. In this sense, the happy ending of *Grün ist die Heide* is predictable: Lüdersen's departure to the city is ultimately averted as he manages to rehabilitate himself both morally and, one supposes, in a more therapeutic sense.

However, as I suggest in my detailed reading of this film in chapter 3, Lüdersen's rehabilitation proves to be a rather laborious process, and his poaching corresponds to an obstinate symptom on the generic level as well. Just as his past as an estate owner haunts his present sense of *zweite Heimat*, so does the devalued other or *un-heimlich* represent a continuing challenge to a genre ostensibly constructed to excise that other. Like Oz, the Heimat of the *Heimatfilm* is both a place "like" home for Lüdersen and the Silesian *Landsmannschaft* (the festival is decked out in the symbolic and sartorial signs of the expellees' former home) and its other, a place that threatens Lüdersen's sense of self. In more broadly generic terms, Heimat in the *Heimatfilm* functions in two ways simultaneously: on the one hand, it affords a colorful flight from a reality deemed lacking into an apparently unrelated fantasy world; on the other hand, it serves as a metaphoric displacement of that reality, whose lack remains legible at different levels of the film text. Thus, when Lüdersen invokes his experience of homelessness to eulogize his recovered sense of Heimat, *homelessness* is the privileged term, magnified by the vast number of Silesians who crowd the image as they mill about the festival. Drawing on the ubiquitous sense of displacement in postwar Germany, Lüdersen's pathos-ridden speech suggests that Heimat is constituted by its absence. Homelessness provides a superior epistemological vantage point from which to gauge the meaning of home. In this sense, Lüdersen's lesson relates to Dorothy's: the value of Heimat can only be known by those who have left it. As a *Heimatfilm*, *Grün ist die Heide* circles around the absence of Heimat just as obsessively as it attempts to drive home the manifest meaning of that term by working through the symptoms of homelessness.

Like Dorothy, then, Lüdersen has had to learn the meaning of home by way of a journey or displacement to a foreign place whose laws the traveler must decipher even as that place offers abundant signs of home. To be sure, the Lüdersens' narrative trajectory from Pomerania to their second home in *Grün ist die Heide* is not as circular as Dorothy's dream/journey from Kansas to Oz and back. This has historical reasons, as the territories in the East from which Lüdersen and his daughter fled had been annexed by Russia and Poland in the aftermath of a war that Germany had perpetrated. On the other hand, precisely this historical situation may help to explain why the same logic of departure and return that motivates Dorothy's trip, the sense of finally arriving back home at the close of the film, also underlies Lüdersen's rediscovery of his lost self in the Lüneburg Heath. If the war had foreclosed the actual return of millions of expellees and made various forms of displacement one of the defining experiences of the postwar years, the *Heimatfilm* was ideally suited to providing an imaginary equivalent of return, a promise of settlement. In this respect, among others, *Grün ist die Heide* functions within the specific historical and ideological contexts of the 1950s; indeed, for all its Gevacolor escapism, the film signals the relevance of those contexts at various junctures—whether symptomatically, as in Lüdersen's poaching, or explicitly, as in the staging of the Heimat festival at which Lüdersen gives his farewell speech.

A mass cultural product, the *Heimatfilm* serves to perform "a transformational work on social and political anxieties and fantasies which must . . . have some effective presence in the mass cultural text in order subsequently to be 'managed' or repressed."[8] While the *Heimatfilm*, like the genre of melodrama from which it frequently borrows, has been criticized for such imaginary solutions to real social problems, Lüdersen's poaching serves as a reminder of the often inconclusive nature of these solutions. At the happy end of many of the films discussed in this study, the promise of Heimat still threatens to be eclipsed by the other it sought to exorcise. *Grün ist die Heide* thus shares with *The Wizard of Oz* a profoundly ambivalent figuration of home as a concept.

HEIMAT: NATION, SPACE, MODERNITY

Tracing related figurations of home in *The Wizard of Oz* and *Grün ist die Heide* allows us to see considerable areas of overlap between the cinematic treatments of home on the one hand and Heimat on the other. Although this overlap is central to the arguments advanced in this study—particularly where I draw on discussions of home in recent literature in human geography—it would be misleading to flatly equate the English term with a German word that many commentators have considered untranslatable. For the purposes of the present book, which explores the role of Heimat in German film history, a glance at the concept of Heimat itself is in order.

The notion of Heimat predates not only the invention of cinema, but also its use as a generic term that would define a corpus of literary or filmic works. Indeed, the "genrification"[9] of Heimat in composites such as *Heimatroman* (Heimat novel), *Heimatliteratur*, and *Heimatfilm* initially depended on readers' or audiences' prior familiarity with a whole culture of Heimat that had begun to consolidate by the middle of the nineteenth century. Not yet codified as a literary genre, this culture initially found expression in the writings of the romantics as well as in political discourse surrounding German regionalism and nationalism. In the emergent popular culture of the nineteenth century, it also formed the focus of the preservationist activities of *Heimatkundler* (local historians) and of entire *Heimatbewegungen* (Heimat movements) which dedicated themselves to embellishing, defending, and extolling the virtues of local landscapes, communities, and customs (eventually putting them on display at the local *Heimatmuseum*).[10] Around the turn of the previous century, Heimat also served as the rallying cry for a conservative revolution in the name of *Heimatkunst* (Heimat art), which advocated an antimodernist, pastoral aesthetics and an antiliberal, nationalist notion of rootedness.[11] In each of these cultural spheres, the term *Heimat* acquired multiple meanings, ranging from conservationist to utopian, from regionalist to nationalist, and from populist to elitist. To engage in the burgeoning discourse on Heimat could entail anything from formulating a new law (e.g., the *Heimatrecht* of the 1820s) or petitioning for more local independence from state government, to penning a sentimental poem or drafting new regional maps, to founding journals with titles like *Heimat* (1900) or *Hochland* (1903), to joining a group of city dwellers for a day hike in the Pfälzerwald. While each of these diverse activities drew on the same term for inspiration and definition, each gave the notion of Heimat a particular spin, leaving us with a dizzying set of meanings. The multiple rebirths of Heimat over the twentieth century have only added to this polysemy. Virtually interchangeable with a racially defined concept of nation during the Third Reich, the notion emerged as a rallying cry for millions of displaced persons reclaiming a "right to Heimat" in the postwar years. It was redefined in line with the social and ecological ideals of the Green Party in the late 1970s, and more recently it has come serve as a trope for identity politics in an increasingly multicultural society.

In the introduction to his well-known lexicon *Keywords*, Raymond Williams defines the object of that book as defining a representative vocabulary, "a shared body of words and meanings in our most general discussions . . . of the practices and institutions which we group as *culture* and *society*."[12] For almost two centuries, the German term *Heimat* has been precisely such a "keyword." It is a notion that has galvanized popular movements and popular audiences, while also attracting scholarly attention from anthropologists, ethnographers, historians, political scientists, sociologists, and film scholars, to name only a few.[13] As Anton Kaes has pointed out, the term is now burdened with emotional connotations almost to the breaking point; Kaes lists among its multiple referents the site of one's lost childhood, of family, and of identity; an unalienated, precapitalist mode of production; romantic ideals of the relationship between country dweller and nature; and "everything that is not distant and foreign." Like no other word, Kaes argues, "*Heimat* encompasses at once kitsch sentiment, false consciousness, and genuine emotional needs."[14] In other words, this keyword has come to accumulate so many meanings—ranging from the mundane to the religious, from the reactionary to the progressive, and from the specific to the unimaginably vague—that it has become difficult to conceive of a lexicon entry that could even begin to claim exhaustive treatment of its function in "the practices and institutions which we group as culture and society."[15] To be sure, the longevity of *Heimat* as a keyword has much to do with this semantic flexibility. One of the defining characteristics of the word may be its adaptability to different contexts. On the other hand, such flexibility poses serious problems for any attempt to pin down its meaning. Consequently, the following remarks on the relation of Heimat to nation, space, and modernity do not pretend to offer an exhaustive definition of the term. Rather, they constitute an attempt to chart some paths on the terrain of Heimat that I consider of particular relevance to the generic logic of the *Heimatfilm*.

Among these paths, the most promising have been explored by historians. Two recent studies of the German idea of Heimat stand out as providing concrete historical material in which to anchor the elusive referentiality of the term. To provide such an anchor is, indeed, Celia Applegate's explicit goal for her groundbreaking study of the meanings of *Heimat* in the Rhineland-Palatinate, a region bordering the Rhine in southwestern Germany. "Instead of generating more definitions for a word that has collected so many," she argues, we should "investigate the history of the word itself." That investigation centers not merely on the bounded region of the Palatinate, but on the use of *Heimat* in larger social and geographical contexts, reaching from alignments and conflicts with neighboring Bavaria to the continued concern with the issue of nationhood. The history of Heimat, Applegate concludes, "means the history of a certain way of talking and thinking about German society and Germanness."[16] Consequently, both Applegate's book and Alon Confino's equally compelling study of the Heimat idea in Württemberg (which borders the Pfalz) devote considerable attention to the ways in which regional activities, politics, and culture invoked a larger national whole. A historically grounded approach to Heimat thus mandates, first, that we consider the relation between Heimat and Germanness, or between the local and the national.

Applegate demonstrates how local associations emerged in the late nineteenth century to carry the idea of Heimat and turn it into a spatial concept that would mediate between the regional and the national. Heimat functioned as a galvanizing notion that reconciled a local world with the larger, more impersonal, national sphere.[17] Historically, that mediation took diverse forms, ranging from an insistence on the specificity of the region against the encroaching demands of the nation-state, to the clear alignment of *Heimat* with *nation* in World War I, to the conflation of the two terms under Fascism. Although these uses of *Heimat* all differed significantly in terms of their political implications for personal, regional, and national identity, the historical persistence of the term highlights the continuing need to articulate the links that mediate between the individual and the nation. As Applegate puts it, "The survival and transformation of *Heimat* reveal to us the struggle to create a national identity out of the diverse materials of a provincially rooted society."[18]

This is where Alon Confino picks up with his reading of Heimat as a "local metaphor" for the nation. Going one step further than Applegate in linking the local with the national, Confino argues that imperial Germany saw the transformation of the idea of Heimat into "an actual representation of the nation." Thus, the peculiarities of local life, as expressed for example in Heimat histories, Heimat postcards, or in the burgeoning Heimat museums across the country, all began to function not only as mediators but also as metaphors and memory for the young German nation as a whole. In this process, representations of locality, region, and nation became interchangeable, forming the basis of an "imagined community" in the minds of Germans. This is not to say that the singularity of local identity was entirely erased or subsumed under concepts of nation, state, or *Volk*. Rather, Heimat facilitated a double view of the local as possessing both a concrete experiential dimension and a more abstract metaphorical function. "Heimatlers," as Confino calls those who propagated this view, "shared the belief in the singularity of local identity and in the capacity of the Heimat idea to represent the singularity and to reconcile it with a notion of Germanness."[19]

Both Confino and Applegate investigate the meaning of Heimat within concisely defined regional contexts, and for good reason: whether we choose to view Heimat as a mediator between the local and the national with Applegate, or as a local metaphor for the national with Confino, the history of this idea involves a particular conceptualization of local space, which can then be related in various ways to a larger whole. Contemporaneous with the founding of the German nation as a unified territory in 1871, the idea of Heimat emerges as an effort to negotiate the abstract concept of the nation in terms of spatial presence. To investigate the notion of Heimat in any of its numerous historical contexts thus involves, second, detailed attention to the characteristic modes of spatiality that define Heimat.

The spatial dimension clings to the semantics of Heimat in virtually all of its historical variants. Heimat "refers to a relation between human beings and space."[20] Though some have emphasized the temporal dimensions of Heimat—whether as memory, as invented tradition, or as an ideal to be realized in the future[21]—an understanding of the particular spatiality of Heimat is necessary to any definition of the term and its attendant practices. Whether one thinks of it as the place of one's childhood, as an elective place of belonging (as suggested by the notion of a *zweite Heimat*), whether it is taken to signify a local, regional, or national territory, or whether it serves to evoke the future or past as a different country, Heimat "aims at a spatial relation," as Hermann Bausinger suggests: "Though it may not be possible to delimit Heimat with any precision, it can be located in space."[22]

How, then, do we define the space of Heimat? What attributes have been taken to characterize Heimat spatiality? A dictionary entry for *Heimat* from 1959 offers a useful point of departure, even though it reduces the polysemic nature of the term to an ostensibly "original" sense. According to this definition, Heimat is to be found wherever people "privilege a small world, which nonetheless encompasses a totality of life [*Lebensganzheit*], and where they perceive any other world as a more or less hostile 'foreign territory' [*Fremde*]."[23] Emphasizing the relationship between space and the capacity of an individual to experience and know space, the author goes on to assert that "the world of Heimat is necessarily small, for only then can it be experienced completely and be open to that complete familiarity in which humans can take comfort in being at home [*beheimatet*]." An earlier influential treatise defined Heimat as "personally lived space."[24] Such definitions of *Heimat* stress its immediacy, its availability to individual experience as a defining element. The geographical scope of Heimat is limited by the ability of humans to experience their surroundings as familiar. In addition, such definitions emphasize the role of an outside against which that small world can be defined. The place of Heimat encompasses everything that is *not* beyond its narrowly defined boundaries. The localism of Heimat, its emphasis on experience, presence, and delimitation suggest that we think of it as place, as a limited terrain that affords its inhabitants respite and protection from incursions originating in the more intangible and abstract spaces beyond its boundaries. As Confino puts it, "Whether through vocabulary changes or through Heimat organizations, Heimatlers attempted to transform the impersonal nation into something manageable, intimate, and 'small.' "[25]

This notion of place found a historically and, some would argue, nationally specific representation in the idea of Heimat. But it is by no means limited to the German context. The spatial dimension outlined in the above definition alerts us to the broader geographical implications of the term. A human geography of Heimat maps onto other definitions of place in terms of limitation, enclosure, familiarity, or even purity. It relates to historical and contemporary examples of exclusive social spaces and practices of "spatial purification," which David Sibley traces through the concepts of home, locality, and nation in *Geographies of Exclusion*. Similarly, many recent discussions of migration and the transnational flows of capital and information have emphasized the retreat to the regional and the resurrection of local boundaries as the corollary of globalization.[26] In the European context, trends towards multiculturalism and the expansion of the European Union have been accompanied by defensive rhetorics and policies designed to fortify the boundaries of "Fortress Europe."[27] Doreen Massey, in her sophisticated critique of the relations between space, place, and gender, has traced exclusionary formulations of place not only in some scholarship on human geography, but also in the emergence of certain kinds of nationalisms, in the marketing of places for investment or tourism, in new urban enclosures, and even in the liberal or leftist rhetorics used to defend particular communities against yuppification. In Massey's useful critical gloss, the notion of place invoked in each of these cases is associated "with stasis and nostalgia, and with an enclosed security." She describes scholarly contributions in human geography that espouse such definitions of place as so many "attempts to fix the meaning of places, to enclose and defend them: they construct singular, fixed and static identities for places, and they interpret places as bounded enclosed spaces defined through counterposition against the Other who is outside."[28]

The nostalgia that Massey identifies in such definitions of place derives from their implicit call for a return to earlier modes of spatiality. They posit a lost sense of place that was allegedly uncomplicated by the complexities of more recent—which is to say modern and postmodern—spatial forms. Like many definitions of Heimat, these conceptualizations of place can be characterized as antimodern and reactionary in the literal sense that they react to the ongoing redefinition of space in modern and postmodern geographies, a process that David Harvey has outlined in terms of the "*compression* of our spatial and temporal worlds."[29] However, where Harvey and other recent commentators have largely tied the effects of time-space compression to the post-Fordist and postmodern dimensions of globalization, closer attention to the spatiality of Heimat serves as a reminder of the modern origins of time-space compression, which Harvey also outlines. Consequently, in tracing the spatial logics of Heimat as an antimodern "attempt to get a grip on the modern world and make [oneself] at home in it,"[30] I draw on recent discussions of place and space such as Harvey's. However, where these discussions have been framed by debates on postmodernism,[31] I adopt a longer view of modernization as a framework that encompasses not only the development of the Heimat idea and the rise of cinema, but also earlier—but not always qualitatively different—forms of the time-space compression more recently diagnosed for the postmodern.[32] As an example, we might compare the telephone and the internet as the emblematic communications technologies of modernity and postmodernity, respectively. Though there are clear technological differences between the two modes of communication, they share a crucial spatial feature that marks them both as modern if we assume a paradigm of "reflexive modernization": both cancel out spatial contiguity as the precondition for instantaneous communication. Like the acceleration of communication, changes in transportation technology, increases in mobility, migration and deterritorialization, urbanization and other spatial transformations date back to the nineteenth century, not just to the 1960s. The spaces of Heimat, I argue, are sites that register these transformations. A third prerequisite for any historically informed discussion of Heimat should thus be to avoid simply reproducing the antimodern rhetoric of Heimat as place, and to pay close attention instead to the place(s) of Heimat in modernity.

Anthony Giddens has provided a particularly useful framework for describing the modern redefinition of spatial regimes, which he describes as a progressive "emptying of space."[33] One of the consequences of modernity, Giddens claims, consists in the fact that "the very tissue of spatial experience alters, conjoining proximity and distance in ways that have few close parallels in prior ages": "The advent of modernity increasingly tears space away from place by fostering relations between 'absent' others . . . . In conditions of modernity, place becomes increasingly *phantasmagoric:* that is to say, locales are thoroughly penetrated by and shaped in terms of social influences quite distant from them. What structures the locale is not simply that which is present on the scene; the 'visible form' of the locale conceals the distanciated relations which determine its nature."[34] In light of such definitions of modernity, it is easy to see the characteristically antimodern impetus fueling nostalgic definitions of *place* and *Heimat*. Against urbanization, such definitions wish to reclaim the romantic solitude of the countryside; against the increase of speed and mobility, or time-space compression, they advocate the longer rhythms of nature and a traditional, static sense of place; against modern forms of "disembedding"—defined by Giddens as the " 'lifting out' of social relations from local contexts of interaction and their restructuring across indefinite spans of time-space"[35]—many definitions of *Heimat* and *place* insist on the spatial horizon of *Gemeinschaft* as structured exclusively through local relations among family members, neighbors, friends, or members of a congregation, for example.[36]

Such definitions of Heimat and place play a central role in the history of the *Heimatfilm*. However, in tracing the antimodern impetus of Heimat and of its spatial dimensions in particular, I am ultimately interested in unraveling the often contradictory cinematic construction of Heimat as a refuge from modernity. Those contradictions remain unresolved, I argue, as long as Heimat is grounded in strictly binary notions of the local as opposed to the foreign, or place as opposed to space, or tradition as opposed to modernity. Unless we question the function of these binaries within the history—and the genre—of Heimat, we are bound to reproduce the contradictory and often reactionary logics of the discourse and of the cinematic practices we have set out to analyze. By contrast, a more dialectical view of these oppositions, which insists on the ways in which their terms are mutually contingent on one another, provides a useful framework in which to account for the *function* of Heimat within modernity, within the cinema.

For this purpose, we must trouble, first, the localism of Heimat, according to which "authentic social existence is, or should be, centered in circumscribed places."[37] In his critique of such localisms in anthropological literature, James Clifford has argued that "human location [is] constituted by displacement as much as by stasis."[38] Such a view is echoed as well in recent work in human geography and in cultural studies on the interpenetration of the local and the global, inside and outside, place and space.[39] It plays a crucial role in Applegate's discussion of Heimat as a mediator between the national and the local. In this respect, it would be misleading to define Heimat solipsistically as a territory organized towards the inside and excluding any consideration of the spaces beyond its reach. On the contrary, the historical purpose of Heimat in the late nineteenth century was precisely to articulate the link between inside and outside on the level of lived, local experience. Those who created and promoted Heimat with the advent of modernity and the nation-state, Applegate points out, "were suggesting a basic affinity between the new, abstract political units and one's home, thus endowing an entity like Germany with the emotional accessibility of a world known to one's five senses."[40]

Second, as I have suggested, we need to remain attentive to the dialectical construction of Heimat in its appeal to premodern traditions. Though recognizable as a desire (whether reactionary, antimodern, or utopian), the implicit longing to return to earlier spatial forms may have no grounding in historical reality. Where the space of Heimat promises to satisfy such longings, it tends to function as an invented tradition. In their well-known discussion of the invention of tradition, Eric Hobsbawm and Terence Ranger have emphasized the modern origins of such traditions. By no means confined to so-called traditional societies, they represent post-traditional ways of constructing usable pasts for a modern present.[41] Heimat, a modern concept "of dubious antiquity" (Applegate), functions according to precisely this logic. Having originated in a period of rapid social transformation, Heimat amounts to a modern notion of tradition, offering a nostalgic view of place. In other words, solipsistic and romantic views of Heimat as place fail to account for the factors that have always shaped that place from outside as much as from within. Their antimodern rhetoric elides the degree to which the place of Heimat has itself been formed historically by the processes of modernity. As David Morley warns, "We are perhaps bedeviled by too stark a contrast between the realm of the traditional and that of the modern, which are often understood as being opposed to each other as stasis is to mobility."[42] This study replaces the habitual treatment of *Heimat* and *Fremde* in binary terms with a more dialectical perspective that allows us to see the mutual interdependence of the two terms, most famously spelled out in Freud's study of the uncanny.

Here, again, Applegate's and Confino's studies prove invaluable. Taking care not to equate the antimodern rhetoric of a few Heimat definitions with the function of the Heimat idea in German history, they amass ample evidence for the imbrication of that idea with various processes of modernization. Beginning with the "essential modernity" (Applegate) of the Heimat statutes of 1825, which tied the right to Heimat (*Heimatrecht*) not to local tradition but to citizenship, the idea of Heimat served to negotiate, rather than simply keep at bay, the modernization of social, economic, and political life in Germany. Heimatlers clearly recognized the moral and use value of local tradition, which they were quick to sell in an emergent tourist market.[43] The modern character of Heimat was also reflected in a selective embrace of the changes associated with modernization. As Applegate puts it, the nostalgia of the Heimat movement for older ways of life and smaller communities "could go hand in hand with an enthusiastic receptivity to present glories, to big, vital cities, to technological wonders and, most of all, to national prestige."[44] Even Friedrich Lienhard, a staunch defender of the reactionary *Heimatkunst* of the turn of the century, claimed in an article devoted to that topic, "We do not wish an escape from the modern, but a *through* [*ein Durch*], a *complement* [*eine Ergänzung*], a broadening and deepening to the human side."[45] Such writing certainly anticipates the "reactionary modernism" that Jeffrey Herf has found in the work of Ernst Jünger and in the Fascist discourse on modernity.[46] But it also serves as a reminder of the historical links between Heimat and modernity. To illustrate that connection, Confino cites a striking passage from a 1914 book on the Heidenheim district in Württemberg. Entitled *Unsere Heimat aus alter und neuer Zeit* (Our Heimat in the Past and Present), the book describes the small town of Giengen an der Brenz. The author explicitly welcomes the fact that progress and increased prosperity are not confined to the cities but have begun to reach the provinces as well, pointing to advances in communication, transportation, and even an "airship hangar and aviation center" about to be built in Heidenheim. Rather than the tranquility of the Black Forest or a picturesque village nestled in the mountains, it is the prospect of a canal connecting the Neckar with the Danube that unleashes the author's unbridled enthusiasm for the future of his Heimat: "New jobs will be created, new factories will be established. Some old things will disappear and new life will flourish out of the ruins. Our times, to be sure, never halt."[47] As Confino points out, the reigning interpretation of Heimat as "wholly antimodern, as a conservative idea that idealized the rural past and ignored modern reality" has until recently excluded consideration of passages such as these.[48] What emerges once one begins to focus on such prose is a driving impulse at the heart of the Heimat movements to reconcile not only the local and the national, but also tradition and modernity. In the fairly modern-sounding words of the Regional Committee for Nature Conservation and Heimat protection of Württemberg, this meant that "Heimat protection and nature conservation mean to harmonize the challenges of progress and the preservation of Heimat's individuality, beauty, remarkableness, and venerableness."[49] In view of such formulations, definitions of Heimat as simply antimodern are inadequate. The point is, rather, to recognize the dialectics of Heimat which, as a reaction to modernization, "both glorified the past and celebrated modernity.... The Heimat idea—

combining an attraction to and celebration of progress with an anxiety over technological change, and a yearning for a past of putative wholeness and authenticity—seems at the center of Germany's experience of modernity."[50]

The history of Heimat reveals an interlocking set of concerns with German nationhood, with the role of space and place for experiencing the nation and historical change, and with the "consequences of modernity"—from the founding of the nation-state through the "disembedding" of local relations to the advent of modern tourism and the *Wirtschaftswunder* (economic miracle) of the Adenauer era. Viewed from this perspective, Heimat indeed becomes, as Applegate suggests, a "map to wider changes in the society," where for two centuries, it has been "at the center of a German moral—and by extension political—discourse about place, belonging, and identity."[51] The present study engages with that discourse as it has impacted the history of German cinema, which is unthinkable without the *Heimatfilm*. In close readings of the ways in which individual representative films mobilize the notion of Heimat, we will reencounter variations of the three aspects that I have highlighted in the history of Heimat. First, much as the Heimat idea emerged in the nineteenth century as a symbolic representation of the nation-state, the *Heimatfilm* of the 1950s in particular has tended to function as a national allegory. In Wolfgang Liebeneiner's *Waldwinter* (1956) as in his *Die Trapp-Familie in Amerika* (1958), for example, we find plots of familial reconstruction that localize the German *Wirtschaftswunder* in the Bavarian Forest and even in America. The question of allegory is equally significant for my reading of Edgar Reitz's *Heimat*, the title of which is superimposed on the image of a stone with the inscription "Made in Germany." Though this clearly invites readings of *Heimat* and of the fictional village of Schabbach as a local metaphor for the (West) German nation, I conclude my analysis of the relationship between space and history in Reitz's film with the suggestion that as part of a larger whole, Heimat does not encompass that whole within the perimeter of the local. Unlike the relatively unspecific landscapes of the *Heimatfilm* of the 1950s, Reitz's Schabbach is localized explicitly enough to maintain the specificity of the local in the face of the national, even as it is portrayed as a node in a series of larger national and indeed transnational networks.

Second, then, the films under consideration are all marked by a recurrent emphasis on questions of space and place. That emphasis is by no means limited to the fictional place which in each case is staged as Heimat; rather, the concern with the spatiality of Heimat is equally apparent in the specific use of profilmic space from the Alpine peaks of *Die Geier-Wally* (1921) to the northern swamps in *Rosen blühen auf dem Heidegrab* (1951). Spatial concerns also figure prominently in editing choices that facilitate transitions between distant locales, or more generally in the genre's manifest concern with issues of transport, motorization, migration, and mobility as central aspects of modernity.[52] In keeping with the historical literature on Heimat, I read this concern not simply in terms of a threat to be kept at bay by reinforcing notions of Heimat as place against the modern transformations of space (though all of the films under discussion do also pursue such a project on some level); rather, I aim to show how different aspects of spatial, economic, social, or cultural modernization leave their mark on the place of Heimat. Like the Heimat movement at the turn of the previous century, the *Heimatfilm* "both glorifies the past and celebrates modernity."[53]

The third recurrent motif in my study of the Heimat film's generic topography is thus its ambivalent engagement with modernity as a process that these films' representation of Heimat both resists and cannot help but reflect. Like the Heimat movement and the Heimat literature that preceded it, I take the *Heimatfilm* to be a specifically modern phenomenon. In one way or another, virtually every film that can be attributed to the genre reacts and responds to the particular processes of modernization that defined German history in the twentieth century. More specifically, in its persistent foregrounding of regional and provincial spaces, of recurrent types of landscapes, and of an ideologically loaded notion of the local, the *Heimatfilm* is a spatial genre like the Western or film noir. As such, I suggest, the *Heimatfilm* responds to the pressing historical question of how to make oneself at home in a world where modernization means, among other things, a fundamental transformation of space and of our sense of place.

In order to give a sense of the evolving role of these concerns in the history of the *Heimatfilm*, I have opted for a chronological approach that keeps these more theoretical considerations constantly in mind. The book is organized in three parts to give an overview of the genre's origins, its evolution, and its shifting cultural functions over the past century. Part I takes a long shot of the *Heimatfilm* and traces its roots in Heimat literature and ideology at the turn of the century; it considers the meeting of Heimat and modernity in the *Bergfilm* of the 1920s and in different uses of Heimat by Nazi cinema. Part II replaces the long view with a series of close-ups of the 1950s, following some of the routes that the cinema of the Adenauer era charts across the domain of Heimat. Here, Heimat becomes a terrain traversed by images of the Nazi past, by the millions of refugees that Nazi Germany and World War II produced, but also by motorists and tourists heralding a new economy. As I argue in chapter 7, this terrain also becomes a battleground for the cold war as well as a crucible for socialist progress in selected East German films of the 1950s. Part III, finally, offers some retrospective views of the *Heimatfilm* after its apparent demise in the early 1960s. Besides the short-lived *Anti-Heimatfilm* after 1968, the most important return to the genre remains Edgar Reitz's *Heimat* of 1984. Reitz's reflexive use of the genre's iconography, its narrative patterns, and its modes of address engages a compelling spatial dialectic of inside and outside, coming and going that has received little attention in the debates about the film's politics of memory. Similar debates have resurfaced around the cinema of the late 1990s, which has turned to notions of German heritage to foster a new consensus about German history. As I suggest in the epilogue, many of these films, too, offer generic retrospectives of the *Heimatfilm*, again requiring us to analyze the uses of that genre in the popular historiography sketched by these films.

By adhering to an underlying chronology, I demonstrate the persistence and the adaptability of the *Heimatfilm* as a popular evergreen in German film history. But this broad overview is deliberately weighted in favor of a closer look at the 1950s. Until recently, the cinema of that decade has remained uncharted territory in most German film histories. In focusing on the genre that dominated the cinematic landscape of the Adenauer era, I hope to contribute to closing that gap. Before embarking on the longer view of the Heimat film's history, therefore, I consider some of the stakes involved in revisiting the preferred genre of the *Wirtschaftswunder*, putting the 1950s in perspective.

PART I

Roots

The place called home was never an unmediated experience.

DOREEN MASSEY

1 Evergreens

The Place of Heimat in German Film History

> The specificity of a nation's cinema might be most readily
> accessible via the genres its audiences preferred.
>
> THOMAS ELSAESSER

Second only to Nazi cinema, which has recently become the object of sustained critical reevaluations, the 1950s arguably remain the quintessential "bad object" of German film historiography. Though the decade is now being reevaluated by cultural historians in particular,[1] the years from 1949 to the Oberhausen Manifesto of 1962 still constitute a gap in the conceptualization of the history of (West) German cinema.[2] Where the cinema of the 1950s does make an appearance in monographs or anthologies, it tends to function historiographically as a postscript to Nazi cinema or simply as a cinematic wasteland awaiting rebuilding by the pioneers of the Young German Cinema. Unlike virtually any other era, and in strong contrast to the success story of the New German Cinema in particular, the decade of the 1950s appears to have yielded no significant auteurs, harbored few compelling institutional developments other than the perennial *Filmkrise,* and produced hardly a stylistic experiment worth mentioning. By the early 1960s, the industry was on the verge of collapse, and critics began to take stock of the preceding decade. Their often caustic attacks on the "aesthetic and political abstinence" as well as the "antiquatedness" of 1950s cinema set the tone for many of the appraisals to follow.[3] Worst of all—particularly when measured against the international visibility of Weimar and the New German Cinema at festivals, in art cinemas, or in the programming of Germany's cultural embassies, the Goethe Institutes—the 1950s seem singularly detached from contemporary developments beyond the German borders: German cinema, it seems, was never so parochial as during the 1950s.

As the French filmmaker Chris Marker commented in 1954 under the title "Adieu au cinéma allemand?" German film at the time amounted to a series of "self-absorbed productions" whose collective logo could have been a lens attached to a navel.[4] In its effort to stake its claim in a market heavily influenced by "American film colonialism"[5] and Allied distributors, the German film industry had turned inward. This protectionist strategy of product differentiation, which the industry pursued deliberately through vertical integration and resistance to foreign imports, is legible even in the film titles that give the decade its bad name. Viewers were invited to a *Rendezvous im Salzkammergut* (1948) and other locations around Salzburg; *Schwarzwaldmädel* (1950) launched a wave of films promising Black Forest *Gemütlichkeit*, from *Schwarzwaldmelodie* (1956) through *Rosel vom Schwarzwald* (1956) to *Schwarzwälder Kirsch* (1958). *Der Förster vom Silberwald* (1955) likewise spawned further Silberwald titles that lured the crowds to the cinematic Alps. To the north, the plains beckoned. *Grün ist die Heide* at the beginning of the decade (1951) and *Wenn die Heide blüht* at its end (1960) bracketed countless films set among blossoming heather in sparsely populated rural areas. Less geographically specific titles still carried the same cachet of the local: *Am Brunnen vor dem Tore* (1952) borrowed the title of a Schubert song to promise romantic serenity, while *Das Schweigen im Walde* (1955) and *Waldwinter* (1956) offered recourse to the peace and quiet of remote forest locations.

Such titles map out the restricted Austro-German geography of a cinema so parochial as to have remained virtually unexportable. Others redundantly point to the idea of Heimat as the key trope that organizes this rural and provincial cinematic landscape: *Heimatglocken* (1952), *Heimatland* (1955), *Sohn ohne Heimat* (1955), . . . *und ewig ruft die Heimat,* (1956), *Lied der Heimat* (1957), *Heimweh* (1957), *Heimatlos* (1958), *Einmal noch die Heimat sehn* (1958), and *Heimat, Deine Lieder* (1959)—these are just some of the Heimat compounds that appeared on theater marquees during the decade. For reasons to be explored in later chapters, the 1950s were singularly obsessed with the notion of Heimat. More specifically, the ready availability of this "keyword" for the German film industry of the time testifies to the successful institutionalization of the *Heimatfilm* as a key genre, which accounts for one in five films produced during the decade.[6] Today, the *Heimatfilm* has become virtually synonymous with the parochialism of German cinema during the Adenauer era, which more than one scholar prefers to remember as "the Dark Ages, nothing but *Heimatfilme* and reaction."[7]

In Anglo-American criticism, the *Heimatfilm* of the 1950s has long enjoyed the curious status of a genre that is "at the same time famous and virtually unknown." While it remains (in)famous for having become "almost synonymous with film in post-Nazi, pre-Oberhausen Germany," until recently, few of the authors who would routinely refer to the genre in this way appeared to have spent much time watching the films themselves.[8] As if to provide further proof of the parochialism of German film production during the 1950s, the films have remained external to the experience of the critics, let alone a broader public beyond German borders. If popular European cinema seldom travels well in the first place, the German films of the 1950s remain a paradigmatic case in point.[9] German cinema "after the war and before the wall," as a recent retrospective called it, remains one of the least-known eras of German film history.[10]

On the other hand, for German film and (especially) television audiences, mention of the *Heimatfilm* will still conjure up a fairly stable set of plots and images, consisting of picturesque Alpine landscapes or herds of sheep roaming the northern plains, of morally upstanding men and girlish women clad in traditional dress trying to track down the sinister poacher whose self-serving obsession threatens the fabric of the local community. Additional associations might include the repeated integration of (pseudo-)traditional *Volksmusik*, whether as part of the plot or as the nondiegetic sound track; lengthy inserts of Alpine flora and fauna, often on the flimsiest motivation; the appeal to forms of humor and general values allegedly held by the peasants who people these films; and perhaps even star pairings, such as Sonja Ziemann and Rudolf Prack (popularly known as "Zie-Prack" at the time) or Anita Gutwell and Rudolf Lenz.

The persistence of these images in the German media landscape for more than half a century is telling and warrants investigation, both in terms of what it says about the function of Heimat during the 1950s and in terms of what it reveals about the lasting, if irritating, cultural relevance of the first postwar decade after the turn of the millennium. Unsurpassed in popularity at the time, the genre of the *Heimatfilm* provided a site where 1950s (film) culture negotiated central concerns with home, space, and belonging in the ongoing process of national reconstruction. In this context, the *Heimatfilm* came to function as a veritable (if selective) map to a postwar national space—not just through the seemingly untouched, spectacular landscapes that provided its locations, but also through the concern with questions of space and place inherent in the trope of Heimat itself, which I discussed in the introduction.

I revisit the *Heimatfilm*, especially that of the 1950s, with an eye for the spatial dialectics of Heimat and modernity. In doing so I have no intention of exculpating, let alone celebrating, the 1950s as a misunderstood decade of subversion, nor do I wish to suggest that we reevaluate the decade by reading it against the grain in the manner of certain strands of French auteur criticism that began to rehabilitate conservative Hollywood directors during the 1950s. However, I do hope to introduce some new frameworks that can bring more nuance to earlier evaluations of the *Heimatfilm*. In particular, focusing on the genre that has come to stand for the cinema of that decade involves placing the 1950s in a threefold perspective regarding that cinema's historical, national, and generic location. In this chapter, I first outline some of the methodological premises involved in such a reframing. Taking into account theoretical concerns with historiography and genre, I then offer a preliminary sketch of the German cinema's long-standing engagement with notions of Heimat, from early brushes with the Heimat movement to the emergence of the *Heimatfilm* as a recognized popular genre and its self-reflexive reinscription in the *Anti-Heimatfilm* of the 1970s and Edgar Reitz's *Heimat* trilogy.

PUTTING THE 1950S IN PERSPECTIVE

Putting the 1950s into perspective requires, first, that we broaden our historical purview. The cinema of the 1950s is not book-ended as neatly as we occasionally like to think by the Nazi or "rubble" years on the one hand and the dawn of the New German Cinema on the other. Clearly, the functioning of *Heimat* as a keyword predates the 1950s, and it has continued to perform this function since the end of that decade. A look at the *Heimatfilm* likewise suggests that numerous cinematic, cultural, and social obsessions of the 1950s originated in earlier epochs and outlasted the end of the Adenauer era. Even a cursory glance at the genre's history reveals a set of striking personal, narrative, stylistic, and other film-historical continuities dating back at least to the 1910s. In other words, we need to correct historically inaccurate definitions which posit that the genre originated in Germany after World War II.[11] Similarly, we need to remain sensitive to the continuities that link this decade to the perpetual reruns of 1950s cinema that have appeared on television screens since the early 1980s, and which inform the proliferating references to Heimat in post-unification cinema. Just as Thomas Elsaesser and Eric Rentschler have recently interrogated the sometimes disconcerting contemporaneity of cinematic legacies from the Weimar and the Nazi eras, we ought to dwell on the "afterlife" of the 1950s at the turn of the millennium as well.[12]

My second reframing of the 1950s has to do with the question of the national. Given the political and territorial reorganization of national identities—and of national cinemas—after Hitler and during the cold war, we need to position the category of the (West) German in relation to these changes. Again taking the *Heimatfilm* as typical, two considerations stand in the foreground. First, we should look south from the Federal Republic and recognize that the cinema of the 1950s, and the *Heimatfilm* in particular, are essentially a German-Austrian coproduction (even if the dependence of the Austrian film industry on the German market for amortization makes this an often rather lopsided affair). Second, if Heimat has always been an ideologically loaded concept in German-speaking countries, during the cold war it became a veritable battle cry. It was used as such not only by the various *Vertriebenenverbände* (federations of expellees), but also by the FRG's official Bundeszentrale für Heimatdienst (Federal Center for Homeland Service) and the short-lived political party Gesamtdeutscher Block/Bund der Heimatvertriebenen und Entrechteten (Pan-German Bloc/Federation of Expellees and Persons Deprived of their Rights), all of which were founded soon after the war.[13] Notions of Heimat also became sites of intense struggles of demarcation in the GDR, and this was not lost on the newly founded, state-controlled DEFA film studio. Placing the German cinema of the 1950s in perspective, then, also requires that we maintain the cold war dual focus on what is "German." Especially with regard to such a long-standing cultural keyword as *Heimat,* an East-West view can yield not only the predictable ideological, and perhaps aesthetic, oppositions between two warring systems, but also significant areas of continuity and overlap and the occasional ideological reversal.

My third perspective on the cinema of the 1950s, finally, is theoretical, and it concerns the question of genre. Scholarship on German cinema, like the historiographies of other "national" cinemas, has traditionally been partial to auteurs. For a long time, standard accounts of the first one hundred years of German cinema celebrated a handful of recognizable directors whose films bear the stamp of their personalities. From the crucial *Autorenfilmjahr* of 1913 through the canonization of directors such as Lang, Murnau, and Pabst in the Weimar years to the international attention devoted to the *Autorenfilm* of the 1960s and 1970s, German film historiography has tended to focus on individual authorship and directorial styles. Significantly, histories of German cinema that chronicle how the baton of aesthetic innovation was relayed from one great artist, group, or period to the next are likely to skip the 1950s altogether.[14] The central role of genre in 1950s cinema, epitomized by the *Heimatfilm,* provides an occasion for revising the auteurist bias and inquiring into the function of genre in German film history. As a period which saw cinema attendance soar one last time before bowing to television as the leading popular medium, and as a decade defined by a steady output of generic fare, the 1950s require a theoretical conception of the role and function of popular genre in the German context.

"GENRIFYING" HEIMAT:
TOWARDS A HISTORY OF THE *HEIMATFILM*

In an influential and often reprinted article from 1984, Rick Altman complained that "genres were always—and continue to be—treated as if they spring full-blown from the head of Zeus."[15] As a consequence, Altman argues, genre theory has tended to hold notions of genre that are wholly synchronic and "fundamentally ahistorical in nature." Accordingly, genre studies are plagued by a gap between increasingly refined—but often ahistorical—*theories* of genre on the one hand, and ostensibly untheorized *histories* on the other. In his most recent publications, Altman has significantly contributed to bridging the gap between theoretical and historical approaches. His book *Film/Genre* provides a series of highly illuminating incursions into the study of genre, now reconceived in "pragmatic" terms. Like the categories of the semantic and the syntactic, through which Altman had previously focused the debate, the category of the pragmatic is drawn from linguistic analysis, where it designates attention to use. Any satisfactory theorization of genre, Altman argues, will have to pay detailed attention not only to the "structures," the "semiotics," the "ritual" or "ideological" functions of a given corpus of texts, but also to the ways in which that corpus becomes constituted through different uses of genre in the first place.[16] The crucial and often neglected historical dimension of genre, then, consists in the simple fact that such uses differ over time. Genres need to be treated as historical constructs rather than as stable, ostensibly self-evident structures; they are "site[s] of struggle among users"[17] rather than ready-made patterns. Consequently, the main categories in which Altman frames his discussions resist transhistorical fixation. He analyzes "genre redefinition," "genre repurposing," and what he calls "genrification" as processes, emphasizes the "discursivity" of genre, asks why "mixed" genres are the rule rather than the exception and how they become established in a "multiplicity of locations." Each of these discussions buttresses his basic claim that "genres and genre functions [have] changed over time."[18]

Altman convincingly shows how the object of genre theory becomes reconfigured once we start paying attention to the different ways and contexts in which genres and generic terms are employed, revised, and dismissed. "Genres are created and sustained," he argues, "by repeated use of generic terminology"—whether in reviews and critical texts or in other venues such as advertising copy, posters, quotations, or intertextual references.[19] Arguing against the tendency of film scholars to blindly accept genre categories which, more often than not, are simply inherited from literature, Altman asks us to investigate the specific development of film genres in their various pragmatic contexts, from production through distribution to reception. Rather than letting the critic generate inclusive generic catalogs based on fuzzy and unargued assumptions about the basic criteria for including or excluding a particular work, Altman suggests, we should ask and document when a particular label was first applied to a given film. When do films with musical elements become "musicals" as opposed to "musical comedies," "musical romances," or the like? At what point, in other words, does the casual adjective *musical* become nominalized to take on the full function of a generic label? With what justification can we call *The Great Train Robbery* (1903)—a film routinely discussed in textbooks as the "first" Western—a Western, when the category was not discursively available until much later in the decade? When, indeed, does the industry recognize the commercial potential of a generic label and begin applying it in the production or marketing phases of a given film? Or can we document the first uses of such labels in the press, to be adopted in turn by the industry for marketing purposes?

To ask such questions is to reorient our search for clues about genre history. In the case of the *Heimatfilm,* such questions lead us well away from the decade of the 1950s, back to the earliest days of cinema and the contemporary cultural context of *Heimatkunst, Heimatliteratur,* and *Heimatbewegung.* While the use of the term *Heimatfilm* as a label during the German cinema's first two decades has yet to be documented, at least one contemporary writer and cinema reformer had explicitly demanded that the "cinematograph" be impressed to the "service of *Heimatkunst*" as early as 1912.[20] In the ongoing efforts of reformers to elevate the artistic potential of the young medium, this author argued that cinema "should above all present the landscapes of the German fatherland and the characteristic beauty of the Heimat." As the principal subjects of such films, which "some cinemas have already been taking successfully in this direction," the author envisioned landscape images, traditional dress, and local architecture—in other words, a cinema rooted in Heimat.

Of course, such images abounded during the early years of cinema, particularly in the nonfiction film among whose "views" Tom Gunning has singled out an obsession with place. Gunning writes of "place films" for the early 1900s, noting the proclivity (among other things) towards natural landscapes. The selection of images in these multi-shot "views," he argues, emulates the tourist album and articulates an aesthetic that would remain remarkably consistent in travelogue films of future decades. "The view of the tourist is recorded here, placing natural or cultural sites on display, but also miming the act of visual appropriation, the natural and cultural consumed *as sights*."[21] Cinema, in these films, was a prosthetic device for the local tourist, its spectacle an invitation to sedentary sightseeing. This function of cinema as a tourist view is central to the history of the *Heimatfilm*, where it resurfaces quite explicitly in films from the late 1950s, such as *Die Mädels vom Immenhof* (1955) or *Gruß und Kuß vom Tegernsee* (1957). In these films, many of which hybridize the Heimat genre with musical or revue formats, Heimat has become a vacation destination for urban tourists where even the locals seem to be on vacation most of the time.[22]

While the "place films" of early cinema anticipate the spectacular construction of Heimat in these later films, the association with Heimat was only latent at the time. Films that seem to prefigure the Heimat genre, such as *Die schönsten Wasserfälle der Ostalpen* (ca. 1905–10) or the landscape views produced by Munich-based Peter Ostermayr during the 1910s, were "place films" featuring local landscapes. Though they showcased the "characteristic beauty" of the Heimat, they were not originally produced or marketed as *Heimatfilme*. Following Altman's call for more historically sensitive treatments of genre, we should question the retroactive assigning of generic terms when Ostermayr, for example, speaks of his early Bavarian "views" as *Heimatfilme*.[23] On the other hand, though few films survive that would allow us to evaluate the links between *Heimatkunst* and the cinema, a number of titles do suggest the presence of such links—even if they remain, in a sense, proto-generic. *Heimatliche Scholle* (1910) is described in censorship documents as a "drama. Peasant boy becomes criminal in the city. Returns home."[24] Even from such a rudimentary description, we can glean a basic pattern that anticipates the constitutive dramaturgical oppositions of many later *Heimatfilme*. Other noteworthy titles include *Heimkehr* (1911), *Wenn die Heimat ruft* (1915), or simply *Heimat*, a title that was used for at least five different films between 1912 and 1919.[25]

By the beginning of the 1920s, we find a critic reviewing *Die Geier-Wally* (1921) complaining that "one can't bear to see any more Tyrolean farms, peasants' huts, open-air dance floors, and village inns." The slight exasperation with which the reviewer lists the film's "overused motifs" (if only to applaud their artful treatment by director E. A. Dupont and set designer Paul Leni) indexes the familiarity of a quasi-generic iconography. By the early 1920s, in other words, the *Heimatfilm* had begun to enter cinematic discourses and practices, with trade papers reporting the founding of a production company named Ostmärkischer Heimatfilm in 1926 and the premiere of a "great German *Heimatfilm*" in 1927.[26] This is not to say, however, that the cinema's imbrication with Heimat discourses had already yielded institutionalized definitions of a Heimat genre. While it is tempting to assume that the genre would soon flourish in the blood-and-soil climate of Nazi ideology, the attribution of generic labels even during the 1930s and 1940s was not as consistent as retrospective filmographies suggest.[27] On the other hand, the term *Heimatfilm* was clearly available to reviewers and the industry alike by the end of the 1920s.

Indeed, not only practitioners like Ostermayr but critics too had begun to apply the term retrospectively by the early 1930s. Theater critic Walter Freisburger, for example, claimed that the label was already common currency during World War I. Likewise, a journalistic retrospective, "Film-Munich," from the early 1930s, recalls that "countless *Heimatfilme* were produced after the end of [World War I]," among them *Almenrausch und Edelweiß* (1918) and *Bergasyl* (1919), both produced by a company named Alpina.[28] Such retrospective datings of the *Heimatfilm* give an indication of the currency of the term by the beginning of the 1930s. Thus, not only was an ideologically loaded idea of Heimat notoriously central to Fascist politics and culture; films of the era, too, were being described with reference to their merits as *Heimatfilme*. The first version of *Grün ist die Heide*, for example, was marketed and reviewed in 1932 as "the first true German *Heimatfilm*," with some critics hoping for more of the same.[29] Elsewhere, one finds a reviewer describing Hans Deppe's *Heideschulmeister Uwe Karsten* (1933) as a wholesome *Heimatfilm* and emphasizing its exemplary role in the German sound film's overall "mission" to achieve the trinity of "German man [and] German song in the German landscape."[30] Oskar Kalbus similarly eulogized Hans Deppe's directorial debut with *Schimmelreiter* (co-directed by Curt Oertel, 1934) as "a *Heimatfilm* of German people, German spaces, German regions!"[31] By 1935, we find Ufa marketing the Peter Ostermayr production of *Der Klosterjäger* as "a new *Heimatfilm*." These proliferating references to Heimat and the *Heimatfilm* in the cinema by the 1930s should dispel the myth that the concept of the *Heimatfilm* did not exist prior to the 1950 surprise hit *Schwarzwaldmädel*.[32]

The relevance of Heimat for cinematic discourse and practice at the time is evident also in films that put notions of Heimat into play even though they may not have been identified as bona fide Heimat films. These would include titles such as *Heimkehr ins Glück* (1933) and *Heimatland* (1939), both of which take overworked businessmen from the city back "home" to the Black Forest, where nature and woman work the humanizing magic of Heimat.[33] Similar films, such as the comedies *Wenn wir alle Engel wären* (1936) and *Spaßvögel* (1938), also play with familiar oppositions of country and city, innocence and seduction, though their definition as *Heimatfilme*

by Francis Courtade and Pierre Cadars must be seen as a retrospective gesture.[34] The relevance of Heimat (which also featured prominently in the
marketing of these films) was also evident, albeit in modified form, in Carl
Fröhlich's *Heimat* (1938): here, the emphasis lies not on landscape and location but on community, as a renowned but world-weary singer (Zarah
Leander) returns to her native village for a last-minute reconciliation with
her father. Yet another sort of appeal to Heimat defines Gustav Ucicky's
infamous *Heimkehr* (1941), which in turn recalled the many *Heim-ins-
Reich* titles produced during the early years of Nazi rule, including Ucicky's
own *Flüchtlinge* (1933) and Paul Wegener's *Ein Mann will nach Deutschland* (1934).[35] While it may be inaccurate, in a pragmatic history of genrification, to subsume these diverse productions under the generic rubric of
Heimatfilm, they contribute to the gradual emergence of that rubric by
virtue of their repeated invocation of various Heimat topoi.

Finally, the search for continuities before the 1950s reveals a textual base
that extends back beyond the turn of the century, notably to the works of
Ludwig Ganghofer, perhaps the most-adapted author in the history of
German cinema,[36] and Ludwig Anzengruber. Though referred to as *Volksfilme* rather than *Heimatfilme* at the time, the first adaptations of these two
authors date back to 1914 (*Der Pfarrer von Kirchfeld*, based on the play by
Anzengruber) and 1918 (*Der Jäger von Fall*, based on Ganghofer's *Hochlandroman* of the same title). The pattern that would follow illustrates the
often short-lived nature of film-historical memory: *Der Pfarrer von Kirchfeld* was remade by the same directors (Jakob Kolm and Luise Fleck) in 1926
and 1937, then by Alfred Lehner in 1955 under the title *Das Mädchen vom
Pfarrhof*, and in 1958 by Gustav Ucicky under the title *Der Priester und das
Mädchen*. Uta Berg-Ganschow has rightly spoken of *Die Geierwally* as an
"evergreen"[37] of the Heimat genre: the 1986 film of that title by Walter
Bockmayer is a queer send-up of the version produced by Ostermayr in
1956, which in turn was a remake of a 1940 remake by Hans Steinhoff of
E. A. Dupont's original 1921 adaptation of Wilhelmine von Hillern's 1875
bestseller by the same title (see figure 1).

The case of *Die Geierwally* suggests not only the relevance of Heimat to
the cinema before the so-called *Heimatfilmwelle* (wave of Heimat films) of
the 1950s, but also its persistence past the watershed of the early 1960s,
which saw the demise of "Papas Kino" and the rise of the Young German
Cinema. Initially, this would have seemed rather unlikely, as a wave of
Bavarian sex comedies with Heimat titles such as *Pudelnackt in Oberbayern*
(1969)[38] or the six-part series *Liebesgrüße aus der Lederhose* (1974–82)
appeared to spell the demise of the Heimat genre proper. Likewise, Peter

Figure 1. Remaking remakes: *Die Geierwally,* 1921, 1940, 1956, and 1986 (clockwise from upper left). Courtesy Stiftung deutsche Kinemathek.

Ostermayr's diatribes against the rising young filmmakers of the late 1950s and early 1960s read very much like an *arrière-garde* battle. Ostermayr retired in 1958 after producing his last film, *Der Schäfer von Trutzberg,* based on the Ludwig Ganghofer novel *Die Trutze von Trutzberg.* By this time a number of future signatories of the Oberhausen Manifesto had begun working in short experimental formats and had had their first brush with the entrenched film industry, in which Ostermayr held a number of key positions, making him a "Bavarian Samuel Goldwyn."[39] These positions, for Ostermayr the crowning achievements of a career that lasted for half a century, were literally representative of "Papas Kino"—both in the sense that Ostermayr was the industry's spokesperson and because his biography made him the incarnation of everything the Oberhauseners wanted to cast aside with their call for "new freedoms."[40] In addition, Ostermayr's standardized output appeared by the late 1950s to be a German version of the *tradition de qualité* that François Truffaut had lambasted in neighboring France: well-made adaptations of canonic literature.[41] Against such schematic procedures and the emphasis on craftsmanship, Truffaut and his colleagues at *Cahiers du Cinéma* famously championed new notions of authorship that would soon be adopted by the young German filmmakers.[42]

It would appear that the rise of the Young German Cinema during the 1960s should have spelled the death of the Ostermayrs and Ganghofers of "Papas Kino" and of the *Heimatfilm* as a genre.[43] And yet it is a sign of the Heimat film's unparalleled persistence that Ganghofer titles continued to be adapted for the screen well into the 1970s, which saw remakes of classic titles such as *Der Herrgottschnitzer von Ammergau* (1973), *Schloß Hubertus* (1973), and *Der Edelweißkönig* (1975). Likewise, a third version of *Grün ist die Heide* (1973), starring the popular singer Roy Black, testified to the unabated popularity of the Heimat genre and to its function in ensuring the survival of "Papas Kino" long after the Oberhausen Manifesto had declared it dead in 1962. Not surprisingly, the new wave of Heimat films in the 1970s also spawned a series of lucrative re-releases during the same years.[44]

Moreover, after the first wave of the Young German Cinema had subsided and filmmakers began to seek new ways of finding and addressing spectators in the late 1960s, the *Heimatfilm* saw a revival of sorts at the hands of its erstwhile detractors. Peter Fleischmann's *Jagdszenen aus Niederbayern* (1969) is usually credited with initiating the reappropriation and repurposing of the genre in the guise of the new or *Anti-Heimatfilm*.[45] A number of notable Young German filmmakers followed suit: Rainer Werner Fassbinder directed *Wildwechsel* (1972), Volker Vogeler made *Jaider, der einsame Jäger* (1971), and Volker Schlöndorff contributed *Der plötzliche Reichtum der armen Leute von Kombach* (1971). In the eyes of the young *Autoren* who now imaginatively inherited the genre from the Ostermayrs and Deppes of "Papas Kino," the *Anti-Heimatfilm*—while aesthetically and ideologically distinct from the "classical" *Heimatfilm* of the 1950s—was explicitly meant to be viewed within the tradition that the *Autoren* were keen to subvert. This return to the genre in the context of the social movements of the late 1960s had as much to do with a nascent new regionalism and a "renaissance of the Heimat feeling"[46] as it did with the established popularity of the *Heimatfilm* itself—a potential which the young filmmakers felt the need to tap, given the poor home box office of their internationally successful productions.

While few, if any, of these productions actually managed to cash in on the genre's popular appeal, Edgar Reitz apparently found the right mixture of nostalgia and critique (that is, of the 1950s *and* the 1970s) in his made-for-TV miniseries *Heimat* (1984). As a film that self-consciously, if not aggressively, signals its generic (and national) lineage even in its choice of title,

Reitz's *Heimat* crystallizes aspects of the genre's development. Both the overwhelming popularity of this series with a domestic television audience (it garnered ratings of up to 26 percent) and the scandalized reactions of critics and scholars owed much to Reitz's decision to face head-on the problem of Heimat as a compromised but stubborn popular cultural formation.

Despite its deliberately drawn out narration and its fifteen-hour screen duration, Reitz's *Heimat* was only the first part of a projected trilogy. Reitz contributed the second part, *Die zweite Heimat,* in 1993; the third installment, entitled *Heimat 3,* coauthored with the East German author Thomas Brussig, premiered at the Venice film festival in 2004. While Reitz seems to have successfully cornered the market for one particular format for the *Heimatfilm* (which he terms the *Filmroman,* or cine-novel), there seems to be no shortage of Heimat productions elsewhere. Wherever we look, German audiovisual culture is saturated with images that only a few decades ago would have been attributed to the *Heimatfilm* proper. On the one hand, the genre still provides the template for the production and reception of films made for theatrical release, such as *Die Siebtelbauern* (1998), *Viehjud Levi* (1999), and, most recently, *Hierankel* (2003). On the other hand, and even more to the point in a pragmatic view of genre history, the *Heimatfilm* appears to have found a new home and new "users" on television. Gerhard Bliersbach dates this return to the 1950s to the evening of September 9, 1980, when a prime-time broadcast of *Grün ist die Heide* (1951) launched a series of *Heimatfilme* on ARD, the leading public TV station.[47] A random sampling of public and commercial programming confirms the continued massive presence of 1950s cinema in German televisual memory, whether in the form of semiannual reruns of *Sissi* (1955) or *Die Trapp-Familie* (1956); old and new soaps such as *Die Schwarzwaldklinik, Der Bergdoktor,* or *Das Erbe der Guldenburgs;* almost nightly prime-time broadcasts of *Volksmusik* shows that have inherited the iconography of the Heimat genre (such as *Musikantenstadl, Musikantenscheune,* or *Kein schöner Land*);[48] regular installments of *Heimatgeschichten* from various German-speaking regions; or the apparent commercial viability of the *Heimatkanal* marketed by Leo Kirch's pay-TV "Premiere World," which offers a continuous mix of 1950s Heimat films, series such as *Der Bergdoktor,* and the occasional Volksmusik show on a twenty-four-hour basis.

From *Heimatliteratur* and *Heimatkunst,* from the *Heimatbewegung* and the cinema reform movement at the turn of the century, through the explosion of the *Heimatfilmwelle* in West Germany during the 1950s, to the repurposing and the reprises since the late 1960s: the process that Altman terms "genrification" appears as a gradual convergence of the Heimat idea, its use as a point of reference in reviews and popular reception, and a growing corpus of films. The diversity of this corpus—which ranges from the documentary to the fictional, from early landscape views or "place films" to propaganda epics, from cinematic operettas to adaptations and remakes of *Heimat* novels, and from *Heimatfilme* to *Anti-Heimatfilme*—begs the question of its coherence. What patterns or continuities, if any, emerge from the history of the *Heimatfilm?* Is there a common concern to these films, and if so, how does that concern register? Are there overlapping narrative patterns, thematic approaches, visual motifs or strategies? Are there personal or institutional continuities to be traced, and if so, do they reveal anything about the aesthetic or textual logics of the *Heimatfilm?*

In answering such questions, the object cannot be to impose unity on a diverse body of films, nor to formulate an essentialist definition of the *Heimatfilm*. Genre development is not monocausal; it involves different directions, detours, and dead ends. Moreover, as Steve Neale has pointed out, the ideological significance of any genre "is always to be sought in a context-specific analysis. It cannot simply be deduced from the nature of the institution responsible for its production and circulation, nor can it ever be known in advance."[49] This insistence on historical context has been central to theorizations of the relationship between genre and ideology, where genre is treated as "one of the privileged mediations between the formal and the historical."[50] To study the *Heimatfilm* as a popular genre in this sense is to investigate the history and the social concerns to which it responds, which it reworks in terms of its formal construction, and to which it has provided imaginary solutions. As Eric Rentschler has rightly suggested, "The *Heimatfilm,* by dint of its persistence throughout the entire span of German film history, acts as a seismograph, one that allows us to gauge enduring presences as they have evolved over the last eighty years."[51]

In the chapters that follow, I set out to reconstruct those "enduring presences." I do so mindful of the competing demands that must structure any theoretically informed genre history. Whether we think of these as formal and historical, synchronic and diachronic demands, or in terms of syntactic, semantic, and pragmatic approaches, my goal is to link theory and history in such a way that the theorization of "enduring presences" and generic patterns does not obliterate questions of historical specificity. On the other hand, if the present study is structured chronologically for this reason, its overriding interest is not to provide a comprehensive history of the genre. Instead, the chapters are organized around case studies, working by example to advance arguments about particular manifestations of the *Heimatfilm* over the course of German film history. As Raymond Williams puts it in

The Country and the City, "It is the coexistence of persistence and change which is really striking and interesting, and which we have to account for without reducing either fact to a form of the other. Or, to put it more theoretically, we have to be able to explain, in related terms, both the persistence and the historicity of concepts."[52] Shifting from the longitudinal view developed above to a series of cross-sections in the consolidation of the genre, I now propose to follow the chronology of German film history with the aim of explaining both the persistence and the historicity of Heimat in the German cinema.

2 Therapeutic Topographies

From Ludwig Ganghofer to the Nazi Heimatfilm

> The less settled, less certain and less free from contradiction modern existence is, the more passionately we desire the heights that stand beyond the good and evil whose presence we are unable to look over and beyond.
>
> GEORG SIMMEL

PROTO-CINEMA: LUDWIG GANGHOFER, PETER OSTERMAYR, AND THE THERAPEUTIC TOPOGRAPHY OF *HOCHLAND*

Bridging the various moments I have touched upon in the history of the *Heimatfilm*, the continuous presence of Peter Ostermayr stands out. Ostermayr personifies the sustained association between Heimat and the cinema from the beginning of the twentieth century through the heyday of the *Heimatfilm* after World War II. Though largely forgotten today, he was widely recognized in the 1950s as the "father of the *Heimatfilm*."[1] Even outspoken critics of the genre would temper their views when speaking of the Ostermayr tradition, which was associated with a particular set of literary sources, high production values, and unflagging continuity.[2] With a career in the film business that dated from the early years of the twentieth century through the 1950s, Ostermayr's activities as the German film industry's self-described "toughest" producer[3] are virtually unmatched in their longevity. Spanning half a century, his career is emblematic of the continuities of German film history even where we have come to expect radical shifts and breaks.

This continuity was assured above all by Ostermayr's prize asset: the rights to the works of Ludwig Ganghofer, which provided Ostermayr with an immense repository of "pre-cinematic illusions."[4] As Germany's most prolific and popular author of Heimat literature, Ganghofer was a lucrative asset for Ostermayr. His novels, having already reached an audience of millions as serial installments in the popular magazine *Die Gartenlaube*, went on to see countless printings in various editions and are still being reprinted today.[5] Keeping in mind the protracted nature of genrification, Ostermayr's acquisition of the rights to Ganghofer's novels in 1918 marks a watershed in the prehistory of the genre. This was to become the single most important deal in the producer's long career of foundings, mergers, and acquisitions. Ganghofer's name, as well as the plots and landscapes of his novels, became a trademark for Ostermayr. To claim, as Ostermayr did in the early 1950s, that Ganghofer "deeply influenced my entire life's work" is to put matters rather mildly; in retrospect it seems fair to say that Ostermayr's identity as a producer was bound to the figure of Ganghofer in a veritable "film marriage," as one article would later put it, arguing that Ostermayr "discovered the photogenic in Ludwig Ganghofer."[6] In this respect, the epithet "Ganghofer-Papst" that was coined in later years seems wholly apposite, despite Ostermayr's repeated protestations.[7]

Not only does the sheer quantity of Ganghofer adaptations that Ostermayr oversaw as producer, scriptwriter, and director account for a growing percentage of his output over the course of his career,[8] but Ostermayr's self-presentation as the rightful cinematic heir to Ganghofer's style, to his particular narrative formulae, and to his pseudo-Alpine worldview betrays a deep-seated affinity between author and producer. Besides acquiring the popularity of Ganghofer as a marketable name, Ostermayr also capitalized on the distinguishing aesthetic and ideological features of Ganghofer's work. In particular, with each new Ganghofer film, Ostermayr brought to the screen Ganghofer's characteristic topography of the Alps as a refuge from the "rotten fruit of the metropolis"[9] in the lowlands. Following a cliché that predates its appearance in Ganghofer's novels, Alpine elevation was synonymous with physical and spiritual well-being.[10] It is difficult to underestimate the constitutive function of this therapeutic topography for the *Heimatfilm* more generally. Popularizing the Alps for a mass readership, Ganghofer's novels also formulated the locational archetypes of the Heimat genre.[11] Ganghofer's imaginary geography of the highlands played a paradigmatic role in the genrification of the *Heimatfilm*.

Ganghofer tended to designate his writings as *Hochland* (highland) novels or novellas.[12] This designation not only indicates the setting of his stories in the Bavarian and Austrian Alps, which was to become a trademark of Ostermayr's films as well; in Ganghofer's and his contemporaries' use, the term *Hochland* was programmatic, functioning as a keyword in the aesthetics and ethics of Heimat around the turn of the century. Propagating a conservative revolution through the idea of *Heimatkunst*, authors such as August Bartels, Heinrich Sohnrey, and Friedrich Lienhard regularly turned to metaphors of elevation in order to champion the *völkisch* renewal of German literature as "neue Höhen-, Volks- und Menschheitskunst" (a new art of elevation, *Volk*, and humanity).[13] One of the central organs of this

movement was the journal *Heimat,* which its founding editor Fritz Lienhard advertised as follows: "To all friends of German literature: Spring! A
breath of fresh air is sweeping the German lands! And Germany's literature
and spiritual life, too, shall be renewed by a breath of fresh air after so many
irritations. From now on, my publishing house shall devote its energies to
providing a home for the new *art of Heimat and of elevation* [*Heimat- und
Höhenkunst*] that is currently blossoming afresh in all German provinces."
The new journal, Lienhard promised, would be an "organ of *Heimatkunst,*"
a "healthy base" for a "pure and strong *Höhenkunst,*" and a bulwark against
the "decline and degeneration of the fin de siècle."[14] The activities of authors
and publicists like Lienhard constituted the beginnings of an antimodern
refusal that can be traced through some forty years from the turn of the
century through the rise of Fascism. Like many uses of *Heimat* from the
turn of the century, *Hochland* needs to be understood as a cipher for different forms of grappling with the transformations of modernity. As Ulrike
Haß puts it in her thought-provoking study of this movement's pastoral
ideology, its "antimodern consciousness functions like a long-term memory
for modern bequests, for that which modernity has left behind."[15]

Ganghofer's beginnings as a popular author predate the programmatic
formulation of a *Heimatkunst* or *Hochland* aesthetics. Nonetheless, his
entire œuvre needs to be seen in the historical and intellectual context outlined by Haß. Where others had turned to images of the forest in what
Simon Schama describes as the "Teutonic romance of the woods,"[16] Ganghofer had found in *Hochland* the "cipher for an ethical and literary search
for higher ground."[17] This upward orientation is motivated autobiographically by Ganghofer himself, who repeatedly describes the epiphanic and
therapeutic function the Alps had for him following blows of depression and
typhus. In his self-stylizations as an unquenchable optimist,[18] Ganghofer
describes journeys to the Bavarian and Austrian Alps (where he would take
up residence later in life) as so many cures, thus anticipating the function of
the mountains in the biography of Arnold Fanck, pioneer of the *Bergfilm.*

Though it is difficult to make out whether Ganghofer translated biographical experience into literature or vice versa,[19] his characters regularly
experience the Alps like their creator did, as an epiphany. When Count
Luitpold is troubled by sorrow in *Der Edelweißkönig,* he needs to move upward: "Let us climb the mountain. I need to go up. The air down here is suf-
focating me."[20] In *Das Schweigen im Walde,* one of Ganghofer's best-known
novels, Count Heinz Ettingen von Berneck flees his "turbulent life" (*Wirbel
des Lebens*) in the "dusty plains and the soot-covered city" for the eponymous quiet in the Tyrolean mountain forests.[21] And *Gewitter im Mai* begins

with the return of a prodigal son from a life at sea (the level of zero elevation) to his birthplace in the mountains: "How beautiful this was, the quiet
rest, far from all unrest out there, after long years in the Heimat again, on
such a morning, in the gentle sun of May."[22] For Ganghofer, the Alpine
Heimat promised renewal for his own health, was a metaphor for spiritual
elevation, and served as a narrative device underpinning characterization
and plot structure in his novels. In the stereotypical plot of Ganghofer's
Hochlandroman the protagonist finds salvation in the mountains, even if
the effects are not always spelled out as explicitly as in the case of Count
Ettingen, who is able to claim after only a few days in the mountains that
"my forest has made me well again! And free!"[23]

This therapeutic approach to topography is the hallmark of Ganghofer's
highland novels. In his worldview, the Alps as Heimat have an almost magical healing power, particularly for those who come to them from the "soot-
covered cities" below. In an era of intense industrialization and urbanization
and increasing social and geographical mobility, the binary topography of
Hochland and lowlands performed a clear ideological function. Mapping
Heimat onto the mountains as a wellspring of youth, beauty, and optimism,
Ganghofer's novels engage in a full-scale critique of the plains as the locus
of modernity. Given the ethical valorization of the mountains over the
depravity of city life in the context of the novels as well as in Ganghofer's
copious autobiographical writings, *Hochland* and Heimat come to stand for
a "retrospective utopia,"[24] an ahistorical place that provides refuge from the
spaces of history below.

If Ganghofer's novels thus participate in the mythologization of Heimat
that has often been identified in the culture and literature of the fin de
siècle, his writings also unwittingly serve to illustrate the paradoxical
nature of Heimat as a modern invention. Conceived as a refuge from modernity, Ganghofer's *Bergheimat* in many ways is contingent on changes
wrought by modernity—from emerging forms of mass communication to
the middle-class culture of leisure and tourism. Likewise, the ahistorical
sense of place held forth by the elevated locations of Heimat is not only
identifiable as a pseudo-feudal past, organized around patriarchal definitions of *Gemeinschaft;* rather, viewed through the tourist's gaze, the ostensibly timeless serenity of the Alps is readily identifiable as an invention of
the fin de siècle. In other words, aspects of the modernity that Ganghofer
decries in the name of *Hochland* and Heimat inevitably appear within precisely those spaces. In keeping with Haß's discussion of antimodern strains
in the literature of the early twentieth century, Ganghofer's writings
appear to function "as a sort of negative language that contains a certain

classificatory knowledge of the character of modernization, a sort of negative imprint."[25]

The "negative imprint" of modernity in Ganghofer's novels takes various forms. *Gewitter im Mai* offers a particularly explicit example. Here, Ganghofer works with a notion of Heimat as "an enclosed world unto itself"[26] that is nevertheless affected by recent social and technological advances, including increased tourism and electrification, the novel's central topic. When the seafaring Poldi returns to his native village, he contemplates the changes wrought during his absence. Motorboats have replaced the old raft to accommodate increased passenger flow across the lake, and on the whole, "much had become different and new" to meet the demands of tourists and the "taste of the city folk."[27] The most visible and fundamental change, however, is in the work of Poldi's childhood friend Domini, who has taken it upon himself to supply the village with electricity; rather than the tranquility of untouched forests, the description of this idyll highlights "poles with telephone and telegraph wires, and over all of the rooftops one could see the plump, green masts of the electric cables."[28] As a result, the novel's protagonist—a son of the Heimat who returns for a vacation and whose career at sea has made him a tourist in the Alps—contemplates an estranged Heimat, where old and new compete.[29] The plot that arises out of this constellation between tradition and technology highlights the nefarious aspects of these changes, to be sure. In the end, the heroine will die, not in the eponymous storm, but by stepping on an "iron snake"—a snapped electric cable. And yet the narrative vilification of technology cannot stave off its impact on the remote idyll. The Heimat that Poldi leaves at the close of the novel has been altered for good. One of the most remarkable devices in this otherwise unremarkable narrative is the unmasking of Poldi's naïveté as he leaves the village in ignorance of his lover's death. As the native-son-turned-tourist casts a parting glance at the village, the narrative supplies us with the equivalent of a picture postcard. In the moonlight, Poldi surveys "the dark Heimat until its last black forests disappeared behind the hills on the banks of the lake."[30] He imbues this vision with the happiness of newfound love, turning again and again to "see just one more little piece of the Heimat, where this lovely happiness waited for him." But Poldi is not privy to the melodramatic climax of the narrative, in which Dorle is electrocuted by the power lines installed and maintained by her fiancé—Poldi's boyhood friend and rival Domini. Poldi's innocence as he contemplates the idyllic location of Heimat thus only heightens the effect for the reader who knows better: the idyll is tainted, the "lovely happiness" lost. On the one hand a melodramatic trick, the character's elation at leaving the picturesque scene of Heimat appears on the other hand as a demystification of the idyll to the reader.

Demystification, if not disenchantment, is also the net outcome of an otherwise wholly "enchanted" novel such as *Der Edelweißkönig*. This text illustrates as clearly as any the affinity between Ganghofer's *Heimatroman* and the fairy tale, a link that has led numerous critics in turn to see in Heimat literature echoes of romanticism, with its emphasis on the supernatural. Early in the novel, the eponymous hero is introduced as a mythic figure, the invisible spirit of the Edelweiß flower. This legend is related by Veverl, a young orphan who lives with her uncle, the *Finkenbauer*. In a tableau-like scene, we see her sitting on the stoop, passing on to her younger cousins the traditional knowledge of the woods and its spirits that she received from her dead father. In keeping with Ganghofer's thoroughly patriarchal gender politics, where healthy, good-looking, nature-loving men pursue healthy, good-looking, girlish women (who *are* nature), Veverl is introduced as "half childlike, half virginal." The novel functions in many ways as a coming-of-age story chronicling her passage from childhood to adulthood.

Focusing on the figure of Veverl, Ganghofer's narrative becomes one of disenchantment. Within the terms of the narrative itself, this process maps onto Veverl's maturation and her transition from the world of the fairy tale to the world of reality (and into marriage). Leaving nothing unsaid in its melodramatic mode,[31] the narration explicitly sums up the destruction of Veverl's "dreamlike world," of which only "ruins" remain in the end: "No Edelweiß king! . . . no miracles or magic! Everything is now only tangible reality!"[32] To be sure, the "tangible reality" from which the novel lifts the veil of myth is none other than Nature herself. It is a mark of Ganghofer's deep-seated biologism that *Der Edelweißkönig* ends by reinstating a festive natural order. The final line of the novel reads, "Da muß a Wandel kommen" (Things must change). In the context of the closing paragraph, the narrator suggests this comment as a corrective to a character's mistaken notion that "the things of life should be different than nature created them." In other words, the *Wandel* or change that the closing line advocates appears to call for a return to a natural, biologically ordained order which cannot and should not be altered by human intervention. Change, in this reading, is only welcome insofar as it reinstates tradition.

But again, the novel also unwittingly registers the permanence of some rifts in this natural idyll of Heimat, rifts that are highlighted by the dramatic action surrounding an illegitimate relationship between a local girl and a count from the city and the subsequent murder of the count by the girl's brother. On an allegorical level, Veverl's final disenchantment signals a shift in the construction of the *Hochland* world itself: as suicide and murder cloud the blissful day-to-day existence of the little Alpine community, the displacement of myth by reality and the unmasking of the *Edelweiß-könig* spell out a subtle detraditionalization of the community. In the larger context of the novel, the rather forced reading of the need for change would appear to make more sense as an echo not of the mountains, but of their demystification. This is not to suggest that we read this or any other of Ganghofer's novels as an enlightenment treatise. But a text such as *Der Edelweißkönig* registers a historical moment of transition in its formal construction and in its privileging of Veverl's coming-of-age story. For all of Ganghofer's profound conservatism and his indebtedness to romanticism, in its unmasking of the supernatural as natural *Der Edelweißkönig* bears the "negative imprint" of modernity.

On the surface of these texts, there can be no question of Ganghofer's antimodern fervor. This is not only a matter of eulogizing forests, celebrating nature, and reinforcing reactionary ideas about gender. Situated in a rural milieu populated by "good" hunters and "bad" poachers, benevolent counts and malevolent rich farmers, childlike, virginal girls and designing women, Ganghofer's texts also envision a social order that has its origins in feudal notions of *Gemeinschaft*. Counts stand at the top of a patriarchal order that is organized around familial ties and traditional loyalties. But the main narrative line in *Schloß Hubertus,* another of Ganghofer's best-known novels, chronicles a count's downfall. Once again, a Ganghofer text thus unwittingly documents the dissolution of traditional hierarchies—whether in the ostensibly timeless realm of Heimat, under the reformist pressures of political modernizers, or in the anonymity of the metropolis. In this regard, Ganghofer's resolutely antiegalitarian worldview, his deep-seated antimodernism, is symptomatic of his historical position as a purveyor of trivial *Heimatliteratur* for modern masses. For as Haß argues, "the [antimodern] ideal of inequality can only find trivial expression from the moment in which it is no longer capable of organizing social reality."[33] Ganghofer's Heimat functions, like other uses of the term, retrospectively; it is, in Haß's terms, the "parting glance" at dissolving feudal traditions.[34]

In characteristically effusive terms, Ganghofer's biographer Vinzenz Chiavacci claims that "Ganghofer's innermost being can only be explained through the magical word *Heimat*."[35] Such a sentence may appear tautological in view of the inflationary use of *Heimat* around the turn of the century in general and in Ganghofer's prose in particular. However, the notion of Heimat does serve to explain some central aspects of Ganghofer's work if we take it to describe the performative contradiction with which I began this study, namely, its function as a modern keyword for antimodernism, a notion that is enabled and haunted by what it dismisses.

HOCHLAND-CINEMA: THE *BERGFILM*

Popularized through the illustrated press, Ganghofer's Alpine novels had fallen on fertile ideological ground in the *Hochland* and Heimat aesthetics of the turn of the century. Under Ostermayr's guidance, these stories were transferred from the mass medium of the nineteenth century to its twentieth-century successor, the cinema. After his initial acquisition of the rights to the novels, Ostermayr managed to exploit Ganghofer's *Hochland* aesthetics three times by producing his first Ganghofer series in the early 1920s, then remaking the same films—now with the new sound technology—as an independent producer for Ufa between 1934 and 1940, and finally producing another set based on the same novels during the 1950s, this time in wide-screen and color (in addition, his Ufa films were re-released in the 1950s).[36] As far as the author and his producer were concerned, the process of adaptation was governed by personal friendship and textual fidelity.[37] Extant prints of Ostermayr's films show a close adherence to Ganghofer's plots, with occasional adjustments in the interest of the economy of cinematic narration. Indeed, in a reversal of standard critiques of literary adaptations, early critics complained of an excessive loyalty to the books. Praising Ostermayr's landscape photography in *Der Edelweißkönig* of 1920 for example, the reviewer for *Film-Kurier* faults the filmmakers for passing up the opportunity to improve the weak motivation of Ganghofer's plot and characters.[38] Such rebukes meant little to Ostermayr, who remained devoted to Ganghofer's worldview. More importantly, however, throughout his long career Ostermayr prided himself on the cinematographic "signature" of his productions. As the early review suggests, the impressive Alpine backdrops took precedence over the thinly motivated plots. In particular, Ostermayr's productions showcase his interest in visually capturing the two factors that had played the greatest role in constituting the Alpine world as a tourist attraction since the late nineteenth century. The first was the pseudo-ethnographic view of the local population, a hierarchically ordered social structure composed of readily identifiable types (e.g., the kind, morally upstanding young man of humble origins; the innocent, girlish young woman; the benevolent or malevolent count; the disgruntled and antisocial poacher; the stern but loving mother). These figures are all dressed in local *Trachten* and move along a seemingly timeless horizon, spatially limited by the surrounding mountains. They are part of a bucolic milieu

that the camera tends to capture in long shots of picturesque Alpine moun-
tainscapes and in the traditional setting of Tyrolean farmhouses or inns
(*Bauernstuben*), whose abundance so exasperated the reviewer of *Die Geier-
Wally* in 1921.

The second factor was the threat of the Alpine sublime. Like the first
adaptation of *Die Geier-Wally* for the cinema, which casts the Alpine village
as a decidedly hostile place (especially for its heroine, who is ostracized,
ridiculed, and literally excommunicated by the locals before a dramatic last-
minute reunion with her lover on the mountain top), Ostermayr's Alpine
world harbors a darker side that competes with the bucolic tranquility of
premodern peasant lifestyles. Personified in the figure of the poacher, this
dark side of the Heimat idyll is also visualized in scenes that treat the Alps
as threatening, overbearing, and sublime. Even where Ganghofer's stories
do not venture into the higher, more dangerous regions of the mountains,
Ostermayr added images of men and women scaling steep cliffs and battling
the elements of nature. Though "man" invariably wins against "nature" in
these climactic struggles, the films incorporate a vision of the Alpine world
as both a thrill and a potential threat to the social fabric.[39]

The visual casting of the mountains in terms of an Alpine sublime
responded not only to a massively increasing tourist interest in Alpine
travel during the 1920s.[40] It was also part of a contemporary generic development in Weimar cinema, where Ostermayr and Ganghofer's *Hochland*
aesthetics intersected with specifically cinematic intertexts. In situating
Ostermayr's work within the (pre)history of the *Heimatfilm*, we must place
his treatment of the Alps as a "domesticated sublime" in the context of the
emerging cycle of films known as the *Bergfilm*. Like the *Heimatfilm*, the
Bergfilm has been held to be an "exclusively German" genre.[41] Usually
attributed to the pioneering efforts of Arnold Fanck and his students Luis
Trenker and Leni Riefenstahl, the *Bergfilm* popularized the cinematic fascination with Alpine landscapes that had already formed a staple of the views,
or "place films" of early cinema.[42] Fanck sought to dynamize the view
aesthetic through a series of technical innovations and heroic stunts and
proceeded to (in)fuse it with often rather vague fictional pretenses in films
like *Der heilige Berg* (1925–26), *Der Kampf ums Matterhorn* (1928), and
Stürme über dem Montblanc (1930).[43]

As Fanck's influence as a teacher suggests, the Bergfilm also initiated a
set of personal continuities which would guarantee that the *Heimatfilm* of
the 1950s was largely the work of seasoned veterans. Eric Rentschler rightly
insists that "continuities of casts, crews, sources, and titles link the *Bergfilm*
with the blood-and-soil productions of the Third Reich as well as the home-

land films of the Adenauer era."[44] Cameramen such as Sepp Allgeier and Hans Schneeberger, who got their start in Fanck's so-called Freiburger Kameraschule in the 1920s, continued to contribute their expertise to Alpine-based productions through the 1950s. Composer Giuseppe Becce supplied the music for Fanck and Trenker and continued to orchestrate majestic images of nature in the films of the 1940s and 1950s. And Harald Reinl, who, like Allgeier and Schneeberger began his career with Fanck, advanced to become one of the most prolific directors of the *Heimatfilm* from the 1950s well into the 1970s.[45]

While these personal continuities again suggest one facet of the Heimat film's genrification, the hallmark of the *Bergfilm* of the 1920s remains its spectacular representation of nature. Though the narrative function of nature shifts from the *Bergfilm* to the *Heimatfilm* proper in ways described below, the staging of natural landscapes for mere spectacle and at the expense of narrative remains a staple of both the *Berg-* and the *Heimatfilm.* This is not to say that the spectacle of the mountains is devoid of meaning in these films; on the contrary, their ideological function has been hotly debated ever since Siegfried Kracauer ventured that Fanck's Alpine vistas were proto-Fascist and that his aerial shots of towering clouds anticipated Leni Riefenstahl's apotheosis of the *Führer* at the beginning of *Triumph des Willens* (1934).[46] While the determinism of such a symptomatic reading remains troubling, Ostermayr's self-exculpatory claim that the cinematic fascination with the Alps was wholly apolitical and therefore innocuous is equally unsatisfactory.[47] Following Rentschler's judicious evaluation of the *Bergfilm,* it becomes apparent that instead of serving either a timeless pastoral ideology or making way for Hitler, the mountain films updated the dialectics of Heimat and modernity that already characterized Ganghofer's novels at the time of their publication in *Die Gartenlaube.*

Focusing in particular on the apparent contradiction between a timeless Alpine sublime and the technological modernity of the cinema, Rentschler discovers a similar constitutive dialectics at work in the *Bergfilm.* In these productions, the Alpine sublime becomes infused with traces of the modern apparatus that pioneers like Arnold Fanck invented (and shouldered) in order to capture the untouched grandeur of nature. Fanck was as interested in technology as he was in nature. Tinkering with ski-mounted cameras or time-lapse photography of Alpine cloud formations, "Mountain films probe the mysteries of nature with the tools of modernity." As contemporary critics noted, Fanck's camera could "at once hallow and . . . penetrate nature. . . . The pristine world of the mountains and a surveying cinematic apparatus do not conflict."[48]

If such a dialectics of nature and representation gives rise to the characteristically modernist aspirations of the *Bergfilm* aesthetics,[49] the profilmic space of the Alps also becomes redefined by signifiers of social, technological, and economic modernization. As Rentschler argues, the characteristic takes of the *Bergfilm* are hardly limited to snow-covered landscapes, billowing clouds, or vast, unpeopled expanses. Rather, the films also "show us tourists, resort hotels, automobiles, airplanes, observatories, and weather stations." In light of both the plots that revolve around these signifiers of modernity and the modernist aesthetics used to capture them, it would be inadequate to limit oneself to a symptomatic reading of the sort advanced by Kracauer. In his view, the mountain film not only presages the apotheosis of Hitler but also represents a general flight from modernity to heroic idealism and antirationalist idolatry.[50] Rentschler's rereading of the mountain film as exemplary product of the interplay between modern and antimodern sensibilities in Weimar Germany, by contrast, emphasizes that "the genre does not simply emanate a virulent anti-modernity nor does it only retreat to a sublime sphere beyond time."[51] Instead, we need to remain attuned to the dialectical link between the *Bergfilm* and the very processes of modernity it ostensibly serves to escape.

Given the constitutive function of location for the *Bergfilm*, this link between the modern and an antimodern timelessness becomes inscribed into the spatial register of these films. The opening sequence of *Stürme über dem Montblanc*, a prototype of the Fanckian *Bergfilm*, provides a particularly complex articulation of this doubly defined space. The film as a whole involves three main locations: a weather station on a mountain peak, an observatory and village in the valley below, and the distant metropolis of Berlin. Each of these spaces, in turn, is associated with one of three characters in the romantic triangle that generates the main intrigue of the film. The blond, muscular Hannes (Sepp Rist) braves the elements and mans the weather station. His friend, the dark Walter (Mathias Wieman), works as an organist in Berlin. Situated dramaturgically, sexually, and spatially between these two men, Hella (Leni Riefenstahl) works at the observatory in the valley.

The implications of this triangulated topography for the film's treatment of the Alps as a timeless natural world are every bit as significant as the homosocial triangulation of the characters, or even the dramatic rescue that finally unites Hannes and Hella at the end of the film. The representation of nature in *Stürme über dem Montblanc* draws heavily on romantic iconography to suggest the sublimity of the Alpine landscape: emphasizing diagonals and stark contrasts of size and color between foreground and background, the landscape dwarfs the human figure and becomes an almost sacred space. Indeed, this metaphor (which we find also in Ganghofer's *Schweigen im Walde*) is literalized by the editing, which links the mountain ranges with a cathedral when Hannes listens to a radio broadcast of his friend's organ playing. The association between the space of the Alps and the space of the church is further enhanced by the sound track, which carries the sacral music Hannes hears over his headphones even after he puts them down and steps outside. Here, the music that was previously a motivated element of the plot takes on a nondiegetic ring as Hannes—and the spectator—contemplate the Alpine panorama to the sounds of an organ.

As these subtle slippages suggest, the opening segment of *Stürme über dem Montblanc* offers a peculiar construction of space. On the one hand, this space is spectacular, rather than narrative. Making minimal use of establishing shots, the film begins with some rather discontinuous editing. We are not able to orient ourselves well in its spatial world. Indeed, we begin to suspect that there is little need for spatial orientation, since the movements of the protagonists within this space are less important than the representation of the Alpine space itself. It is a sign of Fanck's particular modernist aesthetic that the formal characteristics of that space outweigh any representational considerations. Rather than becoming the setting for any dramatic action, these images investigate the Alps for their particular graphic qualities, their fragmented forms, their undulating cloud formations.

At the same time, however, the opening sequence links this abstract, secluded, fragmented, and modernist space of nature to various sites of civilization. On one level, this occurs quite simply, again, through editing: a montage of weather stations in Great Britain, Spain, Italy, Scandinavia, and Germany takes us quickly across a distinctly European geography. Similarly, cross-cutting between the lonely hut atop the mountains and the cathedral in Berlin establishes links between the Alps and civilization with religious overtones. Finally, the match between Hella's view of the moon through a telescope at the observatory in the valley and a slightly longer shot of the moon through Hannes's telescope in the hut creates a remarkable virtual eyeline match. Here, the logic of the editing unites the two protagonists, sitting miles, if not worlds, apart, in their shared gaze at one and the same object. On the diegetic level, in turn, these excursions from the Alpine space to alternate spaces are motivated through the use of technology: the wireless through which Hannes transmits his weather forecast, the radio through which he receives the music, and the optical instrumentation of the telescope, whose elaborate, quasi-cyborganic presentation invokes the movements and the very apparatus of the camera.

This self-reflexive exploration of space takes on further significance when we situate it with respect to the theorizations of the role of space and place in modernity discussed in the introduction. Like Ganghofer before him, Fanck liked to think of the mountains as a therapeutic refuge from modernity, a place free of ethical problems, war, suffering, and pressing social questions.[52] Fanck's intentions notwithstanding, his Alps are hardly a timeless realm of the sublime but exhibit the pull of modernity, where place becomes, in Anthony Giddens's term, "phantasmagoric," that is, the seemingly timeless Alpine locales are shaped by distant social influences.[53] One of these influences is the rise of Alpinism, which took on mass proportions in the urban centers after World War I and during the economic crises of the Weimar Republic. As in the case of Ganghofer's prose at the turn of the century, the Alpine Heimat of the *Bergfilm* was strongly mediated by and for a tourist perspective.[54]

The other distant influence that shapes Alpine space is modern technology. Through the radio and the wireless receiver, the isolated hut on the mountaintop, and the mountain range itself are transformed precisely into the "phantasmagoric" place of modernity. As Giddens points out, what structures such a locale "is not simply that which is present on the scene; the visible form of the locale conceals the distanciated relations which determine its nature."[55] Indeed, while the shot of the Alpine panorama to the nondiegetic sounds of the organ would suggest an invisible penetration of the premodern "place" by modern "space," the montage sequence and the cross-cutting of the hut and the observatory in fact make visible the interpenetration of two different spatial regimes, as civilized "space" invades and transforms natural "place."

Such techniques of mise-en-scène and editing spatialize the underlying dialectic of Fanck's mountain films, where "the challenge is whether the camera can confer on nature the aesthetics of the machine age, and use the mountains . . . to infuse the technological apparatus with the sublime and the elemental."[56] To the degree that Fanck meets this challenge, his films play a transitional role in the history of German cinema and its treatment of Heimat in particular: they link Ganghofer's *Hochland* aesthetics and the *Heimatkunst* movement of the turn of the century with the modernist aesthetics of *Neue Sachlichkeit* that evolved in the 1920s.[57] They also provide a crucial stepping stone in the career of Leni Riefenstahl, who would become, with *Triumph des Willens*, the "official" filmmaker of the Third Reich. The portfolio that brought her this position, however, included not only acting and mountaineering performances for Fanck, but an important contribution to the *Bergfilm* genre as a director.

Riefenstahl's *Das blaue Licht* (1932) counted Hitler as one of its earliest admirers. Although critics have tended to dissociate *Das blaue Licht*, on which Riefenstahl collaborated with Béla Balázs, from her later career under the Nazis, Rentschler is doubtlessly right to see the film instead as a "master text" for the Nazi cinema.[58] Viewed within the trajectory of Heimat, from Ganghofer's *Hochland* novels through militant pastoralism and the *Bergfilm* of the 1920s to the mobilization of Heimat by the Nazis, *Das blaue Licht* serves as a link between the aesthetic modernism of the late Weimar years and the reactionary modernism of the Nazi *Heimatfilm*, discussed below.

Das blaue Licht shares many features of the *Bergfilm* in which Riefenstahl received her training. As in Fanck's films, shots of Alpine panoramas and rolling cloud formations take up significant amounts of screen time, and we follow daring ascents in long shots punctuated by close-ups of hands grasping for holds in the rock formations. However, outside of the dramatic mountaineering sequences, the film introduces a more bucolic rhythm than *Stürme über dem Montblanc* or *Die weisse Hölle vom Piz Palü* (Fanck's 1929 collaboration with G. W. Pabst). *Das blaue Licht* invites us to contemplate an Alpine life structured not only by daring athleticism but also by extended quasi-ethnographic sequences of villagers gathered at a local inn or strapping young farmers wielding a plough. Cut to the tones of an Italian folk song, these images differ from the sublime, heroic Alps visualized by Fanck; instead, they prefigure the folkloric staging of rural life as a tourist attraction in the later *Heimatfilm*.

Continuities of personnel and pragmatic links between the two genres (such as the designation of Ostermayr's mountain dramas as *Heimatfilme*) aside, a number of critics have emphasized the differences between the *Heimatfilm* and the *Bergfilm*. Generally, these distinctions rest on the different function of nature in the two. Whereas the mountain films treat nature as sublime spectacle, we tend to associate the *Heimat* genre with a far more benign, if not innocuous, nature. Nature in the *Bergfilm* calls on heroic masculinities (and on Leni Riefenstahl) to settle individual conflicts by confronting the mountain, whereas in the *Heimatfilm* nature serves as the backdrop for social conflicts and the restoration of community.[59] In view of such antinomies, we might say that *Das blaue Licht* maps the transition from one mode to the other by domesticating nature even as it perpetuates certain romantic iconographies crafted by Riefenstahl's teacher, Arnold Fanck. To be sure, Monte Christallo in *Das blaue Licht* is every bit as fatal as the "holy mountain" of Fanck's film by that title. But the "legend" that Riefenstahl's film constructs around this mountain is grounded much more specifically in broader social processes than is the perfunctory homosocial narrative of *Der heilige Berg*, in which two mountaineers fall to their death for loving the same dancer (played, of course, by Riefenstahl).[60] For all its mystical qualities, *Das blaue Licht* tells a tale of demystification. In so doing it transforms nature from a sublime, unreachable source of "blue light" into an object of rational exploitation. It also transforms a remote Alpine space into a tourist attraction.

Das blaue Licht shifts the tourist's gaze from Fanck's obsession with winter sports and male athleticism to leisure travel and sightseeing. Riefenstahl's film makes this gaze explicit twice in the double opening that frames the narrative: First, a pair of automobilists arrives in the present-day village of Santa Maria, where they are besieged by children peddling crystals and trinkets bearing a woman's picture. They inquire about the woman, and this inquiry sets in motion the flashback to 1866 that contains the film's main narrative. Thus motivated as a mountain tale told for the benefit of modern-day tourists, the flashback repeats precisely this structure. Though the first image we see is of Junta, the woman pictured on the trinkets, we are again introduced to the village of 1866 via a postcard-like long shot that represents the point of view of Vigo, a painter who has come to stay at the local inn. Much like the travelers from the lower reaches in Ganghofer's novels, Vigo sets in motion the main plot of *Das blaue Licht* as a tourist whose perspective will structure our understanding of the film's narrative. The film's local legend, in other words, is twice mediated through the traveler's gaze, Santa Maria's sense of place defined from the outset as a production for tourist consumption.

Vigo the tourist is not the only outsider, however. He shares that role with Junta, played by Riefenstahl herself. In slightly disorienting point-of-view shots that fail to establish her position but make it clear that she is watching, the film shows Junta reacting to the arrival of Vigo. Making sure that she remains unseen in the opening sequence, Junta moves on the periphery of the village throughout the film. She lives in a hut apart from the village and is treated as an outcast by the locals, who at one point chase her from the village calling, "Strega!" (witch). Her somewhat disorienting observation of Vigo's arrival, coupled with her ostracism from the local *Gemeinschaft* and some undertones of the horror film[61] introduce a disquieting note into the unfolding legend. The idyll of Santa Maria is troubled from the outset, the sense of Heimat suffused with multiple traces of the uncanny or *unheimlich*.

The village that we visit with Vigo, then, is by no means untroubled. Instead, it is inhabited by superstitious and tight-lipped villagers in the spell of the eponymous blue light. Every month at the full moon, the sons of the village are drawn mysteriously to the nearby Monte Christallo by a light emanating from its peak, but none have survived the dangerous ascent. Junta, it turns out, is the only one able to scale the mountain and reach a cave of rock crystals that reflects the moon's rays. But after Vigo falls in love with Junta and moves from the village to her remote hut, he discovers her secret and passes it on to the villagers in order to turn a "danger" into a "blessing," as he puts it. Promising Junta he will return, he leaves for the village below, where, unbeknownst to Junta, he gives the villagers a map of her ascent route. This clears the path for an expedition of the village men up the face of Monte Christallo.

The narrative trajectory of *Das blaue Licht* is one of modernization. The painter's cartography dispels the enchantment of the premodern world associated with Junta and replaces it with rational enterprise. Domination by nature gives way to exploitation of nature as the villagers march up the mountain with ladders and buckets to mine its raw materials. An extensive sequence following the excursion shows them celebrating their newfound wealth. As Rentschler puts it, Riefenstahl's film "sanctifies premodern landscapes and documents a village's entry into modernity. In so doing, it enacts a tension between the romantic worship of nature and an enlightened instrumental reason."[62] But this tension exacts a price. Like Fanck's *Bergfilm* before it, *Das blaue Licht* equates woman with nature. But the sacrificial logic of *Das blaue Licht* follows this equation to its fatal end: here, the demystification of nature requires the death of the woman. After discovering that her cave has been mined by the villagers, Junta plunges to her death from the mountain.

Junta thus comes to figure as a token of exchange not only on the formal level, where her image sets the flashback narrative in motion, but also on an ideological level, where the stereotypical association of Heimat with femininity turns into its opposite. In *Das blaue Licht*, both the disenchantment of the village and the establishment of Heimat lore (the crystals peddled by the village children; the tome containing Junta's story, which is produced by the innkeeper; the function of the inn as a local *Heimatmuseum*) are made possible by the exorcism of the woman who serves as a vanishing mediator for modernity. In this sense, *Das blaue Licht* prefigures rather precisely the logic of *Die goldene Stadt* (1942), a melodrama that illustrates the persistence of this gendered sacrificial logic from the *Bergfilm* to the Nazi *Heimatfilm*.

More generally speaking, *Das blaue Licht* updates the dialectics of *Hochland* and modernism that I have been exploring in this chapter. Where Ganghofer had imagined the Alps as a therapeutic escape from the lowlands and Fanck had fused the Alpine sublime with the technology and aesthetics of cinematic modernism, *Das blaue Licht* begins to paint a picture of *Heimat* as a space that unites capitalist modernization with romantic iconography and racist biology. In this respect, we cannot dismiss Kracauer's arguments that the evolution of the mountain films parallels the "surge of pro-Nazi tendencies during the pre-Hitler period," though we may wish to locate such parallels with more precision in the films' complex articulation of modern and antimodern motifs. Kracauer is right to suggest that Junta "conforms to a political regime which relies on intuition, worships nature, and cultivates myths."[63] But Riefenstahl's film as a whole also conforms to a regime that prizes tourism, modern cartography, the rational exploitation of nature for capitalist gain, and female sacrifice. *Das blaue Licht*, in other words, combines "premodern sentiment and modern rationale in a manner that anticipates National Socialism's synthesis of romanticism and technology."[64] Not only would Riefenstahl become one of the Nazis' preferred filmmakers, but her signal contribution to the Heimat genre prefigured some of that genre's varied uses in Nazi cinema.

LOS VON BERLIN OR HEIM INS REICH?

From Ganghofer through Riefenstahl, the therapeutic topography of *Hochland* cast Alpine Heimat as a space of escape, the vanishing point of an antimodern critique. Though this flight was often tinged by an awareness of its impossibility, as I have suggested, its direction was clear. In Friedrich Lienhard's programmatic formulation from around the turn of the century, the goal had been to get "away from Berlin" (*los von Berlin*).[65] The culture of militant pastoralism that developed over the following three decades explicitly advocated the "rebellion of the countryside against Berlin."[66] Pitting "soil" against "metropolis," its proponents subscribed to Martin Heidegger's celebration of the Black Forest as a "creative landscape" (*schöpferische Landschaft*) whose value could trump even the prestige of an invitation to teach at the University of Berlin.[67] Literary debates during the Weimar Republic continuously reinforced the opposition of Berlin to the provinces. In these debates, vindications of the countryside came to stand for the reclamation of culture over civilization, interiority over objectivity, nation over cosmopolitanism, Germanness over Jewishness, rootedness over uprootedness, and Heimat over homelessness.[68] Ganghofer's novels and Ostermayr's films must be located within these discursive coordinates. Their heroes chart the same vectors advocated by the cultural conservatives of the day. Feudal barons and manly mountaineers retreat to the Alps from the cities below, escaping the pressures of urban modernity by scaling mountains. Likewise, Fanck's *Bergfilme* and Riefenstahl's *Das blaue Licht* stage remote villages and mountain peaks as regenerative spaces where moral choices are clear cut, where questions "become simple and essential."[69]

Many of these sentiments were echoed by the National Socialists, whose Heimat rhetoric drew liberally on the tradition of militant pastoralism. Its *völkisch* opposition, encoded in the writings of Ganghofer and in Fanck's films, is commonly held to have paved the way for the rise of National Socialism. Accordingly, there are important continuities between the Heimat tradition from Ganghofer to Fanck and the uses of Heimat under the Nazis. After all, Ganghofer became the Nazi film industry's favorite author, and the personnel of the *Bergfilm* was assured of gainful employment under Goebbels's reign.[70] And yet, the habitual, and in many ways justified, equation of Fascism with antimodern pastoralism should not occlude some crucial redefinitions of Heimat by the Nazis. Besides emphasizing historical and ideological continuities with *völkisch* literature, *Heimatkunst*, and the Heimat movement of the early twentieth century, we need to consider the specificity of Nazi uses of Heimat. I will turn first to the latter perspective, reserving the exploration of some of the continuities that link the Nazi cinema to its forerunners from Ganghofer to Fanck for the concluding section of this chapter.

The (re)definition of Heimat by National Socialist ideologues and by Nazi cinema shows some surprising reversals. On the surface, these might be described as a redirection of Heimat. If the principal vector of Fanck's Alpinism and Lienhard's *Heimatkunst* had been an outward movement of dispersal ("away from Berlin"), the centralization and streamlining (*Gleichschaltung*) of politics under the Nazis brought with them a centripetal movement of concentration. Heimat was defined as a space of return, or *Heimkehr*, as one of the most infamous films of the era would have it. This reversal was legible not only in the early proliferation of plots and images of Germans making their way back *heim ins Reich* in a set of films from 1933–34 that included *Flüchtlinge* (1933), *Ein Mann will nach Deutschland* (1934), and *Der verlorene Sohn* (1934).[71] Later productions like *Der Strom* and the aforementioned *Heimkehr* likewise emphasized the value of Heimat as a space of return, rather than of escape.

This shift manifests a redefinition of the relationship between Heimat and nation during the Third Reich. As Celia Applegate's study of the Heimat idea demonstrates, nation and nationalism around the turn of the century were still tied in important ways to locality. The Heimat movement and its writings suggest, indeed, that allegiance to the local necessarily took precedence over national identification. The appeal of Heimat for those Germans who participated in local Heimat movements around 1900 lay "in its capacity to reconcile communal intimacy with national greatness."[72] The primacy of the provinces became muted only after World War I. As Applegate points out, the language of Heimat became increasingly nationalistic during the Weimar Republic. Defenses of the locality were now linked to the defense of the nation, and the tradition-oriented *Heimatliteratur* took on new *völkisch* undertones during these years.[73] At the same time, however, the Weimar Republic preserved and fostered the tendency to infuse home with republican ideals and to conceive of the nation as an agglomeration of provincials. Citizenship and civic responsibility were tied to place, and local associational activities were taken to be the necessary wellspring of national politics. The educational value of Heimat, according to contemporary treatises such as Eduard Spranger's *Bildungswert der Heimatkunde,* lay not in any ethnic or racial essentialism. Rather, to use a slogan coined in the "new regionalism" of the 1970s, *Heimatkunde* could teach young Weimar citizens the value of "thinking locally," even as it encouraged them to act nationally.[74]

Such localism was anathema to the National Socialists, who, for all their talk of *Heimat* and roots, by and large maintained a distance from local life when it came to formulating national policy or working with local interest groups. Applegate demonstrates convincingly how the Nazi cultivation of Heimat worked against local particularism. Insisting on the absolute priority of the nation, organized "outward and downward" according to the *Führer* principle, the contradictory ideology and cultural politics of the Third Reich replaced the claims of locality with a newly nationalized notion of Heimat. In many cases, this entailed the wholesale destruction of a century's worth of Heimat tradition, to be replaced by a centrally administered notion of Heimat. The gigantic and the national replaced the small and the local as the Nazi reorganization "effectively robbed Heimat activities of their particularity and their local independence, both qualities at the heart of the idea of Heimat itself."[75]

As a result, Heimat and nation became largely synonymous in Nazi usage. Both were defined racially and spatially, or, to use Nazi terminology, through blood and soil. A widely used four-volume textbook entitled *Deutsches Volk, deutsche Heimat,* originally published in 1935, amply illustrates this definition. The first volume, which was in its fifth edition by 1941, provides a natural history of Germany from "Urdeutschland" to "the face of the new *Reich.*" Landscape photography and images of art, architecture, and industry alternate with "characteristic" physiognomies from different German regions, reminiscent of Riefenstahl's close-ups of Alpine peasants in *Das blaue Licht.* The textbook aims to demonstrate how "German Heimat in its present shape is the result of the German people's work over thousands of years."[76] The second volume further anchors this definition of Germany as Heimat in a *völkisch* explication of German history. Its historiographic axioms include a definition of *Volk* as "the unity of blood, language, will, and fate [*Schicksal*]" and of *Heimat* as "the unity of soil [*Boden*] that has been shaped by the work of the people and is populated entirely or predominantly by this people."[77] These are the basic terms of a racial historiography that culminates in the claim that " 'National Socialism is a march into Heimat. . . . Only a people's revolution that seized *all* aspects of life and initiated the march into Heimat, to a renewed unity of blood and soil, could preserve the one thing that gives any politics its sense and its goal: the life of the German people."[78]

Applegate suggests that through the Weimar Republic, "Heimat translated a more ancient sense of place into a modern sense of nation."[79] Through publications like *Deutsches Volk, deutsche Heimat*, the Nazis, by contrast, translated a *völkisch* sense of nation into an archaic sense of place rooted in racist biology. In its racialist language, Nazism cut the notion of Heimat to the measure of its social-biological agenda.[80] Such was also the ideological ambition of a film like *Ewiger Wald*, produced by the National Socialist Party in 1936. The film stages the forest as a biological metaphor for the German people, which is mythologized as eternal and natural. The notion of Heimat figures centrally in this project. After a lyrical montage sequence of forest images opens the film like a Wagnerian overture, displaying the film's theme of natural cycles and growth as well as the technical range of the ten cinematographers involved in the film, we begin in prehistoric times. As a group of men constructs primitive habitations out of logs, the portentous voice-over intones Carl-Maria Holzapfel's heavy-handed lyrics: "From the woods we come/Like the woods we live/From the woods we shape/Heimat and space." The film then makes explicit its Darwinist message by equating the survival of the *Volk* with the survival of the woods—thanks to the exclusion of all that is *rassenfremd* and *krank*. The woods are alternately sacralized through the superimposition of cathedral images and anthropomorphized through the superimposition of soldiers marching for Germany in World War I. The film ends with an apotheosis of the woods as "new *Gemeinschaft*": images reminiscent of the *Volksfest* at the close of numerous Heimat films celebrate a mythological unity of the German *Volk*, as if to illustrate the *völkisch* historiography of *Deutsches Volk, deutsche Heimat* (which first appeared one year prior to the release of *Ewiger Wald*). The program notes matched the bombast of the images: "The people finds itself, a new forest grows: the forest of swastika flags rises up. From its Heimat, from the German forest, the German people has again drawn the power to reach for the sun."[81]

In its mythologization of Heimat, *Ewiger Wald* pulls out all the stops. Biology becomes history, history becomes *ewig*, nature becomes culture, and Germanness is defined in racial terms as the purity of *Volk*, blood, and soil. These conflations have become recognizable as the prototypical Fascist discourse on *Blut und Boden*, which defines Heimat as "rootedness that has been transformed into feeling and spirit. Through the sense of Heimat, the individual, the family, and the group are tied by fate to a piece of land that dominates their soul."[82] Such definitions inform not only the *heim-ins-Reich* films of the early 1930s, *Ewiger Wald* of 1936, and seemingly innocuous Heimat films like *Der Erbförster* (1945); they also underlie one of the signature productions of Nazi cinema, which locates the mythic essentialism of Heimat in a specific historical context.

Gustav Ucicky's propaganda film *Heimkehr* (1941) traces the fate of a group of ethnic Germans suffering persecution in Volhynia, an eastern region of Poland, during the late 1930s. Since the middle of the nineteenth century, Germans had been settling in this region, where they formed a small minority. When Poland was divided between Germany and the Soviet Union, the region fell to the latter, but under a minority repatriation agreement, some 60,000 ethnic Germans were resettled west of the Ukraine. Most ended up in the Warthegau, a region then under German administration.

Out of these events, *Heimkehr* constructs a fictional story that centers heavily on the value of the German *Volksgemeinschaft* as the settlers' true Heimat. Hardly a documentary, as the production company Wien-Film claimed at one point,[83] *Heimkehr* was a massive ideological fantasy. In the words of the scriptwriter, Gerhard Menzel (a Nazi loyalist and renowned playwright who had collaborated with Ucicky on *Flüchtlinge* in 1933), the object was never "mere reporting," but the search for a new aesthetics. Menzel's goal was to portray "the collective fate of the millions of Germans who live far from the Heimat."[84] Indeed, the finished film invokes the topoi of *Heimkehr*, Heimat, and *daheim* for several purposes. It describes the German minority as a beleaguered *Gemeinschaft* whose ties to the village are strong but whose survival is threatened by the Poles. Early on, the film makes that threat explicit by showing the destruction of the German school. Poles drag a blackboard, a globe, and books into the school yard, and a Jewish boy sets the pile ablaze. In a reversal of contemporary reality, Nazi atrocities are projected onto Jews and Poles, casting victims as perpetrators; this reversal structures the propaganda message delivered throughout the film. Indeed, by the end, one German has been lynched by a mob (in a cinema, no less), another has been blinded by a shot in the face, and a German woman has been stoned to death. At the film's climax, the persecution has escalated to a genocidal pitch. Viewers are presented with images of ethnic Germans being carted away on flatbed trucks, huddling under large nets like animals. This is an image already familiar from *Flüchtlinge,* though the audience for *Heimkehr* would not have had to rely on film-historical memory for images of deportation. The same ethnic Germans are then herded into a small cellar with water on the floor, while Poles prepare to fire machine guns from the outside through small window openings. With the deportation of Jews a daily reality in German cities and the Final Solution an imminent decision at the time of the film's Venice premiere in the summer of 1941, the film's "historical unconscious" (Kaes) seems to bubble very close to the surface.[85]

Its intended ("conscious") ideological project, meanwhile, is threefold. First, the racist portrayal of the Poles (and the occasional Jew) as inhuman aggressors against a peace-loving and law-abiding German minority serves as a post-facto legitimization for the invasion of Poland and the Hitler-Stalin pact. Second, the emphasis on German perseverance and the last-minute rescue of the ethnic Germans by Nazi troops in a film from 1941 makes *Heimkehr* an early version of later *Durchhaltefilme,* such as Veit Harlan's *Kolberg* (1945). Third, and most important for our present concerns, the film is an apotheosis of Heimat as a territorially defined *Volksgemeinschaft.* In keeping with the Fascist centralization of the Heimat concept discussed above, *Heimkehr* equates Heimat with nation or *Reich.* This is spelled out in the central monologue of the film, a scene that Goebbels deemed "the best that has ever been shot for film."[86] The preceding scene shows the Germans gathered around the *Volksempfänger* (radio) in a barn, listening to Hitler's declaration of war in the *Reichstag.* This intimate, transgenerational image of a *Gemeinschaft* networked, via the radio, with like-minded Germans "back home" is then broken up by Polish soldiers, who arrest the entire group for meeting illegally. After they have been herded into the prison, where tightly framed low-key shots show some members of the group beginning to despair, fear for their lives, and suffer from claustrophobia, the camera alights on the film's radiant star, Paula Wessely. Her monologue, a *Führerrede* in its own right, summarizes the film's message of safe passage to the German Heimat. As the sound track softly carries the *Deutschlandlied,* Wessely's character Marie articulates the certainty of Heimat:

> Just think, people, what it will be like, just think, when around us there will be lots of Germans—and when you come into a store, people won't talk Yiddish or Polish, but German. And not only the whole village will be German, but all around, everything surrounding us will be German. And

we, we will be right in the middle, inside, in the heart of Germany. . . . We will live again on the good old warm soil of Germany. Home [*daheim*] and at home [*zu Hause*]. And at night, in our beds, we'll awake, and the heart will suddenly know with a sweet shock that we're sleeping right in the middle of Germany, home and at home . . . and all around, millions of German hearts will beat and quietly intone: you're home, home, home with your kin.

What is most remarkable about this pathos-ridden monologue, which was widely reprinted in the press and in publicity material accompanying the film's release, is the redundant use of *Heim* and *deustch* to designate spaces of belonging. *Heimkehr,* the film's title, means safe passage to *daheim,* to a racially homogenous German *Volksgemeinschaft.* At the end of the film, Marie will "drive home" this message one more time, tearfully explaining to her father that because "we never lost the Heimat," the Germans are now "returning home, father, home to our home [*heim nach Hause*]. Isn't that the most precious thing in life, to be allowed to come home, to return [*heim-kehren*]?" The final images show a line of ethnic Germans marching from the left foreground over a vast snow-covered plain towards the radiant sun low on the horizon. In the closing shot, the sun is replaced by an oversized photograph of the *Führer* at the border. The renewed sense of purpose and *Gemeinschaft* that will bring these Germans *heim ins Reich,* however, has already been established at the close of Marie's monologue. Taking her cue, the group spontaneously intones the song "Nach der Heimat möcht' ich wieder" (I want to go back to the Heimat) in three-part harmony. By this point, the song's clichéd lyrics of wandering and homesickness, which form part of a larger Heimat tradition that reaches back well beyond its use in this film, have taken on a clear ideological message. The film makes *Heimkehr* a matter of life and death, a struggle in which the survival of Germans as well as of the *Volk*'s racial purity is at stake. Heimat, the manifest goal of *Heim-kehr,* is the guarantor of this survival.

Heimkehr was a high-profile production. Goebbels had commissioned the film in 1939, and it became the single most expensive project for presti-gious Wien-Film in 1941–42, accounting for fully two-fifths of that sea-son's production budget.[87] A vehicle for Paula Wessely, it also boasted other stars with high box-office value such as Wessely's husband, Attila Hörbiger, and Carl Raddatz. Gerhard Menzel's reputation as scriptwriter was matched by the impressive portfolio of designer Walther Röhrig, who had con-tributed to the expressionist design of *Das Kabinett des Dr. Caligari* (1919) and Fritz Lang's *Der müde Tod* (1921). Like Menzel, he had already collab-orated with Gustav Ucicky on *Flüchtlinge.* Ucicky's reputation as the star director at Wien-Film gave the marketing of *Heimkehr* both an auteurist imprint and the cachet of an accomplished propagandist. Given the high profile of this production and Goebbels's personal involvement from its inception, it is not surprising that *Heimkehr* received the highest *Prädikat* available in the ratings system of the Third Reich: it was "staatspolitisch und künstlerisch besonders wertvoll" and was designated a "Film der Nation."

If *Heimkehr* is in this sense an exemplar of Nazi film politics, it remains but one example of how the cinema of the Third Reich mobilized notions of Heimat. To be sure, propaganda films like *Heimkehr* have long provided some of the canonic test cases for arguments about the political (ab)uses of cinema in the Third Reich. However, for the past decade, scholars of Nazi cinema have been working to revise our image of this era as wholly determined by official propaganda vehicles. As Karsten Witte describes the earlier paradigm, "Again and again critics catalogued and studied a dozen ostentatious propaganda films, but failed to pay attention to the remainder of the films— some of them banal, others quite successful genre films."[88] Conversely, the recent revisions of what Sabine Hake calls the "propaganda studies" paradigm have taken place in large measure around questions of genre and popular cinema and concentrated on the "remainder" identified by Witte.[89]

In this context, it would be misleading to suggest that the *Heimatfilm*, though generally successful, accounted for a majority of Nazi genre films. These were dominated instead by revue films and comedies, melodramas and biopics.[90] Statistical evidence notwithstanding, however, the *Heimatfilm* apparently remains "the genre most frequently associated with Third Reich cinema."[91] In order to understand why this is so, and what this persistent link between Heimat and Fascism in popular (and some scholarly) memory means, we must move beyond the test case of propaganda films like *Heimkehr*. Though these films—as well as invocations of Heimat and *Gemeinschaft* in the *Reichsarbeitsdienst* sequence of *Triumph des Willens*, for example—remain important sites for the official articulation of Heimat in Nazi cinema, we must also investigate the functions of the *Heimatfilm* as a popular genre under Fascism. Here, notions of Heimat are less easily mapped onto Fascist worldviews than was the case with the "Fascist aesthetics" of *Ewiger Wald* or *Heimkehr*.[92] However, in keeping with Witte's influential argument about Nazi cinema more generally, the specificity of the Nazi *Heimatfilm* is not necessarily (or not exclusively) to be sought in the textual, aesthetic appearance of the films themselves, but rather in the historical contexts of their production and circulation. As Witte puts it, we should move from the question of "what constitutes a Fascist film" to an investigation of how film functioned in the context of Fascism.[93]

Once again, the case of Peter Ostermayr is instructive. In particular, it illustrates precisely the function, in the context of Fascism, of a genre that predated the rise of Fascism. From 1933 to 1945, Ostermayr continued working in the format he had established in the early 1920s, exploiting his rights to the Ganghofer novels as an independent producer for Ufa. Having begun to produce sound films in 1931, he turned out technologically updated remakes of his original 1918–20 Ganghofer series in rapid succession. Of the twenty-one Ostermayr productions during the Third Reich years, nine were adaptations of Ganghofer novels, with material drawn from popular Heimat novels by other authors (such as the best-selling *Die Heilige und ihr Narr* by Agnes Günther, or *Frau Sixta* by Ernst Zahn) making up the difference. How should we evaluate these continuities within a history of the Heimat genre, and with respect to its function under Fascism in particular? A brief look ahead to Ostermayr's own evaluation can provide some leads.

The sparse biographical material that has been published on Ostermayr to date describes the postwar years until 1950 as an involuntary creative pause during which the producer worked on his memoirs and tended his garden. As the extensive correspondence in his *Nachlaß* demonstrates, Ostermayr was also busy with his own de-Nazification procedure. As an NSdAP member since May 1933, Ostermayr was required to clear his political record, which involved filing forms with the Allied authorities, explaining pertinent biographical details to their satisfaction, and securing affidavits from untainted friends and colleagues. In this context, Ostermayr's self-description, in particular, is quite revealing for what it says about his conception of the genre on which he had been betting since the early 1920s. Ostermayr's basic line of defense was to point out the continuity of his work, which dated back well beyond the rise of National Socialism. In the often rather restricted logic of the de-Nazification process, the fact that his activities predated Hitler's rise to power was to be taken as proof positive that they were untainted by Fascism. Of course, this begs a number of important questions: If his earlier work, which in many ways prepared and resembled his work in the 1930s, had nothing to do with Nazi propaganda or official party politics, why were the remakes of those early films so enormously successful after 1933? The mere fact that between 1933 and 1945 more films were based on Ganghofer's novels than on the work of any other single author would seem to require some explanation that goes further than simply pointing to their popularity. Furthermore, as some of my earlier examples suggest, links between Heimat and (proto-)Fascist ideologies obviously predated Hitler's rise to power. Ostermayr's autobiographical narratives after the war leave unanswered the question posed so insistently by Siegfried Kracauer during the same years: What was it that helped prepare Hitler, and how was the cinema implicated in this process?

Clearly, one would not expect the practitioner Ostermayr to broach, let alone answer, these questions, which remain difficult and occasionally intractable even in film scholarship. In this respect, it is all the more surprising that Ostermayr does offer some leads when he not only describes himself as an apolitical person, but extends this claim to his films on the basis of their popular appeal. As early as 1936, Walter Freisburger wrote that Ganghofer films (i.e., Ostermayr productions) "always appear when 'high-minded' film production finds the political situation to be serious and unclear—or at least would prefer to wait a bit. During the war, they were called *Heimatfilme*, in 1919 they were *Volksfilme*, and in 1933–34 the emphasis is on Heimat again."[94] In other words, Ostermayr productions must be regarded as political precisely in their ostensible distance from contemporary political events at any given moment. Under these circumstances, Ostermayr's own tendency to equate success with an apolitical stance, if not with outright resistance to official Nazi doctrine, appears rather problematic. In his retrospective self-evaluation, he claims that "my production consisted exclusively of popular [*volkstümlich*] films without any political tendencies whatsoever. . . . In spite of the resistance with which I met, I held onto my down-to-earth [*bodenständig*] popular [*volksverbunden*] production." His activity during the war years, Ostermayr maintained, amounted to nothing but "cultural work for my Bavarian Heimat."[95]

As if notions of *Bodenständigkeit* and *Volk* offered a bulwark against the *Gleichschaltung* imposed by the Nazis, Ostermayr invokes these terms as a level ostensibly below the political. He does so in patent misrecognition of the fact that National Socialism never tired of appealing to precisely these strata of collective consciousness, using them as the basis for an expansionist definition of Heimat, nation, and *Lebensraum*. In this sense, Ostermayr's attempted self-exculpation illustrates precisely the historically specific function of the *Heimatfilm* under National Socialism even where it looked entirely traditional. As Rentschler maintains, "The era's many genre films maintained the appearance of escapist vehicles and innocent recreations while functioning within a larger program."[96] This general assessment holds true for the particular case of Ostermayr's Heimat films as well. By functionalizing the local in the service of the overarching nationalist project at the expense of the often complicated mediations between Heimat and nation that had still obtained around the turn of the century, National Socialism erased the distinction between Heimat and nation. In this situation, to withdraw to the local as a means of self-exculpation becomes disingenuous at best; it becomes downright self-contradictory if it is treated as an act of resistance.

If we follow Witte's argument and focus on the function of cinema under National Socialism rather than on the "Fascist film," then Peter Ostermayr clearly played an integral part in the film industry and its ideological function during the years between 1933 and 1945. By offering the public highly popular images of his "bayerische Heimat" tuned to the unquenchable optimism of Ganghofer's standardized plots, Ostermayr served Ufa well, boasting on more than one occasion that early productions such as *Schloß Hubertus* (1934) and *Der Jäger von Fall* (1936) continued to play well into the war years. But Ostermayr illustrates only one paradigm of the *Heimatfilm* under Fascism, one which needs to be complemented by a second perspective.

As critics have come to realize, what constitutes a Fascist film on the textual level can be very similar to what constitutes a Hollywood film of the same era. In view of this overlap between two apparently opposed culture industries, Eric Rentschler has noted that "Nazi film was traditional through and through."[97] As the example of Ostermayr shows, Nazi film did not overwrite preexisting structures entirely; it remained "traditional" in the manifest continuity of personnel, plots, and motifs. But a different "traditionalism" manifests itself in a number of *Heimatfilme* of the Nazi era that negotiated the dialectics of tradition and modernity in ways consistent with other historical moments of the genre. Films like *Der Strom* (1941) and *Die goldene Stadt* (1942) demonstrate a continuity in terms of the dominant *function* of the *Heimatfilm*. Like many other instances I analyze, these films "engineer" advances of technological modernity in provincial settings, thereby helping to attenuate the impact of change. The difference between these and earlier (or later) films, then, is not so much textual as it is contextual. The political function of such films, while not necessarily legible on their aesthetic surface, nonetheless remains tied to the context of National Socialism. The ideological agenda of the Nazis' cinematic use of Heimat gains sharp contours if we situate it in relation to the discourse of "reactionary modernism" as described by Jeffrey Herf.[98]

DRAINING THE SWAMPS: THE MODERNIZATION OF BLOOD AND SOIL

From the first sound films, *Im Banne der Berge* (1931) and *Gipfelstürmer* (1933), through the majority of the Ganghofer adaptations, Ostermayr's work prolonged the tradition of the *Bergfilm* into the Third Reich. But it was Luis Trenker, a student of Arnold Fanck, who contributed the most faithful update of Fanck's modernist mountain panoramas for the Nazi cinema with *Der verlorene Sohn* (1934). With its striking montages of Alpine attractions like logging and skiing, Trenker's directorial debut remains a compelling example of the mountain film's modernist celebration of the archaic. Though the film ostensibly exorcises the Third Reich's fascination with America by extolling the virtue of an Alpine Heimat, it also imports a distinctly modern dynamism into the mountain world through cinematography and editing. *Der verlorene Sohn* "contrasts the glory of the homeland with the malaise of modern Manhattan."[99] But the famous dissolve that transports the protagonist Tonio from his Alpine peaks to Manhattan with its skyscrapers leaves its mark on the plot as well: it is as if the film downplays the energy of the modern metropolis in languid sequences and contemplative long shots in order to transfer it to the rapidly edited festivities "back home" in the Alpine Heimat. The modernism of *Der verlorene Sohn* tends to undermine its antimodern critique.[100]

Thomas Elsaesser has argued that such films consequently pose "a severe test for any attempt to sharply differentiate between modernism, modernization, and modernity."[101] While *Der verlorene Sohn* implicitly confounds this distinction by playing different cinematic registers and spaces of modernity against one another, other films of the era were quite explicit in advocating a reconciliation, or compromise, between their investment in Heimat tradition on the one hand and modernization on the other. For example, Hans Müller's *Aufruhr der Herzen* (1944), an Alpine drama about the threat of industrialization, begins with a title celebrating the age-old artisanship of the blacksmiths in the small Tyrolean village of Fulpmes. The title already suggests the film's conclusion: while "technological progress" almost kills the village, "the men of Fulpmes, who clung to their old forms of life and their traditions, did everything in order to preserve their artisanship in the new times." The ensuing plot dramatizes and visualizes this conflict between the old and the new. Picturesque images of Alpine valleys and rushing streams introduce us to the Alps as a timeless space where the blacksmiths' tradition seems an organic extension of nature. However, a young investor brings industrial modernity to this idyll. The consequences are drastic: as some villagers are forced to leave in order to make a living, others join to destroy the local smithy in order to make room for the new axe factory. But this symbolic replacement of the old with the new, and of tradition with progress, is soon attenuated by another development linked to modernity: Alpine tourism. As the metropolitan masses invade the mountain world, the blacksmiths find a new market for their quality products. Where the lives of mountaineers depend on them, the factory's mass-produced axes cannot compete with the quality and reliability of hand-wrought iron. The chairman of the Alpenverein recognizes this life-saving difference and grants a lucrative contract to the local blacksmiths. Though the factory owner challenges the deal, the blacksmiths prevail in a dramatic finale. When they march on the next town in order to "preserve our old artisanship," they are vindicated by the judge, who reformulates the film's message: "It cannot be the task of industry to replace artisanship where it still has a role to play. One must not destroy tradition, but preserve it." Significantly, this victory of the old does not come at the expense of the new. Rather, in keeping with a formula at the heart of the Heimat genre, the film ends with an imaginary solution to the conflict between tradition and progress, one which allows for the ostensibly harmonious coexistence of both.

This reconciliation can take various forms—from the negotiated peace between artisanship and technology in *Aufruhr der Herzen*, to the compromise between provincial isolation and the acceptance of a new train connection in *Die Kreuzlschreiber* (1944), to the frequent plots involving reconciliations between old, obstinate peasant patriarchs and young, dynamic, morally upstanding sons and daughters (examples range from the forgettable *Wenn die Sonne wieder scheint* [1943] to the celebrated melodrama *Die goldene Stadt*, to which I return below). A catalog description of *Aufruhr der Herzen* sums up the clichéd logic of compromise that underlies all such plots: "The village has been saved from economic ruin. . . . Tradition and progress find a common path towards the future. After a bitter struggle, the generations are reconciled."[102]

The Alps are not the only space in Nazi cinema where nature, the provincial, and the archaic meet modernity. A similar confrontation plays out in films that negotiate notions of Heimat in the lowlands. Where the *Bergfilm* had featured an elevated sublime landscape and technologized it, these films invert the topography to explore Germany's lower reaches. That exploration can take on the rather unsettling connotations of an expressionist horror film, as in Frank Wysbar's *Fährmann Maria*, which I discuss in a later chapter; or it can be entrusted to an engineer whose task it is to stop a river or drain a swamp, thereby securing and modernizing the landscape for greater agricultural productivity. This is the ideological labor performed in the 1942 production *Der Strom*, a film ostensibly "inspired by love for the German Heimat" and re-released in the 1950s under the title *Wenn du noch eine Heimat hast*.[103] The film was directed by Günther Rittau, whose long experience as cameraman for productions such as Fritz Lang's *Die Nibelungen* (1922–24) and *Metropolis* (1926) or Joe May's *Asphalt* (1928) shows in the impressive cinematography.[104] The plot of *Der Strom* is structured around two brothers who incarnate opposite attitudes towards local tradition, especially when it comes to taming the river that keeps the peasants in check with the recurring threat of floods. Peter relies on the time-honored strategy of manning the dams and only repairing whatever needs fixing in an emergency, whereas Heinrich wants to tame the river through technology. He devises plans to reinforce the dams and adjust the river bed, but when he submits them to the (Weimar) authorities, they are dismissed. Frustrated, he leaves for better opportunities abroad. After spending a decade in North and South America, the prodigal son returns home at the call of the new regime. National Socialism, we are asked to infer, makes up for the failures of the Weimar *Systemzeit* by bringing modern technology to the provinces. The Nazis, not Weimar, are cast as the great modernizers with the good sense to capitalize on the training that America has provided Heinrich and which his homeland denied him during the Weimar years. He agrees to pass up an enticing offer to build a dam in Japan for the job of taming the river that runs through his hometown. An exemplary "new man" for the Nazi era, Heinrich unites worldly expertise with love of Heimat. Consequently, his vision carries the day in the battle with nature. Indeed, he is the only one of three brothers to survive the storm at the film's climax. Whereas the tradition-oriented Peter dies in the flood, Heinrich survives to carry the Heimat towards a new future, triumphing over superstition and tradition in his bid to save the village. The fate of Heimat, this film suggests, is inescapably tied to place and nature; it is best managed, however, not by tradition but by modern engineering.

A similar dynamic characterizes another production from 1942, Veit Harlan's *Die goldene Stadt*. An exemplary melodrama of the Nazi era, *Die goldene Stadt* maps the ideological location of Heimat, even and especially under Fascism, between the push of tradition, located in the countryside, and the pull of modernity, associated with the city. *Die goldene Stadt* ultimately works to bridge these contradictions in an effort to "modernize blood and soil."[105] The film's protagonist is Anna, herself the product of a marriage between city and country: her mother came from the nearby "golden" city of Prague to marry local farmer Jobst. But we soon get an inkling of the troubled, or *unheimlich*, nature of the rural idyll into which Anna's mother married when we learn that she drowned herself in the swamp. Anna's parents' generation still stands for the irreconcilability between country and city, an opposition that is gendered in strikingly contradictory ways by the film.[106] Significantly, *Die goldene Stadt* does not place the blame for this failure only on the threat that the city poses to Heimat (though it does this, too). As I have suggested, the rural space of Heimat itself is described as deficient. Located on the edge of the swamp as a vaguely *unheimlich* threat, the farm is under the tutelage of a stubborn, superstitious, and self-centered patriarch. Jobst embodies the irrationality of tradition, a value that the film significantly does *not* celebrate. Thus, Anna will fare no better than her mother before her. Drawn to the city of her mother, she succumbs to its dangers and becomes pregnant. When she returns to the Heimat, her father refuses her a place in his home, and she follows in her mother's footsteps. According to a fatal patriarchal logic, the rural space of Heimat is threatened both from the outside (the city) and the inside (the swamp, the stubborn patriarch). That space is also defined as unchanging: Jobst opposes the draining of the swamp for the simple reason that the latter "has always been there."

But the film's narrative logic contradicts the irrational traditionalism, embodied by the local patriarch. For in the end, it is neither Jobst nor traditionalism nor the primordial nature of Heimat that wins the day, but the plan to drain the swamp. After rescuers pull Anna's body from the swamp in the penultimate scene, Jobst breaks down and passes the baton of patriarchal tradition to Anna's erstwhile suitor, Thomas (played by Rudolf Prack, who would go on to become one of the key stars of the *Heimatfilm* of the 1950s). In the sacrificial logic of this film, both women have to commit suicide for Jobst to learn that tradition requires change. As a member of the next generation, it is up to the soft-spoken Thomas to administer that change. Thomas, who represents a marriage of provincial tradition with progressive technology, drains the swamp to make way for cornfields, and tradition becomes updated for the future.

In this reading, the most significant image of Harlan's film is arguably its last, which, as Stephen Lowry has pointed out, amounts to an ideological compromise:[107] a vast field of ripening corn swaying in the wind, this is an image of regeneration, of benevolent and productive nature. But it has taken the duration of the film to redefine the countryside as a promising, wholesome site of agricultural production. Up to this point, the film's spatial logic had offered only two equally unappealing alternatives: on the one hand, the countryside, a stifling patriarchal social space as well as a site of primordial, untamed, and dangerous nature; on the other hand, the "golden city" of Prague, presented cinematographically in "festive tones," but with a lure that proves fatal to the heroine.[108] The film's spatial system literally leaves Anna no place to go, other than the swamp in which she finds her death. The final image shows us that very swamp after its transformation into farm-land. Though it comes after the film's melodramatic climax and thus func-tions dramaturgically as an afterthought, it sums up both a central project of the film and the cost of its realization.

In contrast to a propaganda vehicle like *Heimkehr, Die goldene Stadt* contributes to National Socialist ideology not simply by advocating a myth-ical *Blut-und-Boden* definition of the *völkisch* project, but in a far more insidious manner. By championing a reconciliation between tradition and technology, the film exemplifies what Thomas Mann saw as the "really characteristic and dangerous aspect" of National Socialism, namely "its mix-ture of robust modernity and an affirmative stance toward progress com-bined with dreams of the past."[109] Jeffrey Herf has identified this mixture as the defining characteristic of a broader ideology of "reactionary mod-ernism" which was first formulated during the Weimar Republic and was to become a defining feature of Nazi ideology. For all the archaic elements that also played into the latter, and for all the explicit antimodern rhetoric of Fascism, it would be a mistake to equate the Nazi dream of blood and soil with rural nostalgia. Instead, as Herf's term indicates, Nazi modernism com-bined different attitudes towards modernity. In an overview of Germany's history of modernization, Thomas Nipperdey identifies three such attitudes in the Third Reich. These included, first, the antimodern stance that equated modernity with the destruction of *Gemeinschaft*, of the essential (cultural) unity of the *Volk*. In this respect, Fascism was an "antimodernization move-ment." Second, Nipperdey identifies the radicalization of this position. The antidote to modernization was not tradition, but "something prehistoric, archaic." Consequently, the antimodernism of the Nazis itself was not tra-ditional, but "radical, utopian, revolutionary." Third, however, "Fascism was simultaneously hypermodern in its style, its chosen means, and its effects. It was a modernization movement."[110] Herf's notion of "reactionary mod-ernism" is a particularly useful one because it provides a discursive and his-torical framework in which to articulate the simultaneity of the different attitudes towards modernization that Nipperdey identifies.

Reactionary modernists, in Herf's definition, sought to dissociate (tech-nological) modernity from notions of (Western) *Zivilisation* and to align it instead with (German) *Kultur.* Writings by intellectuals such as Ernst Jünger—"reactionary modernism's most interesting proponent from a media-historical perspective"[111]—provided the arguments and many strik-ing images for the reactionary fusion of technology and romanticism. World War I had been for Jünger the crucible of a new era, in which technology took on the authenticity, the beauty, indeed the sublime that the romantics had ascribed to nature. Jünger, Herf notes, "was the first of Germany's right-wing literary intellectuals to separate the idea of *Gemeinschaft* from the slightest hint of preindustrial nostalgia."[112] Technology was now a force to be celebrated, according to Jünger, or at least to be "tamed," as Werner Sombart would put it.[113] Consequently, to the degree that Fascism took Jünger's "magical realism" and Sombart's anti-Semitic defense of German *Kultur* on board, its reactionary modernism distinguished itself from earlier *völkisch* antimodernists, including the Heimat ideologues whose writings had provided the discursive context for Ganghofer's *Hochland* aesthetics around the turn of the century. Though Ganghofer's writings register the advances of modernity in ambivalent ways, as I argued in the previous chapter, they certainly did not embrace progress or "reconcile [themselves] with the machine . . . to see in it not only the useful but the beautiful as well."[114] Reactionary modernism in Jünger's programmatic version celebrated modern technology as "second nature." As such, modernity could be affirmed and yet held to be "no less mysterious than the natural landscape was for the German romantics of the early nineteenth century."[115]

The discourse of reactionary modernism colored many facets of culture, ideology, and politics in the Third Reich and through the end of the Nazi regime. As Herf demonstrates, the main contributors to this discourse were not just prominent Weimar intellectuals like Jünger and Oswald Spengler and other mandarin thinkers such as Carl Schmitt, Hans Freyer, and Werner Sombart. Another group of reactionary modernists that Herf singles out was formed by members of the German engineering profession. Like the more famous philosophers and intellectuals, contributors to journals of the German engineering associations hoped to give technology the aura of *Kultur*. As the agents of such an agenda under National Socialism, engineers strove to legitimate technology even as they distanced themselves from Enlightenment rationality.[116]

This discourse provides an important context for the treatment of modernization in the *Heimatfilm* of the Third Reich in general; it also helps to explain the pivotal role of the engineer in films like *Der Strom* and *Die goldene Stadt*. In the latter, the engineer Leidwein arrives from the city at the beginning of the film to drain the local swamp and reclaim land for agricultural production. He mediates between the two antithetical worlds of the film: a refined urbanite from Prague, he has preserved an appreciation for the countryside and for the values of Heimat (he eulogizes the "simple" life in the country and prefers that Anna wear traditional dresses rather than urban attire). Consequently, the film entrusts its underlying ideological mission to Leidwein as the most "trustworthy" and professional character in the cast. The engineer serves precisely the task of the reactionary modernists by giving technological progress a human face while extolling the virtues of Heimat. He is introduced as a model of moral masculinity who, despite his metropolitan provenance, elicits more sympathy than the farmer Jobst. By vilifying the city as a site of *Zivilisation* but entrusting the space of Heimat to Leidwein's gently modernizing hands (and to Thomas, as the representative of the new generation), *Die goldene Stadt* performs precisely the "selective embrace of modernity" that Herf attributes to reactionary modernism.[117]

In historically specific variations that I will trace in later chapters, the *Heimatfilm* of the 1950s would again take up the project of reactionary modernism. Indeed, the ideologically charged mixture of tradition and modernity marks a significant site of continuity between the Nazi cinema and the productions of the 1950s in particular. Before turning to the latter, however, one particular film deserves our attention, a film that illustrates the transition from Ufa under the Nazis to the cinema of the Adenauer era. German film historiography tends to view the years from the end of World War II until the foundation of two separate German states in 1949 as a hiatus of sorts, defined by *Trümmerfilme*, films that showcase not the beauty of Heimat but the rubble of bombed-out cities. Among this short-lived cycle that is book-ended by the Nazis' last stand in *Kolberg* (1945) and the desperately titled (but never completed) *Das Leben geht weiter* (1945), on the one hand, and by the launching of the *Heimatfilmwelle* with *Schwarzwaldmädel* (1950) and *Grün ist die Heide* (1951), on the other, one "rubble film" stands out for our present purposes. The self-reflexive *Film ohne Titel* of 1947–48, written by Helmut Käutner and directed by Rudolf Jugert, itself the product of a transitional phase in filmmaking, maps a transition from Ufa to Heimat. It does so by once again enacting a compromise between rural tradition and various forms of the "new," even as it paves the way for the rediscovery of the countryside in the early 1950s.

PART II

Routes

When travel . . . becomes a kind of norm, dwelling demands explication.

JAMES CLIFFORD

3 Launching the *Heimatfilmwelle*

From the Trümmerfilm *to* Grün ist die Heide

Her majesty the audience wants such . . . films—it appears that this
is what *Heimatfilme* need to look like.

CAPITO

"DAS IST KITSCH, HERR FRITSCH":
FROM UFA TO RUBBLE TO HEIMAT

Rudolf Jugert's *Film ohne Titel* begins in the country, where we find three
filmmakers gathered under a tree, engrossed in the effort of coming up with
ideas for a "zeitnahe Komödie." A scriptwriter and a director are beset by
doubts about the feasibility of such a project, arguing that any attempt at
producing a "light film" would appear "banal or cynical against the bleak
background of our times." Their star, however, insists on the need for entertainment. Played by Willy Fritsch playing himself, he is keen on using the
project as a vehicle for his well-established image as a romantic lead alongside Lilian Harvey in Ufa films such as *Der Kongreß tanzt* and *Glückskinder.* Consequently, he advocates a continuation of Ufa's successful tradition of lighthearted popular fare, even and particularly for the postwar era:
"People need relaxation: they want to be entertained."

Despite their different ideas about what the postwar audience "needs," all
three agree that there are certain types of films—that is, genres—that it
does not need. To be avoided at all costs are the *Trümmerfilm,* the *Heim-
kehrerfilm,* the fraternization film; nor would Fritsch participate in an anti-
Nazi film ("After all, that would be tactless"), and they share an aversion to
the political film, the propaganda film, and the "bomb film." Once the genre
palette of contemporary German cinema has thus been cleared away like the
rubble blocking the urban streets, *Film ohne Titel* embarks on its main
diegetic material, a narrative embedded within the story about the three
filmmakers. This is initially told not as the plot of the fictional film in the
making, but as the actual story of Martin and Christine, a couple who happen to interrupt the trio in their open-air script development session. Only

gradually will it dawn on the film team—and on the spectator—that this "true" story is actually the kind of tale that merits telling in the postwar years. The scenes from Martin's and Christine's lives during and after the war will become the basis for the as yet untitled film by the threesome under the tree.

The story is that of an urbane, middle-aged man from Hannover who was trained as a carpenter but goes into the antiques business with a young woman named Angelika Rösch. During the final days of the war, he hires Christine as a maid for the bourgeois household he leads with his widowed sister, Viktoria. Christine is introduced as a girl from the country who, unfamiliar with the strict etiquette of a different class, is ill at ease in her new surroundings. The romance that develops between her and Martin foregrounds their seemingly insurmountable differences: Martin represents the urban upper middle class to her rural peasant background; she perceives him as exceedingly *fein*, whereas he initially stumbles over her "simplicity." Feeling out of place, Christine leaves the city to return to her parents' farm when Viktoria reprimands her for her affair with Martin.

Martin, on the other hand, is conscripted in the *Volkssturm*, and his villa is destroyed. Forced out of the city like millions of other refugees, expellees, and returning POWs during those years, he ends up on Christine's farm. Here they rekindle their romance under reversed conditions—now it is Martin who is clearly out of place. A refugee among others, he considers himself a burden to the household. When Christine's father refuses Martin's request for his daughter's hand in marriage, Martin leaves for the city to take up his business partnership with Angelika once more. But he soon realizes that antiques are hardly what a postwar economy needs most, and returns to carpentry for which he was trained, making "simple" furniture. This move initiates his economic recovery and, in more ways than one, clears the path for the final union with Christine.

The self-reflexivity of *Film ohne Titel* obviates the need for the fictional film within the film ever to be made, since we—as viewers of Rudolf Jugert's film—have already witnessed it in the making.[1] However, as a metatext which provides a commentary on postwar filmmaking, the framing device is highly significant. It first sketches an impasse (lack of adequate screenplays, impossibility of comedy formats, inadequacy of available genres, etc.) and then proposes a solution by turning to "a story as real life tells it." In a departure from both the traditions of Ufa advocated (and embodied) by Fritsch, and the expressionist leanings of the *Trümmerfilm* in productions such as *Die Mörder sind unter uns*, *Zwischen gestern und morgen*, and *. . . und über uns der Himmel*, the framing device grounds a renewed

Figure 2. Taking the *Trümmerfilm* to the countryside: *Film ohne Titel* (1948). Courtesy Deutsches Filminstitut–DIF, Frankfurt.

commitment to cinematic realism. Thanks to this strategy, the film won the 1949 Bambi award for most successful film of the year, and Hildegard Knef—ostensibly the incarnation of "real life" in the film—received the award for best actress.

Yet, by virtue of the embedded structure of their self-reflexive narrative, Käutner and Jugert are able to construct the very category of "real life" as part of their fiction, for only the multiplication of narrative levels allows them to introduce the distinction between "real life" and "fiction" in the first place. For all its programmatic commitment to stories "as life tells them," *Film ohne Titel* is scarcely a neo-realist work, but a programmatic fiction about the cinema in a transitional moment. More specifically, it is a film about bringing the cinema home, taking it out of the cities and into the provinces, which hold forth the promise not of reality but of reconciliation, not of reflexivity but of simplicity.

The film's playful structure climaxes when the scriptwriter and Fritsch have caught on to the director's idea of transforming the very story he has been recounting into a film, but before they know how Martin and Christine's story ends. With uncontained excitement, both offer their own views of how to conclude the film. So far, the story has been told by the director in flashbacks introduced by brief transitional voice-overs. As his voice has yielded to the diegetic world that he evokes, we have been allowed to forget his presence and to take the events in Martin's and Christine's lives for "real." Not so in the case of the two endings we are now offered. As the scriptwriter's and Fritsch's excited voices explain the rapid succession of images that flash across the screen, the conclusions they envision could hardly be more different. The scriptwriter insists on avoiding the convention of the happy ending, choosing a starkly expressionist style instead. Suggesting the title *Antiquitäten* for the film,[2] he imagines (and we see) a staccato of images to match his enthusiastic cues: "Hannover. Dusk. Ruins from below. Pan. A bar in the ruins. One hears music. Loud. Aggressive. Interior. Close-ups of faces. A dealer. Bar girls. Now details. Extreme close-ups. A sweaty neck. Glasses. Some thigh . . ." As he continues, his vision materializes in canted camera angles and chiaroscuro lighting; Martin has slipped into the underworld of black markets and alcohol, and in the end he mutely witnesses Christine's wedding to a younger man before he walks off toward the bleak horizon.

Predictably, Willy Fritsch wants nothing to do with this cinematic marriage of expressionism and existentialism, insisting instead that "the happy ending is entirely logical": all it requires is for Martin to become a farmer. The ensuing montage is straight out of an Ufa production, as is the title that Fritsch favors: his suggestion that the film be called *Königskinder* recalls the popular 1936 comedy *Glückskinder*, starring Fritsch himself alongside Lilian Harvey.[3] In Fritsch's scenario, we witness the radiant star chopping wood, wielding the plow, sowing corn, and riding in a horse-drawn carriage against deliberately mediocre rear projections of the passing landscape. The images are brightly lit, the symphonic score is energetic and upbeat, and the close-ups of Fritsch numerous. His version of the film culminates in a double marriage in Christine's village—"in keeping with popular tradition and in authentic traditional dress," as Fritsch insists.

The playwright is not amused. "Das ist Kitsch, Herr Fritsch," he berates the Ufa star. Their dispute is settled, of course, by the director, who once again reminds them to stick to reality and invites them to find out the ending from Christine and Martin themselves at Christine's brother's wedding the following Sunday. With this solution, which brings the internal story up to date with the frame narrative, it appears that we have avoided the excesses of both the hyper-*Trümmerfilm* imagined by the writer and the Ufa comedy imagined by Fritsch; overcoming both of these ostensibly outdated traditions, the appropriate "contemporary comedy" would establish a new discourse on realism. The reviews of Jugert's film picked up precisely this message and certified the currency of this realist discourse.[4]

But the "true story" that carries the day contains more than a bit of both the *Trümmerfilm* and of the kitsch favored by Fritsch. It is, in Robert Shandley's apt words, "the most ingeniously disguised fantasy of them all."[5] The film begins in the closing days of the war, with Hannover under constant bomb attacks and Martin's villa reduced to rubble; the presence of Knef, an actress firmly associated with the *Trümmerfilm*, adds to the narrative and iconographic references to that genre in the film. On the other hand, Fritsch's vision does seem to win the day in the sense that *Film ohne Titel* ends happily with a marriage; even if it is not (yet) Christine and Martin's, it takes place on her parents' farm, showcases an identifiably rural décor, and is accompanied by a continuous sound track of lively dance music. Most importantly, it is a conciliatory ending, one which resolves the tensions and contradictions that had constituted the narrative material of the plot: Martin the city dweller and Christine the farmer's daughter meet literally halfway between Hannover and the countryside as each leaves to find the other. Martin has learned the lesson of "simplicity" and has won over Christine's father with the promise of a secure income. On the meta-cinematic level, the pairing of the young Hilde Knef with the seasoned Willy Fritsch on the dance floor during the wedding clearly signals the successful integration of the old Ufa tradition with the dawn of a new era.[6]

Film ohne Titel, the most successful German film of 1948, is thus quintessentially a transitional film that illustrates the regrouping of (West) German cinema after 1945. Käutner and Jugert provide a clear topography and a sense of direction for that transition. The plot leads ineluctably from the city to the country, and the various reconciliations at its climax take place not in the ruins of the metropolis but in the idyll of the countryside. As Shandley argues, *Film ohne Titel* marks the "end of rubble film discourse" in that it is the first *Trümmerfilm* to leave the metropolis and to name it as the source of conflict.[7] I would add that *Film ohne Titel* is also a premonition of things to come, as the fictional script development on the heath foreshadows the excursions of innumerable production teams into the German landscape during the 1950s. In its reconciliation of Ufa tradition with the *Trümmerfilm*, and in its explicit refusal of current postwar generic categories, *Film ohne Titel* paves the way for the rise of the Heimat genre in the following decade. Though this would scarcely be the "realist" panacea envisioned by the director in (or of) the film, the benefit of hindsight allows us to perceive constitutive features of the *Heimatfilm* within the particular "realism" of this story. Not only is *Film ohne Titel* the first (and last) *Trümmerfilm* to showcase the kind of rural milieu that we associate with the iconography of the *Heimatfilm*; in many respects, it also anticipates the cultural logic of the *Heimatfilm*. That logic centers on a shifting configuration of space and place in the "long decade" of the 1950s. It plays out in the narrative negotiation of the tensions between the city and the country; in the context of massive, often forced mobility as millions of displaced persons crisscross the country, sent by the authorities from overpopulated urban centers to rural communities; and against the backdrop of an emergent postwar consumer economy that is undergoing the "miraculous" transition from *Antiquitäten* to modern supply-and-demand commodity production. All of these transformations are themselves negotiated through a wave of *Heimatfilms* that would be launched only two years after *Film ohne Titel* by Hans Deppe's *Schwarzwaldmädel*. The genre would come into its own with *Grün ist die Heide,* in many ways the prototype of the *Heimatfilm*.

SHOW AND TELL: HEIMAT AS SPECTACLE

Willy Fritsch's dance with Hilde Knef in *Film ohne Titel* was to remain a one-time affair. Knef, whose image and fortune seemed linked to the short-lived *Trümmerfilm*, left Germany for the United States in the 1950s. By contrast, the old Ufa star's staying power, like that of his numerous colleagues in all domains of film production, turned out to be greater than that of the young *Trümmer-Diva*. It is a further mark of the multiple continuities stretching from the Ufa days through the postwar years and into the 1950s that three years after *Film ohne Titel,* we again encounter Fritsch in a signal film of the new decade. He plays the role of a local judge in the 1951 version of *Grün ist die Heide.* From Ufa to the transitional moment of *Film ohne Titel* to the *Heimatfilm,* Fritsch personifies the continuities that connect the different eras of German cinema.[8] *Grün ist die Heide* itself likewise serves this function, reminding us of the longevity and historical embeddedness of the genre. In particular, the film illustrates the personal continuities and the practice of remaking that connect the genre to the Ufa tradition. Directed by Hans Deppe, an established figure in the *Heimatfilm* industry who had worked on numerous projects for Peter Ostermayr throughout the 1930s and 1940s,[9] *Grün ist die Heide* is a faithful remake of Hans Behrendt's 1932 film by the same title. This original version (marketed at the time as "the first true German *Heimatfilm*") had been scripted by Bobby Lüthge, a prolific screenwriter on films ranging from *Fridericus Rex* (1922) and *Hitlerjunge Quex* (1934) to repeated collaborations with Deppe. With Otto Gebühr in the role of Gottfried Lüdersen in the 1951 remake, Fritsch is joined by another seasoned Ufa colleague, one best remembered for his repeated impersonation of

Figure 3. Prototype of the Heimat film: *Grün ist die Heide* (1951). Courtesy Deutsches Filminstitut–DIF, Frankfurt.

Frederick the Great (in *Fridericus Rex, Der Alte Fritz* [1928], and *Fridericus* [1936]).[10]

A popular film with audiences in the 1950s and with television viewers ever since its initial broadcast in 1980, the 1951 version of *Grün ist die Heide* quickly established itself as a "protoype of the *Heimatfilm*."[11] Like the 1932 original, the film features the northern German plains as an idyllic backdrop for the story of Lüder Lüdersen, whose illicit passion for hunting disrupts the peace of the local community. The wayward baron is redeemed when authorities manage to arrest a second poacher who has been killing deer for personal gain. On one level a rural crime story, *Grün ist die Heide* also features the inevitable romantic plot, complicated by the fact that it brings together Lüdersen's daughter Helga (Sonja Ziemann) and the young game warden Rainer (Rudolf Prack) who is charged with apprehending the poacher. Deppe's 1951 version adds a further narrative level by introducing what Lüthge called the "topical, modern motif" of expulsion. In the remake, the Lüdersens are expellees from the Eastern provinces, and the presence of an entire Silesian *Landsmannschaft* in the *Heide* fundamentally transforms the rural community of the original. An itinerant group of singers and a traveling circus troupe round out the eclectic social structure of this ostensibly remote corner of postwar Germany.

As one reviewer put it after witnessing the elaborate premiere of the film at Berlin's Delphi theater, "Her majesty the audience wants such entertainment films—it appears that this is what *Heimatfilme* need to look like."[12] Defined as a prototype from its very first showing, *Grün ist die Heide* has provided numerous scholars with occasion to establish the basic features of the genre. With its mix of narrative and iconographic levels, Deppe's film serves as Gerhard Bliersbach's motto for a retrospective on all of postwar German cinema, which he titles *So grün war die Heide*. In keeping with his attempt to locate a number of exemplary films in the "psychosocial context" of the postwar era, Bliersbach begins his book by reading *Grün ist die Heide* as Freudian wish fulfillment. In hindsight, the film appears to him to be an attempt to substitute the image of a better world for the "unsatisfactory reality" of Germany in 1951. Echoing Kracauer's analysis of Weimar cinema, Bliersbach reads *Grün ist die Heide* as a case study for the nationally overdetermined oedipal constellation of the *Heimatfilm* in the 1950s. The genre, he suggests, allows Germans to rehabilitate broken father figures and to keep West Germany's "children" in line through the kinder, gentler (but no less effective) authority of a maternally coded Heimat.[13]

Bliersbach's psychohistory is idiosyncratic by design. And yet he merely reiterates the cliché of the *Heimatfilm* as itself a clichéd *heile Welt*. To be sure, *Grün ist die Heide* offers plenty of idyllic images, a narrative of reconciliation, and promises of (re)integration. In this sense, the film offers viewers an intact, self-contained world. The community on the heath provides a site to which postwar Germans could retreat in order to heal the wounds of war, forge a new sense of *Gemeinschaft*, and forget the pressing social questions of the day. The village and its surroundings are held together by the voices of the itinerant singers, the bucolic spirit of Hermann Löns, a popular Heimat poet from the turn of the century, and the beauty of the verdant landscape. Social anonymity is reduced to a minimum in this small village, where the judge, the game warden, the pharmacist, and the local estate owner all drink together at the *Stammtisch*. For those who seek comfort in solitude, there is always the nearby forest, a *heile Welt* of flora and fauna.

But this view of the undisturbed idyll is difficult to maintain upon closer inspection. For clearly, all is not well in the Lüneburg Heath, as some early, foreboding images of Lüdersen's poaching and the ensuing plot suggest. We first see Lüdersen in the forest, right after a close-up that shows the game warden musing that he'd give anything to find the poacher. The editing leaves no doubt as to Lüdersen's sinister character, and an ensuing chase sequence in which he flees the warden further indicts him. Though the narrative is organized to motivate Lüdersen's behavior, giving the viewer reasons for his dark habit and exculpating him in the end, the morbid baron remains an irritating presence in the Heimat idyll. Moreover, given the film's rather laborious (re)constitution of social harmony, it is misleading to claim that *Grün ist die Heide* "offers a most unproblematic plot to the movie-going audience," a plot in which "happy country folk in idyllic surroundings feel sheltered in an ordered world."[14] Once a landowner in Silesia, Lüdersen suffers from the quintessential postwar syndrome of *Heimatlosigkeit*, of which his poaching is clearly a symptom.[15] When his vows to stop poaching turn out to be as reliable as an addict's promise to break the habit, his daughter insists that they leave for the anonymity of the city. But even the proposed move to the city, arguably the most radical shock treatment imaginable in the context of a *Heimatfilm*, quickly turns out to be a false lead. What Lüdersen needs is not renewed displacement, but (re)integration. The film works to make over the Lüneburg Heath from a space of *Heimatlosigkeit* and restlessness into Heimat regained.

This is accomplished in the closing sequences of the film, but the integration of Lüdersen and the concomitant stabilization of Heimat turn out to be somewhat perfunctory. While everyone else is still at the *Schützenfest*, Lüdersen takes a final walk in his beloved forest. Here, he happens to track down a second poacher whose transgression makes Lüdersen's habit look like a minor misdemeanor. An employee of the circus has been trapping deer in the woods as food for the lions, allowing him to embezzle the budget for horse meat. Far worse, he has murdered a police officer who had apparently discovered him in the woods. Lüdersen thus appears to cure himself by finding someone else to take the blame. In confronting the poacher-as-murderer, he upholds the law of the community that he himself had been breaking, thus facilitating his own integration into the social fabric of the Heimat.

Significantly, however, by locating the "real" criminal, Lüdersen takes on the function of precisely those authorities (the game warden and the local police) to whose laws he has been told to submit. In a sense, this is tantamount to coming to terms with his own diminished authority as an expellee without private property. But it is not at all obvious that the displacement of the symptom onto another character actually constitutes a cure for Lüdersen himself: we have seen him relapse once, so why not again? As if in recognition of the fact that it generates more contradictions than it settles, the film's "happy" ending is rather abrupt, recalling Douglas Sirk's often-quoted comments on the ironic function of that convention in his melodramas.[16] Indeed, as in so many of Sirk's films from the 1950s, the glimpse of a better future for the protagonist comes at a heavy price. Lüdersen is shot while carrying out the act that is supposed to redeem him. Although the doctor informs his daughter that he will survive, Lüdersen remains absent from the closing images of the film—a sign of the difficulties involved in integrating the "other" into the film's idea of Heimat, and a past like Lüdersen's into the present of the Federal Republic. Instead, the final image is reserved for Sonja Ziemann and Rudolf Prack as representatives of the next generation. While they may represent hopes for a better future, the central story of Lüdersen suggests that all is not well in the Heimat even after its equilibrium has been tentatively regained. As Wilfried von Bredow and Hans-Friedrich Foltin rightly argue, the term *heile Welt*, which critics routinely (and pejoratively) use to characterize the space of the *Heimatfilm*, is actually quite misleading: "*Grün ist die Heide*, like most other Heimat films, is about a *divergence* [from the stable order of things] . . . as a matter of fact, one can hardly speak of a world in which all is well [*heile Welt*]."[17] Commenting on the claustrophobic social world of Sirk's *All That Heaven Allows* (1955), Rainer Werner Fassbinder wrote, "To judge by this film, an American small town is the last place I'd want to go."[18] The same could be said of more than one small German community after reviewing some of the *Heimatfilme* from the same decade.

In this reading, *Grün ist die Heide* is more than merely an escape or wish fulfillment. Instead it indexes some of the very instabilities and contradictions within the spaces that postwar West Germans would preserve as Heimat. Accordingly, a number of scholars have begun to read the *Heimatfilm* of the 1950s as a prism for postwar West German social, political, and cultural history. In all of these readings, *Grün ist die Heide* serves as a key reference, if not as the single representative example of the genre. Depending on a critic's focus, it exemplifies the aesthetic treatment of contemporary legal issues, such as the law to equalize burdens (*Lastenausgleich*); it demonstrates the function of *Heimatfilme* as films for coming to terms with the present; it illustrates the cinematic treatment of displacement and expulsion; it testifies to the genre's role in reconstructing a "moral masculinity" and a "girlish femininity" as socially sanctioned gender stereotypes; and it constructs the space of the heath as a utopian fantasy that affords the positive resolution of contemporary social and ideological concerns about territory and identity.[19] In their shared emphasis on the historical referentiality of the *Heimatfilm*, all of these analyses have contributed to a helpful revision of earlier attacks on the apolitical nature of the genre and on its alleged "holiday from history."[20] From their perspectives as cultural historians, political scientists, and sociologists, these authors have shown to what degree the *Heimatfilm* can serve as an archival source for writing the social, political, and cultural history of the 1950s. My own analyses of *Grün ist die Heide* and of other *Heimatfilme* below join these views by emphasizing the role of displacement, history, and modernity in these films. But I also propose a basic shift in focus by reintroducing some questions concerning methodology and film form which appear to have fallen by the wayside in the writings referenced above.

In particular, I find that available scholarship on *Grün ist die Heide* and on the *Heimatfilm* more generally suffers from a relative lack of attention to the specificity of film as a visual medium. In their readings of the *Heimatfilm*, a number of critics appear to have lent more weight to the illustrated plot synopses generated by distributors than to the films themselves. As a result, recent readings ably distill from the films a catalog of contemporary social concerns (housing, refugees, *Lastenausgleich*) and reactionary motifs (flight from reality, deference to authority, the patriarchal reorganization of postwar West German society). All of these concerns and motifs are undoubtedly relevant to our understanding of the *Heimatfilm*, but the emphasis on plot and action elides the fact that the cinematic "texts" at hand were—and remain—first and foremost a peculiar, generically specific, and qualitatively new kind of visual spectacle.[21] As such, *Heimatfilms* do not merely tell Heimat stories; more importantly, they show Heimat images (and stage Heimat songs) in ways not always immediately connected to the plot. This emphasis on the visual (and on the aural) is readily apparent to the viewer of almost any *Heimatfilm*. Indeed, a host of contemporary reviews explicitly acknowledged the preponderance of image over action and of showing over telling. Thus, to stay with the example of *Grün ist die Heide*, one reviewer argued, "The action is not the essential aspect of this film; it is a *Heimatfilm* in the good sense of the word. Opulent shots in surprisingly tender colors demonstrate the manifold beauties of the Lüneburg Heath in the glow of summer and in the mysterious tissue of white fog. The coarseness of the black elderberry bush, quiet wildlife shots, the colorful depiction of a local festival [*heimatliches Volksfest*] with traditional costumes and customs all delight the connoisseur of this jewel among German landscapes."[22] As in a number of other reviews of the time, the critic redeems the relatively weak construction of the plot with praise for the film's photography and imagery. Like the decision to credit the Austrian landscape as one of the actors in *Der Förster vom Silberwald* (1955), such comments serve as a reminder of the spectacular role of nature in the visual fabric of the *Heimatfilm*. This is not to say that the specific plots of the films are irrelevant altogether; rather, we need to account for the generically specific mixture of narration and description, of diegetically motivated, plot-bound elements and aspects of visual excess.[23] While the allegedly "typical" plot of *Grün ist die Heide* has been submitted to more or less exhaustive ideological critique, few scholars have paused to consider that the Heimat genre can hardly be defined in narrative terms alone. Among recent commentators, only Heide Fehrenbach reminds us that "what is perhaps most striking is the odd presence of visual 'excess' that does nothing to advance the plot" and that "*Heimatfilme* also showcased musical performance."[24] Both of these aspects—the *Heimatfilm*'s visual "excess" and its staging of performance—contribute to the specific forms of visual and aural spectacle that define the genre; any attempt to situate the functions of that genre historically requires that we investigate the role of the spectacular within the formal construction of the films.

To insist on the primacy of the (audio)visual in the genre is by no means to claim that close viewing of the *Heimatfilm* can reveal a hitherto undiscovered aesthetic mastery,[25] but it is important to note that these films drew audiences of millions by virtue of their promise to *visualize* images of Heimat in colorful panoramic formats. For all their "traditional" content, these were decidedly modern productions. Within the context of film history, their logic must be considered on a level with the Western or the widescreen epic, Hollywood's line of defense against the rise of television in the 1950s. In advertising the use of up-to-date color patterns, anamorphic lenses, and the resulting visual pleasures, the *Heimatfilm* of the decade was part of a broader set of strategies for keeping spectators in the theaters, even as these investments were used to produce aesthetic effects that we associate exclusively with the Heimat genre.[26] Likewise, the abundance of musical numbers that appeared in the films, were released on records, and whose lyrics were reprinted in program notes gave the *Heimatfilm* a specific aural dimension that consolidated its generic recognizability. With its emphasis on the visual pleasures of (filmed) landscapes and scenes from rural life, and on the featured *Volkslieder* and *Schlager*, the *Heimatfilm* is clearly a "spectacular" genre of the 1950s.

Grün ist die Heide serves as well as most other Heimat films of the decade to exemplify this staging of visual and aural spectacle. In the following section I ask: How does Deppe's film negotiate the tension between telling about and showing Heimat? What is its distinctive mode of address in the balance between a melodramatic plot and non-narrative spectacle and performance? I then turn to some of the songs featured in *Grün ist die Heide*, arguing that these work according to the same logic as its visual spectacle but add a particular dimension to the representation of Heimat as an imaginary place. My question here is how, in its musical numbers, *Grün ist die Heide* uses the visual cues of profilmic space on the one hand and the diegetic space of lyrics on the other to orchestrate Heimat as a site of audio-visual pleasure for its 1950s audiences.

VISUAL ATTRACTIONS

With *Grün ist die Heide*, producer Kurt Ulrich (Berolina-Film GmbH) and distributor Ilse Kubaschweski (Gloria-Film GmbH) capitalized on their smashing success with Hans Deppe's *Schwarzwaldmädel*, which had premiered a year earlier as "the first German color film."[27] *Schwarzwaldmädel* emphasized color as an attraction in its lush costume ball and revue scenes, as well as in its explorations of the Black Forest in full blossom; as a result, the film had drawn some 14 million spectators by 1952, enjoying an average run of 333 days in the year of its release.[28] *Grün ist die Heide*, referred to by contemporary critics as a "Northern German *Schwarzwaldmädel*," likewise showcased the new Gevacolor process. Publicity kits asked theater owners to design their advertisements for this "German Heimat epic in color" using the color spectrum of the heath as background.[29] Though contemporary critics by and large panned the film for its weak story and acting, they reserved special praise for the "surprisingly good" rendition of color. For *Grün ist die Heide* is as its title promises: green and brown hues vie for prominence with the varying primary colors of Sonja Ziemann's up-to-date fashions.[30] Indeed, the muted natural tones of the countryside (as well as of most of the men's traditional clothing, the game warden's uniforms in particular) supply an ideal backdrop for Ziemann's distinctly modern wardrobe and the corresponding type of femininity embodied by her character. A similar figure-ground relationship also characterizes the various colorful moments of performance that define this film's rather disjunctive narration.

The more or less linear development of the plot surrounding Lüder Lüdersen and his daughter Helga, and the proliferating subplots, are punctuated by non-narrative digressions ranging from contemplations of nature to moments of pure performance. Indeed, the film begins with one such moment as the camera pans down from the sky to three singers and then pans with them as they pass among a herd of sheep and sing the Löns song "Auf der Lüneburger Heide." These opening images turn out to be plot-driven only in retrospect, when the singers end up at the game warden's house, asking for food. Until we reach this point, after several cuts and two verses of the song, the viewer will have subordinated character and narrative to the contemplation of nature imagery. If this imagery, coupled with the lighthearted melody of the song, outlines Heimat as a *locus amoenus*, the subsequent chase sequence in the woods introduces the dark side of Heimat: we shift from the sun-drenched plains and carefree singers to a day-for-night close-up of Lüdersen's brooding figure in the forest. Rainer hears his shot and takes up the pursuit of the unidentified poacher, tracking him to the local estate. Here he confronts Helga, and her troubles begin.

While these images emphasize the spectacular value of both the pro-filmic space and of the cinematic experience, underlining it with dramatic music, they still initiate a plot and move the narrative along. Other sequences go further in defining the function of nature as spectacle by arresting the narrative altogether and substituting the logic of the tableau for that of continuity. At one point, a cut literalizes this logic as we watch a stately buck through the game warden's telescope in an irised shot, then cut to the rendering of a similar animal in an enormous oil painting that adorns the wall at the warden's home. Such cuts emphasize display of the image, not narration of an action. The ubiquitous point-of-view shot, in which one character contemplates or shows another the beautiful landscape, adds a perfunctory narrative motivation for lengthy pans: we look on as Lüdersen gazes over the land he is about to leave, or, in *Der Förster vom Silberwald* (where such shots often become autonomous, uncoupled from any stable point of view imposed by editing), we follow the game warden's gaze as he watches eagles and other wildlife. Another Hans Deppe film of the 1950s combines this motivated gaze with its pictorial function. In *Heideschulmeister Uwe Karsten* (1954), Karsten gives the patrician daughter Ursula Dieven a tour of the *Heide*. As the two stand on a knoll overlooking the landscape, the camera pans 180 degrees from their point of view. "This is the best map," Karsten explains, and then leads her to another tableau, encouraging her to "look, Fräulein Dieven. The wet, gleaming bodies of the horses, the tanned bodies [of boys], the foaming water and the glistening drops. That's joie de vivre, that's life. That is a picture." And indeed, from here we cut to Ursula's sketch of the same motif.

Generally, however, continuity provided by the graphic match of moving image to painting, or by an eyeline match, is the exception. Typically, the tableau sequences of the *Heimatfilm* are far more discontinuous. Though some of these are integrated into the narrative flow as transitional images, they tend to take on a "spectacular" quality in their own right. This is exemplified even more clearly again in *Der Förster vom Silberwald*, a film that was initially conceived as a nature special: in its final form, it occasionally uses the story line as a mere pretext for documentary images of Alpine wildlife.[31] Though some of these images are tied back into the diegesis through point-of-view shots and irises suggesting binoculars, their duration suspends the linearity of story time in favor of pure spectacle. Similarly, a long shot of a shepherd herding his sheep early in *Grün ist die Heide* yields to an entirely unrelated telephoto close-up of grazing deer and then a pan of a tree-lined plain. Even after the camera comes to rest on the three singers at the end of this movement, acting and editing suggest a further type of diversion from narrative continuity. The sequence that follows fails to move the story along, obeying instead a dramaturgy of numbers, or "attractions": we see the three singers clowning around, clearly over-acting a morning routine, at one point even finding a rabbit under one of their hats. The sequence owes more to the circus than to established principles of narrative filmmaking. The most glaring example of such a suspension of plot progression in *Grün ist die Heide* occurs when we are treated to a lengthy series of circus acts under the big top. As part of the local *Schützenfest*, the depiction of which occupies fully one-third of the film's duration, the circus sequence appears to be mandated not by the exigencies of the plot but by the scriptwriter's perceived need for *Buntheit* (colorfulness)[32] and by the dramaturgy of the circus itself as a series of numbers or "attractions." We are treated to acrobats performing to dynamic music (but through a static camera and with little editing), then to a clown number; then we cut to outside the tent to watch the three singers play a prank on a beer vendor. Back inside the tent, we watch two numbers featuring trained horses as the singers sneak into the circus. Finally, the sequence fuses the circus numbers with the singers' gags by using them as audience participants in a magic trick. The link to the narrative context of the film is maintained only through the physical location of the circus in the story space and the presence of a few—though none of the principal—characters at the show.

Fehrenbach suggests that the inclusion of the circus scenes amounts to "little more than a pleasurable distraction—from both the problems internal to the film's plot and those more pressing concerns located outside the walls of the cinema."[33] But while the circus sequence is in this sense typical of the escapism for which the *Heimatfilm* has often been criticized, it is also symptomatic of a defining formal characteristic of the genre. Even if the presence of clowns and acrobats is hardly a hallmark of this genre's semantics, the dramaturgical principle of the circus arguably is. The series of loosely connected numbers or acts provides a model for Bobby Lüthge's avowedly eclectic approach to scriptwriting (which he himself compared to mixing a cocktail);[34] this dramaturgical principle is evident not only in the circus scenes but in the film's combination of various "numbers" according to a logic which occasionally seems to replace narrative causality with a principle of addition. Thus, whereas classical narrative uses the climax to tie up its loose ends, the typical *Heimatfilm* tends instead to lay bare the loose causal structure that connected the preceding scenes. *Grün ist die Heide* ends with a wounded Lüdersen, a VW convertible conspicuous at the close of this film for the absence of motorized transportation up to this point, a horse grazing on the heath after having thrown off its rider, the establishment of the characters played by the starring actors ("Zie-Prack") as a romantic couple, a circus on its way out of town, and the singers, who once again take up their opening song.[35] Though not always as obvious as in *Grün ist die Heide*, which at least one reviewer compared to a variety show,[36] this eclectic mix of ingredients exemplifies the general tendency of the *Heimatfilm* to punctuate a more or less coherent narrative with apparently unmotivated musical offerings and nature shots. The series of gags involving the three itinerant singers is staged exclusively for the benefit of the viewer and fundamentally affects the film's mode of address.[37] The *Schützenfest* itself functions as an extended "number" in the variety dramaturgy of *Grün ist die Heide*, as do the lengthy processions and festivals that conclude any number of films from *Schwarzwaldmädel* to *Am Brunnen vor dem Tore* to *Wenn die Heide blüht*.

In its frequent recourse to visual attractions and the non-narrative register of the spectacular, the *Heimatfilm* evidences traces of what Tom Gunning has described as a "cinema of attraction" and its mode of address in early cinema.[38] In its 1950s guise, this mode is rigidly tamed, to be sure, as it no longer assaults the spectator (as in early and avant-garde cinema) or even the integrity of the narrative, but rather serves to temporarily suspend it, as in the musical, from which the *Heimatfilm* often borrows quite liberally. But the persistence of moments of "attraction" does account for an aspect of the Heimat film's popularity within a longer history of popular entertainment. In this perspective, the *Bergfilm* is an intermediate step in that history. Though critics have questioned its family resemblance to the *Heimatfilm* of the 1950s, as I indicated earlier, the two traditions mesh on the formal level. For all the differences in the kind of nature depicted, the depiction of nature as spectacle remains constant. The specific relationship between the documentary and spectacular quality of the image on the one hand and its place in a fictional narration on the other also places the *Heimatfilm* of the 1950s in the tradition of the *Bergfilm*. The reception of the *Heimatfilm* as a mix of narrative and non-narrative, fictional and documentary reinforces this link. Kracauer's critique of Fanck's "precarious balance between the expressive shapes of nature and the romantic triangles of melodrama" would seem to apply equally well to the *Heimatfilm* of the 1950s.[39] Just as Fanck was criticized for his heavy-handed treatment of fictional narration, so would *Heimatfilme* of the 1950s face challenges to their ability to construct coherent stories. This rarely cast doubt on the attractiveness of their imagery, however.

If we define narrative as a more or less linear causality in space and time, then the suspension of its temporal continuity inevitably redirects our attention to the spatial register. If spectacle knows no time, it always takes place in—and foregrounds—spatial coordinates. Thus, scholarship on the "excesses" of melodrama has focused on the way in which the mise-en-scène of domestic space begins to supply a set of meanings that may differ from, if not subvert, the manifest content of the films' narratives. Likewise, the stylistic excesses of film noir have led critics to explore its particular commentary on the reconfiguration of urban space,[40] and the spectacular construction of landscape in the Western has always been one of the focal points for readings of the genre's negotiation of national space at the frontier. In keeping with such approaches to the spatial logics of individual genres, I would argue, the spectacle of the local in the *Heimatfilm* should direct our attention to its functions in the historical context of the 1950s. On the one hand, as Alisdair King has recently suggested, the *Heimatfilm* offers a symbolic manifestation of the social organization of space during the postwar era, when issues of territory, belonging, identity—and even the recognizability of particular landscapes—were highly volatile concerns.[41] On the other hand, the representation of space in these films might itself be described as volatile. In particular, a host of *Heimatfilme* display a tendency to make the seemingly enclosed space of rural communities function as doubles of distant locales, reinforcing the metaphorical construction of space inherent in the very concept of Heimat. As a result, the spaces of the *Heimatfilm* can be remarkably mobile, and the ostensible rootedness of identity in Heimat turns out to be more easily severed from its original ground than one might expect. The case studies in the following chapters serve to illustrate both the metaphorical doubling of space in the *Heimatfilm* and its negotiation of mobility as the central trope of the 1950s. We can begin to sketch some of the vectors discussed there by returning briefly to the example of *Grün ist die Heide* and shifting from the visual to the aural mode of the spectacular.

AURAL SPECTACLE:
SONG AND SPACE IN THE *HEIMATFILM*

"On the Lüneburg Heath/In the wonderfully beautiful land/I wandered up and down/And many things I found." Introducing the film's location by praising its "wonderful beauty," the opening song of *Grün ist die Heide* functions as a transition from the credits into the diegesis (indeed, the music appears to function as an extradiegetic commentary until the moment when the panning camera picks up the three singers as the source of the music we have been hearing). Such songs praising the beauty of the Heimat were routinely marketed as part of the Heimat film's attraction, the lyrics usually printed in the accompanying program for the benefit of the audience.[42] Besides marking the pragmatic permeability of the Heimat genre with respect to elements of the musical and the *Revuefilm*,[43] these songs contribute significantly to the idyllization of the landscapes and spaces of Heimat. The Heimat extolled by these songs may or may not be located in the diegetic space of the film; various songs praise ostensibly absent spaces as Heimat, while others refer to a generalized notion of Heimat.[44] For all their sentimentalism, these songs expand the diegetic space of Heimat beyond the limited locale that provides the picturesque setting for a given film's plot. To the degree that they universalize notions of Heimat and integrate a lost, or otherwise absent, home in the space of the action, the songs begin to suggest a relatively flexible and hybrid conception of place in the *Heimatfilm*.

Nowhere is this more obvious in *Grün ist die Heide* than in the staging of the *Heimatlied*. In his personal retrospective of the 1950s, Curt Riess quips: "Looking again at the German films of the time, one gets the impression that expulsion from the East had displaced not millions of people, but rather millions of members of singing associations [*Gesangsvereine*]."[45] *Grün ist die Heide* provides a case in point. A crucial scene during the *Schützenfest* shows one of the three itinerant singers (the popular tenor Kurt Reimann playing himself) leading a Silesian *Landsmannschaft* in a heartrending version of the *Heimatlied*. Besides painting an idyllic picture of the Riesengebirge (a mountain range straddling the Polish-Czech border), the song's chorus celebrates those mountains as "deutsches Gebirge" and "my Heimat." Taken on their own, the nostalgic lyrics of this song could easily be read in terms of a revanchist ideological project to reclaim lost regions in the East; in the context of *Grün ist die Heide*, however, the song is staged as a decidedly integrative gesture that makes over the plains of the Lüneburg Heath into a space that can encompass both local and remote traditions.

The song is performed as a surprise for the scores of Silesian expellees at the *Schützenfest*. The sequence immediately preceding the performance is devoted to the programmatic farewell speech of Lüder Lüdersen discussed in the introduction. Claiming to speak for "the many others who have found a second home [Heimat] here among you," Lüdersen implores the locals not to be "too hard on the people who have fled to you. Whoever has not been compelled to leave his home cannot know what it means to be without one [*heimatlos*]." And yet, both his speech and the ensuing song celebrate not *Heimatlosigkeit* or the impossibility of Heimat, but its manifest flexibility, the power to relocate the *heimatlos* subject in an ersatz space that can be redefined as Heimat itself. As if to underscore the ability (and the pressing need) of West German rural communities to integrate even deviant figures such as Lüdersen, the song (announced by Willy Fritsch as "something from the Heimat") unites the locals and the Silesians as members of the same audience. As the camera pans over the attentive faces of the Silesians in their *Trachten*, captures the North Rhine–Westphalian and Silesian flags that adorn the fairgrounds, and then tilts up to the blue sky, the film evokes Silesia as a space that is absent, lost, and yet in important ways also transportable, mobilized by virtue of the folk song's mnemonic power and thanks to the ideological work of the film itself. Another "number" in the cocktail dramaturgy of *Grün ist die Heide,* the song contributes to a characteristic formulation of Heimat as a space that is multiply defined by proximity and distance, community and difference, presence and absence.

As a result, the cinematic space of *Grün ist die Heide* is as heterogeneous as the narrative construction of the film. The Lüneburg Heath according to Deppe is a space crisscrossed by homeless singers, traveling circuses, and migrant refugees. Although the narrative works hard to achieve closure, no single discourse can contain these disparate movements through the space of a Heimat which, I would suggest, is determined as much by what is absent as by what is present. In keeping with Doreen Massey's contention that "it is precisely . . . the presence of the outside within which helps to construct the specificity of the local place,"[46] *Grün ist die Heide* asks us to reconsider the locality of Heimat as a site that has the power to integrate different memories, identities, and itineraries. Its myth is one of integration: here, Silesians coexist peacefully with the locals, vagabonds interact regularly with (and act as relays for) the settled inhabitants, and a circus troupe seems no less out of place than a poaching baron.

This depiction of Heimat as an integrative space presumably accounts in large part for the success of *Grün ist die Heide* and the genre of the *Heimatfilm* on the market, where it managed to reach—or integrate—enormous audiences. While these certainly included the many expellees who found their still open-ended biographies transformed into happily ending stories of successful relocation, the approximately eight million members of this group could only have supplied a fraction of the more than sixteen million who saw the film. Like all popular narratives, the *Heimatfilm* needed a certain degree of polysemy to allow viewers to "read" the film from a variety of different angles and thus to maximize the film's potential on the market. The Heimat of *Grün ist die Heide* thus works not on the level of local history, but as a space for the projection of multiple histories, including not only those of restoration and normalization but also those of the expellees, of otherwise displaced persons, of social, economic, and physical mobility in an ostensibly contained space identified as Heimat.

Among these multiple narratives of reconstruction, *Grün ist die Heide* also references the historical backdrop of World War II. It does so obliquely but in ways that contradict the received image of the *Heimatfilm* as a genre of repression, escape, or forgetting. Lüdersen's displacement is, of course, a result of the war, and while the film does nothing to recall Germany's responsibility for that war, the poacher's pathology certainly reminds us of its effects. Moreover, the investigation of Lüdersen returns several times to the question of gun ownership. The game warden points out that all guns have been collected and no civilian should possess a weapon anymore. Again, the reason for these actions is not referenced—not, one presumes, to hide or forget it, but because it was obvious to the contemporary viewer. Other references to the war and its aftermath are less obvious and appear to work more on the level of the film's historical unconscious. Thus, the game warden's complaint that the poacher is sabotaging his difficult work of "rebuilding" (*wieder aufbauen*) the forest and its fauna makes sense only if we sort out the guiding metaphor, for talk of "rebuilding" makes far less sense in the natural environment than in the bombed-out cities where this was the order of the day. If contemporary viewers did not stop to consider the implications of such a mixed metaphor, it was not because they were forgetful or trying to repress the past, but because they were so familiar with the language of "rebuilding" that would have caused such a slippage in the first place. But perhaps *slippage* is not the right term, either: when the younger of the two game wardens responds to his colleague's complaint with an eagerness to catch the saboteur and sets out to "patrol everything left of the year 1946," he may be thinking in terms of planting cycles and forest husbandry. But one gets the distinct impression that natural history in such films remains inseparable from the most recent events in German history. Nowhere is this more striking than in a film that premiered only a year after *Grün ist die Heide* launched the *Heimatfilmwelle*. *Rosen blühen auf dem Heidegrab*, a *Heimatfilm* that does away with the notion of *heile Welt* altogether, exemplifies the proximity of Heimat, horror, and history in the 1950s.

4 Heimat/Horror/History
Rosen blühen auf dem Heidegrab

> In the genesis of the economic miracle, there was also a purely
> immaterial catalyst: the stream of psychic energy that has not dried
> up to this day, and which has its source in the well-kept secret of the
> corpses built into the foundations of our state.
>
> W. G. SEBALD

HEIMAT AND THE *UNHEIMLICH*

A symptom of his displacement, Lüder Lüdersen's poaching unsettles the
space of Heimat. In the presence of the displaced landowner-turned-poacher,
tranquil images of grazing deer and mist-covered forests give way to sylvan
scenes of alarm and pursuit. At the sound of a shot, the forest idyll turns
into a crime scene, an intractable terrain in which the hunter becomes the
hunted, and which he uses for cover. The heath, a meeting place for lovers
only moments earlier, is now a threatening space—too open for Helga, who
fears that her father's dark secret may be discovered, and too expansive for
the game warden, who takes aim at the poacher but fails to track him down.
Meanwhile, for Lüdersen himself, the forests remain haunted by his memories of Silesia, the Kansas to this Gevacolored Oz in the northern plains of
Germany. "The heath in these films is a place of submersion [*des Untergründigen*]" writes Fritz Göttler, "a *terrain vague*."[1] The *Unheimlich* lurks
beneath the surface of the *Heimatfilm*.

To be sure, the untroubled sylvan idyll is one of the staples of the Heimat
tradition. From its earliest days, *Heimatbewegungen* cleared paths in the
woods for recreation, Ganghofer celebrated the "silence" of the forest in
novels such as *Das Schweigen im Walde*, and *Heimatkunst* extolled the
deutsche Wald as a site of national renewal. By 1936, this "Teutonic
romance of the woods"[2] had taken perhaps its definitive Fascist form in
Hanns Springer's *Ewiger Wald*, which, as I have suggested, asked viewers to
equate the eternity of the forest with the longevity of the German *Volk*. The
same logic obtains in *Der Erbförster* (1945), where an old forester heeds the
good and eternal voice of the forest to defend it as healthy life against its
sick exploitation for milling. And *Der Förster vom Silberwald*, one of the

signature films of the 1950s, strikes the same chord in some rather didactic justifications of traditional hunting and forestry practices. When the young Sissi dutifully recites to Emperor Franz the lesson she has learned from her "Papili" in the first of the three *Sissi* films (1955), she would appear to be formulating the essence of the Heimat film's sylvan ideology: "Should your life ever bring trouble or sorrow, then go through the woods with open eyes. In every tree and brush, in every flower and every animal you will observe the omnipotence of God, which will give you solace and strength."

But this generic image of the forest idyll shades over easily into the dark and *unheimlich* woods presented in fairy tales as a "place of terror."[3] In this view, the pursuit of Lüdersen in *Grün ist die Heide* is a mild preview to the disquieting closing sequence of *Jagdszenen aus Niederbayern* (1968), where an entire village hunts down the protagonist in the forest. Throughout the history of the *Heimatfilm*, the forest is not only a refuge for morally up-standing city folk, but also provides cover to countless smugglers, poachers, and other wayward figures. A film like *Das Schweigen im Walde* (1937) can also turn the forest into a not-so-silent weapon when a frustrated lover ignites the brittle wood and is engulfed by its spectacular flames. And in *Waldwinter,* the embezzling manager of the baron's estate unleashes the power of the venerated forest by setting off an avalanche of stacked tree trunks in a last-ditch effort to shake his pursuers as he flees for the border. Perhaps one of the most psychoanalytically explicit treatments of the forest as *unheimlich* occurs early in Edgar Reitz's *Heimat* (1984), when the vil-lagers happen upon a nude corpse in the woods near the tranquil village of Schabbach. Unexplained and unresolved, the dead woman's body remains an irritant in the topography of the film.

But even more than the forest, it is the swamp that figures within the iconography of Heimat (and not only here) as the site of the *Unheimlich*. In this view, draining the swamp in *Die goldene Stadt* is also a matter of exor-cising the dark aspects of the countryside that the film associates with Heimat and femininity. As early as 1936, a striking film by Frank Wysbar had staged the notion of Heimat as a place haunted by its own likeness by locating it on the borders of a marsh. According to the title card, *Fährmann Maria* is a "legend" about "love that is ready to sacrifice its own life to save the other." Drawing heavily on expressionist technique, favoring lingering close-ups and long landscape shots over dialog and action, Wysbar stages this legend in a liminal space on the northern plains.[4] When the local ferry-man in a remote village dies after having taken Death himself on board his ferry, he is replaced by the young Maria, a woman of unclear provenance who shows up one day in the village looking for work. Along with the job, she inherits the ferryman's house, which is situated on the banks of the river and separated from the village by a swamp. Given the fact that the film associates "the other side" of the river with death from the moment the ageing ferryman picks up his last passenger—a tall, austere, white-haired man clad in black, who catches the dying man as he falls—it is fitting that the central location of the film is a no-man's-land surrounded by bodies of water, beyond which lie both life in the village and death.

Soon after taking up her work, Maria too picks up a charge on "the other side." Responding to a summons from the bell on the riverbank, she finds an exhausted young man who claims that he is being pursued. She falls in love with this "man from the other shore" (borrowing from expressionist drama and cinema, none of the characters besides Maria have names) and treats his wounds and tends to his fever. In a lucid moment, he asks Maria whether she is from the village, and upon hearing that she has "no Heimat," he exclaims: "No Heimat! That is hard for you. To have a Heimat is the greatest fortune one can strive for." His own Heimat, he claims, is on the side of the river where she found him, and with glowing eyes he tells Maria that she should see it some day. Before this union on the other side can come to pass, however, Maria must fulfill the terms of the title card and sacrifice herself when Death demands to be ferried to the victim that she has been hiding. In a lengthy sequence, Maria diverts Death from her house, claiming that her lover is at the village festival. There she dances a frenzied dance with the man in black as the villagers draw back in terror. She tries to shake him by fleeing to a church and ringing the bells, which emit no sound, and finally leads Death back to her house by way of the swamp. At this point, however, her willingness to die in place of the young man turns the tables on Death, who loses his footing and drowns. On the following morning, after a montage of flowers in blossom cut to spirited music, the two lovers can cross to "the other side" and walk off into the vast expanse of the plains, defined by the young man, in the closing words of the film, as "The Heimat!"

Given the association of "the other side" with death, this ending can hardly dispel the *unheimlich* connotations of Heimat (particularly in view of the fact that topographically, the "other side" is virtually indistinguishable from the landscape on "this" side of the river). Reminiscent of Lang's *Der müde Tod*, but also of Murnau's *Nosferatu* (1922), Wysbar's quasisilent feature film inherits Weimar cinema's penchant for the uncanny. In particular, it troubles any idyllic notion of Heimat by equating it with "the other side" and with death. In the film's hybrid generic logic of Heimat and horror, the death of Death by drowning fails to exorcise him from the space of Heimat. As the lovers set off into the sunset, the incarnation of the Freudian *Unheimlich* remains buried alive in the swamp and continues to haunt Heimat below the surface.

Soon after completing *Fährmann Maria*, Wysbar went into exile in Hollywood, where he would remake the film as *The Strangler of the Swamp* (1945). If the horrific undercurrent to Heimat had not been clear enough in the original, *Strangler* turned the expressionist *Heimatfilm* into a bona fide horror film. Many years later, Swiss-German filmmaker Niklaus Schilling debuted with a film that feels like a distant remake of *Fährmann Maria*. Upon its 1972 premiere, film critic Enno Patalas spoke of Schilling's *Nacht-schatten* as "a phantom film, the most beautiful in Germany since Murnau."[5] Like Wysbar's film, *Nachtschatten* takes place on the heath and focuses on an enigmatic woman, Elena Berg. It, too, involves a death in a swamp, and Schilling's debt to the uncanny doppelgängers of Weimar cinema is as pronounced as Wysbar's. The film abounds with déjà vus and doubles, including the dead double of a man who arrives at the woman's house one day with an interest in purchasing it. Arriving from the city in his Mercedes, Jan Eckmann realizes that Elena takes him for the reincarnation of her dead husband, Werner. Although Elena had been acquitted of the charge of murdering Werner, a "shadow clings to her," according to a newspaper clipping. In a dream, Eckmann witnesses his own death as a repetition of Werner's; however, in the end it is Elena who kills herself to join her husband. Like *Fährmann Maria*, Schilling's horrific *Heimatfilm*[6] provides a sustained reflection on the logic of the *Unheimlich* as the double that inhabits *Heimat*.

In the reading that follows, I investigate this logic further. Instead of pursuing images of doubles and the uncanny in expressionist and post-expressionist (Heimat)films such as Wysbar's, or in the reinvention of the expressionist tradition by German filmmakers in the 1970s,[7] where the familiarity of the *Unheimlich* is fairly well established, I am interested here in shedding light on its function in the context of the 1950s *Heimatfilm*. Though this may appear an unlikely site for unearthing the *Unheimlich*, the haunted likeness of Heimat can hover just below its surface. Ingeborg Majer O'Sickey is right to point out that "the *unheimlich* is the 'Other' that Heimat seeks to keep out," but that attempt is not always successful, even in the "Bambified" films of the 1950s.[8] More specifically, the received view of Heimat as a repression mechanism designed to keep the *Unheimlich* at bay fails to account for the pressures that history puts on these films. Haunted by the recent past, the *Heimatfilm* of the 1950s has more to tell us about the uncanny dimension of history than its ostensibly ahistorical landscapes have led critics to believe.

HEIMAT: A HOLIDAY FROM HISTORY?

When the young Heinrich, the protagonist in Heinrich Böll's 1954 novel *Haus ohne Hüter*, wants to escape his oppressive family, the persistent reminders of the past, and the bleak realities of postwar German reconstruction, he goes to the movies: "The cinema was wonderful, it was good and warm. Nobody saw you, nobody could talk to you, and you could do what you couldn't do otherwise: *forget.*"[9]

Forged during the 1950s, this remains our dominant image of German cinema in the Adenauer era: in a repressive society characterized by its "inability to mourn" and by "collective silence and wide-spread amnesia,"[10] cinema was the quintessential site of escape, a place where the past appeared only in the guise of entertainment (if at all), an apolitical and ahistorical locus of forgetting. Criticism of this cinema has been articulated in various ways: first rebuffed by high-minded critics for its lack of artistic merit and its failure to reconnect with international developments after the war,[11] German cinema of the 1950s soon came under even more pointed attack for its reactionary politics of history and memory. "Enjoy a few hours with the unmastered past," quipped Joe Hembus in his biting retrospective from 1961.[12] And writing in the same year, Walther Schmieding reinterpreted the "artistic and political abstinence" of German film as the symptom of a broader longing to take a "holiday from history."[13] The international successes of the New German Cinema, with its historical soul-searching, sealed the indictment of "Papas Kino" for its complete lack of historical conscience.[14]

Whether arguing on aesthetic or political grounds, most critiques of 1950s cinema agree on the *Heimatfilm* as the main generic culprit. As I noted in chapter 1, critics have by and large maintained that during the 1950s, Heimat was the code word for an escape route that led to repression and enabled forgetting in the cinema by performing a "derealization of the past";[15] these films have been seen as an escapist "refuge, unmarked by the consequences of the demolished Third Reich."[16] Indeed, while Germans were engaged in physically transforming Heimat into a "faceless industrial landscape," Klaus Kreimeier argues, the *Heimatfilm* offered them "a counterworld that was ultimately place- and timeless." This genre, he claims, harked back to a "preindustrial stage of production and consciousness which appeared to ensure that the concrete historical experiences of the most recent past—memories of bomb craters, air raid shelters, and landscapes that had been plowed up by total war—paled beside the images [in these films]."[17]

However, as Frank Stern rightly points out, "The perception of the 1950s as a period exclusively defined by social and political restoration, all-embracing anti-intellectualism, historical and moral amnesia, and aesthetic *Spiessbürgertum* may not be sustainable in the light of historical and cultural analysis."[18] Indeed, recent reevaluations of the postwar politics of memory have cast doubt on the "repression approach."[19] Critiques of the *Heimatfilm* as a site for escape had espoused a dominant paradigm of forgetting and repression that dates back to Theodor Adorno's indictment of *Vergangenheitsbewältigung* (coming to terms with the past) for its "empty, cold forgetting."[20] However, in his recent study on Germany's "search for a usable past," Robert Moeller has helpfully insisted on making a distinction between wholesale repression and the partial presence of the past in 1950s culture. West German society during the 1950s may have busied itself with the *Wirtschaftswunder* and worked hard to turn its sights forward, but it did not simply repress or forget the past—rather, it remembered it selectively, strategically. Taking issue with the view that the 1950s were "a decade of historical silence and willing forgetfulness before an explosion of critical self-examination beginning in the late 1960s," Moeller produces evidence from public policy debates, historiographic disputes, the popular press, and the movies to demonstrate the discursive presence of the past. He concludes: "Hardly 'empty, cold, forgetting,' as Adorno charged, West Germans remembered key parts of the first half of the 1940s with extraordinary passion and emotion. Many accounts of Germany's 'most recent history' circulated in the fifties; remembering selectively was not the same as forgetting."[21]

Such an approach to the era entails shifting our attention from the logics of repression to the strategies of remembering: rather than showing what was missing in public discourse at the time, we need to account for what was remembered, and how. Such a revision has begun to produce new evaluations of the culture of the postwar years and the 1950s, among them Moeller's contribution, as well as Heide Fehrenbach's investigations of the role of cinema and spectatorship, Alon Confino's project on the culture of travel in the postwar era, and Frank Biess's work on returning veterans.[22] All of these authors convincingly show to what degree the ostensibly forgotten past played into even the most trivial forms of cultural representation. As Confino and Peter Fritzsche point out in their introduction to a recent volume of essays, *The Work of Memory,* "The years after the war, which are so often uncomplicatedly labeled as years of denial and repression, may be much more important than previously thought for molding the memory of war and genocide. . . . Before and after 1945, the noises of the past reverberated loudly in German society and culture. We may not like the articulation of some of these pasts, but 'silence' is not the right term to describe the presence of the past in modern German history."[23] This chapter aims to substantiate and contribute to this reevaluation of the 1950s by tracing the "noises of the past" where we have come to suspect them least: in the *Heimatfilm*. Without wanting to suggest that all Heimat productions of the era engage with recent German history, I would hope that the following reading has a certain paradigmatic value for further investigations of the links between Heimat and history.[24] Though *Rosen blühen auf dem Heidegrab* is admittedly an extreme case in its melding of Heimat, the wartime past, and the conventions of the horror film, it serves here as a case study designed to focus our critical attention more carefully on the kinds of "absences [that] had a strong presence in West Germany."[25]

MARKETING A TITLE

The portfolio of the small production company König-Film, under the direction of Richard König, mirrors postwar trends in popular cinema. After notable titles such as *Der Ruf* (1949) and . . . *und über uns der Himmel* (1947), König-Film rode the *Heimatfilmwelle* with *Heimat deine Sterne* (1951), *Heimatglocken* (1952), *Die Mühle im Schwarzwälder Tal* (1953), and *Der Fischer vom Heiligensee* (1955). In the cinematic context of the early 1950s, the premiere of the newest König film on Christmas Day in 1952 was a representative, and for that reason inconspicuous, event. Directed by Richard König's brother Hans, the new title, *Rosen blühen auf dem Heidegrab,* promised the audience more of what it had come to expect from prototypical films such as *Schwarzwaldmädel* and *Grün ist die Heide.* The latter had shown the industry "what *Heimatfilme* need[ed] to look like," and *Rosen blühen auf dem Heidegrab* promised similar doses of rural spectacle and melodramatic plot.[26]

The marketing strategy for König's film clearly shows a distributor hoping to capitalize on the success of the Heimat genre, strategically emphasizing those aspects of *Rosen* that made for a generic fit. Advertised as a *Heimat-Ballade* heralding the "breakthrough to the authentic German landscape film,"[27] *Rosen* offers plentiful landscape imagery, no less spectacular for having been captured in black and white. Banking on the association of such imagery with a particular type of Heimat literature, the distributor also sought to associate the film with the name of Hermann Löns, whose writings had inspired the first version of *Grün ist die Heide* in 1932 and whose poems about the Lüneburg Heath had served as the lyrics for songs

Figure 4. Heimat atmosphere: *Rosen blühen auf dem Heidegrab* (1952).

in countless other *Heimatfilme*. Promising "authentic Löns atmosphere," *Rosen* was advertised as a *Heidefilm* of which "Hermann Löns himself could be the author: its romantic images and songs place the story of a young love and of bitter passion in the gilded frame of Heimat."[28] Finally, the film's story itself connects to the Heimat tradition. *Rosen* revolves around provincial lore, challenges to traditional ways of life, and the perpetuation of local heritage. Some fifteen years after *Fährmann Maria*, we are again taken to a small village on the edge of a swamp in the northern plains for a melodramatic plot involving a farmer's daughter, Dorothee (Ruth Niehaus), and her two suitors: the local farmer Dietrich Eschmann (Hermann Schomberg) and the promising young architect Ludwig Amelung (Armin Dahlen).

But for all its generic credentials, *Rosen blühen auf dem Heidegrab* is a *Heimatfilm* with a difference. Both stylistically and thematically, it stands apart from the candy-colored fantasies that we tend to associate with the genre. The cinematography harks back to German expressionism and evokes the low-key lighting and deliberate use of shadows in film noir. In this way, the film infuses its stock Heimat imagery with an unusually somber tone, which is amplified by the plot: barely veiled under the highlighted thematic allusions to Hermann Löns's country prose, *Rosen* ultimately tells a horror story of war, violence, and death. In this respect, too,

König's film is rather more noir and his notion of Heimat more *unheimlich* than its title would lead us to suspect.

The hybridity of *Rosen blühen auf dem Heidegrab* was not lost on the distributors, who tried hard to position it as a *Heimatfilm* but were aware of a "discrepancy between the title and the film." However, in the eyes of the distributor, and of the press that by and large fell in line with the marketing strategy, this discrepancy was exclusively one of aesthetic value: *Rosen* was heralded as a *Heimatfilm* that avoided kitsch in favor of true art.[29] Emphasizing the film's polished cinematography and its use of young acting talent, the distributor impressed upon theater owners and reviewers that despite the lack of an "artistically valuable" title, *Rosen* was indeed an *"artwork."*[30] Advertised as a successful blend of art and the popular, the film was reviewed by the press as a "new German *Heimatfilm*," a *Heimatfilm* "of a different kind" that avoided the "speculative mischief with which the concept of Heimat has been treated."[31] "The title may sound like kitsch," wrote the reviewer for the influential *Film-Dienst*, "but the film is not . . . not a trace of Heimat hokum [*Heimatmache*]."[32]

Such positioning follows a general trend of high-minded film criticism during the 1950s to champion the cause of "art" in the face of German cinema's "primitive mediocrity."[33] However, this strikes me as a symptomatic displacement. I believe that the manifest unease about this film's title and its place in the Heimat genre has its roots elsewhere. If there was anything to be nervous about in marketing this film—and the tone of the press releases and of the reviews suggests that there was—then it was not its over-blown aesthetic pretensions, but rather its *unheimlich* references to the past. In this respect, *Rosen blühen auf dem Heidegrab* is indeed a *Heimatfilm* with a difference.

FLASHBACK: HEIMAT AT WAR

In a triangulation that Heide Fehrenbach has found to be characteristic of the *Heimatfilm* in the 1950s more generally, *Rosen* pits Ludwig, the soft-spoken and "modern" romantic hero, against Eschmann, an older, physically overbearing rival, for the desired woman's affections.[34] More than simply two rivals for Dorothee, the two male leads allegorize opposing scenarios for the (re)configuration of the rural milieu after the war: as a farmer, Eschmann represents the continuity of rural patriarchal heritage, in which Dorothee would move from her parents' farm to his. Ludwig, on the other hand, represents a departure from tradition and a reorganization of provincial space. We first encounter Ludwig in his open convertible, returning to his mother's house in the village after a long absence in the city, where he has been studying architecture. Associated explicitly with the rush to re-build the ruined cities after the war, Ludwig is the prodigal son who brings modern living (and motorized transportation) to the rural backwaters.

The film makes abundantly clear that Ludwig is the "right" match for Dorothee. Although he has no farm to offer in return for her hand in mar-riage, and although their union will doubtlessly alter the thoroughly tradi-tional fabric of local life, Ludwig is the very incarnation of moral masculin-ity, destined to win the day. Unlike Eschmann, who wants to win Dorothee by force, Ludwig serenades her with his guitar; he is represented as a caring son who makes up for the apparently missing father in his family by finan-cially supporting his mother through his work in the city.

Eschmann, by contrast, is an erratic bloc in the Heimat iconography of *Rosen* from the opening sequence to the film's near-fatal end. Played by the towering Hermann Schomberg, Eschmann is repeatedly associated with animals because of his strength, his temper, and his unchecked drives. Low-angle shots and framings that dwarf all other figures by comparison emphasize the excessive masculinity and barely contained violence of this *Viechskerl* (beast), as one character calls him. The frail Ruth Niehaus as Dorothee is a deliberate mismatch for Schomberg's Eschmann, who poses a threat to her from the moment they meet on the heath in the opening sequence. Nor does this threat dissipate over the course of the narrative to make way for the otherwise predictable union of Dorothee and Ludwig; instead, it escalates, erupting at the climax of the film. Unlike *Am Brunnen vor dem Tore*, which dispatches the older character—and by extension the past—by letting him "simply and mercifully disappear" in an off-screen act of suicide,[35] *Rosen blühen auf dem Heidegrab* is over-shadowed by the persistence of a monstrous figure. An embodiment of the past in ways to be discussed, Eschmann also resembles a figure from the cinematic past: like the austere man "from the other side" in *Fährmann Maria*, Eschmann throws up some rather troubling and symptomatic obstacles before the union between moral masculinity and girlish femi-ninity can take place at the forced happy end of this odd *Heimatfilm*. Indeed, the figure of Eschmann is even more disconcerting in its "real" and violent presence than the fantastic personification of death in Wys-bar's film.

Eschmann embodies the past not only in terms of film historical mem-ory, and he is aligned with the past not merely by promising to perpetuate local patriarchal tradition. As part of a whole series of doublings that structure this film, Eschmann also stands for a historical wartime past. This past is first introduced by a flashback in which Eschmann plays no discernable role. One evening, Dorothee and Ludwig return from a stroll on the heath that had taken them to a rose-covered grave. They find the local shepherd in a trance-like state, murmuring to himself, "The swamp beckons." When a talkative salesman from the nearby city inquires about his strange behavior, Ludwig dismisses it as superstition, but Dorothee disagrees, offering what at first sounds like a historical explanation. With a dissolve on Dorothee's face, König takes us into the historical past by recounting a story from the Thirty Years' War.

The year is 1631, Dorothee explains in voice-over. The Swedes have just invaded the same little village on the heath where the present action takes place. Low-angle shots show warriors charging in on horseback. The ensuing images convey a sense of frenzy and pillage: we see burning houses, a flock of geese racing towards the camera, peasants running frantically. These are images of war, and as such they would be familiar to the majority of audiences in the 1950s, who would recognize if not their own experiences from just a few years earlier, then the images and stories of others' experiences that made up public discourse and collective memory at the time. The past thus becomes a metaphor in which the Thirty Years' War stands for World War II. But the evocation of 1631 hides another historical and intertextual reference: *Rosen blühen auf dem Heidegrab* is a remake of Curt von Blachnitzky's 1929 film by the same title. Advertised as a "gripping document of love for humanity and the fatherland," the original contained the flashback structure that is preserved in Hans König's remake; however, Blachnitzky's film located almost the entire action in the past. Whereas König's story about Dorothee and Ludwig is situated in the present and dips into the past only in the brief flashback, the present in Blachnitzky's film functions merely as a framing device: a couple strolls past a grave on the heath, inquires about it, and becomes the diegetic audience for the (hi)story that the film tells. In this version, however, the past is not 300 years old, but only just over a century. Blachnitzky's film takes place in 1806, during the Napoleonic Wars, when "the oppressor's hand weighed heavily on Prussia-Germany."[36]

While there are a number of parallels between the two films, to which I will return, I am concerned here with König's key changes: the 1952 version of *Rosen blühen auf dem Heidegrab* maintains the flashback but significantly reduces its screen duration; and König shifts the historical reference from the Napoleonic Wars to the Thirty Years' War. Both of these changes strike me as symptomatic of an attempt to hide what the film nonetheless names through the doubly displaced historical metaphor—that is, the German experience of World War II. Presumably, to have maintained the reference to Napoleonic troops would, in a sense, have been too "realistic":[37] the reference to French occupation troops would have established a level of cultural verisimilitude that threatened to eclipse the generic verisimilitude of the *Heimatfilm*, which, as will become obvious, is invested in turning history into myth.[38] For the same reason, König could not have granted the historical flashback the same amount of narrative space Blachnitzky did, for this again would have transgressed generic boundaries, turning the *Heimatfilm* the König brothers set out to make and market into a war film.[39]

As Moeller argues in his study of the different war stories that were circulating around the time of König's film, "The devastating outcome of the war allowed West Germans to remember selectively, to tell stories of a past in which they, not others, were the war's most tragic victims."[40] This is true of the war story told in *Rosen blühen auf dem Heidegrab* as well. In both Blachnitzky's and König's versions, the war serves as the backdrop for a far more specific story in which the Germans appear as victims. Both films ultimately treat war only in terms of the occupation of a German village by foreign troops. Thus, after the brief montage showing the invasion of the village by the Swedes, König shifts the pace and focuses on the excesses of the occupying forces, who are shown in low-angle close-ups, drinking, laughing, and lustfully wringing a goose's neck. Dorothee's voice-over narrates the events from the position of the villagers: "Back then one had to be friendly to the foreigners" for fear of reprisals. The key sequence of the flashback shows what these reprisals looked like.

When the Swedish captain witnesses Wilhelmina, a young woman from the village, struggling against one of the occupying soldiers, he intervenes and sends his soldier packing. "Thus, the captain won Wilhelmina's trust," the voice-over explains. However, he abuses this trust just as soon as it has been established. Asking Wilhelmina to guide him across the swamp to the neighboring village, he forces her to stop in the middle of the open plain and rapes her—an event that König renders by cutting to a symbolic shot of dark clouds as the voice-over comments, "Thus fate came to Wilhelmina." But Wilhelmina avenges this fate, leading the captain off the safe path and to his death: together, they drown in the swamp. The suffering of the historical Wilhelmina and her suicidal retribution are subsequently enshrined in a grave erected by an unknown person on the heath and marked with the inscription "Rest in Peace, Wilhelmina."

RAPE AS "FATE": THE RETURN OF THE REPRESSED

Set up as a historical flashback, the story of Wilhelmina ends up as a legend, remembered by the locals by virtue of the *Heidegrab* of the film's title. This legend, which mythologizes the experience of war, occupation, and rape, lies at the heart of König's narrative. The remainder of the film after the flashback functions as a contemporary reenactment of the Wilhelmina legend, with Dorothee taking on the part of Wilhelmina (indeed, Dorothee is a direct descendant of Wilhelmina, and both characters are played by the same actress, Ruth Niehaus). However, whereas in the legend the Swedish captain appeared as both Wilhelmina's protector and as the rapist, in the contemporary version these roles are divided between the two male leads. Ludwig takes on the role of the protector, while Eschmann brings the melodramatically prefigured "fate" of the legend to Dorothee. With Ludwig gone for the day, Eschmann stalks her as she walks across the heath and past the grave. Unaware of his presence, Dorothee lies down and looks up at the sky; cutting to her point of view, the camera shows the same billowing clouds that symbolized Wilhelmina's rape, and then the silhouette of Eschmann's massive figure towering above her. After a brief altercation, Eschmann vents his jealousy over Ludwig, insisting that she shall love him instead, and forces himself on her. Dorothee's screams give way to dramatic music; the "repetition of a 'historical' rape," as a review referred to this climactic moment in the film,[41] is represented by alternating extreme close-ups of Eschmann and of Dorothee, her mouth open in a scream, her eyes wide with fear (see figure 5). In a last effort to force Eschmann off her, she attempts to bite the hand that holds her wrist; then, after a few helpless moans, we see her own clenched hand, in close-up, give way to his overbearing force.

After this drawn out and rather graphic scene, we cut to Ludwig, still in Hamburg, buying an engagement ring in complete ignorance of the horror on the heath. The cross-cutting returns us twice to Dorothee, who remains on her back by Wilhelmina's grave, open-mouthed, thinking, in a voice-over, about what it must be like to be dead. From this point on, she hardly speaks and acts in a trancelike state. Following a highly overdetermined repetition compulsion, she heeds the call of the swamp and retraces the steps of her predecessor and alter ego Wilhelmina. The penultimate sequence of the film reenacts Wilhelmina's revenge on the Swedish captain, showing us Dorothee and Eschmann as they gradually sink lower into the mud; however this time, both the perpetrator and the victim are saved in a last-minute rescue.

Dorothee's repetition compulsion in a plot that is structured around the

Figure 5. Representing rape: Ruth Niehaus as Dorothee in *Rosen blühen auf dem Heidegrab*.

multiple repetitions[42] of a " 'historical' rape" provides the key to the historical function of König's film in 1952. As I have suggested, it is difficult to
imagine that the audience would have failed to see the film itself as a repetition, barely veiled behind multiple references to a distant historical past, of
a far more recent German past. In particular, the graphic representation of
Dorothee's rape, itself a reenactment of a historical/legendary occupation,
would have resonated with the memory of widespread rapes at the end of
World War II. After all, the rape in the story is rather explicitly motivated
as the repetition of the subjugation of a local woman by the captain of a foreign army; although the film refrains from explicitly associating Eschmann
with war and occupation, he does hold the structural position of the occupier
in the reenactment of the Wilhelmina legend. Far better than the melodramatic conceit of a jealous lover, I would contend, this doubling of the local
farmer as occupation soldier helps to explain the brutality and hypermas-
culinity of Eschmann's character. They appear as symptoms of this displacement, referencing the excessive violence of the predominantly Russian
soldiers who committed rapes by the hundreds of thousands at the end of
World War II. Eschmann is not represented in racist terms as "Asiatic," but
there is a manifest continuity between the physical portrayal of this character as a hypersexual beast and much contemporary discourse on Red

Army soldiers. Heavily prefigured in Nazi propaganda that had warned of the "bestial acts of these inhumans [*Unmenschen*]," that discourse continued well into the cold war period to portray Russian soldiers—if not the Soviet people—as "drunken, primitive Mongol[s] who demanded watches, bicycles and women and did not even know that a flush toilet was not a sink."[43]

In order to understand the symptomatic excesses of König's film, we must recall the specific historical discourses surrounding the trope of rape in the postwar years. As Atina Grossmann has demonstrated, these years saw a proliferation of rape stories, told in many different registers. Diaries, memoirs, and novels of the postwar years, as well as records of public policy, document the fact that "these were not, initially at least, rapes that had been silenced."[44] Although the experience of rape may have been surrounded by taboos in many individual cases, and although stories of rape may eventually have circulated privately rather than in public discourse, seven years after the end of the war such stories could still be dredged up readily from the collective unconscious.[45] As Elizabeth Heinemann puts it, "Although discussion of women's rapes became taboo a few years after the end of the war, reference to the rapes hardly disappeared. In fact, they permeated the culture."[46] Indeed, besides König's film, there is substantial evidence to suggest that the memory of rape still lingered close to the surface of public discourse in 1952, to be tapped by political posters, or indeed revisited in publications such as James Wakefield Burke's *The Big Rape* (1951), which appeared in German translation in the same year as König's film.[47]

Dating back to Nazi propaganda and lasting well into the cold war imagery of Germany as the potential victim of Soviet "rape," the trope of rape served as an organizing reference for public discourses in the postwar era. In other words, not only was the experience of rape pervasive among women in the final days of the war; there was also an explosion of speech about the rapes, in which the experiences of individual women who had been victims of rape were transformed into a broader discourse about victimization, race and national identity, public health, and gender. In this respect, the discourses on rape formed an integral part of the selective memory about the war in postwar Germany. As such, the discursivization of the experience of rape contributed to a multifaceted process that Heinemann has usefully described as the "universalization, in West German collective memory, of aspects of the stereotypically female experience of Germany at the end of the war and during the immediate postwar years."[48] In this process, women's experiences provided "potent images for popular representations of the recent past," which served to focus issues of victimization, rebuilding, and morality. In each of these cases, gender-specific experiences were appropriated for the nation as a whole. These different appropriations of female experience ended up forming a complex web of metaphors that "functioned within, and helped to shape, varying strands of [the] emerging [West German national] identity."[49]

Like the discourse on rape, where "multiple and overlapping voices all talked at once, often in the same document,"[50] the discourse on German national identity was fraught with internal contradictions. As part of that discourse, König's film is no exception. Piling up layers of historical referentiality in its multiply embedded narrative, it functions as a historical palimpsest in which voices overlap. This is true in the literal sense that Dorothee will occasionally hear an inner voice or see a vision of Eschmann when others do not, suggesting an overlap between outer and inner reality, between the present and a historical or mythic tense. But there is also an overlap between the different discourses that enable and traverse the film, among them the discourses on rape and on occupation, respectively: a victim of rape, the frail, blond Dorothee becomes an allegorical figure both in the "historical" logic *within* the film—where she stands in for Wilhelmina—and in the historical function *of* the film, where she comes to stand for the victims of far more recent wartime rapes. Given that it already contains an internal allegory on rape, it is difficult not to read *Rosen blühen auf dem Heidegrab* as an allegory itself, one whose melodramatic narrative of female victimization reworks, and contributes to, contemporaneous discourses on German victimhood after World War II.

THE LIVING DEAD: *HEIMATFILM* AS HORROR FILM

But König's film ultimately troubles even this allegory of Dorothee as a victimized *Germania*. What complicates that reading is, on the one hand, the narrative development after the rape (Dorothee's attempted reenactment of Wilhelmina's revenge fails to produce a neat fit with the discourse of female victimization), and, on the other hand, an iconographic dimension that fundamentally unsettles the allegory we have been tracing. Marketed as a *Heimatfilm* with artistic pretensions, *Rosen blühen auf dem Heidegrab* ends up as a horror film in which Eschmann is the monster and Dorothee incorporates the living dead. There are a number of factors contributing to this generic transformation—among them Dorothee's inner visions, the animistic views of nature which superimpose an image of Eschmann on a tree swaying in the wind, and Eschmann's monstrous sexuality. But it is the horrific images of Dorothee as a *Moorleiche* (swamp corpse) at the conclusion of the film which constitute the most disturbing layer of this film's historical palimpsest.

As I have suggested, Dorothee's death is prefigured immediately after the rape scene, as she lies beside Wilhelmina's grave thinking about what it might be like to be dead. Indeed, the convention of showing her hand go limp under Eschmann's grip at first leaves some uncertainty as to her survival. Accordingly, in the close-ups that are intercut with shots of the unsuspecting Ludwig shopping for a ring (to fit Dorothee's lifeless hand), we see Dorothee as both dead and alive—a motionless body under a gravestone, with unblinking eyes and a half-opened mouth, whose disembodied voice articulates a death wish.

This proximity between life and death is driven to an extreme in the final images of the film. Dorothee has led Eschmann to the swamp, where we see them slowly sink into the muck. As a storm brews overhead, the villagers discover their absence and head out to the swamp for a rescue. If the *Heimatfilm* more or less dictates a happy ending, the flashback to Wilhelmina's story has prepared us for the worst, and the transmutation of *Rosen* into a horror film makes Dorothee and Eschmann's rescue less than certain. Even as the returned Ludwig prepares to pull his lover out of the swamp, she disappears entirely into the mud. Ludwig searches for her head below the surface, but his efforts seem futile. When he eventually pulls her out, his act appears less as a rescue than as an exhumation: Dorothee emerges from the swamp a corpse, covered with dirt, mouth agape (see figure 6).

For a few more minutes, we remain uncertain as to Dorothee's fate; bystanders comment that she is no longer alive and that the swamp never returns its victims. Even when the local doctor pulls back Dorothee's mud-covered eyelids to shine his flashlight into her pupils, we receive no indication that would convince us otherwise. In the end, however, both she and Eschmann miraculously survive, and a brief scene at her bed shows her recovery. With Ludwig professing his continued love for her, Dorothee concludes the film with the line "Now they have no power over us anymore, the roses of Wilhelmina."

While this brief epilogue is significant for the ways in which it literally "dispels" the past (i.e., rids it of its spell and the hold it has on the present), it is highly contrived. What stays with the viewer is not the tacked-on image of an angelic Dorothee reunited with her lover in the bright light of her bedroom, but the series of distressing images of a very white and very dirty undead corpse being pulled from its grave. A review in the *Frankfurter Allgemeine Zeitung* complained specifically about these "unappetizingly naturalist scenes of gradual disappearance in the swamp"; intended as a dismissal, the review hit the mark when the author suggested sarcastically that "we should leave it up to psychiatry to examine the sadistic pleasure behind

Figure 6. Exhuming the undead: the *Heimatfilm* as horror film. From *Rosen blühen auf dem Heidegrab*.

[these images]."[51] Like the preceding images of occupation and rape, this even more distressingly graphic image connects with a collective memory of a recent German past littered with dead bodies. That memory was certainly instrumentalized differently from the memory of rape, and it may have been more thoroughly repressed by 1952. But Dorothee's ghost-like re-emergence from the dark waters of the swamp performs a striking return of the repressed.

In numerous films produced by and for the Allied occupation troops during the immediate postwar years, Germans had been admonished by insistent voice-overs not to forget precisely the kinds of images König recalls towards the end of his film. Documentaries produced by the Allies, such as *Deutschland erwache*, a 1945 American production designed for viewing by German POWs, and *Todesmühlen* (1946), in addition to Allied-licensed German newsreels devoted to the same topic,[52] had confronted Germans with indelible images of the liberation of Nazi concentration camps. Besides the piles of corpses that etched themselves on the postwar visual archive (to resurface in literary and cinematic attempts to address the Nazi past after the late 1960s), these films were and remain particularly disturbing on the visual level in two ways: first, they often do not allow the viewer to distinguish between the dead and the living, showing survivors who had been reduced to skeletons; second, a number of these films depicted exhumations, a practice pursued by the Allies at the camps at Hadamar and Schwarzenfeld, among others, in an effort to document Nazi atrocities for later trials.[53] When the Nuremberg trials began in 1946, the court used both the written record and the filmed footage of the camps, and the public was reminded once again of these scenes in daily news reports and broadcasts, as well as weekly newsreels from Nuremberg.

The film's visualization of Dorothee as the living dead thus intersects with a collective visual memory that may have been distorted in many ways but was still very much alive in Germany at the beginning of the 1950s.[54] I do not mean to suggest that we now read Dorothee—or rather her image— as a victim *of* the Germans rather than as the German victim the allegorical readings discussed above would make her. What makes this film so interesting to this day is rather the co-presence of these two images, which do not cancel each other out: German victimhood and the memory of German guilt are in a sense superimposed on one another. Indeed, if we view the corpse as that of the non-Jewish German woman Dorothee is, a third reading imposes itself, one which turns on a fantasy of resurrection rather than exhumation. The troubling scene would then be one of remembrance for the Germans' own dead, for the corpses that, in W. G. Sebald's evocative (and uncanny) image, remain immured in the foundations of the German state, and for whose recovery they provide the "psychic energy." In this view, pulling Dorothee out of the swamp would be a recovery of a different sort— the retrieval of the body of Germans from under the postwar rubble, or the resurrection of the victims of Russian rapes in the East. Drawing on the generic conventions of the horror film, the closing images of *Rosen blühen auf dem Heidegrab* thus add further layers to the historical palimpsest produced by the film, as if to mimic the layered structure of postwar historical memory. The film should dispel any assumption that "memory was sealed off in post-traumatic oblivion behind the 'Zero Hour' of 1945," not to return to public consciousness until the 1960s.[55]

As Dorothee returns to life in her bed at the close of the film, and recollects her fate, she tells Ludwig, "Forget me. Then everything will be okay for you." If we follow standard accounts of West German cinema of the 1950s, Dorothee would appear to be articulating precisely the ideological message of that cinema, and of the *Heimatfilm* above all: forget, and everything will be all right. But these accounts are complicated by a film such as *Rosen blühen auf dem Heidegrab*. As I have suggested, this is not merely a matter of paying closer attention to textual detail; rather, we need to correct received images of the *Heimatfilm* by also insisting on the function of these films as events that arose out of particular sets of discourses, reworked those discourses, and were viewed by a public immersed in those discourses.[56] Thus, whereas a wholly text-centered approach interprets the absence of manifest references to history and the recent past in a given film as an instance of forgetting, a view of the film as an event can help us to reconstruct the (selective) memories that the same film may have put and kept in circulation. These memories, finally, were stored not only in stories about the past, but—just as potently—in a collective visual archive created and sustained by the medium of film itself. Although for different reasons than Ludwig, the viewer would be hard-pressed to heed Dorothee's advice to "forget me" and to erase the image of her return from the dead. Playing out history as a horror scenario on the heath, König's *Heimat-Ballade* makes it difficult to imagine the cinema of the 1950s in Böll's terms, simply as "good," "warm," and as a privileged site for forgetting.

I have suggested that König's film stood apart from other Heimat productions of the era in its explicit thematization of horror on the heath. But I do not mean to suggest that its exceptional status makes it meaningless to broader generic considerations of the *Heimatfilm*. As I argued at the outset of this chapter, *Heimatfilme* have often edged closer to the *Unheimlich* than their handed-down, "Bambified" image would appear to allow. Though this is hardly ever as explicit as in König's film, it is true of other Heimat productions from the 1950s that are surprisingly open to allegorical readings of the past. Josef von Baky's *Via Mala* is one example. A staple text for the *Heimatfilm* tradition, John Knittel's novel by this title was adapted for the screen by Thea von Harbou in 1943 and produced in 1944; its premiere was delayed until after the end of the war (in March of 1945, the Nazis postponed its public release "because of its dark atmosphere").[57] In the vein of early adaptations of *Die Geierwally*, and of roughly contemporary films such as Wolfgang Staudte's *Rose Bernd* (1956), but also anticipating much later developments in the *Heimatfilm* tradition from the 1960s and 1970s, von Baky's *Via Mala* imagines Heimat as a dark place indeed. The provincial idyll we associate with 1950s Heimat is here a reactionary bastion of authoritarianism; instead of high-key interiors and brightly lit panoramas, Baky uses an expressionist mise-en-scène and lighting to stage the patricidal story of the Laurentz family. In a recent reevaluation of this film, critics have seen in *Via Mala* if not a form of "aesthetic resistance . . . and a call to assassinate the tyrant," then at least "a first attempt at 'mastering the past,' the first film of a fatherless society."[58]

Other *Heimatfilme* that followed may have tried to step out of the shadow of history that served as the constitutive, and hardly repressed, element in König's, Baky's, and particularly Staudte's Heimat films noir. But in few cases could they escape historicity altogether, or erect a wholly escapist, place- and timeless counterworld. Re-viewing these films as cultural events that provide imaginary solutions to historical questions, we find the Heimat films of the 1950s and beyond (re)producing the "noise" of history on various levels. Where this history was not the immediate past, it often turned out to be the historical present, a world beyond the ostensibly limited pale of Heimat. In these films, the pressures of history discussed above were compounded by the pressures of contemporary historical change, as discussed in the chapters that follow.

5   Nostalgic Modernization

Locating Home in the Economic Miracle

Everything has been put into motion: people, goods, ideas, values.
ELISABETH PFEIL

When we first encounter the young Ludwig in his new VW convertible, leaving the bustle of the city, *Rosen blühen auf dem Heidegrab* also introduces a secondary character, Albert Berndsen, who shares the road with Ludwig on his motor scooter. A figure apparently included mainly for comic relief in the film's dramaturgy of horror and Heimat, Berndsen also brings into view a subplot that is paradigmatic for the *Heimatfilm* of the 1950s. Berndsen is a persistent but innocuous salesman with a heavy Berlin accent who brings the modern age to the village as a traveling salesman for electric gadgets from razors and shearing knives to vacuum cleaners. Peddling the wares of the nascent *Wirtschaftswunder*, the seemingly laughable figure of Berndsen performs a crucial role in the Heimat film's broader project of what I call nostalgic modernization.

Berndsen enters the main space of the film from "outside": both his accent and his lack of familiarity with local lore mark him as a stranger. Yet his apparently misplaced salesmanship does not serve to ridicule technological advances in the name of tradition. Instead, Berndsen serves to make these advances palatable and to poke fun at the backwardness of rural life. Conspicuously mobile on his scooter, Berndsen the Berliner connects Heimat to the urban centers and tradition with the economic order of the day. Conversely, as an urban interloper, Berndsen becomes the diegetic addressee whose curiosity motivates the telling of the film's central legend. Given the way in which this legend functions as a mise-en-abîme of König's narrative, it is tempting to also see in Berndsen a mirror for the predominantly urban audience of the *Heimatfilm*.[1] Both in his function as traveling salesman and in his role as exterritorial listener, Berndsen illustrates the degree to which a postwar urban modernity, and not some timeless provincialism, provides the central reference points for the cinematic representation of Heimat during the 1950s.

In this chapter, I begin to map some of the key shifts in the configuration of society and culture during the "miracle years" in which the Heimat genre flourished. In this respect, the new consumer goods that Berndsen trades are only the most obvious materialization of the *Wirtschaftswunder*. Having acquired a nostalgic aura in coffee-table publications, they have come to stand, in the popular memory, for the birth of the consumer age. However, they are merely the visible signs of a momentous socioeconomic transformation, jump-started by the Marshall Plan in 1948,[2] which would find expression in countless other facets of everyday life, from technology to architecture to fashion, from the increase in motorization to the beginnings of urban sprawl to the "Americanization" of society and culture. The next chapter will investigate the varying ways in which these transformations played out in the *Heimatfilm* of the 1950s. What follows here is a more general consideration of the stakes involved in the cinematic representation of Heimat during the *Wirtschaftswunder*. After all, Berndsen's role as a gentle modernizer notwithstanding, Heimat would seem to remain a rather obstinate terrain when it comes to mapping social transformations. In order to get a clear sense of how it nonetheless came to fulfill that function, we need to sort out the contradictory image of the 1950s as a decade of both Heimat and the *Wirtschaftswunder*.

BETWEEN PARALYSIS AND DYNAMISM: THE 1950S

Our image of the 1950s and their cinema is shaped by two apparently contradictory views of the politics, economics, culture, and society of the decade. The first of these, which subsumes the repression approach discussed in the previous chapter, highlights the prolonged postwar paralysis of Germany, a diagnosis which tends to extend well into the 1960s. We might call this the restoration approach.[3] Both contemporary glosses and retrospective accounts have led us to think of the first postwar decade in West Germany as utterly static, fearful of any experimentation or change. Such accounts circle around three overlapping trends, all of which privilege a set of conservative values. In this view, the 1950s were the years of reconstruction (*Wiederaufbau*), normalization, and restoration. The success of the Christian Democratic Party's 1957 campaign slogan "Keine Experimente!"—an enduring favorite when it comes to catchwords for the decade—might be attributed to its condensation of these three trends in a politically potent formula. During this era, which became synonymous with the paternal figure of West Germany's first chancellor, Konrad Adenauer, gender roles reverted back to wartime and prewar models after brief shifts in the immediate postwar years;[4] the church reclaimed its role as the nation's moral arbiter (particularly regarding the cinema);[5] and, in one of the most hotly debated developments of the decade, the Federal Republic rearmed, becoming a partner for the West in the cold war. In this view, which Lutz Niethammer has described as the obstinate "myth of the 1950s,"[6] the decade is seen to connect backwards to an era before the Third Reich. Emphasizing the restoration of tendencies dating back as far as the Wilhelmine Empire, or a conservative sense of normalization that would undo the transgressions of the Nazi regime, the restoration approach describes all areas of society, politics, and culture according to a common logic of repression and return.

The famous 1967 account by Alexander and Margarete Mischerlich of the West Germans' "inability to mourn" confirmed Germany's political and moral paralysis through a psychoanalytic diagnosis of widespread repression. Specifically, the Mitscherlichs discerned a collective paralysis, a "psychic immobilism"[7] that had taken hold of the nation. With this diagnosis of withdrawal and arrested development, one associates not only the value attached to Heimat during the 1950s as a "spatially perceived small world turned outside in,"[8] but also the accompanying retreat into domesticity and the private sphere. Given the influence of the Mitscherlich's account on the intellectual culture after 1968, it is not surprising that evaluations of the cinema followed suit. In her introduction to an issue of *Frauen und Film* dedicated to the cinema of the 1950s, Heide Schlüpmann writes of an "aesthetics of paralysis," deliberately echoing Karsten Witte's influential analyses of the static choreographies of the Nazi cinema.[9] Fritz Göttler's nuanced account of postwar cinema neatly sums up received views of this era: "What this cinema is faulted for is, in a word, its immobility. . . . No experiments, no risks, no movement."[10]

However, such views of the decade and its cinema contrast with another version of postwar (film) history, which stresses the dynamism and modernity of the epoch. Taking the modernization approach, social and cultural historians have begun looking at changing patterns of consumption, labor, and mobility, at the rapid technological and industrial advances that captured the imagination of the decade, and at the reorganization of the domestic sphere, but also at patterns of cultural Americanization during the 1950s.[11] Reconstruction, in this view, was not only a matter of restoring the past, but also of marching confidently into the future. Novelty, not normalization, was the order of the day as Germans busied themselves with the

Wirtschaftswunder.[12] As the signature development of the decade, the economic recovery of war-torn Germany would be difficult to describe in terms of stability, stasis, and immobility. Rather, the dominant trope here was the unbridled dynamism of multiple waves: with monetary reform and the Marshall Plan as the driving forces, citizens soon experienced a massive *Konsumwelle* enabled by a *Kaufkraftwelle* and cresting in various *Freß-wellen, Kleidungswellen,* and *Einrichtungswellen.* They dealt with the postwar *Flüchtlingswelle* and soon took to the roads in the *Motorisierungswelle* and the *Reisewelle.* In this view of the era, the *Heimatfilmwelle* that followed the release of *Schwarzwaldmädel* in 1950 was not the epitome of a cinema suffering from paralysis, but part and parcel of a rapidly changing society.

The wave metaphor is problematic in that it suggests the inevitability of a natural catastrophe. But its ubiquity in economics, culture, and society during the 1950s indexes an underlying sense of dynamism that social, psychological, and aesthetic diagnoses of immobility advanced under the restoration approach are liable to miss. Specifically, these approaches fail to account for the many ways in which Germans during the 1950s were on the move. Looking back on the decade in 1961, the influential ethnographer Hermann Bausinger spoke of a "mobile society."[13] After massive postwar migrations had profoundly transformed the human geography of the West German state, other forms of mobility kept up the pace of change. One need only think of the postwar success story of Volkswagen to gauge the impact of motorization, particularly after mid-decade. Likewise, and partly as a consequence of the renewed availability of cars in a consumer society, tourism began to reach mass proportions towards the end of the 1950s. In addition to geographical movement and the role of (labor) mobility as a key asset in the *Wirtschaftswunder,* new (and old) kinds of social mobility played into changing patterns of class and cultural capital. Taking the modernization approach to West Germany during the 1950s, cultural historians and sociologists have come to see in the early years of the Federal Republic signs of a "mobilized society."[14]

How, then, are we to reconcile these two apparently conflicting images of the 1950s as a decade of paralysis on the one hand and of unprecedented mobility on the other? Are these simply two incompatible views that draw on unrelated, but equally valid, archives to substantiate their claims? For example, do increased motorization and the renewal of domesticity simply constitute parallel histories? Or do they intersect? My claim is that they do, and that the *Heimatfilm* is a key site for negotiating both restoration and modernization. Though it may initially appear an unlikely candidate, the notion of Heimat emerges from these films as a dialectical framework that links the two faces of the decade. On the one hand, Heimat is not simply the opposite of change, but also an enabling factor in the lunge towards the new; on the other hand, it is the rapid pace of change, or modernization, that lends Heimat its currency during these years. According to Schildt and Sywottek, the notion of " 'modernization under a conservative guardianship' . . . may ultimately best summarize the Adenauer era."[15] The idea of Heimat and the genre of the *Heimatfilm* served to represent precisely this notion. In this sense, *Heimat* was the ultimate synthetic term of the decade.

This function of Heimat as a synthesis of ostensible contradictions is intimately tied to its function as a spatial category. Both the restoration approach and the modernization approach make broad assumptions about spatiality during the 1950s. While restoration emphasizes the bounded spaces of domesticity and the immutability of provincial life in a parochial nation, modernization evokes displacement, travel, and movement, as well as the general dissociation of "space" from "place." From its representation in the *Heimatfilm* of the decade, the place of Heimat emerges as a space defined by both of these trends at once. Associated at first with the enclosed security of place and with the valorization of domesticity in the early years of the Federal Republic, Heimat also becomes a terrain on which to map patterns of mobility and displacement that define the decade.

Notions of Heimat as physical and geographical place stood at the center of the decade's obsession with domesticity, which is best described in terms of the synthesis mapped above. A place of retreat, the realm of privacy, and a key site for the enforcement of outdated gender norms, the home also became a highly public showcase of the *Wirtschaftswunder* as floor plans were redesigned, new furniture designs, patterns, and fabrics gave birth to the notion of interior decorating, and kitchens were equipped with innovative gadgets. The increased value of "home" dates back to the immediate postwar years, when the physical infrastructure had to be reestablished, bombed cities had to be rebuilt, displaced persons needed to find shelter. Statistics for the year 1946 register only 8.2 million homes to accommodate 13.7 million households.[16] The currency of Heimat over the following decade must be seen as the flip side of this massive experience of homelessness. The first government of the Federal Republic responded to this need with construction, subsidy, and loan programs that generated three million new apartments by 1956; as a result of the so-called apartment miracle (*Wohnungswunder*), most German citizens soon found what the name of a major housing construction company promised: Neue Heimat.[17]

Once the need for domestic living space was met, efforts at reconstructing the home turned from bricks and mortar to the intricacies of interior decorating and style. As average working hours began to decrease after mid-decade, with productivity and spending on the rise, a new culture of leisure further cemented the normative function of domesticity. Publications such as *Film und Frau* and the advertising industry addressed (female) consumers as homemakers, placing a premium on domesticity. With the gradual increase in prosperity and the programmatic expansion of the consumer sphere in Ludwig Erhard's social market economy, female housework turned into a key site for cultural production, as Erica Carter shows in her analysis of gender and consumption in postwar reconstruction.[18] In particular, broad sectors of the population began spending significant time and money on contemporary design—from the celebrated *Nierentisch* (kidney-shaped table) to the newest synthetic materials. As Carter demonstrates, the emerging culture of the home turned housework into a labor of producing aesthetic value and social meaning. Specifically, like the concept of Heimat, the culture of home came to express both a restorative tendency—relegating women (back) to the domestic sphere and signaling a more general social retreat into the private realm—and a thoroughgoing modernization of those spheres, as housewives were called upon to boost the economy by purchasing new technologies designed to rationalize housework and modernize the housewife herself.[19] By the end of the decade, the retreat to the domestic sphere was thus glorified as a specifically modern pursuit, suggesting an overlap between the restorative signature of the 1950s and the headlong push to bring the nation back up to (economic) speed.

If domesticity thus evolved as a "central norm" of the 1950s,[20] it was offset, as I have suggested, by an obsession with mobility. Hardly restricted to trends in travel and postwar relocation, this obsession could reach right into the domestic sphere with self-help brochures instructing modern consumers in "mobile living" (*bewegliches Wohnen*).[21] As a competing norm of the decade, mobility became a signature of postwar modernity. It played into the *Heimatfilm* as well, suggesting that we need to revise the verdict of immobility for the cinema of the decade. Taking a dialectical view of the reconstruction/modernization couplet, the following readings of the *Heimatfilm* draw on cultural histories of the 1950s that stress the "contradictory overlap of traditional factors and unambiguous new beginnings."[22] I trace that overlap in particular through the way in which the "place" of Heimat becomes redefined through the mobility of characters and plots across contemporary geographical, social, and economic landscapes ranging from Silesia in the east to America in the west. In this view, a number of Heimat films reveal not only a conservative or reactionary concern with

Heimat as an archaic realm of settled existence, but also an apparent need to come to terms with various tropes of mobility and displacement that dominate the postwar present—from the plight of expellees faced with the task of resettling in the Federal Republic to the proliferation of late-model convertibles that traverse the tranquility of Heimat scenery; from the relocation of Heimat from the Austrian/German alps to surprisingly similar mountainous regions in Africa and North America, to the bourgeoning tourist plots towards the end of the 1950s. While the mere presence of mobility as a motif does not yet tell us anything about its function, it does tend to undermine received spatial definitions of Heimat as *locus amoenus,* a pastoral idyll untouched by modernity. For as the trajectories charted by characters and objects in these films rise to a sometimes frenzied pace of departure, displacement, and return, it becomes difficult to maintain a solipsistic definition of Heimat as a locale not mediated by distanced relations of time and space. In this view, the function of the *Heimatfilm* is not so much to negate the effects of modernity, as critics have suggested, but rather to model compromise solutions: negotiating the encroaching demands of modernity within the spaces of Heimat, these films allow viewers to imagine postwar reconstruction as a process that embraces both the traditionalism of Heimat and the advances of modernization. Because of its ability to synthesize contradictions that defined the decade, and not because of its promise of escape, the *Heimatfilm* was predestined to become the favorite genre of the *Wirtschaftswunder:* unlike any other fictional format, it responded to, and helped to shape, the decade's double imperative of restoration and modernization.

As films about the restoration of "home," *Heimatfilme* of the 1950s also chart a series of departures. Significantly, many of these departures take place in shiny new convertibles. As a signifier of both mobility and modernity, the car played a central role in the Heimat film's dialectics of dwelling and departure. Private motorization may not be the first building block of the genre that comes to mind, and yet cars are among the most stable elements of a semantics of the 1950s *Heimatfilm* from the moment Sonja Ziemann wins the coveted Ford Taunus cabriolet in *Schwarzwaldmädel* (1950). Whether in *Der Förster vom Silberwald* (1955) or *Heimatland* (1955), in *Schwarzwälder Kirsch* (1958), *Die Trapp-Familie in Amerika* (1958), or *Wenn die Heide blüht* (1960), the *Heimatfilm* appears to engage in a conspicuous motorization of the provinces. Nor are these proliferating convertibles mere functional vehicles for bringing the urban intruder to the countryside or vice versa. At a time when Peter Ostermayr was complaining that "'automobilization' . . . is also to blame for the film crisis," as cars were diverting the time and money of the filmgoing public,[23] the representation of late-model vehicles on screen would appear to have been a matter of commercial viability. As objects of conspicuous consumption, cars in the *Heimatfilm* are invariably signs of the expanding consumer economy engineered by Ludwig Erhard; as prominent signifiers in a genre devoted to the landscapes of tradition, however, cars also profoundly affect the spatial dynamics that characterize the *Heimatfilm*. A film from 1958, when the *Motorisierungswelle* was gathering speed, serves to illustrate this transformation.

CONVERTIBLE PROVINCIALISM: *DIE LANDÄRZTIN*

The opening images of Paul May's *Die Landärztin* must have been a dream come true for the VW marketing department in Wolfsburg. After the credits have rolled over a picture-perfect Alpine landscape seemingly untouched by civilization, the camera pans to follow the approach of a young woman on a motor scooter. As she draws closer, her path is suddenly blocked by a car parked in the middle of a country crossing, and the fluid camera movement comes to rest on the latest model of a VW convertible, which now occupies the lower half of the screen.

From the ensuing exchange between the young woman, Petra (Marianne Koch), and the driver who emerges from the beetle and boasts of his recent purchase, we learn that their acquaintance dates back to medical school. Petra is on her way to take up a position in the nearby village of Kürzlingen as the eponymous country doctor; Dr. Friebe, her colleague and suitor, tries to lure her into his VW for a ride instead, imploring her to return to the city and to the brilliant career that awaits her there. Against his laments that she is jeopardizing her future by taking up a position in a *Kuhdorf* (cow village), she reiterates her reasons for leaving: the country post, she argues, will afford her the opportunity to flee the pressures of specialization and the routinization that she would face in the city. Despite her suitor's protests, she insists that he let her pass, for she has work to do.

Die Landärztin, a film whose mixed reviews all agreed on its generic characterization as a *Heimatfilm*, begins by showcasing the car as a signifier of modernity.[24] Clearly a tribute to a newly motorized society (not to mention a modern form of product placement), the new VW immediately situates the plot of the film not in some timeless provincial tranquility but in a marked *Wirtschaftswunder* present. By the time of May's film, the VW beetle had long passed the magical mark of one million, which had been celebrated in 1955 as an event of global reach. In the context of the *Heimatfilm*, the conspicuous placement of up-to-date modes of private transportation must be viewed against the background of the *Motorisierungswelle* of the mid- to late 1950s, when Germany took to the roads.[25] The increasing and shifting patterns of transportation that West Germans experienced at the time suggest some of the consequences of modernity for a human geography of the 1950s. For example, with the rapid increase in private motorization around 1956, the practice of commuting became much more common. This trend forced a redefinition of the boundaries of the rural and an increasing transformation of non- and sub-urban communities in line with the pressures of urban lifestyles. With regard to newly constructed housing developments on the outskirts of villages and cities, Hannelore Brunhöber points out that traditional neighborly relations were progressively undermined, while distanced and often work-related contacts began to replace proximity as a zone of social exchange.[26]

But the social consequences of private motorization went well beyond the redefinition of spatial relations of proximity and distance. In her study of the profound transformations taking place around notions of mobility and domesticity in France during the same years, Kristin Ross provides some crucial insights into the function of mobility that apply with equal force to the German context. Describing mobility as the "categorical imperative of the economic order," she discerns in the trend towards motorization the "mark of a rupture with the past; every individual must be free to be displaced, and displaceable in function of the exigencies of the economic order."[27] Ross's description is particularly apt inasmuch as she highlights the role of mobility as a spatial and social practice with implications for historical consciousness. As the "mark of a rupture with the past," the new "euphoria of mobility"[28] during the second half of the 1950s in particular served to displace not only recent experiences of forced mobility, but also the expansionist definition of national space and of Heimat that had characterized the Nazi regime. Ross's study of the "headlong, dramatic, and breathless" event of French modernization goes a long way toward suggesting how the "revolution in attitudes toward mobility and displacement" shaped this process.[29] Generating available labor (what Ross calls "l'homme disponible"), changing patterns of transportation and car ownership were literally a driving force in the (re)generation of expanding, flexible labor markets for the growing economy. We must also think of mobility in the sense of increased job mobility as the basis for various forms of social mobility—from the forced retraining of expellees to meet the demands of a new domestic labor market to the readiness to traverse growing distances between home and work.

At the same time, the "rupture with the past" enacted through the newfound mobility was hardly ever complete. As Alon Confino's recent work on travel in postwar Germany suggests, mobility not only effaced memory but also served as its medium as Germany's rekindled tourist industry became a site for contemplating the recent past.[30] Tourism may have been a selective medium of memory, but Confino's analysis shows that it would be wrong to think of postwar travel merely in terms of the repression approach. Rather, tourism "became a metaphor that both claimed the Nazi past and separated the present from it. . . . [It] became a medium for making sense of the past and the present."[31]

By the end of the 1950s, indeed, it had become a mass medium. The *Reisewelle* of the 1950s combined economic dynamism with physical mobility as citizens took to the roads and *Erholungsgebiete* (recreation areas) in newly purchased cars, pitching brand-new tents and booking rooms in the German countryside as well as abroad.[32] Contemporary sociology took note of this development, discerning a shift in patterns of travel by mid-decade. Beginning in 1953, approximately one-third of the adult population of West Germany was once again able to afford at least one annual vacation trip.[33] By the end of the decade, the average citizen was spending up to a month's income on vacation every year.[34] Although popular memory associates 1950s tourism with the rediscovery of Italy (in particular, the island of Capri captured the contemporary imagination even as it remained financially out of reach for most), throughout the decade, roughly two-thirds of all vacation travel took place within the West German borders. At the beginning of the 1950s, sociologists had seen the refugee as embodying a fundamental shift from settled to mobile existence. Towards the end of the decade, the tourist replaced the expellee as the incarnation of the modern "mobile subject" and as an "agent of modernity."[35] Accordingly, it was no longer the literature on refugee families but the sociology of tourism which made broad claims on the relevant prototypes for the era. Remarkably, this literature discovered reversals of the relationship between stasis and mobility, dwelling and travel similar to those that scholarship on refugee families had described earlier in the decade.[36] Mobility, claimed the author of a historical sociology of tourism from 1961, "has replaced stability in all domains. For our society, mobility fulfills the same function as did absolute values and stasis in pre-industrial tradition."[37]

Faced with the dynamics of modernization and motorization during the 1950s, the *Heimatfilm* developed in two distinct directions: while some films took a resolutely antimodern stance that insisted on turning back the clock and offering escapes to premodern idylls untouched by the pressures of economic and social mobilization, others, such as *Die Landärztin*, sought ways to accommodate those pressures within the received iconographic and narrative framework of Heimat. While the former variant may be described as escapist in the traditional sense, offering its viewers a simple, mythical alternative to their postwar present, the latter suggests a more dialectical reading. Films taking their viewers back to mediaeval Alpine settings such as *Die Martinsklause* (1951), *Der Klosterjäger* (1953), and other Ganghofer adaptations and remakes, but also the famous series of *Sissi* films (1955–57) which glamorized the Hapsburg monarchy of the nineteenth century, fit the escapist mold, as do a number of films whose fictional present is difficult to locate and remains remote from the urban viewer's contemporary life. As I have suggested, scholarship on the *Heimatfilm* has tended to focus on this aspect of the genre, emphasizing its tendency to offer viewers a "holiday from history."

Upon closer inspection, however, the postwar present is generally not as remote from the diegetic conceits of the *Heimatfilm* as such views would have us believe. Relatively few *Heimatfilme* are actually situated in an identifiable past the way *Heideschulmeister Uwe Karsten* (1954) (set around the turn of the century) and costume dramas à la *Sissi* are. Instead of generating an antimodern stance by retreating to a glorified past, films like *Die Landärztin* suggest a more complicated—if no less conservative— negotiation of the competing demands of modernity and tradition. While the latter continues to be represented through the constitutive rural spaces, customs, and rhythms of Heimat, the ostensible inertia of provincial tradition is offset by the proliferating tropes of mobility which signal the films' engagement with the economic and social transformations of postwar (West) Germany.

The plot of *Die Landärztin*, as it develops after the meeting of the two motorists in the countryside, provides a case study of the way in which the *Heimatfilm* negotiates antimodern traditionalism with the demands of the "modern" 1950s. At first, as Petra continues on her way to the *Kuhdorf* Kürzlingen, it would seem as if the two vehicles only evoked the motorized postwar present in order to leave it behind once and for all. Connected as it is to Dr. Friebe and his allegiance to the city, which is in turn the site of specialized, routine, and alienated labor, even the shiniest new model cannot entice Petra on her way to a more organic, rooted type of medical practice. By the end of the film, however, we will return to the Volkswagen convertible, the allure of which the opening images have firmly planted in the viewer's mind.

For now, the brief encounter between Petra and Dr. Friebe ends with a victory of the scooter over the convertible; more importantly, however, the encounter has established motorization as a key motif, even as it distributes the means of transportation unevenly according to gender. Although Dr. Friebe has been able to reach this remote country crossing before Petra thanks to the new VW, Petra's availability for rural work is tied to her own mobility on the fashionable scooter, which at the time, was only just being replaced by the car as the predominant means of private transportation.[38] With the signal exception of her gender, Petra represents precisely the "new man" Ross discerns in her analysis of the discourses and images of motorization that circulated in France at the time. It is Petra's mobility that makes her available for work in the countryside in the first place, and we can already surmise that the exorcism of the car and its connotations will not be as complete as Petra's refusal of a lift back to the city might have suggested. Themselves conspicuous signs of the *Motorisierungswelle,* car and scooter serve not only as a signifiers of modernization, but also as vehicles for negotiating its meanings within the spaces of Heimat. Locating the function of motorization and mobility in the *Heimatfilm,* in other words, is not only a matter of determining their semantic presence, but also involves understanding their syntactic relevance. In a reversal of emerging commuter trends, *Die Landärztin* begins with a trajectory from the city to the country. How does that trajectory play out in terms of narrative structure?

Upon her arrival in the idyllic rural community of Kürzlingen, Petra learns that she indeed has her work cut out for her. Before she can perform the kind of services she learned in medical school, she has to work hard to overcome the deep-seated mistrust and reactionary gender politics of the villagers. Shocked to discover that "Dr. Jensen" is a woman, they boycott her office, preferring to travel to the next village or even to be treated by the local veterinarian, Dr. Rinner (Rudolf Prack). Indeed, even the latter is dismissive and more than a little misogynist at first, but when Petra proves her professional skills in an emergency, he joins her cause. This clears the path for a reconciliation between the young newcomer and the villagers, and for the union of country doctor and city doctor in particular; not surprisingly, this union facilitates Petra's acceptance of the offer she had refused in the opening banter with Dr. Friebe: in the film's closing image, Marianne Koch and Rudolf Prack, the stars of the *Heimatfilm,* drive off into the Bavarian sunset in the vet's own VW convertible.

As the film's resolutely up-to-date protagonist, Petra labors under a peculiar double burden: on the one hand, she is a highly qualified female professional who simply wants to do her job in a misogynist rural setting—a basic plot featured two years earlier in Ulrich Erfurth's *Heidemelodie* (1956), where a young female teacher arrives as the successor to the old *Heide-*

schulmeister only to encounter the prejudices and distrust of most the villagers. A similar setup also initiates a later film, *Die Lindenwirtin vom Donaustrand* (1957), in which a young woman arrives by steamboat to take on a position at a local inn, much to the dismay of the villagers who had wanted to see in her the avant-garde of a wave of tourist visitors to their town on the Danube. In each of these cases, the young woman has to overcome entrenched expectations about gender, which invariably results in a partial restoration of gender norms by the film's end. However, her role as initiator of the plot leaves its marks on this restoration: while both Petra in *Die Landärztin* and Helga, the successful pediatrician in *Solange noch die Rosen blühen* (1956) give up their initial independence by falling for the male lead, neither is forced to give up her medical profession. Maintaining their professional commitment, these women therefore also bear the second, larger burden of functioning as agents of modernization charged with bringing the traditional values and norms of a rural community up to speed with the changing reality in the urban centers. Georg Seeßlen describes this double burden of *Heimatfilm* femininity as the "myth of the natural woman." Aside from the "secretary film" of the 1950s, argues Seeßlen, "no other genre describes the role of the woman in the economic miracle with the same precision, demanding two faces of her, both radiant: one gazing in confirmation on the Fascist man, who wants to remain Fascist, and the other turning an eye on the money, on modernization, corruption, and industrialization."[39]

This double task, which occupies Petra throughout *Die Landärztin*, is repeatedly connected to the function of the scooter that has brought her from the city to the rural idyll. As she rides around a conspicuously unmotorized Kürzlingen (hers appears to be the only vehicle in the area besides the vet's VW convertible), the scooter marks her as foreign even as it functions as the misplaced status symbol of a young urban professional. Gradually, Petra earns the trust of a few individuals, who begin appearing on the scooter's back seat. Though the film stages these scenes for comic effect (the priest looks particularly undignified as he straddles the saddle of Petra's "rocket," as he calls it), they contribute to the harmonization it fundamentally aims to achieve. As the villagers come to accept a female doctor in their midst, her form of transportation no longer seems as out of place as it did on the day of her arrival. To the degree that Petra and her motor scooter initially represent the "other" to Heimat, it seems important to note that *Die Landärztin* does not redraw the line that would keep out the modern (in the form of motorization and emancipation) and maintain the integrity of Heimat. Once again, Paul May's film significantly does *not* use the initial opposition between the country and the city to prove the superiority of traditional ways of life over the lifestyle and professionalism of the urban intruder. Nor, of course, does it engage in a full-scale attack on Kürzlingen's patriarchal provincialism.[40] Rather, in chronicling Petra's gradual integration and the locals' grudging acceptance of her professional skill, the film asks its audience to entertain the idea of Heimat as a compromise formation, a space in which the urban reaches the local and modernity meets tradition.

While this harmonization has much to do with character development, it can also be seen as a small-scale transformation of provincial space, which has adapted to the effects of motorization. As the example of *Die Landärztin* suggests, those effects were most tangible in rural areas which were progressively "deprovincialized" by the advent of the automobile. *Die Landärztin* does not block the erosion of differences between urban and rural lifestyles that cultural historians have traced to the 1950s. Instead, the film negotiates this erosion within the realm of Heimat, both on an iconographic and a narrative level. The happy ending, with its union of country vet and city doctor, neatly illustrates the compromise that this film, and the Heimat genre more generally, serve to facilitate. After the requisite marriage, some overly conciliatory speeches, and Petra's public pronouncement that "this is where I belong," the film achieves closure by returning to the vehicle on which it opened. Having transferred her loyalties from the city to the country, Petra can now take the (passenger) seat in a VW convertible that she refused at the outset.

Ross argues that the postwar discourse surrounding cars and mobility is "built around freezing time in the form of reconciling past and future, the old ways and the new. . . . Past and future are one, *you can change without changing.*"[41] There is hardly a better way to describe the role of the convertible in the *Heimatfilm* and in *Die Landärztin* in particular. In this respect, May's film illustrates the links between the *Heimatfilm* of the 1950s and the "reactionary modernism" of a film like *Die goldene Stadt*. The political conservatism of such films consists not in an antimodern stance, but in the selective embrace of the modern and in the mythologization of modernization as a process that will not threaten the underlying sense of continuity and *Gemeinschaft*. In this respect, the *Heimatfilm* contributes decisively to an image of the 1950s as a decade of "modernization under a conservative guardianship." Paul May's film works, like so many others of the decade, towards a negotiated peace between Petra and the villagers, between the pressures of urban modernity and the ostensible inertia of rural tradition.

In the light of such insights, we need to revise spatial commonplaces that would associate the urban with the modern and the rural with the traditional, drawing sharp dividing lines between the two spheres. For the history of motorization, along with the larger history of modernization in the 1950s, begs the question of where to draw such a line. Although the city is not visually present in *Die Landärztin*, the film suggests its presence at every turn—not just in the foregrounding of scooters and cars, but also in the decidedly urban and modern figure of Petra herself. Moreover, while the clear-cut distinction between Heimat and *Fremde* has been a constitutive part of many a definition of *Heimat*, it is worth bearing in mind that feature films rarely offer lexical definitions, but instead use images to tell stories. In other words, as soon as Heimat becomes a narrative and visual topos, the distinction between Heimat and *Fremde* is literally set in motion, subject to visual polysemy, narrative development, revision, and reversals. As a rule, the *Heimatfilm* does not, therefore, maintain the rigid definitional distinction between Heimat and its constitutive other (though it may always invoke that definition as its premise); rather, its ideological function consists precisely in transforming that distinction in the process of narration. These films achieve closure by accomplishing a harmonization between such ostensibly opposed terms as rural and urban, modern and traditional. *Die Landärztin* is doubly emblematic of this process by making it explicit in its references to motorization and by depicting it as a task to be performed by a woman.

HEIMAT IN THE REARVIEW MIRROR:
WENN DIE HEIDE BLÜHT

If motorization and mobility inform the semantic and syntactic construction of the Heimat genre as a space in which to negotiate the impact of modernity without letting go of the old, we can detect a similar dynamics of modernity and tradition on the level of a particular generic form of address.[42] To illustrate this conjunction, let us look at the ending of another *Heimatfilm* which, like that of *Die Landärztin* and so many others, works to resolve the generic conflicts between old and young, men and women, Heimat and *Fremde* through the trope of marriage and the rewriting of these conflicts as harmony and compromise. What this particular film adds to this picture, I would suggest, is a brief glance at the position of the spectator, again situating the genre with regard to the 1950s as a decade of modernization as much as of retrenchment.

At the end of *Wenn die Heide blüht* (1960), a *Heimatfilm* so overburdened with generic stereotypes as to border on the self-reflexive, we witness the establishment of two couples in the genre-typical countryside. The plot has revolved around Rolf, an ageing peasant's prodigal son, who originally

Figure 7. Crowning the *Heidekönigin* in *Wenn die Heide blüht* (1960). Courtesy Deutsches Filminstitut–DIF, Frankfurt.

fled the stifling traditions and the constraining space of his native village for America. After ten years of washing dishes and playing the piano for a living (condensed into some sixty seconds of screen time), news of his father's ill health brings him back home, where he discovers that he has become the prime suspect in the murder of his brother. Shifting from musician to detective, Rolf works hard to exculpate himself, and the climax in the courtroom brings the liberating confession from the old game warden, Harcort: using Rolf's pistol, he shot the brother in self-defense on the night of Rolf's departure. This confession, as well as Harcort's acquittal, clears the way for the union between Rolf and Harcort's daughter Sonja, the assistant to the local vet who is crowned *Heidekönigin* at the requisite *Volksfest* at the film's close (see figure 7).

Besides Harcort, a former soldier of the Wehrmacht who in important ways stands for the generation still tainted by the Nazi years,[43] one other figure hampers the creation of the couple at the end of the film: on the ship back from America, Rolf had encountered a young singer named Vera. A stock figure in the Heimat films of the 1950s, Vera embodies a type of fem-

ininity that differs from the characteristically girlish woman of Heimat in
its over-the-top modernity: we first encounter the singer leaning seduc-
tively against a bar in a luxurious modern ocean liner, richly appointed in
the most stylish interior design of the era. Vera is performing a composition
by Rolf, whose lyrics praise the unbound existence of sailors and traveling
artists like Rolf and Vera themselves.[44] Unlike Sonja back home, Vera is not
defined as a daughter or in other ways tied to a family: she is decidedly independent, a quality which, in the gender logics of the *Heimatfilm*, easily
shades into decadence and uprootedness when it appears in women. Besides
embodying the rootlessness and lack of Heimat that Rolf must overcome by
the end of the film, Vera also represents urban rather than rural culture, the
modernity of the German *Wirtschaftswunder* rather than the idyllic backwardness of Rolf's native village: she is associated with London and Hamburg, where she performs, and when she drives to the village for the
Volksfest, she arrives in a sleek white convertible rather than the traditional
horse-drawn cart.

When Vera is forced to realize that Rolf has learned his Heimat lesson
and decided to stay forever in the provincial idyll he once scorned, she leaves
for Hamburg in her car, accompanied by her persistent but innocuous suitor,
Dr. Erdmann. As they drive off, Vera's convertible is brought to a temporary
halt by a herd of sheep roaming the heath without regard for the existence
of streets. They pause before this idyllic scene, and Vera uses the rearview
mirror to adjust her makeup. The camera aligns with her gaze in the mirror
in a tight close-up, allowing us to witness the kiss between Rolf and Sonja
that seals the narrative.

The shot which frames the "legitimate" couple in the rearview mirror of
the convertible is brief, but odd enough in its composition to stand out in the
otherwise utterly conventional closing sequence of *Wenn die Heide blüht*.
Without making any claims regarding directorial intention, I see this closing as emblematic of some central generic concerns of the *Heimatfilm*, for
this particular shot doubly refracts the viewer's gaze in an interesting way:
we see Rolf and Sonja, ostensibly the very incarnation of Heimat, belonging, and continuity, through the desiring eyes of the woman who moves
outside the space of Heimat, partaking of its spectacle as a tourist at best. In
this regard, Vera's gaze emblematizes that of the predominantly urban audience to whom the *Heimatfilm* was addressed and whom the genre undoubtedly helped to recruit for the newly revived German tourist economy.[45] The
shot is revealing, in other words, for its implicit acknowledgment of the
genre's more general functionalization of Heimat in an avowedly modern
context. We would be wrong to read the *Heimatfilm* simply as an escapist,

antimodern genre without insisting on its own role in the modernization process. Nor is this simply a matter of individual felicitous images such as the one I have just described. We need only think of the role played by color and up-to-date technologies of cinematic spectacle, explicitly signaled in the distribution and marketing discourse surrounding the *Heimatfilm*, in order to gauge the modern impulses that drive its ostensibly antimodern plots. Indeed, as early as 1952, at least one critic had detected the dialectics of the traditional and the contemporary, the rural and the urban in the *Heimatfilm*. Calling films such as *Grün ist die Heide* and *Wenn die Abendglocken läuten* "synthetic Heimat films," Claus Hardt emphasized the *urban* dimensions of the genre. Maria Holst, he observed, had to look fit for Berlin's cosmopolitan boulevards even when playing a local in the village on the heath. The nature of the *Heimatfilm*, in other words, was always already urbanized, "paved over." Accordingly, Hardt saw *Grün ist die Heide* as the protoype of an "Asphalt-*Heimatfilm*": "a pure asphalt product, made by asphalt people for asphalt people."[46]

Despite its troubling invocation of Nazi epithets against the literary modernism of New Objectivity (which the Nazis labeled *Asphaltliteratur*), such an assessment is confirmed metaphorically by the ending of *Wenn die Heide blüht*. Vera's gaze, relayed through the mirror of a parked car, invokes the spectator's situation in front of a screen (if not exactly in a drive-in theater). As the couple leaves in the convertible, the film comes to a close, and the viewer, too, leaves the cinema with a backward glance. Inasmuch as it explicitly, if subtly, references the discursive framework of its exhibition, the *Heimatfilm*, it would appear, offers us the experience of an archaic idyll not on its own terms, but as a distinctly modern, contemporary experience. In the experience of the urban moviegoer, but also of West German society at large, caught in the momentous transformations of the *Wirtschaftswunder*, Heimat exists only as a myth in the rearview mirror of modernity. That myth, incarnated in *Wenn die Heide blüht* by the union of Rolf and Sonja at the film's end, promises its own perpetual regeneration at precisely the moment when it is about to recede into the distance, superseded by the trappings of modernity. As numerous commentators have pointed out, the semantics of Heimat already encode this function: Heimat, Edgar Reitz claims, "is something lost."[47] Or, as Rentschler suggests, "It is only after Heimat ceases to be taken for granted that the notion is articulated."[48] In their obsession with the logics of Heimat, I would suggest, the films of the 1950s (and others of the genre) function to ritualize the passing of a moment when Heimat still existed, negotiating its absence for the progressivist ethos of postwar modernization.

This is again why the genre was so successful during the *Wirtschafts-wunder,* whose effects it made available within the space of Heimat rather than simply keeping them at bay. The spaces we encounter in these films are remote only in a superficial sense; upon closer inspection we see they are regularly suffused with traces of technological and social modernization, yielding a sort of "industrialized provincialism."[49] Accordingly, the comings and goings in films like *Schwarzwaldmädel, Die Landärztin,* or *Wenn die Heide blüht* showcase the most up-to-date, stylish modes of transportation (courtesy of Ford and Volkswagen), making sure to avoid any reference to the detrimental effects of motorization, from congested urban centers to the social effects of long commutes. Indeed, the car appears in the *Heimatfilm* and other films of the 1950s as in a commercial. In a characteristic only-car-on-the-road sequence,[50] the closing image of *Die Landärztin* shows Marianne Koch and Rudolf Prack in their shiny convertible, speeding along a tree-lined highway in the Alps.

If travel and mobility had became the norm by the end of the 1950s, the dynamics of the *Wirtschaftswunder* did not cancel out the other side of the dialectical gamble with Heimat, which brought about the renewed valorization of domesticity, dwelling, stasis. The "norms" of domesticity and of mobility, in other words, must be seen not as exclusive, but as mutually enabling. As we turn from the backdrop of the 1950s as a decade of restoration and modernization to the films of its preferred genre, we need to maintain a dual focus on the logic of Heimat. Rather than tracing the replacement of one norm by another, we must attend to the various ways in which the competing demands of dwelling and travel, of domesticity and mobility, of home and away were negotiated on the terrain of Heimat. As its advertising strategies graphically suggest, the travel industry of the 1950s was at pains to market its products to a population wedded to notions of home. The *Heimatfilm* industry faced the same challenge from the opposite end. To find an audience for its product, this industry would have to find ways of addressing the multiple forms of postwar displacement, movement, and travel even as it extolled the more settled values of stasis associated with Heimat.

This task was undertaken most explicitly in a group of Heimat films that amount to something of a subcycle in the genre and are perhaps best described as *Ferienfilme* (vacation films). Luring urban vacationers to the increasingly numerous recreation areas of the Federal Republic, these films include such titles as *Die Wirtin vom Wörthersee* (1952), *Gruß und Kuß vom Tegernsee* (1957), *Die Mädels vom Immenhof* (1955), and the programmatic *Ferien vom Ich* (1952). Each of these films draws explicitly on the locations, stars, plots, and spectacle of the *Heimatfilm* to rewrite Heimat itself as a travel destination. But even the most "traditional" forms of the *Heimatfilm*, exemplified for many by Ostermayr's productions, deliberately situated their remote Alpine settings in relation to an emerging tourist network. In its publicity for *Die Geierwally* (1956), for example, Ostermayr's revamped postwar company emphasized the role of landscape imagery in "conveying geographical information." Landscape photography in these films, the advertising copy proclaimed, "can thrill us in two ways: on the one hand as a welcome reminder of our own travels, and on the other as suggestion for future vacation destinations."[51]

In other words, the progressive deprovincialization of the rural brought about by motorization, the expansion of the German transport network, and the shifting practices of commuting inevitably left its mark on the *Heimatfilm* even where the genre worked to reverse these trends. In the context of a mobilized West German society, the Heimat topos functioned not only to resist this newfound dynamism, but also to incorporate it. As Germany, like other European countries during these years, saw "the dismantling of all earlier spatial arrangements,"[52] the *Heimatfilm* could not survive by simply transporting an unchanged image of precisely those earlier spatial arrangements, sealed off from contemporary developments (though it did do that, too). Swept up in the various waves of the 1950s, Heimat itself became a mobile concept requiring a new geography of home, place, and community.

That geography, I suggest, was one of nostalgic modernization. In films like *Die Landärztin* or *Wenn die Heide blüht*, as well as in the glut of *Ferienfilme*, the Heimat topos combined the longing for home, restoration, and stability with an affinity towards the economic and geographical mobilization of postwar Germany. It provided a ground for wistful backward glances *and* a headlong rush towards the future without monopolizing either one of these impulses. In calling this negotiated peace between restoration and modernity "nostalgic modernization," I deliberately evoke Jeffrey Herf's study of "reactionary modernism" to indicate a certain overlap between the Heimat ideology of the economic miracle and the selective embrace of modernity by the ideologues of the Third Reich. The *Heimatfilm* of the 1950s shared the impulse to combine antimodern vistas with the economic agenda of modernization. Like the writings of Werner Sombart before them, these films seem to hold the view that modernity can be "tamed." Like *Der Strom* or *Der verlorene Sohn*, they advance images of rural landscapes as the place for that reconciliation.

In spite of these significant parallels, however, I do not see in the *Heimat-*

film of the Adenauer era a simple continuation of the Fascist agenda. What I am calling nostalgic modernization is historically distinct from the discourses and practices of reactionary modernism, and the overlap between the two does not make the 1950s *Heimatfilm* proto- or neo-Fascist. I will reserve the task of mapping the historical specificity of nostalgic modernization for individual readings in which I provide the relevant historical and discursive frameworks for each film. On a more general level, however, we might begin to distinguish 1950s attitudes towards modernization from their Nazi precedents by recalling the specificity of the reactionary modernists' intervention. Nazi propagandists who worked with the vocabulary of reactionary modernism, Herf notes, "were distinct within the panoply of German nationalism for the emphasis they placed on anti-Semitism and the biological foundations they gave to German technological advance."[53] In other words, under Fascism, attitudes towards modernization were inevitably bound up with the larger edifice of Nazi ideology, particularly its racist dimensions. This argument about the historical specificity of reactionary modernism, which Herf develops through a comparison with earlier ideological positions, also holds if we compare it with the 1950s. Though it would be foolish to suggest that anti-Semitism and *völkisch* ideology simply evaporated with the founding of the Federal Republic, or that the Heimat discourse was entirely rechanneled into less nefarious cultural constellations, the realignment of nationalism, modernism, and conservatism took historically specific forms to which we must remain sensitive as we follow it through the films of the decade.

During the 1950s, the Heimat film's ability to (in)fuse change with nostalgia remained linked to the tension between dwelling and mobility, between "roots" and "routes" that I have begun to chart here. The following chapter turns to a number of films by Wolfgang Liebeneiner, one of the most prolific directors of *Heimatfilme* during the Adenauer era.[54] His version of *Waldwinter*, as well as his two films about the Trapp family, offer some revealing perspectives on the geographical and ideological mobility of Heimat itself. Most astonishingly, perhaps, these films showcase the capacity of the Heimat topos to transform (hi)stories of expulsion, emigration, and exile into picturesque narratives of German reconstruction.

6 Expellees, Emigrants, Exiles
Spectacles of Displacement

Today, films are the cultural calling cards of a people. . . . We of
all people, who have been so heavily discredited, should undertake
the serious attempt to use film in order to show the world who we
truly are.

WOLFGANG LIEBENEINER

POSTWAR NOMADOLOGIES

Wolfgang Liebeneiner's *Waldwinter* is a remake of the 1936 version
directed by Fritz Peter Buch. Both films are based on Paul Keller's *Heimatroman* by the same title from 1902. Buch's adaptation is a story of conva-
lescence in the mountains. In the opening sequences, we see the two main
characters leave their modern lives in high society for an escape to the solitude of the countryside. Just married to a "cold and heartless egotist" of a
husband, Marianne von Soden (Hansi Knotek) spontaneously decides to
abandon him on the train en route to their honeymoon. Elsewhere, a jour-
nalist by the name of Werner Peters (Viktor Staal) decides to quit his job in
the city in order to be alone ("What I want above all is peace and solitude")
and to write a novella entitled *Waldwinter*. The ensuing plot, situated in a
castle far removed from the pressures of marriage and work, brings together
the two seekers of solitude in a love story. Resistant to the idea of company
at first, Marianne and Peter gradually realize that they were destined for
each other. A chance encounter in the snow-covered forest, a picturesque ski
outing, and a last-minute rescue in a sublime Alpine storm anchor the
romance in the protagonists' shared appreciation of nature.

Liebeneiner's version treats the original very liberally. Some of the characters retain their names; like Buch, Liebeneiner extols the beauty of nature;
and the reluctant romance remains recognizable. Also, the novel by the
"Silesian Heimat poet Paul Keller" featured prominently in publicity for the
film. In all other respects, however, the script for the remake diverges fundamentally from both the novel and Buch's adaptation. Liebeneiner's film
betrays an interest not in repeating an old plot, let alone in some standard
of fidelity to either the literary source or the previous film. Rather,

135

Liebeneiner set out to "modernize" the plot, as one critic put it.[1] In the director's own words, *Waldwinter* now becomes the story of "the fate of refugees in our time" and of their need to find a new home in the Federal Republic: "After many trials and tribulations, [a] Silesian family regains its old Heimat in the Bavarian forest, its new Heimat."[2] Accordingly, the distributor urged theater owners to advertise *Waldwinter* to local groups of the more than two million Silesians living in the Federal Republic at the time, who ("so we have been assured by well-placed sources") were " 'starved' for a film like this one."[3] As in the case of *Grün ist die Heide* (1951), where screenwriter Bobby Lüthge added the "topical, modern motif" of expellees, the distance between the original and the remake of *Waldwinter* allows us to measure precisely the topicality of Liebeneiner's take.

The updated version of *Waldwinter* begins in 1945 in an idyllic, snow-covered Silesian landscape, replete with young deer and a wooden church. The opening images immediately evoke a sense of Heimat as a space of nature and religion. But the lyrics of a *Volkslied* that accompanies these images suggest that the film's first theme will be one of departure.[4] This theme moves from the sound track to the plot as some villagers leave the Silesian Christmas celebration in the small church. They are awaited by Martin, the grandson of the local baron and a soldier in the retreating Wehrmacht. He has already told a servant that the war "ended a long time ago; the question is merely, When will it be over?" Now he insists that his grandparents leave immediately to avoid getting caught in the approaching front. After a brief deliberation—including a young mother's hesitation to leave with her husband still at war and the baroness's foreboding lament "Who knows whether we will ever see Silesia again"—the baron decides to heed his grandson's advice and take refuge at Falkenstein, his hunting castle in Bavaria. Although some of those present complain about the uncomfortable *alter Kasten* (old shack) of an estate, none can dispute Martin's argument that "there"—in the West—"you'll at least be safe."

Once this decision has been made, one of the villagers comments didactically to a young boy that everyone must wander "from east to west, and from north to south," thus apparently universalizing the themes of displacement and migration that this film will negotiate. This redefinition of the particular as an instance of the universal is certainly no coincidence, given the remapping of the West German landscape through multiple forms of mobility and displacement during the 1950s. However, a contemporary audience would still have understood the historical specificity of universal "wandering." For all their brevity, the exchanges that take place at the beginning of *Waldwinter* would have resonated specifically with the plight of millions of expellees after the war. As such, they serve to establish an intended (but not exclusive) audience for the film in 1957. Just over a decade earlier, many of these expellees would have faced the same decision as the Silesian villagers in the film. Others were also liable to be familiar with images such as the one immediately following, where we watch the villagers depart in a long, shuffling line. Horse-drawn sleds and carts, men and women carrying heavy bundles on their backs and wearing as much of their clothing as possible, trudging over packed snow—these had been recurring images across the German landscape, in newsreels as well as in stories and memories that circulated after the war.[5] As Robert Moeller points out in his perceptive reading of Liebeneiner's film, the memory of expulsion that *Waldwinter* condenses in its opening minutes had become constitutive of postwar West German identity.[6] Indeed, the baroness's uncertainty about ever seeing Silesia again informed various political platforms. Although the opening sequence apparently obliterates the specificity of a forced displacement that Germans brought upon themselves,[7] viewers in the 1950s would have been sure to fill in the blanks. *Waldwinter* can treat the moment of departure so briefly precisely because it was still highly topical at the time of the film's release.

Beginning in the last months of World War II, Germany faced a wave of refugees from the east that profoundly altered the human geography of postwar Germany and of its rural areas in particular. In 1945, roughly six million expellees arrived in the western zones of occupation; with continuing migration—including relocations from East to West Germany—this figure would rise to almost eight million by 1950, and to nine million by the end of the decade.[8] Since housing shortages were particularly acute in the destroyed cities, most of these expellees were relocated to rural areas, where they made up as much as a third of the population and caused population increases by up to 62 percent.[9] While these transformations were particularly radical in the immediate postwar years, the resettlement lasted for a decade and was officially concluded only in 1956.

This is to say nothing of the continued social and political effects of this enormous migration and the challenge of integration that it entailed. The causes of the expulsion of Germans from the east dated back to the expansionist policies of the Germans themselves during the Third Reich and to the politics of the war: between 1939 and 1944, large numbers of Germans had been resettled to the provinces they were now forced to leave. The aftereffects lasted well into the 1950s. Among these was the renewed political charge of the term *Heimat*. Initially banned from organizing collectively, the refugees soon began to form associations, *Landsmannschaften* and *Landesverbände*. They founded a short-lived political party (the Gesamt-deutscher Block/Bund der Heimatvertriebenen und Entrechteten) and adopted a charter asserting the fundamental human "right to Heimat": "We have lost our Heimat. Displaced people [*Heimatlose*] are foreigners on this earth. God has placed human beings in their Heimat. To separate human beings from their Heimat by force is to kill their spirit. We have suffered and experienced this fate. Therefore, we feel called upon to demand that the right to Heimat be recognized and realized as a God-given human right."[10] As Moeller has shown, discourses on postwar expulsion and the integration of expellees into the newly constituted West German state have formed a *basso continuo* to political and historiographic debates throughout the history of the Federal Republic.[11] *Waldwinter* and other films of the era allow us to trace the implications of expulsion for the human geography of the 1950s.

For familiarity with the topic of expulsion was soon not just a matter of historical experience—it rapidly became a generic convention. If the *Heimatfilm* of the 1950s serves to negotiate the impact of mobilization and modernization in the provinces, as I suggested in the previous chapter, it was inevitable that the forced mobility of millions of refugees after the war would leave its trace on the films of the genre well into the first postwar decade. Beginning with *Grün ist die Heide*, populations of *Vertriebene* or individual refugees made regular appearances in the *Heimatfilm*. These appearances were not always staged as reflexively as in Paul May's *Heimat, Deine Lieder* (1959), which incorporates a choir of orphaned expellees singing the *Heimatlied* at a screening of *Schlesien wie es war* before an audience of expelled Silesians in a local inn.[12] Other films wrote the motif of expulsion into their protagonists' biographies, often to bring a remake "up to date," as in *Wenn am Sonntagabend die Dorfmusik spielt* (1953 [1933]), Wolfgang Staudte's version of *Rose Bernd* (1957 [1919]), or even in *Der Förster vom Silberwald*, where we learn that a local hunter—the incarnation of moral virtue, a cultured lover of nature played by Rudolf Prack—learned to play the organ on "our estate in my lost Heimat." In films like *Grün ist die Heide* or in Liebeneiner's version of *Waldwinter*, expellees figured centrally in the plot while also serving as a prominent motif of visual spectacle. But this spectacular function of the expellee could also be dissociated from the narrative altogether, serving instead to charge the films with a wistful tone of loss, as in *Wenn die Heide blüht*, where one sequence shows a group of *Vertriebene* singing a Heimat song and celebrating an old man's seventy-fifth wedding anniversary as evening falls. The only connection of this group of characters to the principal cast is that they live on the farm where the action takes place. Without contributing to that action, they clearly flavor it with a dual sense of nostalgia and topicality.

To indulge in nostalgia for a lost Heimat was only one of the functions of the *Vertriebene* in the *Heimatfilm*. In taking up the issue of refugee migrations, the genre would not only aim to defuse its potentially explosive social and political ramifications; in a remarkable turn, the *Heimatfilm* also managed, as in the case of *Waldwinter,* to fold a whole village of Silesian expellees into its ongoing project of modernizing the provinces. In view of such films, it is insufficient to argue simply that the concrete problems of integrating expellees into the Federal Republic "did not find their way into the world of the *Heimatfilm*."[13] Such an argument holds only at the most literal, reflectionist level. A more allegorical reading shows how the logic, if not the letter, of the refugee phenomenon (and of its economic dimension in particular) finds an imaginary solution in these films. Far from imagining refugee populations simply as an added burden on a suffering population, a film like *Waldwinter* imagines them as the vanguard of postwar modernization, clad, once again, in provincial dress.

The presence of expellees in the *Heimatfilm* was but one instance of this figure's prominence in public discourse throughout the 1950s. *Flüchtlinge*—and by extension the question of displacement and its consequences—figured centrally in contemporary sociology, where they performed a remarkably similar function as in the *Heimatfilm*. At congresses and in influential publications[14]—some of them of lasting impact on the discipline—scholars took the refugee as a figure for "the German of mid-century," treating the plight of expelled families as representative of larger social transformations that they were working to chart.[15] In the words of Elisabeth Pfeil, author of an early, autobiographically colored "psychological and sociological" account of the refugee as the "figure of an epochal transition" (*Gestalt einer Zeitenwende*), "We ask not only what the refugees went through, but also what they caused by entering the world of the settled [*die Welt der Seßhaften*]." The refugee thus becomes "the uprooted human being of our times" and a representative figure for an epoch of displacement, uprootedness, migration.[16]

In the discourses of the decade, the refugee stood for German victimization, as Moeller has amply demonstrated; interestingly, however, sociology also saw the refugee as a figure for new departures, explicitly ascribing to this figure some crucial modernizing impulses. As bearers of the modernization process, refugee families were seen as new social "prototypes"[17] of the postwar era. The experiences of refugee families, while historically specific, were symptomatic of a number of broader trends associated with the impact of modernity on postwar society. This may appear as a striking (even cynical) dehistoricization of that particular plight, but it had far-reaching consequences. Interpreting expulsion as a founding moment of the Federal Republic, even conservative studies of the refugee (family) treated the expellees as case studies for a broad set of irreversible transformations in the fabric of family, economic, and communal life. The sociology of the refugee analyzed the effects of forced mobility, concluding time and again that postwar society as a whole was undergoing a rapid and irreversible process of detraditionalization. Particularly for conservative scholars, to reach such a conclusion was hardly to condone it. But even Helmut Schelsky, a sociologist whose work would be influential in guiding restorative government policy under Adenauer, saw the changes brought about by the refugee phenomenon as radical and ineluctable. Such a diagnosis by a leading conservative scholar of the decade suggests something of the force of this trend. Schelsky's study of expellee families traces the deep transformation of social values and the reshaping of West Germany's social fabric after the war. For Schelsky, as for Pfeil before him, the refugee was the key figure of the era. The refugee family, Schelsky argued, "is not the exception, or opposite, to any constant family structure in German society, but appears to be instead the most advanced and pronounced form of a wholesale transformation in the contemporary German family."[18]

Wandlungen der deutschen Familie in der Gegenwart, which appeared in 1953, is a study of that transformation. Schelsky's findings in this influential project have direct bearing on the question of Heimat during the 1950s. Schelsky and his research team concluded that the influx of refugees had not only irreversibly altered social values, but also shaped the human geography of the new West German state. Writing in the immediate aftermath of the treks, Pfeil had argued that "with a movement of refugees that evacuates entire provinces, [the continued existence of] Heimat itself is drawn into question."[19] Schelsky took this diagnosis one step further by analyzing not only the loss of Heimat to the east and the impact of that loss on the refugee population, but the redefinition of Heimat in the contemporary west. In doing so, he drew into question the very categories of settled existence and tradition that ostensibly constituted the semantic center of Heimat. The distinction between the settled, autochthonous German and the mobile, displaced refugee, Schelsky argued, had replaced class distinctions as the key social category. Likewise, given the defining role of displacement in the refugee family, Schelsky advocated a new focus on the dynamics of geographical, social, and economic movement, and discarded received notions of dwelling and tradition. Accordingly, his analysis followed Pfeil's in diagnosing a profound realignment of the values that anchored social life after the war, among them the values of Heimat and *Fremde*. In spite of its broad popular currency, Schelsky dismissed this opposition as a "dualism of the nineteenth century" which was losing its meaning. Instead, he claimed, careful analysis of the refugee family showed that "the laws of social mobility have long since taken hold of our society."[20] These laws had taken concrete form in the plight of refugee families. For Schelsky, the latter thus emblematized a set of characteristically modern experiences that he defined as "the processes of spatial, social, and intellectual uprooting (*Entwurzelung*) and ensuing increases in mobility."[21] The particular forms of displacement experienced by the families he studied led, in turn, to a redefinition of traditional familial structures, values, and modes of behavior. The massive postwar influx of refugees, in other words, heralded the modernization of family structures across the social spectrum. The postwar family, as exemplified by the *Flüchtlingsfamilie*, exhibited a new sense of social fragmentation (evident in the social isolation of refugee families that had been uprooted from their traditional social networks); a heightened emphasis on social mobility coupled with a new form of "materialism;" an increasing prominence of work in the social life of the family, leading to a "loss" of family values (Schelsky termed this the "de-internalization" [*Entinnerlichung*] of the family); a social leveling of previously hierarchical family structures, based on the overriding need for solidarity among family members, which was perceived as welding together previously differentiated family positions; a leveling off of social differences in what Schelsky famously called the "nivellierte Mittelstandsgesellschaft," where differences based on class and refugee status could be conveniently elided;[22] a "displacement of intra-familial authority towards the woman," as well as an increased role for the woman in the public sphere;[23] and the "objectification" (*Versachlichung*) of traditional values and questions pertaining to choice of marital partner, marital life, parenting, contraception, and so on in reshaping the social fabric of the new West German nation.

For Schelsky, to describe the refugee family as "prototypical" meant to abandon the notion that refugees would gradually adapt to the old familial behaviors and structures of settled peasant or bourgeois families. Indeed, Schelsky held the opposite to be true. With his analysis of the refugee family, Schelsky advocated a sociological paradigm shift in which the traditional hierarchy of settled versus mobile existence would have to be reversed: the figure of the refugee revealed displacement to be the norm, dwelling and stability the exception. Citing the work of René König, another eminent sociologist of the decade, Schelsky argued that "once migrations have exceeded a certain measure, it is no longer the nomad who adapts to his environment, but the environment that adapts to the nomad."[24] Schelsky intended such formulations to describe the modernization of social structures in the wake of World War II. In their emphasis on the constitutive function of displacement and migration, however, Schelsky's observations read like a case study for some far more recent "nomadologies."[25] In particular, by deconstructing nineteenth-century dualisms between dwelling and migration, and oppositions between the traditions of the host country and the impact of arriving refugees, Schelsky anticipated the postmodern revision of spatial paradigms that would view ostensibly foundational categories such as home, Heimat, and the local as derivative of a constitutive nomadism. In these accounts, like in Schelsky's, "Human location [is] constituted by displacement as much as by stasis." Travel, not home, emerges as the ground on which we must locate different, and often provisional, notions of dwelling. As James Clifford puts it, "Once traveling is foregrounded as a cultural practice, then dwelling, too, needs to be reconceived."[26] Both Schelsky's sociology of the refugee and more recent attempts to understand the constitutive role of travel and mobility in modern societies suggest the need to avoid treating home, dwelling, or Heimat as a (territorial) ground, an original or authentic starting place. Instead, we should pay close attention to the function of Heimat as a rhetorical effect, "an artificial, constrained practice of fixation."[27]

As I have argued, German society and culture of the 1950s were subject to forms of displacement and increased mobility that shifted spatial practices and the conventions of locating identities. The *Heimatfilm* is a cultural symptom of these shifts, indicating a profound unsettling of convention and stability. In the context of the 1950s, the genre became a key cultural site for negotiating the meanings of mobility and their implications for contemporary notions of home; in other words, it took on the role of orchestrating the reconceptualization of dwelling for a mass audience. *Waldwinter* took up precisely this project, both highlighting the constitutive function of displacement and eliding it in a hidden cut from Silesia to Bavaria. Barely discernible on the visual level, the transition from the original to the second Heimat becomes the precondition for the Heimat film's dream of modernization without homelessness.

STANDORT HEIMAT:
RELOCATING THE *WIRTSCHAFTSWUNDER*

In 1938, as a result of the Munich accords, which allowed Hitler to annex parts of Czechoslovakia, the Bohemian town of Gablonz (today Jablonec in the Czech Republic) was incorporated into the German Reich. As part of the annexed area, Gablonz was subject to Nazi population policies, which drove Czech nationals out of the Sudetenland and replaced them with ethnic Germans. This administered displacement of an entire population was reversed after 1945, when the Czech government issued the Benes decrees that forced the remaining German population to leave Gablonz. Some 18,000 of these expellees eventually made their way to the Bavarian city of Kaufbeuren and settled on its outskirts. This unique resettling process—in which an entire community was displaced, virtually intact, from its origin to a new destination—was accompanied by a far-reaching business plan, promoted by a particularly enterprising refugee named Erich Huschka. Against the initial resistance of both the local population and the American occupation forces, he managed to secure a lease for a former explosives factory that had been largely demolished by the Americans in November of 1945. Bringing the dominant trade of Gablonz to Bavaria, the refugees founded a glass-blowing and jewelry industry in their new hometown, making a significant contribution to the economic recovery of Kaufbeuren. By 1947, the settlement boasted 92 registered businesses employing a total workforce of 811. In recognition of the geographical and economic transformation it had undergone, on August 8, 1952, the city of Kaufbeuren renamed the area in which the Gablonzer population had settled Kaufbeuren–Neu-Gablonz.[28]

Around the time of its incorporation, Neu-Gablonz published an advertising flyer entitled "Which is the shortest route to New-Gablonz?" (see figure 8). The flyer takes the form of a map, the graphic design of which is overburdened and somewhat confusing—in part because the flyer tries to accomplish too much at once. Its design conflates multiple political, economic, and cultural messages in a single image. In its effort to help potential visitors locate the small town of Neu-Gablonz, the map is dominated by two large arrows. One arrow points out "Rhein-Main Air-Port," Germany's largest port of airbound entry, located in the American zone of occupation.[29] Accessible by land, by sea, but especially by air, Germany is represented as a relay in the circuits of (Western) economic exchange. The second arrow, pointing from the original Gablonz in a black area to the northeast to Neu-Gablonz, is more difficult to read without some knowledge of the town's displaced history. If the arrow pointing to Frankfurt connects to an eco-

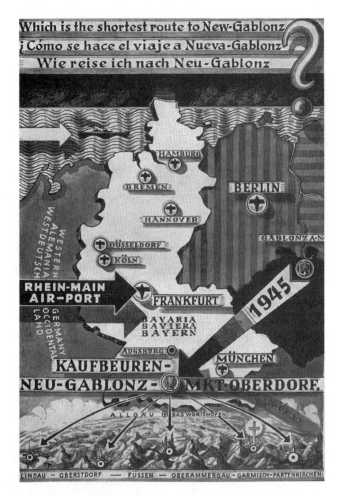

Figure 8. Mapping Heimat as economic *Standort* and tourist attraction: advertisement for Neu-Gablonz, ca. 1952. Courtesy Archiv Neugablonzer Industrie- und Schmuckmuseum.

nomic network, then the arrow pointing to Neu-Gablonz represents a historical migration, as the "1945" label on it would suggest.

Centered at the bottom of the map, Kaufbeuren-Neugablonz appears as a historical destination for the expelled population of Gablonz, but even more prominently as an economic destination for foreign trade from the west. The example of Neugablonz illustrates how the occasionally reactionary politics and values associated with *Vertriebene* as a social group competed with their crucial role in the process of economic reconstruction.

Without in any way discounting the substantial and lasting political impact of eight million new citizens or the many intractable social, political, and cultural problems this raised, the integration of expellees during the 1950s also needs to be considered as a driving factor in Germany's postwar recovery, for these new populations supplied much of the labor force for the economic miracle. Entire so-called *Flüchtlingsindustrien* contributed to the transformation of agrarian states like Bavaria into industrial *Standorte*. The massive population increase represented by the refugees both accelerated and intensified the process of industrialization.[30] As the sociological "prototypes" of postwar displacement, expellees illustrate the degree to which even forced mobility sustained a broader project of modernization.

But the map adds at least one further dimension to this project by situating Neu-Gablonz as a tourist destination, itself a point of departure for day trips to the various sites in the lower Alps listed at the bottom of the image. Here, the graphic register shifts from a geographical map to a topographical panorama. While the design appears even more disjointed as a result, the added message is decipherable nonetheless: as a historically charged economic *Standort*, Neu-Gablonz is worth a trip not only for the goods it has to offer thanks to the hard work of its refugee population, but also for its geographic location. In answering the question "Which is the shortest route to Neu-Gablonz?" the map makes a threefold argument as to why anyone should undertake this journey in the first place: a unique *Standort* in the new Germany, Neu-Gablonz promises a blend of economic modernity, artisan tradition, and Alpine nature.

Liebeneiner's version of *Waldwinter* provides a cinematic fiction with striking parallels to the historical case of Neu-Gablonz. As if to illustrate the postwar (economic) history of Kaufbeuren and the sociology of the refugees who peopled it, *Waldwinter* casts the Silesian refugees as agents of economic progress in the traditional territory of Heimat. Advertising copy for the film might have read, "How do I travel to Falkenstein?" as Liebeneiner's film takes up the threefold project encoded in the Neu-Gablonz flyer: populated by a Silesian community that has relocated intact to the Bavarian mountains, Falkenstein is founded on a historical displacement. Over the course of the film it becomes an economic hotbed: initially threatened by bankruptcy, it emerges as a paradigm of productivity. Extolling tradition and stability in a rural setting, *Waldwinter* works to negotiate the transformation of postwar German society as a result of increased social and economic mobility; as a result, the baron's *alter Kasten* in Bavaria is transformed from a picturesque refugee camp into a cottage industry whose location and product—artisanal Bohemian glass—beckons the film's audience as potential tourists in the *Reisewelle* of the late 1950s.

For all their topical reference to the contemporary plight of refugees, the opening images of *Waldwinter* also set up a subtle but distinct note of pastness, particularly in the structure of the Silesian *Gemeinschaft* that organizes for its westward trek. The resolutely patriarchal organization surrounding the baron and the emphasis on the baron's landed estate suggest that this is still a decidedly premodern form of social organization. Indeed, the way in which the baron generously offers his horses for the trek to his hunting castle, where he will provide free lodging (though presumably in exchange for labor), suggests a feudal mode of production centered on landownership in Silesia and Bavaria. In this regard, it is more than a matter of narrative economy that the baron himself should make the decision to leave Silesia on behalf of what appear to be his subjects—"meine Leute," as he puts it at one point[31]—without regard to the reservations they articulate.

This patriarchal construction of *Gemeinschaft* in Silesia will become the bedrock of a double transformation to be chronicled by the film's story of displacement and modernization. Given that this is a *Heimatfilm*, one is struck by the remarkable ease of the transition from Silesia to Bavaria. Not only is the arduous trek omitted from the narrative once it has been hinted at iconographically, but the cinematic signifier for the central theme of displacement is also buried in the editing of the film. After panning along with the trekkers, the camera tilts down into the snow, only to reverse that motion after a barely perceptible cut. The succeeding shot tilts back up to reveal another snow-covered landscape, all but indistinguishable from the space introduced in the earlier parts of the exposition. A small group of people approaches, the direction of their movement matching that of the long, shuffling line of refugees we just saw, as if to underline the continuity of the cut. A man nails a sign reading "Falkenstein" to a post as a young girl looks on.

For the uninitiated viewer, it is by no means apparent that the cut from one close-up of a snow-covered embankment to the next signifies a move westward in space and forward in time. Until the dialog finally explains that the years in Silesia are long gone, we are unlikely to take the profilmic space as Bavarian, rather than Silesian (or Polish, to be precise). This lag in viewer comprehension serves to attenuate the transition from one Heimat to the next. It also generates a sense of spatial confusion by representing the new Heimat as a replica of the old. Such devices are central to the continuity system, where they ensure narrative and visual economy. However, in the context of a place-centered genre like the *Heimatfilm*, the elision of migration and the visual identification of two different profilmic spaces in a hidden cut or a dissolve take on particular significance. For on a purely visual, often spectacular register, such a transition tends to suggest an irritating equivalence, whereas traditional territorial discourses on Heimat would emphasize its uniqueness as place of origin. Thus, when Luis Trenker superimposes the Alps on the Manhattan skyline in *Der verlorene Sohn,* we are invited to contemplate the possibility that the hero Tonio may be equally at home in New York and in his native mountains; although the film works hard to disprove this assumption, the spectacular assimilation of mountains and modernity remains perhaps the most memorable visual spectacle in a rather spectacular film.[32] Similar unmarked cuts occur in *Heimweh nach Dir; mein grünes Tal* (1960), in which the Alps are matched with the Canadian Rockies; and *Einmal noch die Heimat sehn* (1958), which takes us from the Alps to Africa. In the last we find the hero (Rudolf Lenz) living in an ersatz Heimat that initially looks strikingly similar to his old environment. Again, though the visual and generic register subsequently shifts from Heimat to nature special to ethnographic film, and although we learn that Lenz perceives this (colonial) Heimat as exile, the visual argument implies an unsettling equivalence between home and away, between Heimat and *Fremde.*

Not all Heimat films that employ such cuts treat the implied equivalence of Heimat and *Fremde* as deliberately as *Der verlorene Sohn* or *Die Trapp-Familie in Amerika,* also directed by Liebeneiner, in which the mountains around Salzburg return as the Green Mountains of Vermont. But the implied equivalence is always programmatic, even where it is fleeting, a visual suggestion to be denied by the narrative. The visual attenuation of the transition from Heimat to its other in *Waldwinter* allows Liebeneiner to explore his themes of displacement and modernization without forsaking the commitment to either the old or the new. Like so many films of the era, *Waldwinter* is an exercise in compromise formations that serve to mitigate the impact of modernization without resisting its course.

As the iconographic double of Silesia,[33] the Bavarian landscape becomes a visual metaphor for both the Heimat lost and the nation regained. In keeping with Schelsky's view of the refugee as a new national "prototype," *Waldwinter* stages the baron's Bavarian estate not only as ersatz for Silesia, but also as a local metaphor for the West German nation under reconstruction.[34] Having established the similarity of old and new Heimat, the narrative turns to the central question of how to inhabit that space—that is, of how to reestablish Heimat as a refugee community in West Germany during the 1950s. As we shall see, Liebeneiner's film imagines Falkenstein as a small-scale economic laboratory in which to test various scenarios for a post–Marshall Plan Germany. In keeping with the productivist impulses of the *Wirtschaftswunder*, the film leaves little doubt that the feeling of Heimat is quintessentially a question of economics.

When we first encounter the villagers in Falkenstein, they are in a festive mood, eagerly anticipating the arrival of "the new machine"—a power generator for the glassworks they plan to operate in Falkenstein. But instead, the baron receives a letter from the bank informing him that it has withdrawn its start-up loan for his glassworks. Although the baron is convinced that "his" Silesian craftsmanship could find markets the world over, the economy of Falkenstein threatens to grind to a halt. Without credit from the bank, the baron would not even be able to pay "his" Silesians their wages. Having established this economic impasse, the film explores three competing scenarios for regenerating the local economy. These correspond to different approaches to the reconstruction of West Germany after the war and rubble years. Given the successes of the *Wirtschaftswunder* by the time of the film's making, the ultimate solution to the narrative/national predicament is fairly predictable. In terms of the ideological labor performed by this film, however, it is striking that Liebeneiner's remake deems it necessary to raise and then dismiss alternatives to the productivist ethos of the *Wirtschaftswunder*. More importantly, to the extent that *Falkenstein* serves as a laboratory for postwar recovery, its construction as Heimat has a direct bearing on the outcome of this economic experiment. For it turns out that Heimat can serve to humanize, if not en-gender, the face of progress.

The first suggestion for relieving the baron's debt consists of cutting down more of the valuable forest around Falkenstein. This plan meets with vehement opposition from *Oberförster* Gersternberg. While the sale of lumber apparently helped to rebuild Falkenstein in the years immediately following the war, Gerstenberg insists that he would have prevented even that had he not been in captivity at the time.[35] Gerstenberg, in other words, places the forest's use value higher than its exchange value as lumber. As in countless other Heimat films, the forest features prominently in the visual texture of *Waldwinter*, which takes characters for extended walks in the woods (including a guided tour conducted by Gerstenberg for the baron's grandson Martin). Referred to as the "ur-forest" (*Urwald*) for the age of its magnificent trees, this natural resource is an important part of Falkenstein's patrimony, as well as a trademark of the area of Bavaria where the castle is located. Its depletion would irreversibly damage the very image of the region and hence its attractiveness to potential tourists. In the immediate context of the baron's predicament, however, the sale of lumber seems economically unsound because it would merely stabilize the status quo, enabling the baron to pay his employees but not to make further investments. As we shall see, such a solution is incompatible with the expansionist logics of the *Wirtschaftswunder* and of the film's unfolding plot.

The second suggestion is to turn the castle into a tourist accommodation, a *Schloßhotel*. This plan, pursued with special vigor by the estate manager Stengel, provides for the central intrigue of the film. At first glance, Stengel's suggestion seems to make sense given the economic necessities at hand, as well as the secure future it would afford the baron and his family: a broker has presented an unnamed buyer who would offer to take over all debt and pay an additional amount in cash. This sale, which is almost agreed to by the baron, meets with bitter resistance from Marianne, the baron's adoptive (grand)daughter. In the end, it is averted through the investigations of Martin, who discovers that the would-be buyer is Stengel himself. Prodded by his wife, who dreams of a more fashionable life, Stengel has embezzled the baron's funds with the intention of establishing himself as the owner of Schloßhotel Falkenstein. Before this devious plan is revealed, however, *Waldwinter* has spent a good deal of narrative time exploring the option of transforming the estate into a tourist attraction—a solution clearly favored by other films of the time. Here, however, the transformation of Falkenstein—and by extension of West Germany—into a service economy centered on the tourist exploitation of Heimat is not yet on the agenda. Stengel is apprehended by the police and the hotel alternative is branded as criminal.

The plan that carries the day, after all benefits and drawbacks have been weighed, amounts to an industrialization of the local. With Stengel's arrest, the baron recovers the embezzled funds and is finally able to purchase the generator that will power the new Falkenstein glassworks. This resolution is fairly contrived, arriving almost ex machina at the end of the film; unlike the previous two options, the decision to wait for the necessary funds to materialize is more a matter of faith than of rational deliberation. If the viewer nonetheless perceives that decision as logical and narratively motivated, this has to do with the characters who defend it as well as with the lessons learned by Martin, whose business sense initially tells him to reject it.

Early in the film we are told that it was Marianne who hatched the plan to build the glassworks. Marianne has remained faithfully at her grandparents' side throughout the decade following their flight from Silesia; in Falkenstein, she tends to the household and works towards transforming the estate from a feudal hunting castle into a site for the production of consumer goods. More than any other figure in the film, Marianne combines two qualities that will ensure the survival of Falkenstein and, by extension, of Heimat. Mindful of her own Silesian traditions and dedicated to the preservation of nature (we see her feeding deer in the woods), she "puts a human face on modernization."[36] Like Petra in *Die Landärztin*, Liebeneiner's Marianne embodies the mythical construction of femininity in the *Heimatfilm*. She is "a driving force of modernization, she recognizes and accepts the signs of the times much faster than the men"; simultaneously, however, she is semiotically aligned with nature and with tradition. Incarnating the Heimat film's feminine ideal, Marianne facilitates both economic modernization and ideological restoration.[37]

The "human face" of modernization is precisely the face of Heimat. This becomes evident in the encounters between Marianne and Martin, whose business acumen needs to be "heimatified" by Marianne before he can set things right. A decade after his retreat from the eastern front as a Wehrmacht soldier, we find Martin entering his fiancée's fashionable hat boutique in Paris. He is wearing a smart business suit and has evidently managed to rise from POW to well-traveled business executive. A prodigal son of sorts, Martin is the latter-day incarnation of Schelsky's refugee: his materialist pursuits have led him to forsake his family (fragmentation); he is conspicuously mobile and associated with a "new" woman who has an independent social and business life. Martin has arrived in Schelsky's "leveled-off middleclass society," which his displacement helped to create. But then again, the film noticeably displaces that social transformation from Germany to France, marking its consequences as "foreign" and in need of reintegration. The completion of Martin's Bildungsroman, then, requires the prodigal son to return home and place his business acumen in the service of Heimat.

When Martin is called to come help his grandfather, he arrives from Paris in a car that seems as misplaced in Falkenstein as does his business attire. The baron briefs him on his predicament, but Martin's business sense tells him that the hotel offer is both the most lucrative and the most rational. In complete misrecognition of the situation in the new Heimat, he advises his grandparents to take the money, buy "a nice three-and-a-half bedroom apartment somewhere in Munich and go to the occasional movie or opera." For the baron, this suggestion is unacceptable not only because it seems unlikely that he and his wife would survive for very long in the enclosed space of a petit bourgeois urban home, but also because such a plan disregards the needs of the larger community in Falkenstein. But Martin, the unsentimental businessman, ridicules his grandfather's appeal to the value of responsibility: "Every responsibility ends somewhere," he asserts—implying that this is precisely where a healthy business sense begins. Confronted with the baron's concrete responsibility for "his"

Silesians, Martin coldly reminds him of the mobility of labor under capitalism: as skilled workers, they will easily find jobs elsewhere.

Martin's grandfather is scandalized: "The times may have changed, but morality? For my part, I can observe no change." This view, which the film ultimately endorses by ascribing the baron's values also to Marianne, and later to Martin as well, neatly articulates the film's politics in the context of the *Heimatfilm* as a genre that offers imaginary compromises between radical change and radical conservatism. In adjusting to the changing times of the *Wirtschaftswunder*, Heimat becomes a mobile signifier that can be transported from Silesia to Bavaria, from a feudal past to a Fordist present, from *Gemeinschaft* to *Gesellschaft*. At the same time, the ideological value of Heimat, its morality, remains intact and serves to mask the very transition that it facilitates. It tempers aspects of modernization (such as displacement and increased mobility, increases in production and the threat of alienation, or social fragmentation) with the promise of stability, tradition, and nature. *Waldwinter*'s ideological work consists of letting its viewers have the cake of tradition and eat it too—a goal that still resonates with the Heimat idea from the nineteenth century, when the Heimat movement "attempted to reconcile tenderness with worldliness, looking backward to the past with looking forward to an age of progress."[38] The same strategy resurfaces in the distributor's publicity materials for the film: providing graphics, headlines, and billboard designs, the company asked theater owners to advertise *Waldwinter* not only as "an experience of true love for the Heimat and for nature," but also as "a great, gripping film about the power of our hearts to preserve the old and give shape to the new."[39]

When Marianne casts doubt on the soundness of Martin's judgment, she questions not his calculations, but his values and lack of feeling. As a woman who "sees everything through the lens of sentiment," Marianne accuses Martin of lacking such a view. His business advice "has nothing to do with feeling," she comments angrily, "let alone with such outdated concepts as Heimat, obligation, and responsibility." In a word, this traveling businessman from Paris is *heimatlos:* he "doesn't even know what that is: Heimat, being at home," explains his grandmother. And Marianne caustically remarks that he "has never managed to stay in one place for more than a few days. Why should he make an exception now?" The film will ultimately endorse Marianne's view that the lack of Heimat makes for poor economics. Consequently, Martin has to find reasons to "make an exception" and remain in Falkenstein in order to acquire the values of Heimat. Only then will he be able to make the "right" decision.

Having set up the sparring couple of Keller's novel, the film's unfolding romantic plot closely parallels Martin's education in the values of Heimat. Two further types of experience contribute to that education. First, his walks in the local woods convince Martin (and the viewer) of the need to preserve Falkenstein's natural beauty. Second, as Martin repeatedly looks in on the local families who have brought their skills from one Heimat to the next, he gradually appreciates the value of Silesian craftsmanship and heritage. We see children gathered around the kitchen table producing nutcrackers and three generations of glassblowers preserving the tradition of the so-called *Tränenglas* (delicate glasses that symbolically contain the tears of Hedwig, the Silesian patron saint, who "weeps for all those who have lost their homes"). As he looks on with Marianne, Martin realizes that in their combination of tradition and highly qualified artisanal labor, these cottage industries are poised to take the souvenir market by storm. When the director of a glassworks in a nearby town tells him that his factory is running three shifts and is still unable to meet demand, Martin can finally reconcile business sense with Heimat sense. As Moeller suggests, Martin "slowly comes to understand that in the Heimat, more than the bottom line is at stake."[40]

Indeed, in this film's political economy, learning the lessons of Heimat is the *only* way to ensure the survival of Falkenstein. Heimat *is* the bottom line in the new economic order, its basic exchange value. Untempered by Marianne's "feeling" and by his own insight into the hardly outmoded values of "Heimat, obligation, and responsibility," Martin's imported ways of doing business would have spelled the end of Falkenstein. His views need to be localized for production to begin: "Once restored to the Heimat, he, too, grasps how to wed tradition and modernity."[41] In this sense, the recovery of the baron's funds is no longer a trick ex machina, but the logical outcome of the film's ideological agenda, which advocates a compromise between *Wirtschaftswunder* and Heimat, or the "paradox of the industrialized provinces."[42]

This compromise between the old and the new, between Heimat lost and Heimat regained, between distant and local space is brought home once more in the closing sequences of the film, as the generator is finally transported through the village to the sounds of the local marching band. In the midst of this procession, which is entirely typical of the genre (save for the overtones of a "Soviet rural festival of the 1930s extolling the five-year plan and the electrification of the countryside"),[43] Marianne receives a package from Paris which contains a fashionable hat. Simone, Martin's former lover, has retreated from "this awful forest" to the cold urban modernity of her boutique, but she has left her mark on the Heimat that cast her out. As Moeller puts it, "Tradition did not mean it was necessary to reject generators, world markets, or Parisian fashion."[44] Nor does tradition mean that it is necessary to reclaim lost territory, as the Bund der Vertriebenen was still advocating at the time. Heimat, Liebeneiner reminds us, may be a spatial concept but it is inherently mobile. His film reproduces Schelsky's nomadism and then works to attenuate its impact. Far more than simply fueling nostalgia for lost territories, *Waldwinter* imagines the successful relocation of Heimat in a geographically distant but visually similar place. As in *Grün ist die Heide,* the look and feel of the old Heimat can be matched, home can be transported across generations and across space as easily as across a hidden cut in the film.

The same logic characterizes a pair of Liebeneiner films that take the question of Heimat across the Atlantic to find images of Austria in the Green Mountains of Vermont. Although the underlying (hi)story here is putatively one of exile from Fascism, as opposed to post-Fascist expulsion, the two films once again demonstrate the flexibility of the Heimat topos, the constitutive link between Heimat and displacement, and the role of Heimat in German reconstruction during the "miracle years."

EXILE AS HEIMAT: *DIE TRAPP-FAMILIE IN AMERIKA*

Before *The Sound of Music* (1964), there was *Die Trapp-Familie.* Directed by Wolfgang Liebeneiner, the film topped the German box office in 1957 and has been described as the "climax of the *Heimatfilm-Welle.*"[45] The film's promotional tagline promised that it would trace the family's rise "vom Kloster zum Welterfolg" (from the convent to world success), but *Die Trapp-Familie* only followed the now-famous story up to the point at which the von Trapps reach America. At its climax, a Schubert song, beautifully rendered on Ellis Island, gains the "happy and peaceable family" access to the United States. Even though such access may have been a coveted achievement, this was hardly the promised *Welterfolg* with which the German audience at the time was well acquainted, thanks to extensive coverage of the von Trapps' American success story in the popular press. To chronicle the family's rise to fame (and to capitalize on the film's success in Germany) would require a sequel. Liebeneiner and the star ensemble of the original film obliged, and the 1958 season saw the release of *Die Trapp-Familie in Amerika.*

Besides the continuous narrative line that begins in Austria in *Die Trapp-Familie* and ends in Vermont in *Die Trapp-Familie in Amerika,* the two films also share the same generic appeal. Despite the shift to America and metropolitan New York, the entire family saga works with the conventions of the *Heimatfilm*. Drawing on Liebeneiner's reputation as a director in the genre, the films were distributed by the Gloria company, renowned for its dedication to the cause of Heimat. In addition, all the genre's elements are there:[46] the aristocrat and the priest, children and choirs, a mother running a hotel in Salzburg. Both films treat the ostensible opposition of country and city in ways characteristic of the Heimat genre; they feature the requisite *Trachten*, paraded prominently even on the streets of Manhattan; and both films share the generic use of *Volkslieder* and other vocal music in quasi-musical fashion.[47] *Die Trapp-Familie* is located in the picturesque Alpine landscape of the Salzkammergut, home to over three dozen other *Heimatfilms* of the era.[48] Finally, the dialog repeatedly indexes the relevance of Heimat concerns, as when Maria complains to her husband that their children are "living in a bus"; making explicit the link between *Haus* and Heimat, she explains that "we need nothing as urgently as a house. One cannot be at home in a bus, and every human being needs to be at home somewhere. Whoever has lost his Heimat must see where he can find a new one."

As *Heimatfilme*, both of these films explore a common theme of home. But along the way, they explore related experiences of displacement, settling down, and success in America. In this sense, one might argue that Liebeneiner stages the von Trapps' desire to find their Heimat in America in the double sense of the German word *ankommen*. On the one hand, the films are about the Trapp family's need to *arrive* somewhere, to find a home after having been driven into exile by the annexation of Austria to the Third Reich in 1938. On the other hand, in chronicling the von Trapps' rise to *Welterfolg*, these films are about their desire to *achieve success* with their song, to find their audience. Under conditions of exile, both of these narratives of *ankommen* are nationally overdetermined, for the family remains identifiably Austrian *and* German in ways to be seen, and the popcorn-munching audience is depicted as hyper-American.[49]

Given the rich material for narrating nationality that is contained in the basic story of the von Trapps, it seems rather surprising that *The Sound of Music* should have stopped short of bringing the family to America.[50] Their arrival, after all, as well as the events that followed (including their eventual representation in Liebeneiner's films), were precisely what made the Trapp family famous and their story so full of "human interest," as one German reviewer put it.[51] Unlike Robert Wise, Liebeneiner capitalizes on the international dimensions of the Trapp saga in both of his films. In *Die Trapp-*

Familie, we see the family arrive in America during the final sequence. The second film builds on this climax by foregrounding the von Trapps' search for a new home: under what conditions, the film seems to ask, can America become Heimat for an Austrian family in exile?

Liebeneiner's Trapp films literally go a long way towards redefining the space of Heimat by taking the issue across the Atlantic. Although the two films may seem exceptional in this respect (few other films of the era actually venture into America, though it is regularly referenced in the film culture of the 1950s), I maintain that this only crystallizes the broader spatial logics of the *Heimatfilm*. Moreover, the emphasis on mobility and displacement that drives the narrative of this and other films clearly served a particular set of ideological purposes during the era of German reconstruction. What looks at first glance like a film about America turns out to be another text deeply concerned with the displacement of refugees; likewise, the chronicle of an Austrian family's triumph in America can barely contain the traces of an inverse discourse on the ongoing occupation of Austria and West Germany by the Allies, including questions of social and cultural Americanization. Liebeneiner's films are therefore symptomatic, rather than exceptional, texts which by virtue of their strategies of displacement, condensation, and repression yield significant insights into the function of the *Heimatfilm* as a genre.

My reading of Liebeneiner's two films picks up the German narration where *The Sound of Music* leaves off, to show how Liebeneiner makes over a biography of displacement and exile into a story of Heimat regained. Since I will be leaving the familiar narrative ground of *The Sound of Music,* let me supply a brief sketch of the von Trapps' story as it unfolds under the Statue of Liberty after the flight from Austria. Once they have gained access to the United States, the von Trapps begin touring the country with their familial renditions of Bach and Palestrina. Although they get off to a fairly successful start at the end of the first film, the second opens with redundant representations of failure: small audiences, false optimism, a canceled contract, lack of money, poor living conditions, and so forth. The family eventually auditions for a different agent but is turned down. Even after Maria (Ruth Leuwerik) manages to change the agent's mind thanks to some innovative research on what she calls "sex appeal for concerts," the *Welterfolg* still refuses to materialize. To be sure, the new management's professional publicity has filled the concert halls; but when it comes time to applaud, only a handful of nuns express their enthusiasm for the children's angelic song. The capacity crowds ostentatiously continue to chew on their popcorn. Finally, a nostalgic stop in the pastoral idyll of the Vermont countryside throws the family off schedule. They arrive late for that evening's concert and are forced to improvise, only to discover that less means more: on the spur of the moment, Maria changes the program, substituting German *Volkslieder* and American folk songs for the sacral music favored by Father Wasner, the accompanying priest. A montage sequence convinces us of the lasting effect of this shift, and after Maria's monologue on the need for Heimat, the *Welterfolg* is crowned with the acquisition of an old barn in Vermont. Once Maria has faced down the threat of her family's expulsion from their newfound Heimat, the film concludes with an impromptu performance by the Singing Trapp Family in the INS building in New York.[52] At the close of the heartrending delivery of the Schubert song "Kein schöner Land in dieser Zeit," all that is left is for Ruth Leuwerik to turn to face the camera and take leave of the spectator with a personal "Auf Wiedersehen."

The final song is quite economical in its repetition of the film's terms: not only do we see the von Trapps in full Austrian garb, doing what they do best as they get into familiar choir formation and take their respective notes from Father Wasner; in addition, as the sound track continues to carry the harmony of the *Volkslied*, the film provides two contemplative inserts of the locales that constitute America in the story, thus constructing a tight syntagmatic chain of cinematic space in order to bring about the film's closure. From the singing family and its audience in—of all places—the Bureau of Immigration and Naturalization, Liebeneiner's film takes us to a high-angle shot of Manhattan which dissolves into an image of the rolling hills of Vermont.[53] From there, another dissolve brings us back to the scene of the song, where well-dressed clerks emerge from the (not so) busy government offices to form a circle around the choir in the hallway. Of course, this again cements the narrative teleology which has just led us to the promised *Welterfolg:* whereas in the opening scenes of the film, the family could hardly fill a single row in the concert houses in which it appeared, the von Trapps' song is now vested with a communicative power that spontaneously recruits its audience even in the most unlikely venues. As the family's toddler looks on from his red-and-white pram, framed against a background of parasols in red, white, and blue, the success story ends with the embrace of the Austrian family by an America that is multiply coded as a public sphere and its law (the INS), as the country of the American dream[54] and as a seemingly spontaneous form of *Gemeinschaft* welded together by the performance of the *Volkslied*. To her own "surprise," Maria is suddenly able to refer to this newfound (or better: regained) sense of community and to the Green Mountains of Vermont as "zu Hause," thereby articulating the complex and astonishing ideological work that the narrative has performed: through a set of narrative transformations that remain to be traced, America has apparently been made over into that quintessentially German parochial structure of feeling called Heimat.

This tour de force leaves its marks on the narrative. When the camera zooms in for the final close-up of the film's star, aided by an aural "close-up" on the sound track, the sense of closure is suddenly undermined by Ruth Leuwerik's "Auf Wiedersehen." Addressed directly to the camera, this farewell ruptures the diegesis and begs a question: From whom is she taking her leave? On the one hand, this device is motivated intertextually, repeating and varying Leuwerik's "Gute Nacht" at the end of *Die Trapp-Familie.* Moreover, the zoom and the final close-up emphasize Leuwerik's role as the romantic lead of the films, which were explicitly conceived as star vehicles for her. The direct address is also generically motivated if we read the film as the proto-musical that it is, where the gaze at the camera is "allowed" by the conventions of the genre. But given the fact that this is one of only two moments in the entire film where this particular device is employed,[55] the final words appear far more as a break with convention, foregrounding their unique mode of address which exists *outside* of the preceding story. By addressing the spectator directly (even if only to take leave of her or him), the film's "closure" opens up the question of reception, asking us to reconstruct the discursive or pragmatic space in which the seemingly intimate exchange between Leuwerik and her spectator takes place.

"WIE ZU HAUSE": HEIMAT AND ITS DOUBLE

Taking this final moment as a cue for the form of the film's narration, it becomes apparent that the entire plot of coming to fame in America is not as self-contained as it might seem. The principal formal device by which the narration achieves this effect consists in redoubling the American plot to map out a 1950s narrative of Germany. This would begin to explain, for instance, why the film hardly even pretends to represent the historical moment depicted in the memoirs on which it is based. Or, to be more precise: the story seems to lose its historicity the minute it arrives in America—a significant aspect not merely because of the image of America it projects (I will return to this below), but also because, as Fredric Jameson points out, "Historical inaccuracy . . . can provide a suggestive lead towards ideological function." Jameson reads such instances as symptoms of the "resistance of the 'logic of the content,' of the substance of historicity in question, to the narrative and ideological paradigm into which it has been thereby forcibly assimilated."[56]

Let us retrace the ways in which the narrative gradually weighs its historical anchor. At first, as in *The Sound of Music* (though with slightly less dramatic effect), the historical moment is clear: a clichéd image of an old radio with Hitler's voice booming into the parlor is all it takes to inform us of the date. But from the moment the film fades in on the Statue of Liberty, visible behind the bars of the detention center on Ellis Island, all references to a historical past are eliminated. Liebeneiner uses 1950s settings and automobiles, suddenly skipping more than a decade, not to mention the cataclysm of World War II. Within the terms of the narrative, this apparent lack of concern for historically motivated continuity makes possible some highly anachronistic encounters. The sequences in New York emphasize the modern character of this city, and the display windows of department stores reflect its skyscrapers but no war-time shortages of consumer goods. The most glaring anachronism, however, noticed by at least one critic at the time, occurs in a scene in Central Park, where Maria runs into a friendly chimney sweep. They strike up a conversation in which he identifies himself as a GI just back from Cologne. The historical makeover is complete when he begins to reminisce about German women in authentic "Frollein-Deutsch."[57] In a historical short-circuit, we thus move from the early years of the Nazi regime and the question of exile to the time of the film's making. By the same token, its release in Germany also operates a well-known form of ideological release from the immediate past, confronting not Fascism but at best its aftermath in the form of occupation.

The anachronistic presence of a GI in the plot also raises the question of location, as the ambiguous treatment of history unsettles the coordinates of cinematic space. Have we really left Austria? Has the GI in fact returned to America, or is he perhaps still fulfilling some mission in postwar Germany even as the film's narrative places him in Central Park? A brief sequence towards the end of the film begins to provide some orientation in this awkwardly de- or rehistoricized space. Setting up the central plot point that converts the hapless family singers into an overnight sensation, this sequence finds a dejected Trapp family driving through the Vermont countryside, where, as their American driver explains, "They produce nothing but tombstones." Ever the irrepressible optimist, however, Maria sees something else that will cause both the driver and the narrative to stop for a brief pause. As the children pile out of the car to play in the meadow and the grown-ups amble into the hilly landscape, Maria asks, "Doesn't it remind you a bit of the Salzkammergut?" The camera tracks in on her pensive face

Figure 9. Projecting Austria in the Green Mountains of Vermont: *Die Trapp-Familie in Amerika* (1958).

as she says, "Just like back home [*wie zu Hause*]: I can picture everything right here." After a few incongruous images of the children yodeling on the surrounding hilltops, we cut to a brief montage of images from the previous film, dissolving into each other as so many memories before Maria's mind's eye. "Wie zu Hause," she sighs again as she snaps out of her daydream (see figure 9).

For all its brevity, the scene has metatextual implications. Maria's pensive remark provides a key to the way in which Liebeneiner relocates the Heimat genre in America. The audience is asked to read the images of America twice over, superimposing the image of an Austrian or German Heimat onto the profilmic locations in Vermont, just as Maria does. Such a refraction of America through the Austrian/German lens dovetails with other cinematic treatments of America. As Eric Rentschler points out, America has tended to function in German film "as a playground for the imagination, as a mirror that reflects and intensifies the preoccupations and imported conflicts of its visitors."[58] As I have suggested, the principal preoccupation that Liebeneiner's film imports to America is that of Heimat itself. This should be no cause for surprise in an exile narrative, where the need to make oneself at home in new surroundings is likely to involve re-creating the home left behind. And indeed, the von Trapps' historical plight in America was one of exile, hardly a stopover on the way back home. But this is no film about exile, at least not in the historical sense where the possibility of return would be blocked by Nazi occupation. Indeed, for that historical condition of exile to have any structural relevance after Cologne-based GIs have returned to the United States, the narrative would have to develop explanatory frameworks which lie entirely beyond its frame of reference.[59] It is therefore not the longing to return that structures the narrative, but rather the need to adapt, and thus to deal with the American present.

This is one reason why *Die Trapp-Familie in Amerika* is in important ways more of a *Heimatfilm* than an exile narrative. For even though it follows the family to America, Liebeneiner's film still moves within the conventions of the Heimat genre, which not only permits the opposition of Heimat to its "other," but tends to require such opposition for the purpose of reinforcing the value of the former. What is unusual about the von Trapps' itinerary within the Heimat tradition is that the family never comes back, at least not to Salzburg. In films like *Die Rose vom Wörthersee, Schwarzwaldmelodie, Wenn die Heide blüht*, and, again, *Der verlorene Sohn*, journeys to America (and the American metropolis in particular) function merely as a step on the way towards the fullness of the original Heimat. Liebeneiner's film, however, disavows the possibility of a return to (that) originary fullness, exhibiting an obsession with continued mobility instead.

The Americanized Heimat scenario is further complicated by the fact that the apparent dehistoricization of the American space simultaneously opens it up for a rehistoricization into a narrative of the German 1950s. In this respect, it is simply insufficient to claim that "the dimension of history is foreign" to the *Heimatfilm*;[60] the question to be asked is, rather, what *kind* of history the genre serves to write. While nothing in the film suggests that the von Trapps' exile is due to the terrors of the Nazi regime in Germany and Austria, there are a number of cues which suggest the historically distinct form of deterritorialization we already discovered in *Waldwinter*. The von Trapps' fall from aristocratic grace in Austria due to financial ruin, their apparent cultural disorientation, and even their songs mark them as displaced in the specific sense of the postwar European pandemonium. They are not refugees from Hitler but belong to the social group of *Vertriebene*. This might begin to explain the paradoxical narrative contrivance whereby the return to Austria is never discussed, although the condition of *Heimatlosigkeit* remains the family's central preoccupation. Under the terms of a narrative economy that replaces the loss of the Austrian Heimat with a diffusely articulated inability to get back to where they came from, the von Trapps' "exile" echoes that of the postwar refugees from Eastern Europe. Another cinematic parapraxis similar to the appearance of the GI in Central Park alerts us to this slippage. During an impromptu performance by the children in their New York tenement building, Liebeneiner includes a pair of refugees from Danzig in the cliché of multicultural America that makes up the spontaneous audience; the presence of a Pomeranian couple also suggests that the distinctly American mythology of the melting pot doubles here as an imaginary solution to the pressing sociopolitical need to integrate refugee populations in postwar Germany.

But the film stages another sort of return to the Heimat even as it forecloses the recovery of lost origins. In the end, we see the family refurbishing a large house that looks suspiciously like a Tyrolean farmhouse in a Vermont countryside that looks suspiciously like the Salzkammergut, or "wie zu Hause." As Rentschler suggests in his reading of America as a topos of German film, "The closer one looks, the more familiar the foreign experience becomes."[61] Thus, the parallels that make the impossible possible— namely, a German *Heimatfilm* literally superimposed on an American setting—are signaled not only by the dissolving images from Salzburg that Maria imaginarily superimposes on the Vermont landscape; they are made fully obvious in the reconstruction of the farmhouse. We may be in the Green Mountains, but the presence of Austria is signaled by the installation of the same red and white shutters that had decorated the Salzburg house. This achievement is celebrated of course with joyous song—the only song, in fact, that has no diegetic audience, making this the most purely "musical" performance. But again, there is a slight discrepancy between the levels of the cinematic narrative. While the result of the family's combined efforts is reminiscent of a feudal Austrian existence, the lyrics of the song speak of individual initiative and diligent work, with a chorus that runs, "Do you know what we will harvest,/as compensation for our efforts?/A little house with a garden,/even if it's just small./A little house with a garden/shall be our Heimat, our new Heimat!"

The *Heimatfilm* of the 1950s has often been criticized for being "false" and full of kitsch. Scenes such as this one would appear to be a case in point. Forced acting ruptures the fictional framework, ideology and its aesthetic representation do not line up neatly, even the image and the sound track do not seem to cohere (the actors' voices are no match for the synchronized angelic singing voices of the Regensburger Domspatzen). But as Georg Seeßlen conjectures, some of the old *Heimatfilme* remain fascinating precisely because of "their not-yet-perfection . . . their transparency; they were so honest in their reactionary appearance, they had no idea how perfectly people can be duped."[62] Accordingly, such jarring moments tend to reveal these films' historical unconscious with particular clarity. To take only the disjunction between the sound track and the image: clearly, the song's chorus is hardly fitting for the von Trapps' new Heimat—neither in Austria nor in Vermont do their living arrangements resemble the modesty of suburban real estate evoked by the song. But again, the answer to a problem raised by one narrative level is to be found on the historical plane that it allegorizes—which is to say, in the German 1950s that the film has conscientiously evoked. In a manner recognizable to most German and Austrian audiences of the 1950s, the von Trapps are literally staking a claim to a piece of real estate and rebuilding a dilapidated (though not bombed out) house. As part of a film that chronicles the family's slow but inevitable return to fame and fortune, this scene reenacts the ongoing *Wirtschaftswunder* activity of reconstruction. To find a referent for a "Häuschen mit Garten" and for the work ethic of the song's lyrics, German audience members had only to leave the theater and return to their own reconstruction efforts in the German economic miracle. At the end of the rainbow of the American dream, Liebeneiner's film suggests, we will find the *Wirtschaftswunder* pot of gold.[63]

The persistent doubling of geographical, economic, and political referents for the images and the plot of Liebeneiner's film has significant implications for its definition of Heimat. In particular, the film's emphasis on displacement is far from exceptional within the context of the *Heimatfilm*. The spectacle of "place" in the *Heimatfilm* often doubles as the spectacle of a displacement which it cannot contain. Indeed, this doubling is repeatedly spelled out in the Heimat film's construction of space. Like *Waldwinter*, but for a different geographical constellation, *Die Trapp-Familie in Amerika* is thus exemplary in that it makes explicit a metaphoric treatment of space whereby one particular diegetic or profilmic place is made to stand for another. Liebeneiner's film stretches, but by no means breaks, the function of Heimat—in this case Vermont—as a "local metaphor"for the (German/Austrian) nation. Like the representation of Kansas through Oz, the Green Mountains double for the Alps, just as the northern plains come to signify Silesia in *Grün ist die Heide* and the Bavarian Heimat regained in *Waldwinter* is indistinguishable from the snow-covered landscape left behind in Silesia. No matter how small and contained, space in the *Heimatfilm* is surprisingly often double, more than itself.

"SEX APPEAL FOR CONCERTS":
AMERICANIZING THE *HEIMATFILM*

Die Trapp-Familie in Amerika, I have suggested, makes over Vermont into Heimat: familiar images of Heimat de-exoticize the New World, allowing the von Trapps to "export" the concerns of the *Wirtschaftswunder,* the reintegration of *Vertriebene,* and even the memory of occupation. But there is a further layer in this spatial palimpsest. While exporting Heimat to America, Liebeneiner also imports the pressing issue of American modernity itself to the German genre that would appear most inimical to the ongoing Americanization of Germany after World War II. Though clearly attenuated by its link with the Heimat topos, the question of Americanization again pushes the locational politics of the film, asking us to read the family's engagement *in* America in terms of a German engagement *with* America. In this sense, the von Trapps' inability to return begins to suggest the irreversibility of Americanization itself. Where Rentschler argues that "America figures as a way station for travelers whose manifest destiny lies elsewhere,"[64] the Trapp film reminds its German spectators that their manifest destiny has become inseparable from the American way station itself.

The film actually connects its two narrative levels, as if in recognition of the fact that the *Wirtschaftswunder* pot of gold would still be full of worthless reichsmarks had it not been for currency reform and the Marshall Plan. If the von Trapps' success story repeatedly connotes the German *Wirtschaftswunder* at the height of which the film was made, how does it stage the continuing American presence in Germany? For the von Trapps are Americanized in the United States, and once again, a refugee serves as the "prototype" for a larger development. The family's negotiation of an American cultural economy allegorizes the contemporary struggle over the meanings of America in Germany. What is at issue, then, is the degree to which the German star/Austrian character (and ultimately the Heimat genre itself) will accept that Americanization: does she use it to her advantage or resist it by insisting on a rigid distinction between self and other, between the values of Heimat and those of American modernity?

On the most obvious level, the von Trapps depend on American money to get their familial economy back in gear. No matter how great its talents, the Singing Trapp Family would fail were it not for John D. Hammerfield, owner of uncounted oil rigs. Twice he intervenes on behalf of the family to keep its recovery on track. But while the paternal, pragmatic, and moneyed figure of Hammerfield stands in for Uncle Sam's helping hand in the reconstruction of the German (national) family, the film also constructs a more subtle discourse of the von Trapps' Americanization, which is staged in terms of sexual and cultural negotiations.

In his study on the Americanization of 1950s German youth culture, Kaspar Maase provides a useful framework for understanding the process of cultural Americanization more generally.[65] Drawing on the work of Michel de Certeau and the Birmingham School, Maase reads the imbrication of American and German culture in postwar Germany in "tactical" terms. From this point of view, the American presence in Germany offers a grab bag of cultural signifiers which are selectively appropriated in different ways by different people in different situations. Thus, contemporary youth cultures used the semiotics of American fashion, American music, and American stars to develop subcultural lifestyles which strongly polarized postwar German society along generational lines. Maase's methodology not only undercuts globalizing, top-down notions of cultural imperialism, but also emphasizes the social role of cultural self-fashioning within nationally defined systems of signification.

Take, for instance, the example of fashion itself, which in the 1950s was still closely bound up with the film industry and its various tie-ins. Not only did the James Dean and Marlon Brando images of the mid-1950s have a significant impact on the youth subcultures that Maase studies; in addition, the newly revitalized magazine business quickly discovered a market for film and fashion magazines such as *Film und Frau* and *Film- und Mode Revue*. Juxtaposing star gossip, serialized film narratives, and photos showcasing the season's fashions in Hollywood, these magazines created an Americanizing narrative of their own. If Hollywood played a part in that process, it was largely through the display of fashions that were clearly marked as American. In this respect, the grab-bag status of American icons takes on the specific connotations of the display window, a conjunction that has led film theorists to speculate about the affinities between spectatorship and consumption.[66] But if such a relationship exists, then what is being consumed (or at least contemplated in the cinematic shop window) within the postwar German context is precisely the American status of these fashions.

The *Heimatfilm*, by contrast, would appear to produce fashion at the other end of the line: the spectacle of traditional dress that colors these films suggests nothing if not Germanic traditions. This is what accounts for the incongruity of the Trapp family parading dirndls and feathered Tyrolean hats in America. The film repeatedly suggests that this is precisely the family's problem. With their anachronistic Austrian fashions, the von Trapps don't seem to know how to dress for success. In front of a manager's office, Maria catches her eldest son staring at life-size photographs of women in scant bikinis. "Perhaps we should sing like this," he suggests. Surprisingly, Maria joins her son in front of the posters to contemplate his suggestion before dismissing it. This scene prepares us for a later one at a different manager's office, where Maria inquires of several women what her family is missing. When the agent's assistant responds (after sizing her up from head to toe) that "you haven't a bit of sex appeal," Maria decides to go shopping. After a brief look at clothing in glamorous department store windows, she winds up in a bookstore where red and white tiles evoke the Austrian flag until two star-spangled blue dresses swirl across the screen.

Maria timidly asks a salesman about books on sex appeal, "especially for concerts." The clerk tells her that "you can't read about sex appeal," but she insists. The clerk decides to let the women handle this and fetches one of the assistants in the blue-and-white dresses. Informed of Maria's problem, she asks Maria to "look at me," thus turning the research project from discourse and books to performance and visual spectacle. There is a cut to a medium close-up of the assistant's legs, which she exposes to just below the knee by slightly lifting her petticoat. Another clerk, also in a blue dress, joins in to show off her version of sex appeal; the following shots alternate between the two assistants' swirling dresses and swinging hips, and reverse shots to Maria's quizzical gaze. The salesman ends the brief fashion show by pointing out, "Look: that's sex appeal!" To which Maria incredulously replies, "For concerts?" The friendly Americans clarify that "to have sex appeal means to display your feminine charms," but when Maria despairingly pulls up the hem of her dress (*over* her knees) it is only to insist that "I don't sing with the back of my knee!" The little dilemma has its own happy end, for upon taking in Ruth Leuwerik's exposed legs, the experts from the bookstore immediately exclaim, "She has it! *That's* sex appeal."

The repeated invitation to "look at me" marks sex appeal as pure spectacle and femininity as "to-be-looked-at-ness."[67] But significantly, the scene is staged for a woman who is shopping for American sexuality, and, by extension, for success. In this respect, her awkward request for "sex appeal for concerts" merely underlines her pragmatic attitude towards the spectacle she see(k)s: for her, the American way of "display[ing] your feminine charms" has a distinct use value. Consequently, the following scene shows Leuwerik somewhere in Central Park, trying out the habitus that the bookstore performance has specifically marked as American. Like the Halbstarken in Germany who took up James Dean's poses and Elvis's hairstyle, Maria is appropriating a style, while the perennial dirndl continues to mark her otherness.

Significantly, the film raises the question of American sex appeal only to

lose sight of it once Maria has tried it on. For the real problem lies elsewhere: As the varying moments of the Trapp family singers' success and
failure amply illustrate, the cultural appeal of their concerts hinges not so
much on how they perform, but on what they sing. Thus, the progression to
Welterfolg is accompanied by contentious negotiations over the family's
repertoire, where Bach and Palestrina fight an uphill battle against folk
songs and the *Volkslied*. Behind the shifting contents of the concert program
loom the embattled positions of high and low, European and American culture. Mass appeal may come about without sex appeal, but it cannot avoid
facing the question of the popular itself.

Matters of taste can replace class categories as forms of distinction;[68] but
of course there may also be significant areas of overlap. The von Trapps'
aristocratic background would seem to forbid stooping to the levels of popular culture and public entertainment. Back in Austria, the baron had
insisted, "My family will not work in the entertainment industry!" As we
know, he couldn't be further off the mark; but then, in a way characteristic
of many postwar cinematic narratives, Baron von Trapp has little to say in
this group anyway. As if to confirm Schelsky's analysis of the refugee family, it is Maria who makes all the important decisions, gets the contracts,
arranges for the acquisition of the house, and at crucial moments determines
the program for the performances. Her only real rival in this respect is the
secondary figure of Father Wasner, the priest who directs the choir and
favors the sacred music that has become synonymous with high German
culture. Thanks to his interventions, the subplot of the Americanization of
Germany is neatly paralleled by the von Trapps' own mission in America,
"to familiarize America with the old masters of church music," as Wasner
puts it.

But Maria is better attuned to the anachronism of this mission. After a
concert for an audience of twelve, three of whom leave before the end, Maria
asks Patrick, the family's Irish American driver, for advice on how to polish
up their act. The scene is framed by two prominent shots of a glittering
jukebox whose selection of contemporary American tunes supplies a commentary of its own for the ensuing conversation. Patrick suggests that perhaps Palestrina simply will not draw the crowds to the concert halls. In
response, Maria overrules Father Wasner, suggesting, "Maybe Patrick is
right. Too . . . well, too difficult. Maybe hard for Americans to grasp, no?"
On one level, such exchanges echo the priest's missionary spirit even as
they refute it: in an attitude that remains a staple of German/European
anti-Americanism to this day, Maria is suggesting that to be successful
would mean for the cultured musicians to stoop to the level of the American

ignoranti. But again, the ensuing narrative does not bear out such literal readings. For despite the priest's insistence ("But we can't sing *pop songs* [*Schlager*]!"), the film's turning points are brought about not by Palestrina and Bach, but by the German *Volkslied* and Ruth Leuwerik's rendition of "Oh, Susanna."[69] Of course, that particular performance can be read as the von Trapps' Americanization only in the hybrid sense suggested by Maase; for although the response of the diegetic audience suggests that the family singers have finally "arrived" and been accepted in the New World, there remains the strongly incongruous impression of Ruth Leuwerik strumming her guitar in full Austrian dress, with her children, directed by the faithful priest, singing the backup vocals.

Another instance of the falseness of the *Heimatfilm*, this performance again signals a programmatic aspect at the heart of the genre. Even in its striking incongruity, the scene telegraphs a desire for compromise and harmonization in an ideological, rather than just musical, sense. Where the missionary spirit of the high cultural priest sees only the choice between good and evil, Maria reconciles European heritage with American folklore. In this sense, Maria's ability to improvise, her pragmatic hybridization of the familiar and the foreign, "high" and "low" parallels the logic of Americanization itself as analyzed by Maase: what impressed youths of the 1950s about American idols such as Elvis Presley "was their ability to sell themselves, and their commitment to market values instead of moral messages." Such a pragmatic approach to cultural representation "ran counter to the German 'idealist' tradition of adhering to principles and ideological polarizations of friends and foes, clearing the way for a more relaxed and compromising approach to social conflicts of interest."[70]

As I have suggested, Liebeneiner's film negotiates Americanization circuitously, by displacing it from Germany to America itself and treating the question within the generic framework of a strangely deterritorialized, or Americanized, *Heimatfilm*. As Maria's willingness to try on a popular American habitus suggests, the resulting cinematic hybrid shares something of the "relaxed and compromising approach to social conflicts of interest" that German youth culture discerned in contemporary pop-cultural images and sounds from America. And yet there remains a distinction to be made between the compromises involved in Americanization according to Maase and the generic investment in compromise formations that we encounter in the *Heimatfilm*. Whereas the youth-cultural negotiation of American "signs" during the 1950s prefigured the struggles for liberalization and democratization of German politics and society during the 1960s, a *Heimatfilm* like *Die Trapp-Familie in Amerika* makes its peace with

America in order to harness its consequences. Trying on and then discarding some "sex appeal for concerts," Maria selectively embraces American modernity in the overarching project of regaining a sense of Heimat. Liebeneiner's film invokes the tropes of Heimat to show that "one can acquire America's good features while avoiding its corruption, one can modernize without losing the national (or regional) identity."[71] Accommodating some postwar forms of displacement and even the mobilization of Heimat itself, the film once again reassures its audience that traditions and the German sense of Heimat "are both conserved and gone beyond; past and future are one, you can change without changing."[72]

Maria's nostalgic Americanization on her way to *Welterfolg* thus has political implications for the reconstruction of West German identities. Among other things, Liebeneiner's film draws on tropes of Heimat to bring those identities in line with Adenauer's policies of Western integration in the cold war. Moreover, in weaving together Heimat and Americanization, *Die Trapp-Familie in Amerika* plots both of these cultural phenomena within a complex web of economics, politics, (cultural) consumption, and heritage. Emphasizing the mobility of Heimat and prefiguring that of the postwar German tourist, the film highlights the links between Heimat and travel, dwelling and mobility, that are at the heart of Germany's postwar reconstruction.

These issues have long been seen as specific to the Federal Republic, and the assumption that Americanization was a Western phenomenon has been axiomatic in Maase's and other accounts of Americanization. But as Uta Poiger demonstrates in a recent study of America's cultural impact on postwar Germany, the United States served as a mirror for both the West and the East. Contemplating its respective past and present but especially its future, in this mirror, "*Each* Germany laid claim to a German heritage and tried to define what it meant to be German."[73] Consequently, Poiger approaches the issue of Americanization in a comparative vein, looking to write the history of popular culture in the postwar Germanies on either side of the iron curtain. Given the different impact of American culture on the two states that emerged in 1949, Americanization is a particularly fertile concept for such a comparison. But Poiger's methodological premise extends past the study of Americanization. "In writing the histories of the two Germanies," she argues, "we need to employ concepts that make meaningful comparisons possible, concepts that allow us to think about fundamental differences between the two Cold War enemies as well as similarities between them."[74] Though the concept of Heimat may appear an unlikely candidate for this task, I suggest that it is perfectly suited for, and even demands, such comparisons. The official rhetoric of the East may have been at pains to exorcise Heimat discourse as a vestige of late-bourgeois ideology, but this purge was hardly complete. Heimat remained a concern for pedagogues and became an operative concept in the writing of local history and in state-sponsored cultural activities. As it became the object of a diffuse socialist politics of Heimat, the concept also informed a series of films produced by the East German DEFA studios over the course of the 1950s. These films can profitably be viewed as cold war cousins of the established *Heimatfilm* in the West. The following chapter takes a closer look at three such films in particular: Konrad Wolf's *Einmal ist keinmal* (1955), Martin Hellwig's *Das verurteilte Dorf* (1951), and Kurt Maetzig's epic *Schlösser und Katen* (1957).

7   Collectivizing the Local

DEFA and the Question of Heimat in the 1950s

And we love the Heimat, the beautiful
And we protect her, for she belongs to the people
For she belongs to our people.

GDR YOUTH SONG

Feelings of Heimat are an important factor in the creation of a
socialist society.

KULTURPOLITISCHES WÖRTERBUCH

In November of 1955, the East German distributor Progress announced the premiere of a new DEFA film at the Babylon theater in Berlin. The evening featured Richard Groschopp's *52 Wochen sind ein Jahr*, based on Jurij Brezan's novel by the same title. The film chronicles a year in the life of Krestan Serbin, an aging farmer who is working toward the day when he can retire and leave the farm to his daughter, Lena. The film is set in the Lausitz region of East Germany, home to an ethnic minority, the Sorbs. A prologue informs us of their persecution under Fascism, a plight that has ostensibly been reversed with the founding of the GDR. As if to convince us of their new, happier life, the film is suffused with images of rural bliss that bring together the rhythms of nature with local traditions. One line of the narrative concerns Lena's work to restore a traditional Sorbian folk song, and we are repeatedly treated to images of the Sorbs, dressed in *Trachten*, singing and dancing. The Progress advertisement for the film encapsulates this iconographic and narrative image by showing the faces of an older farm couple and two younger women, one of them wearing a traditional head-dress, grouped around the title, which is set in *Fraktur*; a horse-drawn carriage rounds out the picture (see figure 10). Publicity materials summed up the film's main attraction with the words "A gripping film from the beautiful German Heimat."

From today's point of view, it seems almost cynical that the film accompanying this one on the theater's double bill was *Das erste Atomkraftwerk der Welt* (The World's First Nuclear Power Plant). At first glance, what could have been further apart than the tradition-bound rural idyll promised by

Figure 10. Marketing a *Heimatfilm* in the GDR: Progress Film-Vertrieb advertisement for *52 Wochen sind ein Jahr* (1955). Courtesy Bundesarchiv-Filmarchiv, call no. BA-FA 20265.

Groschopp's film and a documentary about the latest advances in nuclear technology? And yet a second glance at *52 Wochen sind ein Jahr* reveals that for all its emphasis on tradition, this particular *Heimatfilm* is not entirely irreconcilable with the faith in progress exuded by *Das erste Atomkraftwerk der Welt*. For Krestan Serbin's life undergoes a significant change over the course of the film. In the beginning, he works solely for himself, stubborn in his insistence on preserving and passing on his hard-earned property. But the end of the film shows a "new" Krestan lugging away the fieldstones that separate his plot from the surrounding land. Resisting the reactionary forces that wanted to enlist him for their cause, Krestan has come around and joined the agricultural collective (Landwirtschaftliche Produktionsgenossenschaft, or LPG). In more ways than one, this clears the path towards a brighter future. As the film didactically asserts, collectivization is not only ideologically desirable, it is also crucial to increasing productivity—a lesson that Krestan boils down to the formula "small field, small bread—large field, large bread." As a result of this agricultural revolution, which also involves the full-scale technologization of agriculture (one sequence shows us Krestan evaluating new tractors at the agricultural fair in Leipzig), Krestan no longer has to work as hard. In addition, his daughter can now realize her dream of studying at the university rather than being bound to tradition through the inheritance of her father's plot. If it has not exactly yielded to a nuclear reactor, after fifty-two weeks of story time the Lausitz region has come to embrace both technological and social modernization within its traditional structures.

The juxtaposition of these two films in one program may therefore not have been all that surprising to a contemporary audience. But from a film-historiographical point of view, the advertising copy for Groschopp's film might give us pause. The advertisement for a DEFA *Heimatfilm* in 1955 challenges us to reassess one of the most basic assumptions about the genre: namely, that after the end of World War II the *Heimatfilm* was confined to the Federal Republic.[1] This assumption is based, in turn, on the lack of comparative approaches to cinema in East and West Germany more generally. Aside from numerous stock-takings of DEFA subsequent to its demise in the early 1990s[2] (as well as of the New German Cinema after its less certain disappearance from the domestic and international scene),[3] we must also focus on the relationship between the two traditions.[4] For too long, East and West German cinema have been considered beyond comparison. Especially for the 1950s, the anti-Fascist traditions of DEFA and the studio's apparent commitment to confronting the past, however selectively, appeared wholly incompatible with the fantasy productions of the West. The dominant historiographical narrative has attributed to West German cinema of the 1950s nothing but restorative tendencies, a complete lack of stylistic innovation, and a refusal to confront the past, while holding up DEFA cinema as the inheritor of expressionism and the guardian of an anti-Fascist historical consciousness. The two traditions have been viewed as irreconcilable parts of a "torn screen" under a "divided heaven."[5]

And yet, during the 1950s, the torn screen occasionally served as a set of mirrors. It is worth keeping in mind that the Zonengrenze, the border dividing East and West, remained relatively permeable throughout the 1950s. This allowed for some surprising forms of interzonal exchange—however lopsided—in terms of film practice, personnel, plots, and salient tropes.[6] To be sure, this was hardly ever a mutually sustained relationship, and animosity often outweighed the potential for convergence, let alone cooperation. However, the connections persisted throughout the decade, to be severed fully only by the building of the wall in 1961. While it would be misleading to suggest that the two postwar German film industries were defined by mutual influence or cooperation, any account of German film history in the 1950s in particular should be mindful of the multiple exchanges taking place during that decade—including the persistent struggles of two states locked in cold war combat, but also the travel of films, genres, and even audiences across the Zonengrenze.

Some of the reasons for the persistence of certain similarities are rather obvious. During the 1950s, the division was recent enough for filmmakers and cultural practitioners more generally to draw on shared traditions, even if these were officially taboo or had simply been disavowed by the socialist state in its definition of itself as inheritor of anti-Fascism. Indeed, in the case of cinema, DEFA arguably benefited from an even greater continuity of film production under the Nazis than did the West, where the dismantling of a centralized film industry was conducted much more thoroughly and with more lasting effect than in the East. DEFA was licensed by the Soviet occupation forces in 1946, and with Babelsberg in the Soviet sector, the new studio could work with the infrastructure and some of the personnel from the Ufa years. This is the institutional basis for Barton Byg's claim that there "was less of a rupture in cultural identity in 1945 in the East than in the West, despite the socialist rhetoric of the 'New Germany.'"[7] Particularly surprising in this respect are some of the personal continuities, including the work of prominent Ufa directors such as Arthur Maria Rabenalt, Werner Klingler, and especially the king of the West German *Heimatfilm*, Hans Deppe, who got his postwar start at DEFA. Moreover, as Byg and others have noted, the official self-definition of the GDR as an anti-Fascist state could serve as a sort of ideological amnesty for German cultural symbols and practices that otherwise might have been tainted by Nazi Germany. In this context, even "such concepts as folk, nation, Heimat . . . could eventually be given socialist content."[8]

Focusing on three films from the 1950s, this chapter investigates what it meant to give Heimat a socialist content. For this purpose, I have chosen to maintain a focus on the redefinition of rural space that characterizes many Heimat films in the West. It also represented a key component of the political agenda as East German authorities charted a rocky course of land reform and collectivization from the early postwar years through April 25, 1960, when the Volkskammer declared the process of collectivization complete.[9] Although the three films differ in their look and their appeal— ranging from a musical comedy to an anti-Western propaganda film to an epic chronicle of the postwar decade—they all share a more or less explicit commitment to the *Aufbau* ethic of the young socialist republic. Rather than stemming the tide of socialist change through a retreat into a late-bourgeois concept of Heimat, these films stage local place and rural space as the very crucible of socialist progress. Their political agenda certainly differs from that of their cousins in the West; nonetheless, these films draw on the same ideological potential of Heimat: its ability to attenuate change and put a human face on progress.

CROSSING THE ZONENGRENZE: *EINMAL IST KEINMAL*

On the outskirts of Klingenthal, a small village in the Erzgebirge, an urbane, bespectacled young man literally stumbles out of a train into a haystack. As he desperately looks for his glasses in the hay, a sleek convertible pulls up and a woman with a French accent offers her help and a lift to Berlin. The young man refuses both, waits for the woman to leave, finds his glasses and turns to the camera to explain the premise of the film we are about to see. Identifying himself as a composer by calling who has had to earn his living by playing the piano in a band, he confesses that he's "sick of band music." As the sound track begins to register the song of the birds in the surrounding countryside, the young composer dreamily enumerates his reasons for undertaking the long journey from Düsseldorf to the Erzgebirge—even though everybody from "drüben"[10] had warned him about spending his vacation there: "ah—peace, nature, solitude—and [the birds are joined by symphonic music on the sound track] music. Deep music. True music. Serious music. Bach, Stravinsky, Beethoven. Symphonies, rhapsodies!"

The young man's mounting enthusiasm is staged against—and seems to

Figure 11. Peter Weselin (Horst Drinda) on his way to Klingenthal in *Einmal ist Keinmal* (1955). Courtesy Bundesarchiv-Filmarchiv, call no. 3405.

gain momentum from—a backdrop of rural bliss, from the hay that cushioned his fall, the birds that accompany his musings, and a few panoramic shots of the valley below to two brief inserts of a squirrel and a woodpecker who inhabit a forest that enchants the accidental tourist. In no particular hurry, our protagonist wanders through the idyll and eventually lies down for a nap in the grass, only to be awakened by the kiss of a young woman who finds him while picking berries in the woods with a friend. In the ensuing chase scene, he clumsily tries to catch up with the two giggling women but is abruptly stopped when he bumps into a low-hanging branch. As he looks up, we see a long shot of the village of Klingenthal nestled between green mountains and framed by the branches of the tree under which the protagonist is standing: we have arrived at the locale where the action of the film will unfold after a brief fade to black.

This mildly self-reflexive opening of Konrad Wolf's 1955 debut film *Einmal ist keinmal*[11] (which thematically evokes the opening of Rudolf Schündler's *Wenn am Sonntagabend die Dorfmusik spielt* [1953]) serves to establish a number of crucial elements of the ensuing plot, its generic appeal, and of the film's iconography. Both Peter Weselin's monologue (including his direct address to the camera) and the deliberate use of the sound track, which hovers between the subjective and the nondiegetic, set the stage for a musical comedy, as do the credits, which show the members of the cast as cartoon characters marching across the screen with instruments. In its play with different styles and genres of music, the opening also begins to sketch the central conflict of a film that will revolve around disparate musical tastes, notably between the serious and popular, the traditional and the modern. Finally, in its emphasis on a seemingly enchanted rural space, the opening asks us to locate the film and its narrative conflicts within the generic space of the *Heimatfilm*. At least one contemporary reviewer did so with all the requisite enthusiasm.[12] Although Konrad Wolf spent much of his career trying to disavow this film as a kind of false start, and although critics have subsequently tended to either overlook this part of Wolf's œuvre or to dismiss it as a "colorful little work,"[13] contemporary reviews were by and large quite favorable, occasionally even exuberant, in their response to the way *Einmal ist keinmal* combines landscapes, music, and love to offer one of DEFA's most successful and daring comedies to date.[14]

At first glance, then, it would seem that *Einmal ist keinmal* fits comfortably into the generic developments of the 1950s as a rather typical hybrid of musical, comedy, and Heimat. In ways that remain to be shown, Wolf's film is indeed an almost classical *Heimatfilm* by virtue of its many similarities to recently established prototypes such as *Grün ist die Heide, Der Förster vom Silberwald*, and *Schwarzwaldmädel*. On the other hand, *Einmal ist keinmal* also differs fundamentally from these films in that it geographically redefines the idea of Heimat. In the prototypical *Heimatfilm* of the 1950s, the foreign "other" of Heimat usually appears synonymous with urban space and metropolitan lifestyles, if not with America as the ultimate form of cosmopolitanism. This opposition between the local and the urban, in turn, outweighs the distinction among such different locales as the heath, the Black Forest, or the Austrian Alps. *Einmal ist keinmal,* on the other hand, not only pits Klingenthal against Düsseldorf, but the Erzgebirge against its counterparts in the Federal Republic. With Wolf's film, we cross the Zonengrenze from the West to explore the lure of the local in the eastern half of Germany. This basic geographical (and by extension, geopolitical) shift is sketched for the viewer in a brief prologue in which the local glue manufacturer, Herr Edeltanne, receives a telegram from his nephew "from the West," thus marking Edeltanne's hometown of Klingenthal as an East German village. His exclamation "I'm off to meet him" is followed by a cut to the image of a train running from right to left, ostensibly carrying Edeltanne on his westward path towards his nephew. Almost instantly, though, the image flips 180 degrees. Now we see a train running in the opposite direction, back to Klingenthal.[15] Here we first encounter Peter Weselin (Horst Drinda), the prodigal nephew from "drüben," engrossed in a tortured dream about music under the proud but concerned eyes of his uncle. Before they arrive at their destination, Peter stumbles off the train and into the picturesque countryside.

Produced by DEFA at the height of the West German *Heimatfilmwelle* in the mid-1950s and directed by the man who, along with Kurt Maetzig, was to become the most celebrated auteur of GDR cinema, *Einmal ist keinmal* is remarkable for the way in which it begins to rewrite Heimat for a socialist context. As if to illustrate this labor of resignification, Wolf's film reworks both the syntax and the semantics of the Western *Heimatfilm*. *Einmal ist keinmal* does not simply imitate that model; rather, the film, which was praised by the government's film control board for undertaking a "successful step on the way to a new genre," renegotiates the value of Heimat for a socialist cultural politics.

This relationship of proximity *and* divergence is particularly evident in the film's narrative logic, which borrows and reworks some of the central features of the West German *Heimatfilm*. Through the thick, horn-rimmed glasses of his endearingly naïve Western protagonist, Wolf lets us observe the gradual integration of Peter as the "foreigner" into the fabric of a socialist Heimat. Like any number of similar films from the Federal Republic, the plot of *Einmal ist keinmal* is set into motion by the arrival of a young artist from the city. His presence upsets the balance of the closely knit *Gemeinschaft* in the village as he challenges the existing hierarchy, traditional assumptions about artistic value, and time-honored local customs surrounding the annual musical celebrations in Klingenthal.

Peter first comes to Klingenthal—and, by extension, to socialism—like a foreigner who is unable to read the signs. After the chase through the forest has brought him to the village, Peter follows Anna (Brigitte Krause), the redhead who kissed him, into the local accordion factory. When the doorman asks him what he wants, Peter quickly glances at the sign identifying the factory as a collectively owned business, or "volkseigener Betrieb" (VEB). In his need to improvise, he asks to see "Director Veb, please," thus revealing his national and class background. By the end of the film, however, he is celebrated as the winner of a competition at the Klingenthaler Musiktage and, just as importantly, he has won Anna's favor. The motif of the stranger who arrives in the village, needs to learn how to negotiate its customs, and gets the local girl in the end is familiar enough from the history of the *Heimatfilm*; however, as Peter Hoff points out, *Einmal ist keinmal* tacitly politicizes this motif by giving it national and class connotations.

Just as the film maps the relationship between Heimat and *Fremde* onto
East and West Germany, so does the integration of the "foreigner" into the
Heimat imply a process of successful socialist reeducation. Peter succeeds
only in the East. More importantly, he learns that the popular, which, in the
form of band music and boogie-woogie, he despised, resides with the working class. Indeed, the film spells out the advantages of East over West in relatively didactic terms, even as it couches this lesson in the format of a musical comedy. The West stands for alienated working conditions and the
boogie-woogie of a capitalist culture industry, whereas Klingenthal, home of
the accordion factory VEB Klingenthaler Akkordeonwerke, promises the
organic integration of local tradition, high art, and popular folklore.[16]

Characteristically, *Einmal ist keinmal* chronicles Peter's Eastern reeducation through a number of compromise formations. On the one hand, his trip
to the East opens up new perspectives, both amorous and musical. Not only
does his sojourn in Klingenthal and its picturesque surroundings enable
Peter to compose the piece of "deep," "true," and "serious" music that he
dreamed of back in Düsseldorf (a central scene shows him composing his
rhapsody on a bench in the rural idyll of the Erzgebirge). In his quest for
Anna, he also comes into contact with a version of the popular that apparently differs fundamentally from the syncopated American band music he
has come to disdain in the West. Having first refused to compose a *Schlager*
for Anna's band, Peter ultimately succumbs to her stubborn but proud character, which provides the inspiration for the foxtrot "Anna, dein Charakter."
The composition has already been hinted at by the film's sound track and
becomes its signature tune. Like his rhapsody, which has its premiere at the
Volksfest that concludes the film, and like the waltz that Peter also composes
for the festivities, the foxtrot is locally based. While the rhapsody reworks
what is allegedly an old folk song (the "Einmal ist keinmal" of the film's
title, sung by Anna and her companion in the woods at the beginning of the
film), the foxtrot memorializes the stubborn but loveable character of Anna,
the embodiment of local custom, charm, and tradition. As the dominant
motif of the film, Peter's compositions demonstrate how the hero succeeds
by virtue of his ability to compromise between the old and the new, the high
and the low, the classical and the local. "Deep," "true," and "serious" music,
it turns out, can be symphonic while making use of local material. As in
Liebeneiner's film about the Trapp family, success depends on the ability to
negotiate the new in the language of tradition. Characterized as a mandarin
upon his arrival (in this respect, he measures up to Father Wasner's missionary zeal to "acquaint the Americans with the old masters" of German
church music), Peter is able to develop a softer stance on the distinction

between high and popular art, taking on board motifs from local popular culture that will assure him success on all fronts. Not surprisingly, the catalyst for this compromise is once again a woman.

Wolf's film, though unique in many respects, is hardly the only example of a GDR *Heimatfilm*. The same generic framework echoes through a number of other DEFA projects from the 1950s, whether *Der Ochse von Kulm* (1955), a projected but never completed film by Konrad Wolf entitled *Weg in die Heimat*, or *Verspielte Heimat* (1971). In other instances, the discourse surrounding the film linked it explicitly to a concern with Heimat. This was the case with *52 Wochen sind ein Jahr*, which, as I have suggested, was marked as regional from the beginning. As "A film from the Lausitz region," it shows us "Sorbian Heimat, and this gives the film its special attraction." The press consequently described *52 Wochen sind ein Jahr* as "a good *Heimatfilm* [that] depicts what is new in our people as well as their new problems."[17]

Not all of the films under discussion here can be assimilated to the *Heimatfilm* as "automatically" as *Einmal ist keinmal* or *52 Wochen sind ein Jahr*; in keeping with a pragmatic approach that would avoid essentializing the Heimat genre, I have deliberately broadened the frame to capture films that relate to the issue of Heimat and to the genre in more circuitous but no less telling ways. While I consider explicit, literal attribution of a genre label to be an important—indeed a sufficient—criterion for including a particular film, I do not perceive the availability of such labels as necessary for this purpose. Thus, to single out *Einmal ist keinmal* as the only instance of a GDR *Heimatfilm* is to restrict the generic criteria to a few iconographic and narrative elements.[18] If these are essentialized as necessary conditions of the genre, they conceal a host of films which, while not identical with their Western counterparts, entertain a complicated but dynamic relationship with some of the aspects of the genre that I have identified as salient in the West. Thus, as in earlier chapters, I advocate here a heuristic definition of the *Heimatfilm* that allows for multiple overlapping generic criteria, rather than essentializing a limited and often untheorized set of "typical" generic aspects for classificatory purposes. From this perspective, a closer look at a range of DEFA films and their cultural and political contexts in the GDR of the 1950s reveals a sustained discourse on Heimat and its connotations of the provincial, the rural, and the national as more or less contained spaces of belonging. While the films that I discuss arguably fall short of a full-fledged generic coherence that would allow us to speak of a DEFA *Heimatfilm* in its own right, a comparative look at these films, along with their Western counterparts, can contribute substantially to our understanding of the ideological functions of Heimat in German film history.

RESIGNIFYING HEIMAT IN THE *AUFBAU* YEARS

Notions of Heimat, I have argued, were crucial to reconstruction in the West. But the GDR, too, pressed the local, the provincial, and the rural into the service of an overarching project of socialist reconstruction, or *Aufbau*. Despite the new regime's democratic centralism, Celia Applegate's claim that "Germany was rebuilt from the regions outward and upward"[19] holds true for the East as well. The geopolitics of occupation resulted not only in the resizing and eventual division of the defeated nation, but also in its increased regionalization. As in the West, the political geography of postwar East Germany was complemented by widespread discursive attention to issues of place, Heimat, and belonging. The films I discuss here represent only one medium in which this discourse materialized, and they need to be understood in the context of a diffuse socialist politics of Heimat articulated simultaneously across a range of different sites. These included such diverse texts and activities as anthologies of Heimat poems,[20] a well-known Heimat song of the GDR youth organization, scholarly work on "the love of Heimat as an essential goal of our patriotic education" (and later, Günter Lange's classic *Heimat: Realität und Aufgabe*), state directives for the treatment of Heimat in schools and other pedagogical institutions,[21] and the practical efforts of the Deutscher Kulturbund to foster interest in local history.[22] Additionally, as in the West, the notion of Heimat played a central role in the ongoing effort to accommodate scores of displaced persons from the east. Though official parlance differed—in the GDR, one spoke of *Umsiedler* (resettlers) rather than of *Vertriebene*—here, too, the postwar presence of millions of displaced people reinforced the discursive value of notions of Heimat and belonging.[23] Finally, to the degree that "the task of winning the hearts and minds of the populace for Heimat and *Vaterland* was seen primarily as that of the artistic media," as Harry Blunk has suggested, the films themselves must be regarded as key participants in the discursive construction of Heimat in the GDR of the 1950s.[24]

Needless to say, the goals of these Heimat endeavors differed from those of their Western counterparts—most obviously, perhaps, in the way in which discussions of Heimat were used to decry the reactionary and idealist Heimat culture in the West. This is the function of the uncle, Edeltanne, in Wolf's film. As his name suggests, this character is treated ironically from the beginning. He appears as the representative of an outdated Heimat culture who laments that "Klingenthal just isn't its good old self anymore." With his bourgeois apartment, his stilted speech, his amateurish love poems, and a complete lack of self-awareness, Edeltanne blunders through the plot as a pointedly anachronistic figure. Multiple misunderstandings with his nephew reveal Edeltanne's inability to read the signs of the times.[25] He is a figure from the past who will recede into anonymity with the dawn of a new musical and political era. But in addition to his temporal dislocation, he is in the wrong place. More than Peter, who will successfully negotiate the transition from West to East by the end of the film, one is tempted to read Edeltanne as a delegate from the *Heimatfilm* in the other half of the country, where his antics would look considerably less out of place. In Klingenthal, by contrast, Edeltanne winds up in a sanatorium, where he is treated to a series of mud baths against his will. Although the film stages this fate as a practical joke, it is difficult to escape its allegorical implications for the dynamics of tradition and change. In its renewal of folk customs and Heimat feelings, the film suggests, the GDR will have to put to rest the old traditions that are still alive and well in the West.

Other contemporary texts are less lighthearted in their critique of West German notions of Heimat. A pertinent dissertation from 1957, for example, repeatedly engages with literature from the West in order to demonstrate its hopeless relativism, its biologism, and its continuity with the *Blut-und-Boden* rhetoric of the Nazi era.[26] From a socialist point of view, the "imperialist" definitions of Heimat in the West rob it of its "objective" character in order to legitimize the actual *Heimatlosigkeit* under capitalism and to prepare the population for renewed warfare.[27] According to this logic, the ideology of Heimat in the West served merely to reproduce existing class relations by fostering acceptance of the status quo at home and an imperialist stance abroad. The discursive emphasis on "peace and quiet" was seen to foreclose the development of any revolutionary consciousness.[28]

In many respects, the Eastern critique of the Western ideology of Heimat seems wholly apposite. As I have argued, the films of the 1950s stage Heimat as a milieu that naturalizes processes of modernization and makes the economic miracle available to the provinces. In this respect, Heimat served the ideological purpose of providing seemingly constant images for rapidly changing social conditions. As a compensatory space for the ongoing process of modernization, Heimat in these films was hardly a concept through which to articulate a critique of social reality, much less to imagine a different future. And yet this is precisely the intended upshot of the Eastern ideology critique of Heimat. Here, redefinitions of the concept aim explicitly at making Heimat a site for socialist change. As the writer Hermann Kant would later remark, "A word was still spelled the same, but one used it for a different way of thinking."[29] On one level, this resignification merely required stressing the collectivity involved in the notion of Heimat by expanding (or just renaming) the acknowledged role of family and *Gemeinschaft* to include socialist collectives such as youth groups (the Pioniergruppe) and the class collective itself, emphasizing their function "for the creation and development of a love of Heimat."[30]

From here, it was only a short step to the overriding concern of the *Aufbau* years with collectivization, particularly in rural areas. According to the Eastern ideology critique, the West elaborated its diffuse theories of Heimat only to hide its absence in an alienated society dominated by class conflict. Consequently, it fell to socialism to facilitate the revival of a "really existing" Heimat by making sure no part of it was privately owned. This was the lesson contained, for instance, in the song "Unsre Heimat," quoted in the epigraph to this chapter. Written by Herbert Keller, it was an early and enduring classic of the GDR youth organization Junge Pioniere. Its lyrics, which are still familiar to most Germans who were brought up in the GDR, assert that Heimat extends beyond the realm of cities and villages into the beauty of nature. More importantly, the concluding lines point out that this inclusive idea of Heimat requires protection as a collective good. The song reinforces the value of Heimat for the project of constructing an imagined community in which "we" all work together for its protection as an inalienable common possession.

As the essential object of collective ownership, the Eastern variant of Heimat presupposes two further aspects, to which it was discursively linked: a Marxist definition of labor, and the process of land reform that was initiated in 1945 and lasted throughout the 1950s. By contrast to the late-bourgeois definition of Heimat, which writers in the East decried as hopelessly idealist, the concept was to be put back on its feet by anchoring it in the process of labor as an activity of appropriation.[31] As opposed to metaphysical definitions that posit Heimat as part of the human condition, the Marxist version insisted on the fact that Heimat was not a given but needed to be won or appropriated through an active process. As the concept of Heimat was thus stripped of its layers of late-bourgeois ideology, it was simultaneously subjected to a process of socialist resignification, which burdened the concept with an array of meanings ranging from collectivization to the ideal of a socialist international, from labor as the active appropriation of nature to the future of the socialist project itself.[32] As opposed to the backwards-looking temporality of the Western Heimat concept, the Eastern counterpart was charged with a forward-looking utopian dimension, making it once again an ideal site for the negotiation of spatial transformation.

Ironically, this process produced a concept that was no less vague than its often maligned Western counterpart. Günter Lange's critique of late-bourgeois definitions of Heimat, for example, applies in equal measure to his own endeavors to fill the term with new, socialist meaning. For the "revanchist ideologues" in the West, Lange argues, Heimat "remains an empty political-ideological formula, to be filled with an always diffuse content, the accentuation of which changes in accordance with existing power relations."[33] The same could be said of Lange's own account, which equates Heimat with everything from the immediate family to the socialist world system of the future; likewise, Sigrid Schwarz's dissertation confuses means and ends when she begins by claiming to reexamine the notion of Heimat with the tools of historical materialism and ends up reproducing historical materialism itself, seen through the lens of Heimat.

In other words, as in the West, the notion of Heimat appears to be of little analytical value when we turn to the films in question, since definitions that equate Heimat with the whole of political economy clearly lack the requisite specificity. Rather, the trope of Heimat provided a site for the articulation of a number of discourses that circled around questions of home and belonging, provincial and rural space, ownership, tradition, and change. In reading DEFA productions as *Heimatfilms*, my goal is thus not so much to prove the appropriateness of this label, but rather to demonstrate the degree to which these films intersected with, and were energized by, the discourses that flourished around the notion of Heimat in the GDR of the 1950s. This proliferating discursive activity testifies to the flexibility and to the perceived centrality of this notion in both East and West; it appears that neither state could afford simply to cast the idea aside in its effort at reconstruction. The transformation and modernization of rural space was simply too important for this project, even as it took entirely different ideological shape in the two Germanies. The film industries on either side of the Zonengrenze reflected and contributed to this situation.

LOCATING THE COLD WAR: *DAS VERURTEILTE DORF*

A look to the east during the 1950s reveals a remarkable concentration on the village as the crucible of socialist society during the *Aufbau* years. As if the official doctrines on realism required carefully circumscribed settings for their didactic purposes, a host of DEFA films produced during this decade used the village as a microcosm for larger developments. This is to say nothing about the particular form their plots could take—for all the recurring aspects of the films under discussion, their generic "look" could be quite varied. As in the West, where the *Heimatfilm* could be coupled with generic registers from the dramatic to the historical to (musical) comedy, Eastern productions that centered on the importance of rural locale ranged from comedies such as *Einmal ist keinmal, Der Ochse von Kulm,* and *Was wäre, wenn* (1960) through the more or less didactic plots of *Freies Land* (DEFA's first film, a semidocumentary feature from 1946) or *52 Wochen sind ein Jahr,* to the outright propaganda of *Das verurteilte Dorf* and the high drama of Kurt Maetzig's *Schlösser und Katen.* For all their differences, however, these films converge in their shared attempt to chronicle "the change in village life," as a reviewer for *52 Wochen sind ein Jahr* put it.[34]

Das verurteilte Dorf, whose title announces a tale about village life, mobilizes Heimat as a defense against the threat of renewed warfare. One of only six films produced by DEFA in 1952, *Das verurteilte Dorf* was based on a newspaper report about plans to turn the West German village of Hammelburg into an American air force base. Although the completed film replaces Hammelburg with the fictional Bärenweiler, the place and time of the action remain clearly identified as West Germany in the year 1950. *Das verurteilte Dorf* thus represents the first foray into the territory of the Federal Republic by a DEFA plot. As Ralf Schenk rightly remarks, it does so without much regard for poetic or psychological nuance.[35] Rather, held up at the First Film Conference of September 1952 as a model for the socialist film of the future, *Das verurteilte Dorf* works with a set of blunt but effective binary oppositions to satisfy the official demands on propaganda in the GDR. Situating its action in a small village in the West, the film locates the cold war in a propagandistic vein, seeking to "actively develop the Marxist-Leninist worldview and the communist morale" of the viewer.[36]

The film opens with the image of a map, on which a magnifying glass picks out the hamlet Bärenweiler. Although this image, which was used in modified form for publicity, is something of a stock motif in film language, it signals this particular film's concern with a politics of location. Bärenweiler, we are to understand, is representative of other such villages. This is "not just Bärenweiler," as one review puts it,[37] but also a local metaphor for the nation as a whole. In the words of the protagonist, "Actually, this is about much more."

The film will progressively amplify the representative function of the village up to the much-touted crowd scenes full of *Volksfrontpathos* (pathos of a popular front) at its end. In the beginning, however, Bärenweiler is a sleepy little village crisscrossed by geese and hay wagons, where the gossiping postman makes his rounds and knows everyone (and the contents of their mail). The drama begins to unfold with the delivery of two letters: the first announces the return of POW Heinz Weimann five years after the war's end. A "man of the people" and a hard worker, the figure of Heinz furnishes the "positive hero" for the film's celebrated socialist realism.[38] The second letter introduces the central conflict: it informs the local mayor of plans to evacuate the village and expropriate the surrounding fields for an airfield for American occupying forces.

As news of this plan spreads, the villagers react with shock and helplessness, expressed first in an exchange between the distraught mayor and a representative of the state government, and then in the villagers' short-sighted reasoning when they believe that a simple letter signed by all might change the Americans' minds. When this plan fails, the local priest—a decidedly fatherly figure with a self-described "peasant's stubbornness," played by Eduard von Winterstein—attempts to solicit the bishop's support, only to be reminded of his duty to "give to the emperor what the emperor is due." Realizing the inadequacy of their individual uncoordinated actions, the villagers convene and decide that their plight requires greater visibility. They muster the support of the surrounding villages as well as of the workers in the nearby city and stage a rally in the state capital. However, at the command of the American general, who marches in wearing sunglasses and chewing gum, the demonstration is forcefully dispersed by the police. Although their demands have been refused, the inhabitants of Bärenweiler have won their first victory: in a series of rapid cuts, which a contemporary analysis of the script celebrates as "an overwhelming image of the solidarity of working people in the fight for peace,"[39] the mayor of Bärenweiler receives a string of telegrams from all over the country, including the Eastern half. Entire villages, but also factories and local collectives show their support and testify to the whole nation's solidarity with Bärenweiler.

But the Americans are not swayed. Early one morning, the military police arrive in the village to clear out the inhabitants. When the villagers refuse to leave, the police arrest Heinz as the protest leader. This leads the workers in charge of building the airfield to go on strike. The situation escalates, and to the sound of ominous music, the Americans once again head to Bärenweiler, setting a four-hour ultimatum for the evacuation of the village. While some begin packing their belongings and loading them onto carts in images still familiar from the long treks of refugees heading west, an older woman hangs herself in desperation. This strengthens the villagers' resolve to head off the American threat, setting the stage for the final showdown between the power of arms and the citizens' right to Heimat. Bärenweiler's church bells summon support from the surrounding villages, and a young woman manages to get a message out to the workers, who return from the city to help face down the threat. Realizing that they cannot afford further escalation and overwhelmed by the unity they face, the Americans get in their Jeeps and drive away.

The press hailed *Das verurteilte Dorf* as a "breakthrough in German filmmaking." Reviewers found lavish praise for the film's story, its politics, and its form. They commended it as an "exemplary film," a model of socialist realism for DEFA films to come, repeatedly likened its images and its treatment of the masses to Eisenstein's *Battleship Potemkin* (1925), and echoed the party line on aggressive pacifism by calling *Das verurteilte Dorf* a "passionate weapon for peace."[40] The film received not only the coveted Nationalpreis of 1952, but also the Weltfriedenspreis for the following year—the only occasion on which this distinction was bestowed upon a DEFA film. As one reviewer recalled on the thirty-fifth anniversary of the founding of the GDR, *Das verurteilte Dorf* "was not only a big box office success, it was a political event."[41]

What were the factors that contributed to this event? As a piece of cold war propaganda the film set out to achieve two goals: on the one hand, *Das verurteilte Dorf* militates against the threat of a third world war; on the other hand, it aims to reinforce the perception of an overwhelming solidarity among peasants, workers, and upstanding citizens in the West with the socialist commitment to world peace in the GDR. The latter goal and the attendant assumption of a revolutionary situation in the Federal Republic, in particular, may have represented a "complete misapprehension of [contemporary political] reality."[42] Nonetheless, the film succeeded as a "political event." It did so, I would argue, by capitalizing on the notion of Heimat and its various connotations against the backdrop of the cold war. In other words, the burning questions to which *Das verurteilte Dorf* proposed a set of propagandistic answers fundamentally concerned the location, the extent, and the endangerment of Heimat during the cold war.

The relevance of these concerns became explicit in a number of reviews. The official party newspaper *Neues Deutschland*, for instance, praised the film as an "epos of national resistance against the American occupiers, of the Germans' love for their Heimat."[43] More importantly, though, the concern with Heimat is inscribed into the narrative and the iconography of the film at crucial junctures, serving as the principal motivating force behind the heroic story of resistance that is being told. For this purpose, the film takes care to establish the force field of Heimat early on. The opening sequence depicts a serene rural idyll of meadows, orchards, *Fachwerkhäuser* and a small church—images so (stereo)typical that one reviewer spoke of the beginning as a *Volkslied*.[44] The feeling that these images are meant to evoke is one of home, collectivity, and unity—or so claimed another review, which identified them as the very essence of a (unified) German Heimat: "Immediately, we feel 'at home,' every detail is dear to us and familiar. This is Germany. Our Heimat, unsullied by barriers and not torn apart by any Zonengrenze."[45]

Moreover, the first action to take place in this setting is one of home-coming. In a scene that had already become a staple of the postwar cinema, we see Heinz returning from imprisonment to his aged mother, mending the broken family and reestablishing the continuity of its lineage. Heinz can think of nothing he would rather do than "work my field in peace and quiet" and dance with Käthe, his hometown honey. The images illustrate this commitment to Heimat by showing Heinz behind his plow, accompa-nied by the sound of horn music. A montage of Heinz sowing and then har-vesting corn in his field brings us through the year's nature-bound rhythm to Bärenweiler's Erntedankfest. Featuring festive decorations, people in tra-ditional dress, and a parade, this German thanksgiving is depicted in images straight out of any Hans Deppe film (save for the lack of color), as if to gen-eralize Heinz's earlier sigh of relief at having returned: "There's no place like home" ("Es geht nichts über zu Hause"), he enthuses as his mother dotes on him and some locals gather around her kitchen table.

Only after this overdetermined sense of community, security, and home has been established does the news of the American threat spread through the village—a threat which the viewer now equates with a threat to the value of Heimat itself. A group of villagers working the harvest are the first to see the Americans. From a wagon loaded with wheat, we follow Heinz's gaze to two dark limousines on the nearby road. The villagers stop their work as suddenly as the music on the sound track ends, yielding to their aural point of view: we hear fragments of dialog in American English. When the limousines depart, we are left, like the villagers, with the impression of a vague threat. This key scene works with strong contrasts, as the ominous dark limousines and the Americans with their military demeanor and dark sunglasses "invade" the bright and expansive countryside of the peaceful peasants.

Again, the specific fate of Bärenweiler recedes behind its role as a generic locale, now under siege. Bärenweiler, remarks the reviewer for *Neues Deutschland*, "stands for all German villages, for all cities, for our threat-ened Heimat itself."[46] Heimat, in this reading, becomes a word for an endan-gered space. Its deprivation amounts to an attack on inalienable values of peace and *Gemeinschaft*. Clearly, this is a calculated effect: the threat of the Americans appears all the greater and the more inhumane for the effort that the film expends on first establishing Heinz's right to a sense of home after the war and the ensuing years of imprisonment. Accordingly, the villagers' petition to the American military authorities explicitly bases its appeal on the universal values of "humanity and human rights whose defense is among the glorious traditions of your country."

Such appeals, as well as the film as a whole, are staged against a historical situation in which the right to Heimat is anything but universal, and where the very invocation of any such right is always linked to the massive reality of displacement. Though the threat to Bärenweiler may have been based on a factual story, it is hardly representative of the many other kinds of evacuation, expulsion, and homelessness faced by millions in the war and postwar years. The film's reference to such forms of displacement is characteristic of broader postwar discourses of German victimization (even if, in the end, the victims are victorious). As Robert Moeller points out for the Western context, the war stories that circulated in postwar Germany amounted to a highly "abbreviated" account of National Socialism, according to which "all Germans were ultimately victims of a war that Hitler had started but everyone lost."[47] While the official anti-Fascism of the East German state tempered this sense of victimhood by infusing it with stories of heroic resistance, Germans as either perpetrators or bystanders remain absent in the discursive landscapes on both sides of the inner-German border. By making a former POW the "positive hero" of its story, emphasizing his right to the security of home after ten horrific years, the film taps a widespread tendency in both East and West Germany to reestablish national identity on the basis of the memory of German victimization. Heimat had always played a prominent role in this project; as a film that capitalizes on a nationalist discourse of Heimat and German victimhood, *Das verurteilte Dorf* appeared to critics as a national epos par excellence—a "real *Deutschland*-song that moves our hearts passionately . . . a unique patriotic document."[48]

The film continues its valorization of Heimat as an endangered space when the workers and peasants unite to march on the capital. As the first demonstration of the unity that will ultimately assure the victory of Bärenweiler and all victims of American aggression, this sequence is particularly crucial to the development of the plot. Shot from below, we see the demonstrators as a towering presence. Their banners read "Hands Off Our Heimat" and "We Won't Give Up Our Heimat." By this point, the defense of Heimat has become a matter of active resistance against a military force. The politics of occupation, let alone the fact that occupation was the result of liberation from Fascism by the Allies, play no role in this cold war scenario. Chants of "Amis go home!" mingle with calls to leave "Germany to the Germans."[49] When the police use force to disperse the crowd, a particularly didactic image shows a poster advocating "Peace in our Heimat!" being trampled underfoot. It is only fitting, then, that the final victory of the village be described as the victory of *Heimatliebe* itself. According to one review, this was the core of the film's realist message: the locals' "love of their Heimat soil is authentic—a reality that neither the Americans nor Adenauer can get around."[50]

The drama and propaganda of *Das verurteilte Dorf* work with a clearly structured set of binary oppositions. Plot structures and characterization clearly draw the lines in the cold war battlefield between the sinister Americans—identified by the press as "Interventen"—and an idealized German resistance united behind the "positive hero" Heinz. Pitting peace-loving villagers against warmongering American occupiers, the film allegorizes a number of other cold war divisions as well: Bärenweiler represents the cause of the country against the city, socialism against capitalism, the collective against the monopolies of the military-industrial complex, German unity against division, and peace against (cold) war. The place of Heimat in this clearly divided cognitive map of postwar Germany is unmistakable. The film aligns it with the first terms of these oppositions, making Heimat the crucible not only of village life, but also of peace, the collective, and of any scenario for German unification.

While the place of Heimat in the rigid cold war scenario of *Das verurteilte Dorf* seems clear enough, it is worth pointing out that the film also contributes to the resignification of Heimat outlined above. For all of its rural idylls, inalienable traditions, and even the occasional biologistic assumption of some soil-based identity,[51] Heimat in *Das verurteilte Dorf* is clearly a space of transformation, not of retrenchment. To be sure, the basic story of the film is familiar from the history of Heimat as an antimodern sense of place—the village's resistance to the construction of the airfield represents a refusal not only of remilitarization but also of modernization. However, in a process that I describe as characteristic of the *Heimatfilm* throughout this study, this outward resistance to change does not leave the space of Heimat itself unchanged. Indeed, this lesson is part of the socialist-realist project of *Das verurteilte Dorf*, which chronicles the politicization of Heimat. Characters such as the peasants, the mayor, and the priest conform to the socialist-realist demands for the "typical" by virtue of their ability to develop a revolutionary consciousness. Shown as passive, anticommunist, and fundamentally apolitical in the beginning, the villagers join in a process of politicization that determines the outcome of the film and serves to transform the very face of Heimat. *Das verurteilte Dorf* neatly encapsulates this project in the development of a set of three characters who might be taken as representative of three different aspects of Heimat. In a subplot of the film, the protagonist Heinz is pitted against the figure of Vollmer. Like Heinz, Vollmer served in the military, but unlike the protagonist, he has failed to develop the pacifist and collectivist ideals that Heinz brings home from Soviet captivity. Together with two war comrades, Vollmer prepares for the imminent reestablishment of a German army and enthuses, "If we maintain this tempo [of remilitarization], we'll soon be back on our estate in Mecklenburg." Vollmer the Junker thus stands for the reactionary forces in the West whose commitment to Heimat is tantamount to a renewed imperialist war against the East. Heinz, the incarnation of all that is positive about Heimat, radiates an active commitment to his hometown of Bärenweiler. Vollmer, who is not "rooted" there but arrived as a refugee from the East in 1945, can think of nothing better than to leave this *Drecknest* for a military career in the city.

The schematic opposition between these two figures is triangulated and ultimately resolved through the figure of Käthe. Though she had originally promised to wait for Heinz to return from the military, her father has forced her to marry Vollmer in the meantime. Marital tensions escalate with Heinz's return and with Vollmer's evolving plans for their move to Frankfurt. When Käthe first signs the petition for Bärenweiler against Vollmer's will and then refuses to come with him to the city ("What would I do in the city? I couldn't stand it for even a week!"), she comes into her own as an exemplary figure for Heimat. The development of Käthe's character provides the model for the development of a "Marxist-Leninist worldview and communist morale." As she joins the march to the city, first hesitantly and then triumphantly, she seals Vollmer's fate as well as that of his outdated ideals. In Käthe we witness how the new, socialist Heimat overcomes the old. Needless to say, the (re)establishment of the couple of Heinz and Käthe by the end of the film only reinforces this message.

This replacement of an old Heimat with its new, socialist counterpart, which I have described here in terms of character development, defines the overall project of the film. In the beginning, the local *Gemeinschaft* seems helpless, lacking both the arguments and the force to articulate its right to Heimat. But by the end of the film, the villagers are able to formulate that right in terms, and on behalf, of a series of interlocking collectives of which they are now an integral part. They have come to experience themselves as the necessary basis for a democratic society in which the local collective is joined by neighboring villages, by the workers in the nearby city, and ultimately by the entire German labor force. Far from solipsistic or isolationist, the new Heimat, in other words, becomes a space that is essentially inter-connected with its various "others" and which is therefore capable of refracting the national cause in the prism of the local. In sketching this politicization of Heimat, *Das verurteilte Dorf* negotiates a series of funda-mental transformations (including the *Entgrenzung* or de-limitation of a previously limited Heimat) within the confines of the local. As in *Einmal ist keinmal*, the logic of Heimat again depends on a successful articulation of tradition *and* change, using the local setting to bring home the benefits of socialist transformation. In other words, the "pacifist" message that won the film the Weltfriedenspreis and its Heimat message are two sides of the same propagandistic coin. In the eyes of the press, the film is a "unique patriotic document" for precisely this reason, "as it reveals the simple and profound truth: the defense of peace is the rescue of Heimat."[52]

COLLECTIVIZING HEIMAT: *SCHLÖSSER UND KATEN*

If *Das verurteilte Dorf* offers a schematic translation of propaganda imper-atives into cinematic narrative, *Schlösser und Katen* impressed critics with its absence of "construction and schematism." *Schlösser und Katen* was DEFA's hundredth film and Kurt Maetzig's first after his pair of monumen-tal Ernst Thälmann biopics (1954–55). It differs from the biopics especially in terms of its careful characterizations of a broad ensemble of different fig-ures. To this day, it remains an impressive document of an era, full of psy-chological detail. A two-part village epic, *Schlösser und Katen* traces a fitful process of reconstruction from the end of World War II through the mid-1950s. As we will see, notions of Heimat again stand at the heart of that process.

The setting is Holzendorf, a small village in northern Germany, in 1945. The local count has recently left in the wake of the war; now the villagers must reorganize the management of the estate and the cultivation of the land surrounding it. In the ensuing months and years, a number of con-flicting models for the survival of Holzendorf are proposed. Some suggest that the estate should rightly pass into the hands of Annegret, the illegiti-mate daughter of the count and his maid, Marthe. This possibility is pursued with particular persistence by a man known locally as "der krumme Anton" because of his hunchback. During Marthe's pregnancy, Anton had agreed to marry Marthe and to accept paternity for Annegret in exchange for a docu-ment in which the count promised to make the illegitimate child his right-ful heir upon her marriage. This piece of paper—referred to by the charac-ters simply as "der Schein"[53]—functions as a central motif of the film as it is passed from hand to hand, creating numerous misunderstandings, generating false hopes, and dashing others. Though neither Marthe nor Annegret knows of this document at the beginning of the film, Anton's intrigue receives the backing of the devious estate inspector Bröker, who wants to marry off his son to Annegret in order to benefit from her position. However, when Annegret learns of the promissory note, she feels that she has been abused by Anton's and Bröker's interests. Together with the young Heinz, she flees the village to study in the anonymity of the big city. As the camera lingers on the departing couple in a long shot of the rural landscape dotted by some newly acquired tractors, the German flag billowing prominently in the foreground,[54] a villager comments with an air of disappointment, "They'll have their child, get married, go to school, furnish the apartment, electric stove. . . . The city lets nobody return."

This image of a small, intrigue-ridden rural community that is being robbed of its young population by the lure of the city closes the first part of *Schlösser und Katen*, entitled "Der krumme Anton." This is a film rife with the generic concerns and images of Heimat: the abiding concern with tradition and modernization, family intrigue surrounding questions of heritage and legitimacy, the narrative importance of the opposition between the countryside and the city, and the ongoing negotiation of the meaning of the local are all familiar motifs from the films discussed so far. Similarly, the elaborate mise-en-scène of rural and agricultural scenes links Maetzig's film to the Heimat genre—from the credits that come up against a billowing tree to Anton and Marthe wielding their plow on the windy plain, from the community conducting its affairs after Sunday church, to the joint effort to bring in the harvest and the requisite parade replete with the sound of horns. All of these images would seem at first glance to derive from the same iconographic stock as the images in *Waldwinter, Die Trapp-Familie, Rosen blühen auf dem Heidegrab,* or *Wenn die Heide blüht.*[55]

The second part of the film provides additional material for such a generic pedigree. Its title, "Annegrets Heimkehr," already signals its concern with home and belonging. As the film opens, we see Annegret coming back to mend broken familial ties (while in the city, she had ceased to correspond even with her mother). The upbeat and idyllic images of Annegret's approach to Holzendorf in a horse-drawn carriage further underline the valorization of *Heimkehr.* The film's happy ending includes not only an Erntedankfest, but the marriage of Annegret and Heinz, which functions to integrate the community one more time. The mending of broken ties and the reestablishment of an inclusive *Gemeinschaft* reaches its poignant climax with the last line of the film, as Annegret calls for a glass for "my father"—referring not to the count, of course, but to "der krumme Anton." By the film's end, even the wayward social outcast whom "nobody wants, not even the police" has been rehabilitated, and Holzendorf celebrates a sense of Heimat regained.

However, *Schlösser und Katen* is again a *Heimatfilm* with a difference. For all its affinities with the genre, *Schlösser und Katen* clearly diverges from its typical concerns in some crucial respects. To the degree that *Schlösser und Katen* is indeed a "prototype for films about 'Heimat in socialism,'"[56] it exemplifies not only some remarkable parallels with Western developments, but also the labor of resignification that makes the notion of Heimat such an "important factor in the creation of a socialist society." As a chronicle of the postwar years, *Schlösser und Katen* lets us witness the complicated transformation of Heimat from its late-bourgeois abuses during and after the war into a future-oriented space of collective responsibility, a motor for the *Aufbau* of socialism during the 1950s.

Shot in an expressive black and white, and with a total duration of over three hours, the film takes its time to explore Heimat as a space full of contradictions, solutions, and new complications. While reviewers tended to complain about the unaccustomed length of the film and the multiplying layers of its narrative, they did acknowledge Maetzig's particularly nuanced portrait of the postwar years. Committed to balancing the celebration of successful steps towards a new socialist society with a reminder of its failures and dead ends, Maetzig's film is indeed a far cry from the propagandistic narrative of *Das verurteilte Dorf*. This is evident from the very beginning, where we are presented with an image of turmoil and transition, rather than with the lyric serenity of the opening scenes in *Das verurteilte Dorf*, let alone the tranquility we might associate with the picturesque openings of Western Heimat films. Maetzig's village chronicle begins in 1945, with the war in its final stages. After the credits have rolled (to foreboding symphonic music) against a tree blowing in the wind and silhouetted against a cloudy sky, we cut to a raucous party at the count's estate. Eventually, the estate inspector Bröker interrupts the festivities to announce that the British army will withdraw westward to the final demarcation line, to be replaced permanently by Soviet occupational troops. At this announcement, all hell breaks loose. Shouts of "Die Russen kommen!" punctuate the panic that ensues. The nobility, most of the evacuees from the east who had been housed temporarily in the stables, and some of the peasants take flight. The camera captures these scenes with few establishing shots, letting groups of people crisscross the frame of the image in medium shots as they scurry for their belongings and leave the estate with no discernible plan. With the din of screaming people and barking dogs in the background, herds of animals are set loose, adding to the mayhem. At the outset of the film, Holzendorf is hardly a stable, peaceful rural community.

After this tumultuous beginning, the actual arrival of the Soviet troops reshuffles the local hierarchy and reintroduces a certain sense of settledness. The few remaining communists who had apparently hidden their political convictions under the Nazi regime are given administrative offices by the occupational troops and are charged with finding housing for the scores of *Umsiedler* camping on the grounds of the estate. Though there is still a high degree of fluctuation among the inhabitants of Holzendorf, making this a transitory space, a relatively stable ensemble of characters begins to take shape. The film will tell their interlocking stories. Besides Kalle, Jens, and Hede, the upstanding communists who take on the labor of running and reorganizing the village, there are two principal families: the Brökers, who remain torn between staying in Holzendorf to hold out for a better future and fleeing across the "green border" to the West, if not to Canada; and Annegret's patchwork family, consisting of her mother Marthe and Anton the hunchback, whom she believes to be her biological father. The group is rounded out by the family of the hard-working *Umsiedlerin* Christel, who will rise to become chair of the new LPG; and by the young Heinz, a *Heimkehrer* who arrives from Soviet captivity in search of his mother. Having found her, in one of the most melodramatic moments of the film, Heinz turns out to be a young man full of useful practical knowledge and boundless energy. He represents a new generation that will build the socialist state from below and is the rival to the young Ekkehart Bröker, who has been promised Annegret's hand in marriage by his father and by Anton.

Once this ensemble is in place and the transition to peace has been accomplished with some remaining, others fleeing, and still others arriving, the narrative focuses on the large and small issues involved in creating a socialist Heimat. The traditional agricultural community of Holzendorf naturally takes great interest in questions concerning the ownership and cultivation of land. Crucial moments in the transition from private ownership to large-scale collectivization consequently make for central plot points in the film. Of particular importance are two scenes from the first and second parts, respectively, that portray first the redistribution of land according to the directives of the *Bodenreform* and then its collectivization as Holzendorf reorganizes its agriculture into an LPG. Both of these scenes, which echo each other in their mise-en-scène, represent moments of high tension as the successive reforms are visualized on parcel maps of the surrounding land. As the so-called *Neubauern* first receive, and later yield, their own plots, the politics of land reform and collectivization are not only localized in the exemplary village of Holzendorf, but also individualized: each gain or cessation of landownership becomes part of an individual story that remains to be reconciled with the abstract rationality of the state directive. In keeping with the socialist theorization of Heimat, it only becomes possible to speak of the latter when the state's rationality becomes concrete, when the national is mirrored and appropriated at the level of the local and is thus infused into the characters' sense of place.[57]

Under the official motto "Farmhands Become Farmers" (Jeder Knecht soll Bauer werden), the first of these two scenes enacts the subdivision of the lands seized from the count. The resulting plots are distributed to a host of *Neubauern* through a lottery. Even Marthe, whom Anton attempts to hold back, can finally realize her dream of owning "a piece of land and a few animals and something that belongs to *me*." The two principal characters to refuse the partition and reappropriation of land are Bröker, who would prefer instant collectivization of larger plots, and Anton, who remains suspicious of all change for fear of losing Annegret's ostensible claim to the estate. Both Bröker and Anton reflect deep-seated insecurities about the political future of East Germany. Repeatedly, they insist on the possibility that the transition to socialism is only temporary and that the clock will ultimately be rewound. On this basis, they refuse to participate in the project of rebuilding Heimat on a new foundation, hoping instead to gain by remaining loyal to the old.

In contrast to *Freies Land* or *52 Wochen sind ein Jahr*, this film does not portray the *Bodenreform* as an unmitigated success. Rather, *Schlösser und Katen* emphasizes the contradictory nature of the process and the need for improvement. Here, land reform clearly fails to create a society of equals; in particular, the distinction between the remaining *Großbauern* of the prewar era, who continue to hold land of their own, and the newly created *Neubauern* still carries significant social weight. Wary of the representatives of the old order, the *Neubauern* also have to overcome differences among themselves, for the luck of the draw has left some, like Marthe, with small plots and poor soil. From the lottery, we cut to a particularly melodramatic scene showing Marthe and Anton plowing their field in the distance. We see them only as silhouettes, tiny figures lost on the horizon between the expanse of land they are attempting to till and the overbearing sky, which fills two-thirds of the screen (see figure 12). It is Sunday, and while others congregate in the church, Marthe and Anton are forced to work the land to

Figure 12. Heimat between land reform and collectivization: *Schlösser und Katen* (1957). Courtesy Bundesarchiv-Filmarchiv, call no. 14446.

make ends meet. The music underlines the hopelessness of their situation as their cow breaks down and Anton takes its place at the plow.

The sequence has an important function for the film's goal of showing the development of a socialist consciousness, politics "in statu nascendi," as Maetzig put it:[58] while we empathize with Marthe's persistent dream of landownership, images such as this prove that she cannot make it on her own. Conveyed to the viewer in a single, well-crafted sequence, this realization takes the characters several years. Only gradually do the Holzendorfers see that the redistribution of land needs to be accompanied by the reorganization of labor in the village. But again, opinions on how to go about this differ. While some want to press ahead with further collectivization, others remain skeptical. Predictably, the *Großbauern* resist any attempts at collective labor (let alone ownership), since they depend on the availability of wage laborers for the cultivation of their own land.

Collectivization, which essentially annuls the results of the land reform in the name of equality and higher productivity, is staged to evoke the moment it *revokes*. Again, we see the villagers gathered tensely around a map of the land surrounding Holzendorf. Again the deliberations on how to proceed are not easy. And again, the character of Marthe serves to focalize the difficulties of these transitions. Her refusal to yield the plot of land she has been working so hard leaves a dark rectangle in the middle of the map on the floor, meaning that the collective will have to till around this "appendix," as one farmer calls it. Marthe's intransigence conflicts with the efficiency of the new machinery, suggesting that higher productivity depends not only on advances in the means of production, but also on each individual's insights into the economic necessity of collectivization. Only once she has come around to a fully developed socialist worldview—fostered, as we shall see, by the next generation—will Marthe finally sign up for collectivization.

As a dominant motif of the film, the gradual transformation of the means of agricultural production links fiction to politics, story time to historical time, and the local to the national. Without using documentary material, the film's realist aesthetic emphasizes the representative function of Holzendorf and the perceived historical accuracy of *Schlösser und Katen* as either a chronicle or a *Gegenwartsfilm* (film about the present). The film's realism was noted in its reception, which was dominated by tropes of authenticity: "That's exactly how it was," claimed the *Bauern-Echo*.[59] Contemporary responses amounted to a celebration of the bright present after a laborious past. Viewers and reviewers situated themselves in a temporal perspective that corresponds roughly to the endpoint of the film, when all of the contradictions have been solved, the past laid to rest, and there is a bright future ahead. Although Maetzig himself appears to have had some reservations about the neatness of this ending, which leaves behind the commitment to a logic of successive contradictions without permanent resolution, we now need to consider the face of Heimat after the transformations that the film has chronicled. Given the initial disarray of Holzendorf after the count's departure, the contradictions involved in successive phases of land reform, and the intrigue surrounding Annegret's position as the count's illegitimate daughter, does the film suggest any master narrative that would help us arrange its disparate and occasionally episodic moments into a coherent whole? What solutions does it offer to the contradictions it chronicles?

While a Western *Heimatfilm* built around similar motifs would have been likely to bring the question of heritage back into play towards the end of the film, this is not an option for Maetzig. Although the countess returns to her former hunting grounds, or *heimatliche Gefilde*, once in the second part, and though the worker uprising of June 17, 1953, poses one last dramatic challenge to the stabilization of the new order in Holzendorf, the role of the count is limited to that of an absent personification of the old order. A film like *Waldwinter* already chronicles the replacement of a feudal order by a new mode of production. *Schlösser und Katen* had to be even stricter in writing off the lure of the old. On the other hand, while Maetzig's work hardly emulates Liebeneiner's film of the same year in integrating the expellees from the East into a functioning capitalist economy, the two films share an underlying commitment to social and economic modernization— adjusted for the different meanings of that term under capitalism and socialism, respectively. Indeed, while this commitment may appear somewhat elusive in Western productions, it becomes an explicit motif in *Schlösser und Katen.*

Among the impressive ensemble of characters in Maetzig's film, one stands out as the embodiment of progress. This becomes evident especially in part two, which brings home a heroine of modernization. Together with the young Heinz, the local engineer and tractor repairman, Annegret represents the victory of science over nature, and of the new over the old. As in any number of *Heimatfilme* from the West, this function is tied to generation and gender. Though hardly a representative of the type of girlish femininity that characterizes the figures played by Sonja Ziemann and others in the West, Karla Runkehl's Annegret is decidedly a member of the young generation and a "new woman" for the GDR of the 1950s. As such, she serves to articulate a resolute ideal of progress without sacrificing the sense of the local that any such progress will threaten.

It is no accident that this task should fall to the daughter of Marthe, whose refusal to bow to the new order is as stubborn as it is motivated for the viewer. Unlike other enemies of change, such as Bröker and the various *Großbauern*, Marthe is clearly a figure designed with a view towards maintaining the viewer's sympathy; this serves to raise the stakes for her conversion to a socialist worldview at the hands of her own daughter. An exchange between Annegret and Marthe focuses the concerns raised by the negotiation between the old and the new. After Annegret's return and the ensuing reconciliation of mother and daughter, we witness the two women engaged in the everyday chores of peasant life. As they feed the chickens and sweep out the coop, Marthe exudes a basic contentment with the way things are beginning to fall back into place. With her daughter back in the fold, all she desires is stability, a couple of pigs, and a horse. Annegret, the recently graduated *Zootechnikerin* (veterinary technician), however, has more ambitious dreams: "Fatten up some pigs. Around two or three thousand of them." When her mother responds with exasperation, Annegret outlines her dream for the imminent future of Holzendorf, which she envisions as "rich . . . and clean, and not a fly in the stable anymore, nor in the parlor. And the people are all doctors and engineers. And in the evenings, I want to go to the theater, or to the movies, or to a concert." Marthe, gaping at her daughter's hubris, quickly concludes, "The city has spoiled you."

Needless to say, Annegret ultimately wins the argument. In the beginning, she has to work hard to regain the trust of the locals because Bröker has discredited her with gossip about her education ("studied, knows nothing, and is smarter than all of us combined") and about her alleged plans to inherit Holzendorf on the basis of the ominous *Schein*. Repeatedly, Annegret tries to go about her work, only to encounter a lack of cooperation if not downright aggression from the villagers. Even Jens and Kalle, the communist leaders of the village, mistrust her. In order to regain her reputation and her self-esteem, and to realize the project of modernization which she embodies more than any other figure in the film, Annegret needs to lose a double stigma in the eyes of the locals: she needs to dispel the negative connotations of having left Holzendorf for the city, and she needs to dispel the assumption that she has an interest in realizing Anton's plans for her to become the countess for whom she is taken upon her return.

These trials of Annegret at the diegetic level correspond in no way to her position in the eyes of the viewer. The film characterizes her as an innocent victim of Anton's and Bröker's intrigue who nonetheless takes her life into her own hands. The flow of story information keeps us better informed than any single character, ensuring that we understand the figure of Annegret as the well-intentioned incarnation of progress. The happy ending reinstates her as the luminous figure whose *Heimkehr* to Holzendorf and whose marriage to the young Heinz mark the beginning of a brighter, cleaner, and more efficient future. With Annegret in its midst, Holzendorf will become a community without flies and with cultural diversions for hard-working peasants-turned-engineers.

Maetzig's epic film exemplifies the degree to which the importance of the regional in DEFA cinema had an agropolitical dimension, which is equally present (though often less convincingly narrativized) in many of the other films discussed here. Different in their generic appeal and their didactic approach, all of these films work through "local" plots in order to establish and promote the redistribution and collectivization of land as one of the major concerns of the 1950s. An early documentary that took its title from the propaganda slogan *Junkerland in Bauernhand* (Junker land in the hands of farmers) describes the goal of a process that would last well into the 1950s. As this process was couched explicitly in a rhetoric and in images of modernization as socialist progress, the films under discussion once again underline the function of the local in the service of an overarching impulse of modernization. Whereas it is driven by capital in the West, this process is celebrated as the achievement of "Arbeiter und Bauern" in the East. Aside from this obviously central distinction I would argue that the main difference between East and West is thus not the presence or absence of the modern within the space of Heimat. Rather, the films differ in the degree to which they take on the force of modernization as their explicit *telos*, to be negotiated within the boundaries of the local (as in the East), or as a hidden conflict to be naturalized in the terms of the narrative (as in the West).

In other words, the rural plots—or *Ackerfilme*[60]—produced by DEFA during the 1950s differ from their Western counterparts in many respects, but like the *Heimatfilm* in the West, they work towards the modernization of rural spaces. The difference lies in their degree of self-consciousness. Both Bärenweiler and Holzendorf are literally representative villages, local metaphors for the national project of collectivization. This project is one of modernization both in the (social) sense that it transforms local space by opening it up to the national and in the (economic) sense that collectivization yields higher productivity. Where it touched explicitly on the trope of Heimat, this project required a reflexive approach to a term that was otherwise highly suspect for its late-bourgeois connotations. In order to function within DEFA's socialist agenda, Heimat needed to be rethought, if not reinvented. Figures like Edeltanne served to criticize its backwardness, clearing the way for its renewal by a socialist new (wo)man such as Annegret. Finally, in the parameters set by the cold war and as part of the resignification of Heimat, the local needed to be redefined against its "Fascist" and "imperialist" abuses in the West. It would take approximately another decade until this comprehensive critique of Heimat would travel back across the border. In the late 1960s, however, a handful of young filmmakers in the Federal Republic launched their own resignification as they (re)turned to the *Heimatfilm* in the context of the New Left and the New German Cinema.

PART III

Retrospects

Heimat is something lost.
EDGAR REITZ

8 Inside/Out

Spaces of History in Edgar Reitz's Heimat

It is now hard to think of Heimat in West Germany without thinking of the film *Heimat*.

ANTON KAES

Any contemporary narrative which ignores the urgency of the spatial dimension is incomplete and acquires the oversimplified character of a fable.

EDWARD SOJA

BROKEN IDYLLS: THE *ANTI-HEIMATFILM*

"Suddenly, they're back again: the valleys and the mountain peaks, the forests and the meadows, the pastures and fields."[1] Writing in *Die Zeit* in 1972, Wolf Donner noted a rebirth of the motifs and characters of the *Heimatfilm* on West German screens. After the early successes of the Young German Cinema, which included ambitious literary adaptations such as Volker Schlöndorff's *Der junge Törleß* (1966) and complex formal experiments such as Alexander Kluge's *Abschied von Gestern* (1966), here was a surprising run of films by young directors featuring hunters and priests, God-fearing villagers and local barons. Had not the renewal of West German cinema after the Oberhausen Manifesto of 1962 been premised on the rejection of the *Altfilm*, or "Papas Kino," epitomized by the *Heimatfilm* of the 1950s? Yet at the end of the 1960s, a number of *Jungfilmer* had begun turning out films that again centered on rural locales and tight-knit communities. But as Donner also noted, this was where the parallels with the *Heimatfilm* of the Adenauer era ended. Rather than a rebirth of the old, Donner saw in these films the birth of "the critical *Heimatfilm*—a new genre."[2]

In many ways, though, the generic coherence of these new interventions remains elusive. They included Bavarian Westerns such as *Jaider, der einsame Jäger* (1970), horror films such as *Lenz* and, later, Niklaus Schilling's *Nachtschatten* (1972), Brechtian costume films such Schlöndorff's *Der plötzliche Reichtum der armen Leute von Kombach* (1971), or theatrical adaptations such as Peter Fleischmann's *Jagdszenen aus Niederbayern* (1968), based on Martin Sperr's play from 1965, in the tradition of the *kritisches Volksstück*.[3] Though *Jagdszenen* has been credited with initiating this cycle of films—variously referred to as "critical," "new," or *Anti-Heimatfilme*—later films were by no means modeled on it in the same formulaic way in which, say, *Grün ist die Heide* reworked the ingredients of *Schwarzwaldmädel*. Only Rainer Werner Fassbinder followed in Fleischmann's steps by adapting Marieluise Fleisser's *Pioniere in Ingolstadt* (1971) and Franz Xaver Kroetz's *Wildwechsel* (1972); other directors were more inclined to marry the tropes of the *Heimatfilm* with the *Autorenfilm*'s mandate for originality. Thus, Reinhard Hauff co-wrote and directed *Matthias Kneissl* (1971), and Uwe Brandner wrote and directed *Ich liebe dich—ich töte dich* (1971). Consequently, what united these films was not so much the traditional signs of genre—such as shared narrative modes or iconographic repertoires—but rather a common generic reference. In their attempt to find an audience for a new German cinema, the *Jungfilmer* had turned to the *Heimatfilm* as an established popular tradition; the "new genre" was defined by the way in which it quoted the old.

This was an inheritance that the new directors wanted to turn upside down in a classic example of what Rick Altman calls "genre repurposing."[4] Given their political allegiances, which pitted them against "Papas Kino" and with the New Left of the late 1960s and early 1970s, these filmmakers all turned to the formulae of the *Heimatfilm* with an eye towards their subversion. Looking back on the brief cycle of *Anti-Heimatfilme* a decade later, Volker Vogeler, the director of *Jaider*, provided a graphic description of what motivated him and his colleagues at the time: "The present was visceral anger [*eine Wut im Bauch*]. . . . In our cinema, the *Autorenfilm* had come into crisis. We didn't have enough of an audience. We searched for a new narrative cinema and turned to the *Heimatfilm*. Until then [this had been] the most successful German genre. A welcome lie about an intact world [*heile Welt*]. We took the genre and its myths and turned them on their heads until the blood began to flow."[5] The image is fitting in its ambivalence. By turning the *Heimatfilm* on its head, the young directors wanted to stimulate reflection; in keeping with the politics of the generation of 1968, they also wanted to reveal the violent streaks that had remained buried under the repressive cloak of the Adenauer era. In previous chapters I argued that this "repression approach" does not hold up to close scrutiny of the 1950s, and that we may need to revise our habitual associations of the *Heimatfilm* of the 1950s with a *heile Welt*. But for the filmmakers who set out to inherit the genre in the late 1960s, when the Mitscherlichs had just formulated their diagnosis of the "inability to mourn," such associations were certainly a truism.

In other words, the infuriation at the politics, economics, and aesthetics of "Papas Kino" which the *Jungfilmer* had voiced in the Oberhausen Manifesto was still palpable in their appropriation of the *Heimatfilm*. When crafting their films, they went to great lengths to show the illusory nature of any Heimat idyll from the outset, to highlight the simmering violence that lurked in the provinces, and to confront audiences with Heimat histories of oppression rather than social harmony. The aesthetic means they employed could vary from Fleischmann's biting irony when he edits images of a filthy pigsty to lighthearted yodeling on the sound track, to the studied didacticism of the voice-over in *Der plötzliche Reichtum der armen Leute von Kombach*.

Such differences coalesced in an overriding formal penchant towards distanciation. A Brechtian impulse united most of these films on a formal level. Eric Rentschler has cataloged some of the formal principles that characterize these films despite their apparent diversity. He identifies, first, the self-reflexive use of the image as medium; second, the "textuality" of these films, the proliferation of intertextual references; and third, "the dynamic array of visual—and aural—earmarks inherent to the *Anti-Heimatfilm*."[6] Among the latter, Rentschler lists the studied use of lateral tracking shots, depth of field, and sound, as well as the recurrence of the long take. Taken together, these innovations are recognizable as part of a larger formal arsenal of the New German Cinema and other new waves of the 1960s. In a generic history of the *Heimatfilm*, they become legible as reversals of long-standing traditions. The emphasis on aesthetic openness and distanciation overturns the genre's perceived proclivity towards closure and enclosure; where panorama shots were included for spectacle and visual pleasure in the 1950s, *Kombach*'s tracking shots are designed to provoke reflection; Schlöndorff's modernist approach to the sound track replaces the use of folk and revue music as colorful background in a film like *Schwarzwaldmädel*.

The revisions also extended, of course, to the narrative contents generally associated with the *Heimatfilm*. Rather than focusing on expelled barons like Lüdersen or the patriarch in *Waldwinter*, the *Jungfilmer* brought the instruments of the *Heimatfilm* to bear on "people of humble origins, the lower classes, the exploited, the forever defeated and the rebellious."[7] Zooming in on the disenfranchised victims of German history in an effort to rewrite that history, their films offered revisionist accounts of class, as in Schlöndorff's *Kombach*; of the relationship between the individual and the state, as in *Matthias Kneissl*; or of sexuality, as in Fleischmann's *Jagdszenen*. What united these different approaches was a common interest in writing history from below. In the words of a reviewer of *Kombach*, these films centered on peasants "who survived the age of Martin Luther but did not live long enough to be energized by the age of Karl Marx."[8]

At the same time they were rewriting German history, however, the new *Heimatfilme* also investigated the German present from a position that *was* energized by Karl Marx. The resulting diagnosis of provincial life was bleak. Although the *Heimatfilm* of the 1950s had much more to say about the postwar present than the critics of escapism would have us believe, its picture of the Adenauer era was ruled by an imperative of harmony. Its use of Heimat as a space in which tradition could safely meet modernity allowed only for the idyllic reinscription of social problems and for their imaginary solution in the provincial microcosm. The new *Heimatfilm*, by contrast, staged the local as a site of profound social ruptures, of unreconciled hierarchies and stark class divisions, of prejudice and backwardness. Every bit as allegorical as the films of the 1950s, films like *Jagdszenen* suggested that the countryside was the seat of abiding Fascist mentalities. Fleischmann explicitly wished to indict the "everyday Fascism" that the New Left had detected in the Federal Republic at large. As a consequence, *Jagdszenen* is occasionally so bitter in its critique as to fall back into the friend/foe schemata that had informed the narrative logic of the *Heimatfilm* in the 1950s, merely reversing its polarities.[9] As the critic Günter Pflaum put it in a review of Fleischmann's film, its basic attitude was marred by a fatal "rejection of and animosity towards the characters and their milieu."[10]

To the degree that films like *Jagdszenen* were diatribes against the narrow-mindedness, provincialism, and bigotry of country life, these were indeed *Anti-Heimatfilme* more than anything else. And yet, critics like Donner, who preferred to speak of the "new" or "critical" *Heimatfilm*, could point to significant areas of overlap with the earlier tradition. Such continuities manifested themselves especially in the conception of space as a social and geographic microcosm with porous boundaries. Though the new *Heimatfilm* turned the values of staying and leaving upside down, it shared the genre's long-standing commitment to analyzing the social dynamics of the local, staged against a rural backdrop. The difference, of course, lay in the fact that the *Jungfilmer* conceived of the countryside as a prison. As Daniel Alexander Schacht points out in his study of the cycle, "The restricted village world of the new *Heimatfilme* is *unheimlich*, not Heimat as a place of security."[11] *Die Fremde*, traditionally the negative of the homeliness and security of Heimat, becomes revalorized in these films as a safe haven, its indeterminacy vastly preferable to the known oppression back home. By contrast, Heimat now became "the epitome of spatial boundaries, mental barriers, and material confinement."[12]

The *Anti-Heimatfilm* and its New Left agendas remained a passing phenomenon in the early 1970s, soon to be eclipsed by new waves of Ganghofer adaptations on the one hand, and on the other by more internationally successful productions in other genres by some of the same filmmakers who had participated in the brief revival.[13] It was not until the intervention of Edgar Reitz in the early 1980s that the notion of Heimat again struck a resonant chord both with an enthusiastic following at home and with an often very critical audience abroad. As Reitz's breakthrough to international fame some twenty years after he had co-signed the Oberhausen Manifesto, the fifteen-hour miniseries *Heimat* fused the legacy of the *Heimatfilm* from the 1950s with its revisions. The result was a film that was both reflexive and, in the eyes of some, naïve.[14] The notoriety that came with international recognition of Reitz's magnum opus had much to do with his conscious, and occasionally somewhat defensive, engagement with the Heimat tradition. In particular, I will suggest, Reitz once again reworked the formal devices and narrative patterns that had occupied the creators of the new *Heimatfilm* a decade earlier. His turn to Heimat as a social microcosm, his investigation of the boundaries that separate this space from a more or less defined outside, and his attention to the vectors that nonetheless link the world of the village to the history of the nation all owe equal debts to the work of Fleischmann, Hauff, and Vogeler, as well as to the *Heimatfilm* of the Adenauer era. In its remapping of Heimat geography, Reitz's film not only subsumes numerous aspects of the *Anti-Heimatfilm*, but also affords us a vantage point from which to review more generally the developments I trace in this book. Conversely, in returning to a film that has been so heavily debated by critics and scholars since its release in the early 1980s, the background elaborated in the preceding pages also allows us to shed some new light on these debates.

GEOGRAPHY LESSONS

In the second episode of Edgar Reitz's *Heimat*, entitled "Die Mitte der Welt," we are treated to a brief lesson in Heimat geography. This episode picks up the chronicle of the fictional village Schabbach, which the pilot episode had charted from the end of World War I to the late years of the Weimar Republic. After the unexplained departure of Paul, one of the central characters, life in Schabbach has returned to normal, only to be interrupted by the arrival of a young Frenchwoman on horseback. Her desire to visit the count of a nearby chateau that has been in ruins for over a century tests the locals' limited knowledge of French as well as their resourcefulness in providing a "room with a bath" before the advent of modern plumbing. As the villagers gather in front of the inn to debate the extraordinary event, the innkeeper remarks that "if you ride form Paris to Berlin, you have to go through Shabbach." In answer to the incredulous comments of some bystanders, the village mayor Alois Wiegand begins drawing some lines in the dirt to demonstrate that Schabbach is really the heart of Europe: "Here's Paris, and here's Berlin. And here's Schabbach. And the middle runs right through it. Draw a line from the North Pole to the South Pole, that goes through Schabbach, too." Reflecting on this revelation, a local exclaims: "Wir wisse gar net zu schätze, wo wir hier wohne!" (We don't know how to value where we're living), to which the mayor and would-be geographer replies, "I'm telling you, we're the center of the world."

What are we to make of a Heimat geography that situates the tiny village of Schabbach—and by extension the generic space of Heimat—at the center of the world? On the surface, the lesson is sophistic, since any point on the globe is on a line from the North to the South Pole. This sophistry—or is it just the limited intelligence of country bumpkins?—gives the lie to the locational hubris that envisions Schabbach as a global epicenter. The scene is patently ironic, as is the episode's title. In this view, both serve only to reinforce the provincialism that we would expect of a Schabbach or of cinematic treatments of Heimat more generally.

On the other hand, by connecting Schabbach to Paris and Berlin, by situating it on an imaginary map of the world, this little geography lesson alerts us to a fact far too often overlooked in discussions of Heimat and the *Heimatfilm*. No matter how retrograde, no matter how idyllic, and contrary to what superficial treatments of the genre have suggested, the spaces of *Heimat* need to be defined relationally. They do not exist in self-contained isolation from larger networks of circulation. Consequently, we must remain attentive to the role of these larger urban, industrial, modern networks within the cultural geography of Heimat, as well as to the role of Heimat within those networks. Reitz's film, I suggest, has the advantage of making explicit this relational mapping of Heimat. An important dimension of his contribution concerns the fact that notions of home have "always in one way or another been open; constructed out of movement, communication, social relations which always stretch beyond [the place called home]."[15] Focusing on Reitz's translation of movement, communication, and social relations into the formal, cinematic terms of his epic "cine-novel,"[16] this chapter aims to trace the location and dislocation of Heimat in *Heimat*.

PATTERNS OF GENRE AND RECEPTION

In an uncharacteristic twist on typical patterns of reception for the New German Cinema, *Heimat* was a hit with its home audience when it was first broadcast in 1984 but has troubled critics both in Germany and abroad. Here was a film made for television by a signatory of the Oberhausen Manifesto which garnered ratings of up to a quarter of the entire German population and has spawned a fan base on the internet;[17] and yet *Heimat* also drew sharp attacks as "an example of the current reactionary cultural climate" and a "dangerous whitewash of German history."[18] Applauded by filmmakers in Germany as a "requiem for the small people," Reitz's ambitious narrativization of Heimat left others irritated, if not enraged, for its "blatant tokenism," its "born-again German nostalgia," and his "unproblematic use of 'we', 'us', and 'our.'"[19] If, as Miriam Hansen claimed at the time, "The most significant aspect of *Heimat* [was] its reception," then we need to begin by elucidating what was at stake in the divergent responses to Reitz's series.[20]

In taking this point of departure, however, my purpose is not merely to recontextualize *Heimat* with the benefit of hindsight. Rather, I wish to return to Reitz's film, and to aspects of its formal construction in particular, in order to shift our focus back to what I consider a central preoccupation of *Heimat*. Often overlooked in the heated debates on Reitz's politics of history and memory, the film elaborates a sustained argument about the role and transformation of provincial space in German history. The questions to be asked of Reitz's series, in other words, go beyond those raised by the critics, who were by and large concerned with Reitz's politics of memory and his self-proclaimed role as "chronicler" of German national history. While these are admittedly central concerns of the series involving high political stakes, they need to be linked to questions derived from the longer history of the *Heimatfilm* concerning the function of space in *Heimat*. Such issues are implicit in critiques of the way Reitz locates Heimat "on the fringes of history,"[21] if not in a "place outside of history" altogether.[22] We should pose them explicitly: What is the role of the provincial in the series and what kinds of stories are told in that space? What boundaries are erected around Heimat, and how permeable are they? How does the film construct its profilmic space as well as the spatial compass of its *fabula*? To what degree does the series rely on a clear-cut distinction between inside and out, between proximity and distance, staying and leaving—a central category in Reitz's own reflections on his film?[23]

These are the questions a spatial reading of *Heimat* has to pursue, and I will propose some answers in looking more closely at Reitz's film. In the course of this review, I hope to reveal how *Heimat* foregrounds the historical dimension of provincialism, thereby offering an argument about the spatial sedimentations of historical time. A closer look at Reitz's insistent spatialization of history, I suggest, has the potential to reorient a discussion that has tended to elide the film's spatial historiography and which has focused instead on the temporal dimensions of memory, narrative, and historical discourse.

By the time of the series' initial broadcast, a number of discursive frameworks for the reception of *Heimat* were already firmly in place. These frameworks have been implicit in much of the literature on *Heimat,* and at least one recent publication provides a useful overview of them.[24] For the purpose of outlining the stakes involved in the debates on the film, I will therefore limit myself to a brief summary of the salient discursive contexts that have framed the discussion. These have been, first, the generic framework of the *Heimatfilm,* including the subcycle of the *Anti-Heimatfilm* discussed at the beginning of this chapter; second, the renewed attention to questions of *Heimat* and regionalism in German society and culture during the 1970s; third, the New German Cinema's "historiographic turn" towards the end of that decade; and fourth, a renewed public discourse on historiography more generally during the early 1980s.

The reception of *Heimat* was inevitably colored by a set of generic expectations that "help render films, and the elements within them, intelligible and therefore explicable."[25] Confronted with a TV miniseries that signaled its generic heritage even in its title, viewers were bound to look for the traditions of the *Heimatfilm* in Edgar Reitz's *Heimat.* They could find them in the film's rural milieu, its emphasis on the family as the basic narrative unit, and in its appeal to tradition and the continuities generated by female work in particular. Drawing the broadcast audience into an extended meditation on the notion of Heimat, Reitz's film traced familiar patterns of departure and return, stasis and mobility. Even the series' occasional avant-garde flights of fancy apparently did no harm to its appeal as mass entertainment for the German national audience. To claim that "the film basically doesn't differ much from the mainstream *Heimatfilm*" may be to overstate the case and to willfully overlook some of its innovative aspects.[26] But critics have been right to insist that some of the driving narrative conflicts between rich, obnoxious locals and less well-to-do but quintessentially good locals might have been taken straight from *Der Meineidbauer* or *Waldwinter.* On the other hand, Reitz's treatment of these conflicts was clearly filtered through the interventions of his colleagues a decade earlier: its interest in the gradual dissolution of Heimat marks the series as an *Anti-Heimatfilm* as well. The history of the genre thus provided templates for viewing the film either as 1950s-inspired nostalgia or as a post-1968 critique.

While the generic pedigree of *Heimat* inevitably has some bearing on how we read the film, so did the general "renaissance of Heimat feeling" in the late 1970s and early 1980s.[27] The divisive reception of *Heimat* must be seen against the backdrop of a new regionalism, the emergence of the peace movement, and the early political successes of the Greens.[28] Faced with the increasing internationalization of market economies, new volleys in the cold war (fought with particular intensity on East and West German territory), and the ever-present threat of nuclear catastrophe, the German left had taken an interest in the politics of the local. *Heimat* was arguably the most exposed manifestation of this new "Heimat feeling."

In addition, *Heimat* was part of a larger historiographic turn in German cinema. As Thomas Elsaesser puts it, "The New German Cinema discovered the past when filmmakers found history in the home and fascism around the family table. . . . The royal road in the 1970s of West German cinema to German history was family history."[29] In turning to Heimat as an organizing concept and to the *Heimatfilm* as a generic pedigree, Reitz's film seemed to beg the question of what, exactly, constituted the New German Cinema's "historical imaginary": Did *Heimat* exemplify a new type of history from below, did it help to undo tired meta-narratives about the German past? Or was this the German version of *la mode rétro*, a growing fascination with the Nazi past in which critics also implicated films such as Rainer Werner Fassbinder's *Lili Marleen?*[30] Especially given the nostalgic tone of *Heimat*, critics quickly began to wonder about Reitz's selective approach to German history and about the apparent desire for "normalization" driving that approach.

Such questions were inevitable given the timing of *Heimat* and the currency of historiographic questions in the West German public sphere of the 1980s. The initial broadcast of the series (on which Reitz had begun working in the late 1970s) coincided with the historians' debate of the mid-1980s.[31] With its focus on historical revisionism and on the relativization of the Holocaust in particular, this debate functioned as a discursive template on which to map—and evaluate—Reitz's film. Just as the historian Ernst Nolte had attempted to demote the uniqueness of the Holocaust to the status of a reaction, a copy of an earlier "Asiatic" deed, so did Reitz's chronicle of small-town life seem to relativize the Holocaust in its apparently naïve focus on the local. If this was local history, then it left critics with the feel-

ing that "the historical context [was] missing."[32] In the discursive context of
the historians' debate, *Heimat* was thus closely scrutinized not only for its
overt nostalgia, but also for its sins of omission and for its stance on the
revisionism that was at the heart of that debate.

The historiographic stakes of *Heimat* were further compounded by
Reitz's self-alignment with contemporary trends in *Alltagsgeschichte* (history of everyday life) and oral history. Reitz's commitment to a microhistorical approach in his research and in his published writings on *Heimat*
positioned him at the center of a debate on methodology which again had
far-ranging political implications. Here, the questions of uniqueness, selec-
tivity, and omission that defined the historians' debate resurfaced in terms
of historiographical perspective. What was to be gained, and what was lost,
in shifting from a macro- to a microhistorical approach? Especially regarding the history of the Third Reich, how would the oral historian maintain
his or her critical distance and avoid simply "sketching loving historical
miniatures of everyday life?"[33] As an "emblem for [the] *alltagsgeschichtlich*
approach to the writing of history,"[34] *Heimat* inevitably became caught up
in these polemics. Critics wondered out loud whether Reitz's dissolution of
history into individual stories "merely documents a projection" or whether
"these stories, narrated from the bottom up, capture something historical?
What are legitimate modes of narrating history in film?"[35]

In the discursive logics that framed much of the debate on the film, "legitimate" often turned out to mean comprehensive. Reitz has repeatedly been
taken to task for generating a historical vista that was judged to be lacking
on the basis of preconceived notions of macrohistorical accuracy. These
notions will always carry a specific political weight when it comes to interpreting Nazism and its aftermath, and Reitz's obviously selective narrative
maps all too easily onto a broader desire to "normalize" the German past by
"forgetting" its more problematic and traumatic aspects. On the other hand,
I think Alon Confino is right to criticize what he perceives as a "shift of the
discussion about the film from what really happens in it to what should have
happened, but did not."[36] Given the historiographic contexts outlined above,
this shift was all but inevitable at the time of *Heimat*'s release; with the benefit of hindsight it does seem glaringly obvious, though, that debates focused
far more on what Gertrud Koch identified as the structuring and predictable
"fade-outs"[37] of the film than on the sounds and images that it did comprise.
As Confino puts it, "The critics have faulted the film for sins of omission, at
times at the expense of paying attention to plot and action. And by concen-
trating on what does not take place in the film, we risk losing the meaning
of what does." [38] In other words, if we wish to gain any perspective on the

basic critique that charges Reitz with reactionary nostalgia for a local past uncomplicated by the course of national history, we need to return not only to a historically informed notion of Heimat, but, more importantly, to the film itself. Though reception was undoubtedly an important aspect of *Heimat* in its own right, Jim Hoberman clearly overstated the case when he insisted that it was "far more interesting than the film itself."[39] The interest lies, rather, in the occasional divergence of reception from the logic of the text itself, a divergence only close reading can reveal.

"THE CALL OF FARAWAY PLACES": FIGURATIONS OF SPACE AND MODERNITY IN *HEIMAT*

Where critics have taken the trouble to look at the film in any detail, Reitz's "sins of omission" would appear to consist especially in an elliptical structuring of historical time. Working on the assumption that "in *Heimat*, the main protagonist is time itself,"[40] these critics have taken *Heimat* to task for its idyllic reinscription of "cyclical" or "folkloric time," which functions according to the organic rhythms of nature, storytelling, memory, and experience. The implication has been that Reitz mourns the loss of this sense of time through a fundamentally elegiac, pastoral narrative that bemoans the gradual destruction of Heimat under the pressures of modernity. This view involves two related claims: first, that Reitz imagines Heimat as something intact and retrievable at the beginning, eroding over the time spanned by the historical narrative, and irretrievable by the film's end; second, critics have repeatedly held that the pressures under which Heimat crumbles all come to Schabbach from the outside (that is, from the metropolitan centers), and specifically through Fascism, portrayed as "originating in a Berlin brothel."[41] Accordingly, to many it appears that Heimat constructs its story of loss by projecting blame outward, to the point where the Reich appears "as the destroyer of Heimat."[42] Eric Santner sums up the logic of this argument when he writes: "The narrative figuration of experience and bereavement in the film orbits around the fantasy of a realm of cultural purity and authenticity, a place where the autochthonic voice of experience has not yet been harrowed by the ... plow of history."[43]

This notion of temporal decay is all too familiar in its distinction between an uncontaminated past, which belongs to memory (and which can be evoked by the mnemonic powers of the cinema), and the present, which belongs to the symbolic order of history and modernity. Such a reading finds support in Reitz's copious writings on his own activities as a filmmaker, which he describes as a kind of "memory work" that is essentially concerned with the problem of time and with the need to reconnect to earlier modes of experience buried by the culture industry.[44] These writings are indeed vulnerable to critiques of revisionism and nostalgia, and some of them are downright shocking, as Gertrud Koch rightly asserts, "in that they betray an amazing decline of historical sensibility."[45] But it seems to me that the same critiques are misdirected when leveled against the film itself rather than at Reitz's written interventions in the critical debates *on* the film. In particular, the emphasis on the temporality of *Heimat*, and on the nostalgic privileging of the "good" past over the "modern" present, fails to take into account Reitz's manifest—though less reflexive—concern with space.

Although the question of space is central to the very definition of Heimat, as I argued in previous chapters, few commentaries on Reitz's film have taken up that question other than in a cursory way.[46] Where they do address the geography of *Heimat*, it is either in a metaphorical sense or it has been to emphasize, if only in passing, the closed world of *Heimat*. Santner, for example, emphasizes the sharp line that protects the "idyllic matrix" of Heimat as a "realm of cultural purity" from intrusion by various "outsiders" and "others." Quoting Mikhail Bakhtin, Santner describes the world of *Heimat* as a "spatial corner of the world where the fathers and grandfathers lived and where one's children and their children will live. This little spatial world is limited and sufficient unto itself, not linked in any intrinsic way with other places, with the rest of the world."[47]

Given the ironic, self-reflexive inscription of Schabbach as the "center of the world," I have doubts as to whether *Heimat* really does constitute the de-linked "little spatial world" Bakhtin describes. According to Santner, Reitz generates that world as a way of maintaining its integrity, fending off intrusion or change, and scapegoating outsiders for any form of change that does occur.[48] In this reading, Heimat can only be maintained by "violently excluding from its territory the representative agent of an external threat or aggression."[49] To the degree that the external threat is defined here—as in most Heimat films—in terms of modernization, Reitz's film would then indeed be nothing but a nostalgic return (through experience and memory) to local traditionalism, a celebration of the provincial as independent from, and resistant to, the "plow of history." But I would suggest that another spatial reading of the film is possible, one which emphasizes the tension between nostalgia and critique inscribed into the film's play between home and away, inside and outside.

Heimat signals its concern with space on several levels, beginning with the title of the first episode, called "Fernweh" (The Call of Faraway Places). At first glance, this choice of title would appear to constitute a misnomer: the primordial longing associated with Heimat, the series's title, would have to be *Heimweh*, the desire to return home, not *Fernweh*, the desire to leave home.[50] If there is a directionality to Heimat—that is, if the concept of Heimat doesn't refer to an entirely static, self-contained sense of place to begin with—then should the primary impulse not be inward? Is Heimat not by definition a centripetal force, a "spatially perceived small world turned outside in"?[51] Isn't Heimat a notion that harnesses *Fernweh* and redirects it towards hearth and home as the center of gravity?

Such notions of Heimat do play a role in Reitz's film, as I will show. But the decision to begin the series with "Fernweh" and to save a title like "Mitte der Welt" for the second episode, signals another dimension at the heart of the topic. In addition to turning the world "outside in," this series will also chart a vector from the inside out and negotiate the desire for leaving home.[52] From the outset, there is thus a double directionality that corresponds to two distinct articulations of space as centripetal on the one hand and centrifugal on the other. The first images of the film, for example, carefully retrace the steps of an emotional return. We open with a homecoming, a distinct trajectory from the outside—France, the battlefields of World War I—to the inside, as Paul, a returning soldier, takes up his place at the anvil in his father's forge. This movement, which gathers speed as Paul draws closer to home in the opening sequence, initiates the centripetal organization of Heimat space. In this view, the narrative of *Heimat* encompasses a space that is best described as a series of concentric rings around Maria's kitchen, and whose gravitational pull the film's second sequence will soon establish. On the other hand, however, from the very beginning of the fifteen-hour narrative, the centripetal place of Heimat competes with a centrifugal directionality in the spatial logics of Reitz's film, signaled by the *Fernweh* title. Aligned with different aspects of modernization, the proliferating manifestations of centrifugal movement and space in *Heimat* exert a pull on the film's notions of home, hearth, and belonging that draws into question any enclosed definition of its organizing concept.[53] For all its unique and homely qualities, Schabbach is connected to a bigger picture from the outset. The very first minutes of this extended narrative, then, already go a long way toward suggesting that inside and out are not going to be easily separable, diametrically opposed notions in this film. The simple, static notion of place that its title may promise will turn out to be part of a carefully constructed spatial dialectic.

Reitz's film carries through this deconstruction of Heimat place in its careful and detailed construction of space through mise-en-scène, editing, and especially cinematography. Even the most cursory viewing of the film reveals a sustained formal concern with the relationship between inside and outside, enclosed and open spaces as the camera looks in and out through windows, as it switches from highly subjective points of view to positions of lofty omniscience, and as it travels in circles around characters and objects and charts vectors of departure and return on long open roads leading into the distance. This treatment of space is remarkable enough for its innovative aesthetic choices. Its significance ultimately lies, however, in the deconstruction of received spatial binaries, from the distinction between inside and outside, centripetal and centrifugal space to the topography of Heimat and *Fremde* itself. Emphasizing the interplay between open and closed spaces, it gestures towards "a progressive notion of home, Heimat, and community, which does not necessarily depend on the exclusion of all forms of otherness, as inherently threatening to its own internally coherent self-identity."[54]

If the opening shots of Paul's homecoming already suggest a fundamental spatial ambivalence, the extended scene that follows further elaborates the dialectic between inside and outside. After Paul arrives at his father's side in the forge, Reitz makes a cinematic beeline for the kitchen. The function of this fifteen-minute scene, which serves as a kind of extended establishing shot that enables the narration of Heimat, is not merely, as Elsaesser suggests, to "establish the interactive, productive, and reproductive time that knits the families together."[55] Although the leisurely timing of the kitchen scene does initiate the viewer into the film's unique temporality, I would argue that its main function is to establish a particular sense of space to which the film will return, which it will invest with meaning, and which it will expand over fifteen hours of screen time. In many ways, the kitchen will turn out to be the epicenter of *Heimat*, around which its characters and its stories revolve.

The gravitational pull of this kitchen is centered around a pillar at the end of the kitchen table. Paul leans against this pillar as the villagers flock in to greet the prodigal son. Initially, the camera takes up a position behind Paul's right shoulder, allowing us to observe with him—and with his slightly detached, curious gaze—the ongoing activities in this busy space. His mother Katharina and his sister Pauline prepare some food and exhort him to eat; his brother Eduard sits at the window reading the newspaper. Gradually other villagers appear, inquiring about Paul, discussing the years of the war, snippets of the day's news provided by Eduard, and local gossip. As the characters move about the increasingly crowded kitchen, the camera follows them and takes up various positions that gradually, if imperceptibly, describe a circle around the central pillar. Once Eduard moves from a window opposite the door to the second window behind Paul's back, the camera has come full circle as it frames Paul's left shoulder from behind in a reverse shot marking his reaction to an item read out loud by his brother. Gradually circling around the kitchen's central pillar and around the figure of Paul, the placement and movements of the camera thus underscore the concentric and centripetal construction of space, anchoring the notion of *Heimat* that the film will develop as if around a magnetic pole. We are immediately aware that this is a place to which the story will return over and over again, a place where large- and small-scale events become telescoped into the inner sanctum of Heimat.

But if space is in this sense centered and at rest around the kitchen as its inner sanctum, evoking a premodern sense of immediacy and tradition, the kitchen sequence also offers a number of cues for a second reading of space that will gain equal importance over the course of *Heimat*. The ability of the community that repeatedly assembles in this kitchen to anchor Heimat around the Simon family's table is also called into question. Clearly traumatized by the war, Paul, for one, is an unstable center in the kitchen scene. He drifts in and out of the ostensible warmth of this *Gemeinschaft,* and his hallucinatory encounter with the ghost of a neighbor provides a stark contrast to the seemingly harmless banter around him. Paul's trauma indeed can be understood as the basis for his *Fernweh,* a sensibility that the opening of the film marks as coterminous with any longing to return. Moreover, as a metonymic representation of the film's notion of Heimat, the kitchen itself is "open" to the outside in ways that conventional readings of *Heimat* would not allow. Although it carefully circles the interior, Reitz's camera cannot contain the intimacy of the kitchen as a metonymic place of Heimat. Nor is this really the singular intention of the scene, whose construction of the kitchen space hovers between intimate and claustrophobic to begin with.

The second, centrifugal aspect of the kitchen sequence is particularly apparent in the role played by Paul's brother Eduard—for a long time Reitz's favorite character in the film, and the protagonist of the first two episodes, according to the director.[56] Reitz positions Eduard at the kitchen window as he comments on the events outside and reads aloud from the local newspaper. Again and again, the camera returns to him as if to a relay station for the world beyond the kitchen. In the larger context of *Heimat,* this device is important in two ways: first, Eduard's position at the window introduces the cinematographic motif of shots framed through windows, looking out or looking in.[57] For example, in an over-the-shoulder shot of Eduard leaning out of the window, we see Wiegand ride by on his newly acquired motorcycle, which in turn becomes the object of gossip among the people gathered inside the kitchen. This self-reflexive positioning of the camera to articulate the relationship between inside and outside is amplified by a number of relatively unmotivated shots later in the kitchen scene of a boy named Hänschen Betz, who peers into the kitchen window from outside with his one good eye. The cinematic motif of shooting through windows is hardly unique to *Heimat* (Fassbinder's signature shots using windows and doorways as interior framing devices come to mind). But I would argue that this motif takes on a special relevance in a film so insistently concerned with distinctions between home and away, self and other. The window motif miniaturizes those overriding concerns by cutting back and forth across the threshold that divides inside from out, asking viewers to look in on the enclosed world of home, comfort, and belonging from the outside, but also to look out from that same world to the goings-on beyond the local. By connecting the kitchen space to the outside world and gesturing beyond its ostensible warmth, Reitz has already begun to explode the sense of place that his film investigates. This project will be picked up quite explicitly in later scenes that treat Heimat as a space phantasmagorically connected to national geography, that emphasize the centrifugal force of telephone wires and highways that link Heimat and *Fremde,* or that emphatically de-idyllize the landscapes of *Heimat* using time-lapse photography to emulate the speed of a military jet on a reconnaissance mission.

Eduard's other important function in the opening kitchen scene is related to the newspaper from which he reads. His occupation with a mass medium that transports the world at large into the Simons' kitchen prefigures the series' preoccupation with the spatial consequences of technological advances in communications media. As they fuss over Paul, the villagers learn about Mayday in London, shootings in Russia, and a streetcar robbery by Spartacists in Munich. Like Wiegand's motorcycle, these events in "faraway places" become the object of sometimes heated and occasionally hilarious local debate. Pauline reacts to the news from Munich with the relieved exclamation "Thank God we don't have a streetcar here in Schabbach!" and her aunt Marie-Goot decides firmly that "I will never go to the city as long as I live." Although such comments may reveal the limited and conservative worldview of the characters, they also begin to give the viewer a sense of the broader horizon in which to place them, asking the viewer to take up a position that is not identical or even aligned with that of the characters, no matter how great his or her sympathy for them may be.[58] By having Eduard read out events going on elsewhere, Reitz does more than merely provide some historical color for his fiction; rather, he lays the groundwork for a

Heimat narrative constructed on the understanding that "the place called home was never an unmediated experience."[59] The "mediation" of home through the history of the media is one of the stories that Reitz's film tells quite explicitly, reflexively, and with as much fascination as with nostalgia. An early shot shows the mail carrier "pedaling hard [on his bike] to connect Schabbach with the outside world."[60] Subsequently, Schabbach acquires radio reception, becomes electrified and increasingly motorized, and is connected to the telephone grid. In this process, the places of *Heimat* become remapped onto an expanding network of modernization. The effects of the history of communication register most acutely in terms of eroding spatial boundaries and the remapping of premodern place onto distant relations in modern space.[61]

A later scene again links this remapping to the window motif. In episode three, entitled "Weihnachten wie noch nie," the community has gathered in the local church. Wiegand has chosen to stay home and put on a record as he decorates the Christmas tree. A medium close-up from outside his window frames Wiegand inside. Although the camera is positioned at great distance from the window, using a long focal length, the sound track places us right inside the room as Wiegand selects the record and starts the gramophone. Aligned visually with the camera on the outside, the viewer is simultaneously positioned aurally on the inside. Wiegand's slightly theatrical gestures as he puts on the record suggest that he is engaging in a symbolic ritual act (the hackneyed poetry that issues from Wiegand's gramophone amounts to a Nazified Christmas sermon). Isolated from his immediate neighbors and held in the tight frame of his window, Wiegand forsakes the local community gathered in the nearby church and instead joins the absent community of the "we" addressed by the speaker on the record. Framed acoustically by the "Horst-Wessel-Lied" and a Christmas carol, the record constructs an imaginary community united under the leadership of God and *Führer*. This community is national in the Fascist sense of the word: a "pure" ethnic group, defined in terms of a *völkisch* "we" who "must and want to liberate the country, in order to be of pure German stock." Invoking the expansionist rhetoric of *Lebensraum*, this racist conception of community both exceeds the confines of Schabbach in its disembodied form as a recording and is impersonated within the village by Wiegand as he assumes his Hitler pose in the window.

The scene evokes a stock image from German (and Hollywood) films dealing with National Socialism in which the disembodied recorded voice of Fascism, broadcast via a diegetic radio, serves to anchor the historical fiction in (quasi-)documentary evidence. Reitz's use of a historical SA Christmas record performs precisely this function, as it "authorizes" its local fiction, using an *objet trouvé* to document an aspect of everyday life under Fascism. But in the present context, this "documentarizing" gesture also works to establish a particular spatial argument. Not only do we witness Wiegand from the outside, but hear from the inside; as the record continues to play, the camera eventually leaves Wiegand's home and focuses on the deserted, snow-covered streets of Schabbach. In the viewer's perception, the diegetic source of the radio speech thus fades from view, and the latter becomes part of an extradiegetic sound track that breaks the boundaries of the fiction as it crosses the closed window that would separate "us" from Wiegand. As the voice continues to invoke a *völkisch* community over the images of Schabbach, the audiovisual construction of the scene emblematizes the reach of the Nazi regime, mediated through communications technology, *across* spatial boundaries of inside and outside.

The use of technology in this scene to generate an absent or distant community that becomes telescoped into Schabbach through the figure of Wiegand mirrors another use of technology in *Heimat*, namely to generate local forms of community in which villagers interact with distant events. The key technologies in this respect are the radio and the telephone. Significantly, Reitz does not treat these media as threatening aspects of modernization that atomize the public sphere, fostering individualization and a wholesale retreat to the private. Rather, historical innovations in communications technologies tend to prompt village gatherings and foster collectivity. A quintessential example occurs early on, when Paul first completes the construction of his radio and the entire community gathers at a nearby ruin to partake in the broadcast of a mass from Cologne. Generating a "public sphere . . . focused around a technological invention,"[62] this scene provides the mirror image of Wiegand's recorded Christmas. Whereas the record provides a local source that links Wiegand to an absent community, the radio captures a distant source that underlines the present community in Schabbach. The scene at the ruin illustrates the communal function of the radio, as well as its ability to fold spatial distance into relations of proximity.

Both of these aspects of radio are taken up again in the penultimate episode, "Die stolzen Jahre." A particularly wistful episode that replays a number of earlier narrative events as so many internal memories of *Heimat*, "Die stolzen Jahre" reiterates the scene at the ruin in the way it stages a live broadcast of Paul's half brother Hermann's debut as a composer with a composition entitled "Bindungen." The performance of the piece at the radio station provides a continuous sound track that ties together listeners in different locales, from the studio audience in the town of Baden-

Baden to the villagers in Schabbach who have gathered in the local pub to listen to the broadcast. The live transmission allows Reitz to cut between various locales in Schabbach and the studio without forsaking continuity; the dispersed listeners come together as a simultaneous audience. However, due in large part to the modernism of Hermann's composition, the integrative power of radio is also drawn into question as the villagers, with the exception of Glasisch-Karl, the village idiot, fail to comprehend what they are hearing. This disintegrative moment is most poignant in the phone call—also during the broadcast—of Hermann's mother Maria to her son Anton, both of whom have chosen to listen to the broadcast in the privacy of their own homes. Whereas Anton scorns his half-brother's art but nevertheless has his family around him to share the event, Maria sits alone in her kitchen. Listening to the avant-garde composition and failing to recognize its strangeness and beauty, Maria despairs at what she senses is an insuperable generation gap. Indeed, this split between mother and son is more than just a matter of generational difference in tastes. Rather, given Hermann's manifest mobility (later in the episode he stops by his mother's kitchen "on the way from Paris to Berlin," directly evoking the global remapping of Schabbach in "Die Mitte der Welt"), and given Maria's apparent inability to leave Schabbach other than "with the finger on the map," as she puts it, the broken emotional *Bindung* illustrates the costs of linking Schabbach to other places and of geographically expanding the horizon of home and family.

It is no coincidence that during the broadcast of Hermann's composition, Maria communicates this realization to Anton (and to the viewer) via telephone. Even more than records or radios, the telephone networks Schabbach and maps it in relation to an invisible yet determining spatial grid. Here, the quintessential example occurs in the episode entitled "Heimatfront," which features the *Fernehe* of Anton and Martha. If marriage would appear to be one of the cornerstones of Heimat as a place of *Gemeinschaft* determined by relations of proximity and presence, then the *Fernehe*—a marriage by proxy and at long distance—would be a safe indication that Heimat now functions according to a larger, emphatically modern logic of space. No longer requiring the presence of both partners, this type of marriage wrests time from place by allowing temporal simultaneity (Anton and Martha make their vows at the same time) in the face of spatial distance (Martha is in Schabbach, Anton at the eastern front). The mediating technology that seals this long-distance marriage is the long-distance telephone call that allows "the Heimat [to] reach every soldier via telephone." As Wiegand holds the receiver, waiting for the call to the front to go through, his son

Wilfried muses, "Who would think, crossing the fields from Schabbach, that these telephone wires are part of a network that covers all of Europe." As in the earlier gramophone scene, however, the camera does not stay inside the parlor for the duration of Wilfried's speech; instead, Reitz cuts to the telephone wires Wilfried invokes, and the camera follows them into the snowy distance as if to intimate the larger network onto which Schabbach is being mapped through the new technology.

The extensive attention that *Heimat* devotes to the telephone has a number of implications. In the *Fernehe* scene, it links Schabbach to war and war to modernization. As such, the telephone becomes the agent of what Anthony Giddens calls "disembedding," enabling marriage at a distance and undoing the links between intimacy and proximity, interaction and presence. But again, communication at a distance is imagined in *Heimat* as a collective endeavor. The phone call is by no means a private affair: in Schabbach, the receiver gets passed around a room full of guests, and in a parody of the imaginary community generated by the telephone, Anton's new mother-in-law (whom he has never met) waves to him when her presence is mentioned to Anton over the phone. On Anton's end, the conversation is even more directly hooked into a broader public, as it is filmed for the weekly newsreel from the front. In a series of highly self-reflexive shots, we watch the spot and the focus being adjusted, and the captain in charge of the filming gives last-minute stage instructions to Anton, whose conversation with his bride consequently turns from helpless to ridiculous. The difference between the communities at either end is obvious. While the camaraderie at the front is clearly staged and mediated by the demands not only of the telephone but also of the film medium and of the propaganda effort that it serves, the community in Schabbach is utterly authentic by comparison. Instead of foregrounding the alienating effects of technology, Schabbach integrates the telephone into its communal fabric, all but naturalizing its effect.

The scene of the *Fernehe* spells out the spatial consequences of telecommunication. As David Morley points out in an article on the relationship between household, family, community, and nation, communications technologies such as the telephone have "the simultaneous capacity to articulate together that which is separate (to bring the outside world into the home) but, by the same token, to transgress the . . . boundary which protects the privacy and solidarity of the home from the flux and threat of the outside world."[63] Such a spatial reading of technology's ability to alter relations of proximity and distance goes a long way toward explaining the significance of the extended *Fernehe* sequence and its emphasis on linking bride and groom, home front and war front through a phone call. It also suggests that we revise the geographical location of Heimat at the center of the world and situate Schabbach instead within a far more decentered network of communication and transportation that "spans all of Europe" but no longer maps onto the straightforward coordinates of North, South, and metro-poles.

As I have been suggesting, Reitz's film repeatedly illustrates this aspect of the general process that Giddens describes as "disembedding." Importantly, Reitz shows this process to take place not just "elsewhere"; neither modernity nor Fascism is simply imported from the metropolis and its brothels, but both are located within the community of Heimat. In the spatial logics of Reitz's film, Heimat provides no sanctuary against disembedding or modernity. However, in the recurring motif of the communal use of modern technologies, Heimat does serve more than once to hide the consequences of modernity, whether we describe them as alienation, individualization, or more generally as disembedding. Much like the *Heimatfilm* of the 1950s in this respect, Reitz's *Heimat* mitigates the effects of modernization. As in the case of earlier films such as *Waldwinter* or *Die Landärztin*, the point is not that Reitz "fails to embrace the complexity of modernity," as critics have claimed.[64] Rather, the problem lies in the way Reitz treats that complexity by folding it back into the lure of Heimat as a premodern space.

HEIMAT AS SPATIAL METONYM

In my reading, what is ultimately at stake in Reitz's film is the relationship between nation and Heimat redefined as a relationship between history and space. The first set of terms, *Heimat* and *nation,* is familiar enough, and it has provided the focal point for virtually all discussions of the film to date. Reitz himself has maintained more than once that "Heimat and nation . . . are contradictory terms."[65] But this is a disingenuous claim for a film that superimposes the title *Heimat* on the phrase "Made in Germany," which is chiseled in stone. If there is one common theme to the multifaceted reception of Reitz's film, it has been the tendency to read Schabbach as Germany. In these allegorical readings, *Heimat* represents a local metaphor for the nation. All of the discursive frameworks outlined earlier favored such a reading, none more so than the contemporary cinematic intertexts. Thomas Elsaesser has even described the array of allegorical films from the New German Cinema as a genre that "filters public events through their private repercussions." This genre, he argues, "virtually imposes itself whenever Fascism, the War or the post-war period are dramatized."[66] Elsaesser also notes a danger inherent in this genre, however, in that it trades on "an all-too-ready symbolism: Germany is linked to the feminine, motherhood, sisterhood; the land, the regions, the seasons come to stand for the nation, and History along with women and the family are reclaimed as Nature."[67] To the degree that *Heimat* centers on Maria as a living calendar, turns historical time into cyclical and biographical time, and makes the family the measure of all things social and political, the allegorical implications of this film are troubling indeed. Particularly if we read Maria as another Germania, as Eric Rentschler suggests, *Heimat* joins a representative list of New German Films whose mise-en-scène of national history overlaps in disturbing ways with the revisionist discourses of the contemporary historians' debate. In each case, the emphasis is routinely on victimhood rather than on perpetration, on daily life at the expense of big politics, on nature rather than on history, and on some version of Heimat competing with the repressed dimension of the Holocaust.[68]

In *Heimat*, these generic slippages and their historiographic implications are further compounded by the long history of a concept that has tended to function as a metaphor for the nation. If Alon Confino is right to read "the Heimat idea as a symbolic representation of the nation-state,"[69] then Heimat is itself already an allegory. Preestablished historically and culturally as a microcosmic representation of the greater whole, the Heimat allegory then becomes allegorized once over in Reitz's narrative. His film retells German history from below, as if through a camera obscura that captures the "German" panorama in a small box labeled Schabbach. But as Confino's work also suggests, the structure at the heart of Heimat as a local metaphor is not so much that of a microcosm that could substitute for the larger world as it is one of association: "The network of local, regional, and national Heimat associations corresponded to the constitutive metaphor of the Heimat idea—the metaphor of the whole and its parts."[70] This is to say that the constitutive metaphor of the Heimat idea is actually not a metaphor at all, but a metonymy.

This distinction is significant for the way in which we read *Heimat*. As elements of figurative speech, metaphors "involve a transfer of meaning from the word that properly possesses it to another word which belongs to some shared category of meaning."[71] As a metaphor, Heimat would share in the meaning of nation, a meaning that is transferred from the greater whole to the smaller world as its microcosmic mirror image. Metonymy, by contrast, tends to assume a more complex set of articulations involving the relationship between individual parts and a greater whole. As Thomas McLaughlin points out, "Metonymy does not call for the magical sharing of meaning that a metaphor implies; instead, it relies on connections that build up over time and the associations of usage." Metonymy, he suggests, "places us in the historical world of events and situations, whereas metaphor asserts connections on the basis of a deep logic that underlies any use of words."[72]

Read metonymically, Heimat relates to nation *not* on the level of similarity where one can substitute for the other, as metaphorical readings claim. Rather, the constitutive relationship here is one of contiguity, and as such it necessarily involves a spatial dimension. Viewing the space of *Heimat* as a metonymic construction allows us to avoid two common misreadings, neither of which is borne out by a closer look at the film. The first would claim that Heimat is coextensive with Germany, a comprehensive metaphor for the greater whole which could be faulted for any number of "sins of omission." The second misreading, upheld by Reitz himself, among others, posits Heimat and Germany simply as binary opposites.[73] In the proposed metonymic reading, by contrast, Heimat functions as one of many parts that make up a larger whole as so many links in a chain. Schabbach is clearly *linked* in numerous ways to the national—by telephone wires, roadways, and railways, by vectors of departure and return, by imaginary maps of the world and equally imaginary journeys on those maps. To the degree that Schabbach is not spatially isolated but connected to larger networks of culture, society, and nation, Heimat appears as a spatial metonym whose links to the outside we must follow as carefully as its construction of an internal space of Heimat.

In this respect, it is no coincidence that one of the central events in the history of Schabbach, with repercussions reaching outward to the Reich and inward, deep into the family structure of the Simons, is the building of the *Reichshöhenstraße*, the highway that gives the fourth episode of *Heimat* its title. Conceived as a network that would cover all of Germany and redefine the very nature of national space, the *Reichsautobahn* was designed as a metonymical project from the start; the *Reichshöhenstraße* in the Hunsrück would become one part of a whole, "all structures would fit together as individual links in a chain spanning the Reich."[74] The construction of the highway brings workers, engineers, money, and travelers into the village; inevitably, it also carries those same workers and others back out and transports anonymous travelers through the region. Like the historical project on which it is modeled, the *Reichshöhenstrasse* becomes "medium and message in one, a means to conquer spatial distance that also transforms the meaning of the territory it traversed."[75] This is made explicit at the beginning of episode five, when some villagers contemplate the passing cars on the nearby highway and reflect on the changes it has wrought in local geography: "The road used to lead from one village to the next," comments

Glasisch-Karl; "Now it goes past them." "That's modern times for you," responds another villager, explaining that the drivers cannot be bothered with too many curves and stops.[76] But Glasisch-Karl is trying to get at something else: with the new road, travel itself has become a far more abstract experience, one that takes the driver down highways and across interchanges rather than through villages and across town squares. As Edward Dimendberg rightly suggests, the "highway may well be the pre-eminent centrifugal space of the twentieth century."[77] In the *Reichshöhen-straße* episode, Reitz couples that outward direction with a reference to Schabbach as an enclosed world, cut off from centrifugal space. As another would-be cultural geographer of Heimat puts it in the film: "Anyone who goes from Paris to Berlin does not pass through Schabbach anymore as he used to. Many people will come here to the Hunsrück whom we will never get to see."

The heated debates around *Heimat* testify to the fact that it remains one of the most intriguing interpretations of German history in recent years. To my mind, this has as much to do with Reitz's nuanced deconstruction of place as with his treatment of memory or with the function of *Heimat* as a historical chronicle. Reitz maps a transformation of space under modernity, and if there is an overall trajectory of deterioration in *Heimat*, this should not lead us to conclude that Reitz constructs a stable myth of origin, an uncontaminated place only transformed into modern space by the plow of history. As Karsten Witte observed in his review of the film, Reitz "does not offer an idyll of the provinces. He merely illuminates, with increasing beauty and precision, the breeding-places of German history. . . . Heimat is not a place of rest; rather a transit camp for the utopia of social harmony."[78] Because Reitz depicts Heimat as a space that has always been imbricated in the ongoing process of modernization, his film does not merely duplicate Heimat ideology but also allows us to interrogate its abiding mythological function in German culture.

Epilogue

Heimat, Heritage, and the Invention of Tradition

"Home" has become a scattered, damaged, hydra-various concept in our present travails. There is so much to yearn for. There are so few rainbows any more. How hard can we expect even a pair of magic shoes to work?

SALMAN RUSHDIE

HEIMAT/COUNTRY

At the conclusion of *The Country and the City,* Raymond Williams notes the astonishing persistence of these two opposing terms. Writing in 1973, Williams already saw "us" (he was writing mainly about Britain and the British) living in many forms of social and physical organization that are no longer adequately described as either "the city" or "the country;" and yet, "The ideas and the images of country and city retain their great force."[1] Indeed, for the twentieth century, Williams notes an inverse relationship between the declining economic importance of the countryside and the unabated cultural importance of rural ideas.[2] Among the latter, I submit, we must now also include ideas and images of Heimat, which overlap in many significant ways with the cultural representations of country that Williams studies. Both *country* and *Heimat* are terms used to convey primarily rural notions of place which go beyond the physical structure of a home even as they signify home for certain people in certain instances. Like the notion of country, Heimat is often contrasted to the city, and like the English word *country,* the German term *Heimat* has occasionally come to stand— whether metonymically or metaphorically—for the broader concept of nation. Heimat continues to function, like the representations of the country that Williams studies, as an image of the past, and both concepts still tend to be associated with an idea of childhood and an "ideally shared communal memory."[3] Just as earlier pastoral images of country persist in the present, so does the notion of Heimat retain its force almost two centuries after it first gained currency in German culture and society.

Beyond such similarities of denotation and connotation, however, the terms *Heimat* and *country* seem capable of serving quite similar ideological

227

purposes. In particular, both terms play a crucial role in what Eric Hobsbawm and Terence Ranger have famously described as the "invention of tradition." As they define it, the invention of tradition yields "a set of practices, normally governed by overtly or tacitly accepted rules and of a ritual or symbolic nature, which seek to inculcate certain values and norms of behavior by repetition, which automatically implies continuity with the past."[4] The formation of cinematic genres might be seen as just such a process; what I have referred to, following Altman's work on film genre, as the gradual genrification of Heimat in German cinema could also be described as the invention and reinvention of (cinematic) tradition. However, Hobsbawm's and Ranger's memorable phrase also suggests two further aspects, which are perhaps less visible in, but no less pertinent to, genre theory. First, their discussion offers a model for thinking about the relation between tradition and modernity that lies at the heart of the genre. "Invented traditions," they suggest, "are responses to novel situations which take the form of reference to old situations, or which establish their own past by quasi-obligatory repetition."[5] In this view, the "invention of tradition" itself constitutes a modern phenomenon, and we "should expect it to occur more frequently when a rapid transformation of society weakens or destroys the social patterns for which 'old' traditions had been designed." Williams repeatedly makes a similar point about the proliferation of ostensibly timeless ideas of the country, and I have endeavored to demonstrate a parallel development in my repeated emphasis on the modernity of Heimat, whether in the aesthetic modernism of the mountain film or the motorization of the provinces in the 1950s. The images of the *Heimatfilm* may celebrate the traditional and even the archaic; but its generic logic follows that of invented traditions which are hardly the prerogative of what we think of as "traditional" societies; on the contrary, the greater the lunge toward the new, it seems, the quicker the recourse to the invention of tradition. Second, the "invention of tradition" is for Hobsbawm and Ranger essentially a construction of the past for present purposes. As opposed to some organic notion of tradition, which views the present as merely an effect of the past, Hobsbawm and Ranger insist that " 'traditions' which appear or claim to be old are often quite recent in origin and sometimes invented."[6] As Williams also argues, every present constructs for itself the past—usually a past country, or Heimat—that it needs. Applegate's and Confino's studies of the Heimat idea at the turn of the century likewise foreground this strategy at the heart of Heimat historiography, and the same assumption underlies my readings of the Heimat genre in this book.

But if traditions, Heimat, or the country are all constructions of the past for present purposes, then their analysis has much to tell us about a given present. Raymond Williams argues this fact very persuasively in his study, which remains invaluable for its methodological approach. Images of the country and the city, he maintains, are symptoms (what he calls "partial interpreters") of actual social relations and forms of consciousness, ways of responding to the accelerated social development under conditions of modernity and capitalism. Heimat, I have argued, must be read as a symptom of the same process, and Williams's analysis remains strikingly valid if for the country/city dichotomy we substitute the opposition of Heimat and *Fremde.* Though Williams follows a broader historical trajectory than I have traced in this book, he similarly emphasizes the ways in which historical changes have affected the relational meanings of *country* and *city.* This leaves room for the many and often contradictory meanings that such terms have accrued. Thus, like Heimat, the country has been taken to represent "the idea of a natural way of life: of peace, innocence, and simple virtue" while also designating "a place of backwardness, ignorance, limitation."[7] Which definition prevails and how we ultimately use notions of country or Heimat becomes, in Williams's words, a "problem of perspective." As he sets out to define the end of a particular rural form of life that would still have coincided with clear notions of the country, Williams self-consciously traces those notions back from the mid-twentieth century to the Garden of Eden by way of the eighteenth-century pastoral and the "organic society" of the Middle Ages. Each earlier manifestation in this endless regression appears more remote, more idyllic and more ideal than the previous one. But before the meaning of such idylls dissolves, or congeals into nothing but the "well-known habit of using the past, the 'good old days,' as a stick to beat the present," Williams insists that we analyze the meaning of the regressive movement itself: "Old England, settlement, the rural virtues—all these, in fact, mean different things at different times, and quite different values are being brought into question. We . . . need precise analysis of each kind of retrospect as it comes."[8]

In this study, I have aimed to treat selected films from the Heimat genre as such "retrospects," analyzing them for what each cinematic invocation of the "timeless" idyll tells us about a particular historical construction of place, community, and historical change. I have traced the shifts from Ganghofer's antimodern topographies through the reactionary modernism of Nazi *Heimatfilm*s to the genre's various ways of negotiating the conflicting demands of restoration and modernization during the 1950s, and I have used Edgar Reitz's *Heimat* as a vantage point in the early 1980s from which to reevaluate the Heimat film's spatial histories. But my overall argument parallels Williams's approach in another way as well. Williams goes one step beyond the injunction to historicize, asking us also to probe for a common denominator that links all variation and historical specificity. The persistence of binaries such as country and city or Heimat and *Fremde* as keywords through which we give meaning to social experience suggests "some permanent or effectively permanent need, to which the changing interpretations speak."[9]

Williams's analysis remains compelling precisely for its dialectical approach. Linking historical variations in the rural imaginary to a seemingly persistent need for unalienated forms of existence—and linking that need, in turn, to the specific historical realities of capitalism—Williams aims to "explain, in related terms, both the persistence and the historicity of concepts."[10] As important as the patterns of historical variation are the historical constants, the "effectively permanent need" that motivates the different invocations and aesthetic treatments of Heimat. As I suggested at the outset, the history of the Heimat concept extends well beyond its genrification in the cinema. Designating a sense of "personally lived space," Heimat has consistently been linked to changing configurations of geographical and social space. In this history, the term initially comes to signify a spatially bound sense of belonging, settlement, and home, as opposed to experiences of migration, displacement, and other forms of unsettling mobility. The dialectical link between Heimat and mobility, indeed, has been traced back to its earliest documented usage and is evident in the currency of Heimat during the second half of the nineteenth century, which witnessed great increases in social and geographical mobility.[11] As I argue with reference to the postwar "nomadologies" of the 1950s, the nexus between migration and Heimat reappears most clearly during the Adenauer era, when the genre of the *Heimatfilm* routinely grapples with the reconfiguration of Germany and Germanness after the repatriation of millions of *Vertriebene* or *Umsiedler* and with the surge of mobility afforded by the *Wirtschaftswunder*. But this nexus obtains throughout the history of the genre: it is one of the underlying convictions of this study that increases in mobility and dislocation increase the currency of Heimat, indexing an "effectively permanent need" for a sense of security, spatial stability, and "personally lived space." The principal function of the Heimat genre, then, is both to *compensate* for the perceived loss of home and to *shape* the experience of that loss through representation.

Given the dialectics of Heimat and dislocation, I would disagree with Peter Sloterdijk's diagnosis of our globalized present, in which he claims that "the end of the settled civilizations marks the beginning of a global age of permanent crisis for the concept of Heimat."[12] On the contrary, the history of this term and of its cinematic uses suggests that we should remain especially attentive today to the logic that links processes of disembedding, globalization, and mobility on the one hand with cultural or political (re)turns to Heimat on the other. Far from entering into crisis during moments of intense social transformation and increasing mobility, Heimat gains its cultural currency precisely at these junctures. For it is during these times that its function as "an organizing ideology for people quietly seeking a haven from the uncertainties of modern life" is most readily invoked.[13] We might describe this as the ritual aspect of Heimat, which serves to index and manage a perceived loss of home. In a 1999 lecture on the place of Heimat, Bernhard Schlink articulated this ritual function quite precisely. The experience of Heimat, he claimed, "is made when whatever Heimat might be is missing or stands in for something that is missing." As processes of disembedding exacerbate this lack, Heimat becomes a privileged compensatory site that would ritualize social transformations. Contra Sloterdijk, Schlink offers a more dialectical reading of the social function of Heimat when he notes that the Heimat idea "gains in importance in the age of internationalization and globalization."[14] This dialectic is born out by an incessant stream of publications that explicitly thematize the use value of Heimat for the global age.[15] It may also help to explain the proliferation of heritage films in European cinema, films whose German variant overlaps in significant ways with the generic history I have traced in this book.

HEIMAT/HERITAGE/HISTORY

Recent years have seen a renewed surge in images of the past in the cinema. In light of the genre history outlined in the preceding pages, it is difficult not to perceive these films as continuing and rewriting the historiographies of the *Heimatfilm*. For example, films like *Sonnenallee* (1999) or *Good Bye Lenin!* (2003) appear to have successfully tapped the widespread phenomenon of *Ostalgie*, or nostalgia for the defunct GDR, in ways that evoke the sentimental return to the past in many a *Heimatfilm*. Leonie Naughton even argues that West German productions after 1989 recast the history of the GDR as a lost Heimat. Films such as *Der Brocken* (1992), *Wir können auch anders* (1993), or the "Trabi comedies" of the early 1990s, Naughton argues, turn to Heimat in order to provide their audiences sentimental and reassuring reflections of national identity. More specifically, Naughton makes a case for the narcissistic function of these films for the West. Constructing the GDR as West Germany's idyllic past, they generated new mythologies of Heimat and held up an "Eastern" mirror to the Federal Republic, in which it could contemplate its ideal image.[16]

While Naughton uses the notion of Heimat in interesting ways to explain the cultural work performed by these films, it remains a heuristic device. She turns to the Heimat idea as an interpretive framework that she borrows ready-made from scholarly literature, and applies it to a set of disparate Western-backed films from the 1990s. Though these films use some clichés that we have come to associate with the *Heimatfilm* of the 1950s (such as its escapism or its ostensibly apolitical nature), it is difficult to see how they would amount to a full-scale "reappropriation" and "restoration" of the *Heimatfilm*, as Naughton claims.[17] Far more interesting for the history and theory of the genre that I have elaborated in this study is the glut of recent cinematic spectacles that circle explicitly and obsessively around the overlap between Heimat, heritage, and German history. By way of conclusion, I would like to cast a glance at these recent developments, since I believe that the German cinema's long-standing love affair with Heimat informs cinematic constructions of the past for the postwall present as well.

As Eric Rentschler has suggested, much of postwall German cinema has been defined by an overriding drive for consensus. "Quite emphatically," he writes, "the most prominent directors of the post-wall era aim to please, which is to say that they consciously solicit a new German consensus. In this sense, the cinema they champion is one with a decidedly affirmative calling."[18] Noting similar trends, a number of critics have held the revival of genre filmmaking during the 1990s accountable for the bland and provincial, ultimately harmless appearance of postwall German cinema. It is difficult to overlook the echoes of the 1950s in such descriptions. Sabine Hake spells out the historical parallels quite explicitly, noting that filmmakers seeking to address post-unification concerns turned to the genres of the postwar period to craft another "Zero Hour."[19] As it did in the 1950s, the return to genre in the 1990s would appear to signal a desire for "normalization" at the expense of historical retrospection.[20]

The history of the *Heimatfilm* that I have elaborated in this study offers a crucial vantage point for evaluating such claims. With the "miracle years" as its center of gravity, this history serves to confirm the diagnosis of a comeback of the 1950s; at the same time, however, placing the present in the perspective of the *Heimatfilm* allows us to specify more carefully the relation between genre and (the perceived absence of) history after 1989. Three aspects require our attention here. First, we should avoid reproducing the critical shorthand that equates the 1950s and its preferred genre with a lack of historical consciousness. As I demonstrate in my readings of both prototypical 1950s fare such as *Grün ist die Heide* and less familiar but equally revealing cases such as *Rosen blühen auf dem Heidegrab*, historical retrospection is not as alien to these films as talk of a "holiday from history" or the "repression approach" to the Adenauer era have led us to believe. Second, since the end of the 1990s, certain forms of historical retrospection have hardly been absent from German cinema, but instead seem to have become its hallmark. After the *Beziehungskomödien* of the early part of the decade, history was back on German screens with films like *Comedian Harmonists* (1997), *Meschugge* (1998), *Aimée und Jaguar* (1999), *Marlene* (2000), the recent Oscar-winner *Nirgendwo in Afrika* (2001), and Sönke Wortmann's *Das Wunder von Bern* (2003). To be sure, these films' shared interest in German history does not exclude them from the affirmative mode that Rentschler traces back to Doris Dörrie's *Männer* (1985). On the contrary: we can witness in such films the reach of the normalizing imperative as the cinema rewrites even the most fractious periods of German history in terms of consensus. To the degree that these recent developments overlap with the history of the *Heimatfilm*, a third observation imposes itself: As a generic template for historical consciousness, Heimat appears ready-made for the German cinema's postwall revisionist impulses. This is nowhere more obvious than in the ideological remix of Heimat and heritage that has characterized much recent filmmaking in Germany.

Lutz Koepnick has described the recent glut of historical fictions as "German Heritage Films."[21] He adopts the notion of "heritage" from the British context, where it has been used to describe a cycle of films dating from the 1980s and 1990s. Viewed against the film-historical backdrop I have surveyed in this book, Koepnick's apt reference bears further elaboration, for it reveals a striking set of links to the history of the *Heimatfilm*. As Andrew Higson points out, films like *A Passage to India* (1984), *A Room with a View* (1986), or *Howards End* (1992), all adapted from novels by E M. Forster, provided "artful projections of an elite, conservative vision of the national past."[22] Their investment in mise-en-scène, rural spectacle, and high production values brings to mind a number of films from the Heimat tradition. One immediately thinks of the *Sissi* trilogy of the 1950s, but lesser productions like *Waldwinter* certainly display heritage properties (the Silesian landowner's estate in the Bavarian Forest) with as much prominence as do the more recent Merchant-Ivory productions. The predominance in heritage films of character, place, atmosphere, and milieu over dramatic, goal-directed action is also familiar from any number of films discussed in this book, from Fanck's Alpine spectacle to the logic of "attractions" that governs *Grün ist die Heide*. Likewise, the pervasive sense of loss, the nostalgia that radiates from the "old" landscapes of the Forster adaptations resonates directly with the invocation of Heimat as something lost, from Wolfgang Liebeneiner to Edgar Reitz. It is more than coincidence that *Heimat* was first broadcast in Germany just as the heritage genre was on the rise in Britain. For all the apparent differences between Reitz's epic and, say, *A Room with a View,* a detailed comparison could reveal an important set of aesthetic, ideological, and historiographic parallels that further substantiate the links between cinematic modes of Heimat and heritage.[23]

With the German heritage films of the 1990s, however, this link becomes charged with specific historical implications, and the spatial dynamics of Heimat take on the temporal charge of nostalgia. In a reversal and a popularization of the New German Cinema's representations of German history, heritage films have offered audiences melodramatic visions of history, including of the Nazi era, which allow strikingly positive identifications.[24] Drawing on the spectacular qualities and the overall tone of both Heimat and heritage, 1990s films by Joseph Vilsmaier and Max Färberböck, among others, restage the German past as a site of reconciliation. As Koepnick notes, Jewish figures play a seminal role in the heritage cinema's strategies of consensus and nostalgia. Many of these films go back to scenes of German-Jewish cooperation during the 1920s and 1930s in order to "reconstruct the nation's narrative and reintegrate German Jews into hegemonic definitions of German cultural identity."[25] Films like *Comedian Harmonists* and *Aimée und Jaguar* provide key examples of this logic at their melodramatic climaxes, as both films allow German viewers to revisit anti-Semitism and the Nazi past from a disturbingly philo-Semitic vantage point. German audiences turn out in massive support of Jewish performers under the Nazis in *Comedian Harmonists,* as if to suggest a submerged tradition of popular resistance against the anti-Semitic policies of the Nazi state. And when the non-Jewish Lily Wust (Aimée) implores her lover Felice not to leave her upon learning of her Jewishness in *Aimée und Jaguar,* the burden of representation shifts from the historical plight of the Jew to the non-Jewish German's wounded narcissism.[26] Behind the histories of German-Jewish symbiosis that these films set out to recall for their audiences lies the broader project of redefining German identity for the postwall present. For what typifies heritage filmmaking in general and the chronicling of German-Jewish relations in these films in particular "is the production of usable and consumable pasts, of history as a site of comfort and orientation."[27] Germans can take comfort in viewing themselves as fans of Jewish singers and as Jaguar's wounded lover.

This conciliatory project also informs Caroline Link's *Nirgendwo in*

Afrika, an "exterritorialized" Heimat-and-heritage film that takes the German-Jewish question out of Germany altogether and locates it in the scorched plains and British colonial institutions of Kenya during World War II.[28] The film tells the story of the African exile of a young German Jewish couple and their daughter Regina. In opulent images reminiscent of both heritage productions and Heimat films (the cinematography is by Edgar Reitz's longtime cameraman Gernot Roll), Link follows the slow acclimatization of the Redlich family from Breslau in their "new Heimat."[29] This process is described as one of hardships, suffering, and setbacks, but also one of transformation and liberation. Jettel, the mother, in particular grows in exile to find a new kind of independence that eluded her in her role as bourgeois housewife back in Breslau. And Regine grows into a self-assured young teenager who mediates between her parents and their Kenyan surroundings. Told from her point of view, this is the coming-of-age story of a German Jewish girl living in an exile that strains her parents' marriage almost to the breaking point. The film provides a powerful account of the loss of home and the effects of exile on the micro level of a couple's relationship and a young girl's adolescence.

But like the von Trapps in Amerika, the Redlichs do double duty. The story of "Die Redlich-Familie in Afrika" may be more urgent by comparison, given the threat of racial persecution (rather than, as in Baron von Trapp's case, ideological conviction and economic necessity). Nevertheless, the logic of the two films, the rewriting of Heimat through narratives of exile, remains comparable if we adjust for the different historical and discursive contexts of their production. Both films are based on published autobiographies whose temporal and geographical distance they turn into backdrops for far more contemporary German stories. In the case of the von Trapps, that story is one of postwar reconstruction and Americanization; in Link's film, Africa becomes "a mystical locus of European transformation, [and] the Africans represent at best eager guides along this path."[30] In keeping with the heritage genre, the film tells a story driven by the need for German-Jewish consensus over half a century after any hopes for such consensus were irreparably shattered. As Kristin Kopp points out in her incisive reading of the film, Link takes the story of Germans and Jews to Africa in order to validate a "hyphenated" German-Jewish identity, promising the exiles' return in the end. This allegorical logic was captured unwittingly by a reviewer who described *Nirgendwo in Afrika* as a "*Heimatfilm* that plays in two worlds but knows only one longing."[31] What this longing might be remains more ambiguous than the formulation suggests (the father's longing to return and take up work in Frankfurt, for instance, is the object of much debate and emotional tension within the film); but the melodramatic inscription of longing itself, the diffuse desire to define a sense of home—whether in Africa, Breslau, or Frankfurt—makes this a *Heimatfilm* in the mode of heritage.

Link's film was celebrated by the German press as a model for German cinema in the new millennium.[32] The film's success at the 2003 Academy Awards will certainly fan the collective elation at having found a recipe for blending the popular and the national in ways that can attract international—that is, American—audiences as well. But the revisionist strategies that struck a chord with viewers both at home and in Hollywood should also give us pause. Kopp identifies such strategies in the deflection of anti-Semitism from the Germans to the British, the deflation of the horrors of the Holocaust, and a baffling imperviousness to colonial history. Invested in telling a story of exile and Heimat, the film appears blind to its function as a "neocolonial fantasy" structured by asymmetrical attributions of "authenticity."[33] German-Jewish reconciliation, it appears, is only possible against the backdrop of absolute otherness. To Kopp's trenchant analysis we should add the revisionist function of the Heimat topos, familiar from a long generic history. By imagining exile as a space of German-Jewish *Gemeinschaft* in the past (even as it excludes the local population from that space), *Nirgendwo in Afrika* also fantasizes about this possibility "somewhere in Germany" in the present.[34] Like the *Heimatfilm* of the 1950s, *Nirgendwo in Afrika* stages its spectacle in locations that seem remote only at first glance. Upon closer inspection, they turn out to be key sites for the negotiation of German cultural and political identities.

This is true even when the fusion of Heimat and heritage is not driven by the same revisionist impulses as in Link's, Färberböck's, or, especially, Vilsmaier's films. A number of important contributions have explored the spaces of Heimat in order to reconstruct cultural and political identities beyond the model of consensus, choosing to emphasize an agonistic construction (and destruction) of local *Gemeinschaft* instead. In this vein, postwall productions ranging from Stefan Ruzowitzky's *Die Siebtelbauern* (1998) and Didi Danquart's *Viehjud Levi* (1999) to Sebastian Steinbichler's *Hierankel* (2003) productively continue the tradition of the critical *Heimatfilm*, using the genre for the merciless mise-en-scène of local pasts. Along the way, they unearth familial taboos, class tensions and, in the case of Danquart's important film, rural anti-Semitism of the 1930s. *Viehjud Levi*, indeed, may offer the best example of how to fuse the traditions of the *Heimatfilm* with German history while at the same time refusing the nostalgic sense of community offered in other heritage films of the 1990s. Chronicling the exorcism of the Jewish cattle trader Levi from the Black

Forest, *Viehjud Levi* ends not with a reconciliation, but with the violent expulsion of the Jew. Danquart manages to stage the Heimat film's favorite idyll as the site of historical rupture. Remote though it may be, the film's unnamed hamlet becomes a touchstone of the German twentieth century.[35]

This, then, is the place of Heimat in German cinema. A historically charged term whose properly cinematic pedigree dates back to the beginnings of the twentieth century, Heimat remains a key site in our ever-expanding audiovisual present. After its gradual genrification during the first half of the century, its virtual monopoly on the cinematic landscape during the Adenauer years, and its various repurposings since the late 1960s, the *Heimatfilm* has become a fixture of German cinema and a potent cultural instrument, notwithstanding its dismissal as low culture, kitsch, and popular entertainment. That instrument continues to be played in different ways by the participants in the pragmatics of genre, from filmmakers and marketers to critics and audiences. As my brief examples from the postwall era suggest, two trends are readily discernible at present: on the one hand, Heimat and heritage serve to rewrite German history in terms of consensus and nostalgia, serving a broader agenda of "normalization" in the emerging cultural constellation of the Berlin Republic.[36] On the other hand, Heimat can remain a site of disruption, a microcosmic locale that resists integration into overly conciliatory frameworks. Which functions of Heimat prevail, and which meanings we ascribe to the term in any given instance, will ultimately hinge on its spatio-temporal construction either as an enclosed sense of place, of fuzzy warmth and nostalgic cathexis, or as a space that preserves the traces of the historical movements which constitute it. If home has become, in Rushdie's words, "damaged" and "hydra-various," we are not served well by representations of Heimat that simply disavow this state of affairs by imagining some simple plenitude. The most promising explorations of this concept will be those that manage to make its proliferating meanings productive and confront its historical failures as much as its promises. Undoubtedly, the Heimat genre still has a lot of mileage as German cinema enters its second century. If we heed its most impressive manifestations, but also if we care to look closely at its more mundane and troubling appearances, we find that the *Heimatfilm* sets into motion all the hydra-various historical meanings of this damaged concept. The most productive aspect of the genre's history may turn out to be its proof that, when it comes to fixing the meaning of Heimat, there is no place like home.

Notes

INTRODUCTION

Epigraph: Jean Améry, "How Much Home Does a Person Need?" 48.

1. Salman Rushdie, *The Wizard of Oz*, 56, 10.

2. Ibid., 14.

3. Sigmund Freud, "The Uncanny," 220. For a recent Freudian reading of *The Wizard of Oz*, see Elisabeth Bronfen, *Heimweh*, chap. 4.

4. I leave the term *Heimat* untranslated for obvious reasons, and, except in references to the word itself (as here) or to film titles, in roman type.

5. Hans Günther Pflaum, "Auf der Suche nach Heimat," 23.

6. Thomas Elsaesser, *New German Cinema*, 141. In his dissertation "Genre and Ideology," Tassilo Schneider entitles his chapter on the *Heimatfilm* simply "The German Genre."

7. All translations, unless otherwise indicated, are my own.

8. Fredric Jameson, "Reification and Utopia in Mass Culture," 25.

9. I take this term from Rick Altman's *Film/Genre*, which usefully insists on the historicity of genres. I present a more detailed discussion of Altman's genre theory and its relevance to the study of the *Heimatfilm* in chap. 1.

10. On the history of the Heimat movement, see Celia Applegate, *A Nation of Provincials*; Alon Confino, *The Nation as Local Metaphor*; Edeltraud Klueting, ed., *Antimodernismus und Reform*.

11. On *Heimatkunst*, see Karlheinz Rossbacher, *Heimatkunstbewegung und Heimatroman*; for exemplary studies of some authors of *Heimatliteratur*, see Peter Mettenleiter, *Destruktion der Heimatdichtung*; and on the conservative ideology that fueled these aesthetic programs, see Fritz Richard Stern, *The Politics of Cultural Despair*, and Ulrike Haß, *Militante Pastorale*.

12. Raymond Williams, *Keywords*, 15; emphasis in original.

13. For an exhaustive bibliography on Heimat from a variety of disciplinary standpoints, see Bundeszentrale für politische Bildung, ed., *Heimat*.

14. Anton Kaes, *From Hitler to Heimat*, 165–66.

15. This is not to say that such entries have not been attempted—any major German language encyclopedia will include and define the term.

16. Applegate, *A Nation of Provincials,* 5, 6.

17. Ibid., 115.

18. Ibid., 19.

19. Confino, *The Nation as Local Metaphor,* 98, 107.

20. Rolf Petri, "Deutsche Heimat 1850–1950."

21. The most famous future-oriented definition of Heimat as a utopian space beyond alienation remains Ernst Bloch's concluding line of *Das Prinzip Hoffnung,* where he speaks of Heimat in his characteristically utopian language of "not yet" ("noch nicht"). Heimat, he suggests, must be seen as something that shines into our childhood, but in which nobody has yet been ("worin noch niemand war"). *Das Prinzip Hoffnung,* vol. 3, 1628.

22. Hermann Bausinger, "Heimat und Identität," 202, 9.

23. Oskar Köhler, "Heimat," in *Staatslexikon,* vol. 4, quoted in Wilfried von Bredow and Hans-Friedrich Foltin, *Zwiespältige Zufluchten,* 26.

24. Kurt Stavenhagen, *Heimat als Lebenssinn,* 45.

25. Confino, *The Nation as Local Metaphor,* 133.

26. See David Morley, *Home Territories;* Hamid Naficy, ed., *Home, Exile, Homeland.*

27. See David Morley and Kevin Robbins, *Spaces of Identity,* especially chap. 5, "No Place Like Heimat: Images of Home(Land)."

28. Doreen Massey, *Space, Place and Gender,* 167–68.

29. See David Harvey, *The Condition of Postmodernity,* 241; emphasis in original. See also Edward W. Soja, *Postmodern Geographies.*

30. Marshall Berman, *All That Is Solid Melts into Air,* 5.

31. For a collection that brings together many participants in these discussions, see Michael Dear and Steven Flusty, eds., *The Spaces of Postmodernity.*

32. In this respect, I share the view of sociologists such as Anthony Giddens, Ulrich Beck, and Scott Lash, who prefer to speak not of postmodernity but of "reflexive modernization," defined as the ability of "one kind of modernity [to] undercut and change another." Beck argues that where industrial society modernizes tradition, reflexive modernization implies the modernization of industrial society itself. Beck, Giddens, and Lash, *Reflexive Modernization.* See also Beck, *Risk Society.*

33. Anthony Giddens, *The Consequences of Modernity,* 18.

34. Ibid., 140, 18–19.

35. Ibid., 21.

36. These are some of the relations that characterize *Gemeinschaft* as opposed to the more contractual and potentially distanced relations that make up the associational form of *Gesellschaft* according to Ferdinand Tönnies's well-known definition. See Tönnies, *Gemeinschaft und Gesellschaft.* The conceptual link between Heimat and *Gemeinschaft* is established explicitly in Stavenhagen, *Heimat als Lebenssinn.*

37. James Clifford, *Routes,* 3.

38. Ibid., 2–3.

39. See Massey, *Space, Place and Gender;* see also Arjun Appadurai, *Modernity at Large;* Alf Dirlik, "The Global in the Local."

40. Applegate, *A Nation of Provincials,* 10–11.

41. Eric Hobsbawm and Terence Ranger, *The Invention of Tradition,* 2. See also Anthony Giddens, "Living in a Post-Traditional Society."

42. Morley, *Home Territories,* 42.

43. See Confino, *The Nation as Local Metaphor,* 119.

44. Applegate, *A Nation of Provincials,* 62.

45. Friedrich Lienhard, "Heimatkunst?"1396.

46. Jeffrey Herf, *Reactionary Modernism.*

47. Quoted in Confino, *The Nation as Local Metaphor,* 121.

48. Ibid. A notable exception is Hermann Bausinger's 1961 book *Volkskultur in der technischen Welt,* published in English in 1990 as *Folk Culture in a World of Technology.*

49. Confino, *The Nation as Local Metaphor,* 121.

50. Ibid., 122.

51. Applegate, *A Nation of Provincials,* 6, 4.

52. "The modern subject is a subject on the move. Central to the idea of modernity is that of movement, that modern societies have brought about striking changes in the nature and experience of motion or travel." John Urry, *Consuming Places,* 141.

53. Confino, *The Nation as Local Metaphor,* 121.

CHAPTER 1

Epigraph: Thomas Elsaesser, "Early German Cinema," 27.

1. See, among others, Heide Fehrenbach, *Cinema in Democratizing Germany;* Uta Poiger, *Jazz, Rock, and Rebels;* Robert G. Moeller, *War Stories;* Hanna Schissler, ed., *The Miracle Years.* Erica Carter has likewise made an important contribution to this scholarship, though her book *How German Is She?* is informed more by the methods and concepts of British cultural studies than by those of cultural history. All of these books either focus on film (Fehrenbach) or offer chapters on film as a significant material source for the cultural historian.

2. An important recent exception in English is Sabine Hake's comprehensive overview, *German National Cinema.* A forthcoming anthology edited jointly by John Davidson and Hake, *German Cinema of the 1950s,* also promises to fill in some of the remaining gaps. Also, a number of dissertations completed during the 1990s consider some of the decade's production from a perspective informed by film studies: see, for example, Temby Caprio, "Women's Film Culture in the Federal Republic of Germany," and Tassilo Schneider, "Genre and Ideology." In German, a number of useful essays or chapters are available, among them Fritz Göttler, "Westdeutscher Nachkriegsfilm"; Ulrich Kurowski, "1945–1960"; Georg Seeßlen, "Der Heimatfilm" and "Durch die Heimat und so

weiter." In addition, there is a glut of memoirs by stars and other members of the industry in the vein of Curt Riess's *Das gibt's nur einmal*. The standard work on the *Heimatfilm* remains Willi Höfig, *Der deutsche Heimatfilm*.

3. The first quote is from Walter Schmieding, *Kunst oder Kasse*, 27. The attack on the German cinema's "antiquatedness" makes up the bulk of a total of all of two pages that Ulrich Gregor and Enno Patalas dedicate to recent German cinema in their book *Geschichte des Films* (262–64). For the most sarcastic diatribe, see Joe Hembus, *Der deutsche Film kann gar nicht besser sein*.

4. Chris Marker, "Adieu au cinéma allemand?"

5. The term is from Klaus Kreimeier, "Die Ökonomie der Gefühle," 228.

6. This often-quoted statistic is derived from Willi Höfig's study of three hundred Heimat films produced between 1947 and 1960, with 1952 and 1956 yielding record percentages of 33 and 36 percent, respectively. See Höfig, *Der deutsche Heimatfilm*, 166.

7. Rick McCormick, quoted in Hanna Schissler's introduction to *The Miracle Years*, 7.

8. Both quotes are from Schneider, "Genre and Ideology," 144. Writing in 1994, Schneider rightly makes exceptions of Eric Rentschler and Anton Kaes, and one should add that in the meantime, some of the work on film by cultural historians has begun to rectify the situation (see the sources cited in note 1). Individual articles devoted to the genre over the past decade include Alisdair King, "Placing *Green Is the Heath*"; Ted Rippey, Melissa Sundell, and Suzanne Townley, "'Ein wunderbares Heute'"; Ingeborg Majer O'Sickey, "Framing the *Unheimlich*."

9. By definition, popular European cinema is at a disadvantage on the international market, which remains dominated by Hollywood and international art cinema. For numerous institutional, aesthetic, economic, and cultural reasons, popular films from countries other than the United States have tended to fall through the cracks of international exhibition practices and the protocols of film studies, which allow for little overlap between the European and the popular. Films of European provenance that travel internationally (even within Europe) tend to be categorized as art cinema, whereas the notion of popular cinema in global markets has long been seen as synonymous with Hollywood. As the editors of a special issue of *The Velvet Light Trap* devoted to the topic of popular national cinema put it, "By equating national cinemas and the art cinema, film studies has (until recently) ignored attempts by institutions and individuals to create indigenous popular film in the face of Hollywood's hegemony." Meanwhile, the exceptions that continue to prove this rule are proliferating; Hong Kong and Bollywood cinema provide perhaps the most notable current examples. See Editors, "Introduction"; see also Natasa Durovicová, "Some Thoughts at an Intersection of the Popular and the National." Dimitris Eleftheriotis explores different constellations of the popular across a number of European contexts in *Popular Cinemas of Europe*. See also Richard Dyer and Ginette Vincendeau, *Popular European Cinema*.

10. Put together by the Film Society at Lincoln Center in 2003, this series included freshly minted thirty-five-millimeter prints, with subtitles, of *Schwarzwaldmädel, Ich denke oft an Piroschka, Sissi, Die Trapp-Familie in Amerika, Das Wirtshaus im Spessart,* and *Rosen blühen auf dem Heidegrab,* to list only the titles most immediately relevant to the question of Heimat. Likewise, a touring series of films from the 1950s assembled by the Film Society at Lincoln Center has been made available. In addition, the Goethe Institut and InterNationes have recently compiled a package of subtitled sixteen-millimeter Heimat films available for rental. To claim that these efforts substantially increase the visibility of postwar (West) German cinema in the United States is not to say that such films have been entirely unavailable in this country. The German Language Video Center in Indianapolis has apparently specialized in producing unsubtitled NTSC copies of the canonic (and not so canonic) works from the 1930s to the 1950s, and the international DVD market now supplies a steady trickle of *Heimatfilm* releases, though generally on German Region 2 discs without subtitles.

11. Somewhat surprisingly, we find such an assertion in the entry "Heimatfilm" in Georg Seeßlen and Bernt Kling, *Unterhaltung,* vol. 2, 169. In his important essays on the genre, Seeßlen's history is far more nuanced (see note 2).

12. See Eric Rentschler, *The Ministry of Illusion,* and Thomas Elsaesser, *Weimar Cinema and After.*

13. The Bundeszentrale für Heimatdienst was founded in 1952; the Gesamtdeutscher Block/Bund der Heimatvertriebenen und Entrechteten achieved 5.9 percent of the vote in 1953 and 4.9 percent in 1957, before it was integrated into the CDU.

14. "A film historiography which conceives of European cinema as a cinema of *auteurs* is merely consistent in jumping from, roughly, 1930 to 1970 in the case of Germany since, during the intermittent period, German cinema is presumably lacking the kinds of films (or *auteurs*) it would need to have in order to be considered part of film history at all." Schneider, "Genre and Ideology," 50.

15. Rick Altman, "A Semantic/Syntactic Approach to Film Genre," 28.

16. Indeed, Altman even draws into question the primacy of the corpus as the place where genres are ultimately located. Altman, *Film/Genre,* 84.

17. Ibid., 99.

18. Ibid., 179. On the role of genre as process rather than structure, see also Steve Neale's many interventions, from *Genre* to *Genre and Hollywood.*

19. Altman, *Film/Genre,* 84.

20. Wilhelm Spickernagel, "Der Kinematograph im Dienste der Heimatkunst," 234.

21. See Tom Gunning, "Before Documentary," 15; emphasis in original.

22. See Gertrud Koch, "Wir tanzen in den Urlaub"; Seeßlen, "Durch die Heimat und so weiter."

23. Quoted in Ulrich Kurowski and Sylvia Wolf, *Das Münchner Film- und Kinobuch,* 14.

24. Herbert Birett, *Das Filmangebot in Deutschland*. Birett's detailed filmographic research can also be consulted online at www.kinematographie.de.

25. Ibid. I have been suggesting that the proliferation of Heimat titles needs to be seen in the context of *Heimatkunst* and the Heimat movement from the late nineteenth and early twentieth centuries; with the opening up of a home front (*Heimatfront*) and stories of returning (*heimkehrend*) soldiers, however, World War I supplied another important context for these developments.

26. "Wer kennt den 'Ostmärkischen Heimatfilm,'"; "Die heutige Berliner Uraufführung."

27. Karl Kraatz's *Deutscher Film Katalog*, for instance, lists thirty-nine *Heimatfilme* for the period from 1930 to 1945. However, the filmography is incomplete and the classificatory scheme somewhat arbitrary, and one is tempted to surmise that the generic rubrics were determined far more by the climate of the 1950s than by the contexts of their production and reception in the 1930s and 1940s.

28. Walter Jerven, "Film-München von einst: Ein Rückblick über vergilbte Blätter," reprinted in Kurowski and Wolf, *Das Münchner Film- und Kinobuch*, 48–49.

29. See Oly, "Grün ist die Heide," 8: "Wir haben ja bisher so wenige ausgesprochene Heimatfilme, hier ist einer, und es wäre gar nicht so übel, wenn nach all den meist recht dummen Filmmoden nun einmal der Heimatfilm Mode würde."

30. Fritz Stege, "Heideschulmeister Uwe Karsten," quoted in Oskar Kalbus, *Vom Werden deutscher Filmkunst*, 58.

31. Kalbus, *Vom Werden deutscher Filmkunst*, 109.

32. This claim is advanced by Manfred Barthel in his history of postwar German cinema, where he dates the origin of the label to 1951. The popular history was marketed as an insider account by an expert who "simply could not remain silent any longer" in the face of "so much misinformation about the German cinema after 1945" (dust jacket). Barthel, *So war es wirklich*, 89–90.

33. *Heimatland* starred Hansi Knoteck, a regular in Peter Ostermayr's productions, and prominently featured a *Heimatlied*. Based, like many Heimat films of the 1950s, on an operetta, it was marketed as a "happy and gay Ufa film" depicting "the love of a young girl whose loyalty to the Heimat wins the day against all obstacles. Through its contemporary popular appeal [*zeitnahe Volkstümlichkeit*] and its images of the Black Forest, it offers the viewer a beautiful experience" (press kit in Bundesarchiv/Filmarchiv, Berlin).

34. Cf. Francis Courtade and Pierre Cadars, *Geschichte des Films im Dritten Reich*, 267–68.

35. Eric Rentschler rightly describes these films as intertexts for another film with a heavy investment in notions of Heimat: Luis Trenker's *Der verlorene Sohn* of the same year. See Rentschler, *The Ministry of Illusion*, 73–96. I discuss *Heimkehr* in chap. 3.

36. While there are no statistics to back up this claim for the entirety of

German film history, a count undertaken by Patrick Vonderau places Ganghofer at the top of the list of authors adapted for the screen for the years from 1933 to 1945.

37. Uta Berg-Ganschow, "Der Widerspenstigen Zähmung," 25.

38. The title is a play on the comedy *I A in Oberbayern*, first directed by Franz Seitz in 1936 and then in 1956 by Hans Albin, who was also the director of *Pudelnackt in Oberbayern*. Other continuities among the three titles include the appearance of Beppo Brem in each (he plays himself in the 1969 version).

39. "Zum Tode Peter Ostermayrs." His merits at retirement included the Bundesverdienstkreuz (Federal Cross of Merit), which he received in 1953; he also had influential positions as honorary president of the Association of German Film Producers and chairman of the board of Bavaria Studios.

40. Oberhausen Manifesto, quoted in Eric Rentschler, ed., *West German Filmmakers on Film*, 2. When Ostermayr went on a crusade against what he considered the poor quality of the work produced by the young generation, he chided newcomers for "wanting to imprint the film with the signature of their personality." Peter Ostermayr, "Bessere Autoren, bessere Filme."

41. On Ostermayr's insistence on quality and craftsmanship, see Walter Butry, *Münchner Porträts*, 35–36.

42. François Truffaut, "A Certain Tendency in the French Cinema."

43. Indeed, one might argue that the Oberhauseners' desire to liberate themselves from *all* conventions amounted to proclaiming the death of the convention of genre itself.

44. See "Die Heimatfilm-Welle rollt wieder"; Kai Krüger, "Im Kino darf wieder geweint werden."

45. The two seminal publications on the topic are Eric Rentschler's chapter "Calamity Prevails over the Country: Young German Filmmakers Revisit the Homeland" in his *West German Film in the Course of Time*, 103–28; and Daniel Alexander Schacht, *Fluchtpunkt Provinz*.

46. Bredow and Foltin, *Zwiespältige Zufluchten*; Jürgen Bolten, "Heimat im Aufwind."

47. Gerhard Bliersbach, *So grün war die Heide*, 33. Reaching almost half of all television-viewing households in the Federal Republic (47 percent), for a total of over seventeen million viewers, *Grün ist die Heide* was the most successful feature film broadcast by ARD in 1980. In the competition between the two public stations, it was runner-up only to ZDF's *Jäger von Fall* (based on the Ganghofer novel), which garnered 49 percent. See Bredow and Foltin, *Zwiespältige Zufluchten*, 107.

48. See Georg Seeßlen's acerbic remarks about these shows in *Volks Tümlichkeit*, 19–45.

49. Neale, *Genre*, 65.

50. Fredric Jameson, *Signatures of the Visible*, 101.

51. Rentschler, *West German Film in the Course of Time*, 104.

52. Raymond Williams, *The Country and the City*, 288.

CHAPTER 2

Epigraph: Georg Simmel, "The Alpine Journey," 221.

1. Marlen Sinjen, "Der Vater des Heimatfilms."

2. See Claus Hardt, "Der heimatlose Heimatfilm."

3. Peter Ostermayr, "Wie alles anfing . . . und wurde," unpublished typescript, Peter Ostermayr Archiv (henceforth POA), Munich.

4. Hans Schwerte, "Ganghofers Gesundung," 164.

5. The last available estimates of Ganghofer's circulation from the 1970s put the total number of published volumes somewhere around twenty-five million. See Mettenleiter, *Destruktion der Heimatdichtung*, 366. More precise figures are difficult to come by due to the proliferation of publishers after the texts entered the public domain. A selection of works is available online through Projekt Gutenberg-de at http://www.gutenberg.spiegel.de/autoren/ganghofe.htm.

6. E.M., "Film-Ehe mit Ganghofer."

7. Ostermayr, "Wie alles anfing . . . und wurde," unpublished typescript, POA, Munich.

8. During the Weimar era, Ganghofer's contributions remained limited to the *Ganghofer-Serie* of the late 1910s and early 1920s. During the Third Reich, Ganghofer already accounted for over one-third of Ostermayr's production; after the war, Ostermayr's rekindled production company was practically synonymous with *Ganghofer-Filme:* nine of the thirteen films Ostermayr produced before he retired were based on Ganghofer novels. Ostermayr directed some of the first adaptations in the early 1920s before dedicating himself mainly to production. Films he produced for Ufa during the 1930s, such as *Gewitter im Mai* and *Der Edelweißkönig,* however, still include his name in the credits for *Mit-Regie,* or co-directorship.

9. Ganghofer used this phrase to characterize the scandal-mongering Baroness Pranckha, from whom the protagonist, Count Ettingen, has fled in *Das Schweigen im Walde.* It appears in a passage in which the count contemplates his newfound Alpine love interest, Lolo Petri, who appears by contrast to the rotting city fruit as "a pure, beautiful flower of the mountains." Ganghofer, *Das Schweigen im Walde,* 289.

10. See Schwerte, "Ganghofers Gesundung."

11. Gertraud Steiner, "Von der Heimatdichtung zum Heimatfilm," 82.

12. On the designation *Hochland* see Schwerte, "Ganghofers Gesundung," 166–69. One of the key publishing venues of the *Heimatkunst* movement, the journal *Heimat,* was originally to be called *Hochland,* which Friedrich Lienhard preferred to the term *Heimatkunst.* In an article from 1900, Lienhard explained his resignation from the editorial board of *Heimat* as follows: "Because I find a *Hochland* of the spirit and the heart, a distinguished and great culture . . . far more desirable than the comforts of a Heimat regained, though of course we needn't give up the latter for that reason." Friedrich Lienhard, "Heimatkunst?" Although the editors settled on *Heimat* against Lienhard's wishes, a journal with the title *Hochland* began publication in 1903 under the editorship of Carl Muth.

13. Adolf Bartels, "Heimatkunst," 19. For overviews of the literature and ideology of the *Heimatkunst* movement around the turn of the century, see Martin Travers, *Critics of Modernity;* Rossbacher, *Heimatkunstbewegung;* Haß, *Militante Pastorale;* F. R. Stern, *The Politics of Cultural Despair.*

14. The advertisement appears in Fritz Lienhard, *Die Vorherrschaft Berlins;* emphasis in original.

15. Haß, *Militante Pastorale,* 27.

16. Simon Schama, *Landscape and Memory,* 107. See also Haß, *Militante Pastorale,* 189–204.

17. Schwerte, "Ganghofers Gesundung," 169.

18. See Ludwig Ganghofer, *Lebenslauf eines Optimisten.* Or, in the formulation of a character in *Der Jäger von Fall,* "Der Traurige stirbt allweil früher als der Lustige. Dös is a Naturgesetz" (The one who is sad will always die before the one who is happy. That's a law of nature). Ganghofer, *Der Jäger von Fall,* 152.

19. For an argument favoring the former reading, see Schwerte, "Ganghofers Gesundung." Mettenleiter argues the inverse, showing the formulaic construction of Ganghofer's autobiographical writings to be modeled on the plots of his novels. Mettenleiter, *Destruktion der Heimatdichtung.*

20. Ganghofer, *Edelweißkönig,* 270.

21. Ganghofer, *Das Schweigen im Walde,* 5, 24.

22. Ganghofer, *Gewitter im Mai,* 7.

23. Ganghofer, *Das Schweigen im Walde,* 156. Similar passages abound in this and other novels; for a related and representative case of such miraculous healing, see Friedrich Lienhard's exclamation upon arriving in the Alps for the first time after a youth spent in Berlin, "bent over double, both spiritually and bodily": "O *Hochland,* my *Hochland!* Tears streamed over my hollow cheeks like those of a child who has found his mother again, like those of a convalescent who for the first time strolls through a spring garden again." Friedrich Lienhard, *Wasgaufahrten,* 156.

24. Mettenleiter, *Destruktion der Heimatdichtung,* 335.

25. Haß, *Militante Pastorale,* 19.

26. Ganghofer, *Gewitter im Mai,* 7.

27. Ibid., 21.

28. Ibid.

29. A visit to the house of the local weaver, who shows off her new electric light, prompts Poldi to muse about the comic aspect of the opposition between tradition and technology: "Dorle's little sitting room—and Edison's spirit of invention! Here and there, the Old World and the New! How these things come together." Ibid., 45.

30. Ibid., 165.

31. "The desire to express all seems a fundamental characteristic of the melodramatic mode. Nothing is spared because nothing is left unsaid." Peter Brooks, *The Melodramatic Imagination,* 4.

32. Ganghofer, *Edelweißkönig,* 345.

33. Haß, *Militante Pastorale,* 36.

34. "Heimat has to do with the long story of the dissolution of feudal traditions . . . and always represented a parting glance [*Trennungsschmerz*]." Ibid., 187. In addition to the above considerations of content, form, and ideology, the original publishing venue for most of Ganghofer's novels puts his antimodernism in a somewhat more dialectical light than his reactionary approach to plot, language, and gender would suggest. *Die Gartenlaube*, which serialized Ganghofer's texts and catapulted him to lasting fame, was deeply implicated in the modern invention of the German nation. The journal itself was part and parcel of a process of modernization that the stories would hold at bay. The magazine's popular mix of nostalgia and modernity, as well as its pioneering role in the modernization of the press, provided a distinctly modern outlet for Ganghofer's antimodernism. For all of Ganghofer's celebration of mountain solitude, his mass success made him an "early representative of the entertainment industry" (Mettenleiter, *Destruktion der Heimatdichtung*, 368). On the importance of *Die Gartenlaube* to nineteenth- and early-twentieth-century popular (and national) culture, see Kirsten Belgum, *Popularizing the Nation*.

35. Vinzenz Chiavacci, *Ludwig Ganghofer*, 9.

36. In addition to his exclusive rights as a producer, Ostermayr was involved as director on some films, beginning with the first Ganghofer series from 1918 on, and then as co-director of his Ufa productions (e.g., *Gewitter im Mai* [with Hans Deppe, 1937] and *Das Schweigen im Walde* [also with Deppe, 1937]).

37. Although Ganghofer died soon after the deal with Ostermayr was struck, he approved of the first films of the Ganghofer series. Both the contract and the friendship with the producer were renewed by Ganghofer's son August after Ganghofer's death.

38. Leonhard Adelt, "Filmkritik."

39. While Ganghofer's *Das Schweigen im Walde* does contain the flaming woods and the narrow escape over the cliff that concludes Ostermayr's film version, *Gewitter im Mai*, for example, involves no mountaineering feats. Ostermayr's adaptation of this novel in the same year, however, brings the conflict between Poldi and Domini to a head by sending one up the mountain to be saved from a storm by the other.

40. Membership in the Alpenverein tripled from 1919 to 1923; see Christian Rapp, *Höhenrausch*, 35.

41. Siegfried Kracauer, *From Caligari to Hitler*, 110.

42. Fanck's first film, indeed, appears to have been such a "view," in which the role of the camera was signaled in advance by the title, *Erste Besteigung des Monte Rosa mit Filmkamera und Skiern* (First Ascent of Monte Rosa with Film Camera and Skis, 1913). The film is assumed to have been lost. See Jan-Christopher Horak, "Dr. Arnold Fanck: Träume vom Wolkenmeer und einer guten Stube," in *Berge, Licht und Traum*, 15–67.

43. In his important article on the *Bergfilm*, Eric Rentschler paraphrases Siegfried Kracauer's critique of the mountain films for their jarring mismatch of image and narrative: "For all their masterful imagistic immediacy, these films

are seriously inept—and misguided—in their negotiation of narrative terrain" ("Mountains and Modernity," 142).

44. Ibid., 141.

45. Other significant personal continuities would necessarily include Hans Deppe, the "king of the *Heimatfilm*," as a 1998 exhibit at Berlin's Schwules Museum affectionately called him. Deppe had more remakes to his credit than any other director. He tops Höfig's list of Heimat film directors, having contributed ten films to the genre between 1947 and 1960, and fourteen during his career before 1947.

46. Kracauer, *From Caligari to Hitler*, 257–58.

47. I discuss Ostermayr's strategies for his own (and his films') de-Nazification in the next section.

48. Rentschler, *The Ministry of Illusion*, 36.

49. Rentschler explicitly underlines the "cinematic modernism" of Fanck's images (ibid.). See also Thomas Elsaesser, "Moderne und Modernisierung" and *Weimar Cinema and After.*

50. Kracauer, *From Caligari to Hitler*, 112–14.

51. Rentschler, "Mountains and Modernity," 139.

52. In a radio speech from 1931 advertising his latest feature, *Der weisse Rausch*, Fanck promised that his film "will not confront you with any problems . . . whether spiritual or ethical, nor problems of love, with the suffering they inevitably bring, nor with war and struggle, need, or social questions." Quoted in Jan-Christopher Horak, ed., *Berge, Licht und Traum*, 153.

53. Giddens, *The Consequences of Modernity*, 18.

54. See Rapp, *Höhenrausch*; see also Kracauer, *From Caligari to Hitler*, 111.

55. Giddens, *The Consequences of Modernity*, 19.

56. Elsaesser, *Weimar Cinema and After*, 392.

57. Ibid.

58. Rentschler, *The Ministry of Illusion*, 31.

59. See Thomas Jacobs, "Der Bergfilm als Heimatfilm"; Horak, "Dr. Arnold Fanck," in *Berge, Licht und Traum*; Rapp, *Höhenrausch*, 8.

60. There are, however, a number of parallels between the two films, including the name of one of the male leads—Vigo—as well as Hans Schneeberger's cinematography.

61. See Rentschler, *The Ministry of Illusion*, 31–32.

62. Ibid., 38.

63. Kracauer, *From Caligari to Hitler*, 257, 259.

64. Rentschler, *The Ministry of Illusion*, 43.

65. Friedrich Lienhard, "Los von Berlin?"

66. Wilhelm Stapel, "The Intellectual and His People." The text dates from 1930.

67. Martin Heidegger, "Creative Landscape."

68. See Jochen Meyer, ed., *Berlin/Provinz.*

69. Heidegger, "Creative Landscape," 427.

70. Riefenstahl's case is only the most famous one; Goebbels actively courted Luis Trenker, Giuseppe Becce contributed heavily to the sound track for the Third Reich, and cameramen like Sepp Allgeier, who had worked on virtually all of Fanck's films in the 1920s, moved easily from *Triumph des Willens* (1934) to *Friesennot* (1935) to Ostermayr productions like *Standschütze Bruggler* (1936) to Heimat comedies like *Das sündige Dorf* (1940).

71. See Rentschler, *The Ministry of Illusion*, 73–96.

72. Celia Applegate, "The Question of Heimat in the Weimar Republic," 67.

73. See Ulrike Haß, "Vom 'Aufstand der Landschaft gegen Berlin.'"

74. Eduard Spranger, *Der Bildungswert der Heimatkunde* (originally published in 1923).

75. Applegate, *A Nation of Provincials*, 205.

76. Fritz Wächtler, *Deutsches Volk, deutsche Heimat*, vol. 1, 7.

77. Ibid., vol. 2, 7.

78. Ibid., vol. 2, 71.

79. Applegate, "The Question of Heimat in the Weimar Republic," 67.

80. Rudy Koshar, "The Antinomies of *Heimat*," 131.

81. Press kit, Bundesarchiv/Filmarchiv, Berlin.

82. Max Hildebert Boehm, *Das eigenständige Volk*, 100.

83. Gerald Trimmel, *Heimkehr*, 64.

84. Program notes for the German premiere; facsimile in ibid., 304.

85. In one particularly stunning instance, one of the prisoners considers the Germans' plight from the perspective of bystanders. Having been deported, imprisoned, and herded into a basement, he suddenly reflects on his status as victim: "People locked up in a basement and gunned down with a machine gun through the window. And you're lying in bed without knowing of this. Or you don't want to know of it." It is difficult to decide in retrospect whether the film's images of persecution coupled with explicit reflections on the bystanders' denial would have overlaid or evoked identical scenes of deportation, not of German settlers, but of German Jews (both in Poland and "back home") in the public consciousness.

86. Quoted in Trimmel, *Heimkehr*, 63.

87. Ibid., 64.

88. Karsten Witte, "Film im Nationalsozialismus," 119.

89. See Rentschler, *The Ministry of Illusion*; Linda Schulte-Sasse, *Entertaining the Third Reich*; Sabine Hake, *Popular Cinema of the Third Reich*; Antje Ascheid, *Hitler's Heroines*.

90. David Welch, *Propaganda and the German Cinema*.

91. Hake, *Popular Cinema of the Third Reich*, 76.

92. Susan Sontag, "Fascinating Fascism," in *Under the Sign of Saturn*, 71–105.

93. Witte, "Film im Nationalsozialismus," 119.

94. Walter Freisburger, *Theater im Film*, 25.

95. Unpublished manuscripts ca. 1950, POA, catalog nos. D305002 and D305029.

96. Rentschler, *The Ministry of Illusion*, 16.

97. Ibid., 23.

98. Jeffrey Herf, *Reactionary Modernism*.

99. Rentschler, *The Ministry of Illusion*, 87.

100. See Elsaesser, *Weimar Cinema and After*, 393.

101. Ibid., 386.

102. Kraatz, *Deutscher Film Katalog*, 316.

103. Terra-Film press kit, Deutsches Filminstitut–DIF Frankfurt.

104. In Cadars and Courtade's survey, the film ranks as "one of the most vivid and beautiful films of the entire Nazi production" (*Geschichte des Films im Dritten Reich*, 173).

105. Stephen Lowry, "Ideology and Excess in Nazi Melodrama," 143.

106. See Ascheid, *Hitler's Heroines*, 69–78.

107. Lowry, "Ideology and Excess in Nazi Melodrama," 145.

108. Ascheid, *Hitler's Heroines*, 74.

109. Thomas Mann, "Deutschland und die Deutschen," quoted in Herf, *Reactionary Modernism*, 2.

110. Thomas Nipperdey, "Probleme der Modernisierung in Deutschland," 57.

111. Elsaesser, *Weimar Cinema and After*, 400.

112. Herf, *Reactionary Modernism*, 80.

113. Quoted in ibid., 150–51.

114. Ernst Jünger, *Feuer und Blut* (1929), quoted in ibid., 79.

115. Herf, *Reactionary Modernism*, 85.

116. Ibid., 155.

117. Ibid., 22.

CHAPTER 3

Epigraph: Capito, "Zutaten."

1. Indeed, we return to their deliberations for increasingly short periods of screen time, and for long stretches we are reminded of their presence/present only through brief interjections bracketed by dissolves from, and back to, the embedded story. Only at the very end does the narrative return for good to the time and space of the frame.

2. This was apparently the working title of Jugert and Käutner's film during production.

3. On *Glückskinder* in the context of Ufa under the Nazis, see Rentschler, *The Ministry of Illusion*, 99–122.

4. Robert R. Shandley, *Rubble Films*, 157–58.

5. Ibid., 155.

6. More than any other actress of the time, Knef had symbolized this departure ever since her debut in *Die Mörder sind unter uns* (see Johannes von Moltke and Hans J. Wulff, "Trümmer-Diva"); she would be replaced in this nationally symbolic function only by Romy Schneider in the successful *Sissi* films of the 1950s.

7. Shandley, *Rubble Films,* 160.

8. On these continuities see Hans-Peter Kochenrath, "Kontinuität im deutschen Film."

9. Deppe's other films included *Schloß Hubertus* (1934), *Die Heilige und ihr Narr* (1935), *Der Jäger von Fall* (1936), *Gewitter im Mai* (1937), *Die kluge Schwiegermutter* (1939), *Der laufende Berg* (1941), and *Der Ochsenkrieg* (1942).

10. Hans Stüwe, who played Lüder Lüdersen in the 1951 remake of *Grün ist die Heide,* had been a prominent actor under the Nazis, working for a number of Ostermayr productions in the 1930s as well as in the self-reflexive *Heimatfilm* about filmmaking on the heath entitled *Dahinten in der Heide* (1936) and in the revue *Es war eine rauschende Ballnacht,* where he starred alongside Zarah Leander and Marika Rökk.

11. Claudius Seidl, *Der deutsche Film der fünfziger Jahre,* 187.

12. Capito, "Zutaten."

13. Bliersbach, *So grün war die Heide,* 33–46.

14. Manfred K. Wolfram, "Film in the Federal Republic of Germany," 372.

15. Bliersbach mentions "melancholia" and reads Lüdersen's poaching as "revenge" for his expulsion from the East. Bliersbach, *So grün war die Heide,* 39.

16. Douglas Sirk, *Sirk on Sirk.* King justifiably speaks of the film's "many false endings" ("Placing *Green Is the Heath,*" 140).

17. Bredow and Foltin, *Zwiespältige Zufluchten,* 120.

18. Rainer Werner Fassbinder, *The Anarchy of the Imagination,* 78.

19. See, respectively, Bärbel Westermann, *Nationale Identität im Spielfilm der fünfziger Jahre,* 189–203; Bredow and Foltin, *Zwiespältige Zufluchten,* 107–15; Moeller, *War Stories,* 132, 134; Fehrenbach, *Cinema in Democratizing Germany,* 161; King, "Placing *Green Is the Heath.*"

20. The phrase is Walter Schmieding's and appears as a chapter heading in his bitter 1961 retrospective of the cinema of the preceding decade, *Kunst oder Kasse.*

21. Bliersbach notes in his introduction that the plot summary is something he wishes to avoid; his descriptions and "Gefühls-Analysen," however, tend to be rather eclectic and associative, driven by an interest in the representation of family and/or national conflict.

22. "Grün ist die Heide" in *Evangelischer Film-Beobachter* 411 (1951).

23. Indeed, a "classical" conception of narrative, derived either from Hollywood or, more locally, from Ufa models, may not be the dominant paradigm here at all. Given the prominence of the operetta or the *Revue* as sources for the *Heimatfilm,* we might expect quite different relations between spectacle and narration. At times, indeed, it seems as though narration is entirely subordinated to a logics of display, moving the aesthetics of the *Heimatfilm* closer to those of a Heimat museum than of a Heimat novel.

24. Fehrenbach, *Cinema in Democratizing Germany,* 152.

25. See Wolfgang Liebeneiner's self-serving comments at the time in "Film-industrie und Filmkunst sind zweierlei!"

26. Peter Ostermayr's productions are again emblematic; see, for example, his patented Garutso-Plastorama lenses, advertised in his annual production company newsletter, *Peter-Ostermayr-Express,* in 1954. If the narratives of Ganghofer remained his trademark, their specific visualization was his actual trade.

27. The claim that this was the first German color film is not true, of course; it was merely the first such film after the war.

28. Höfig, *Der deutsche Heimatfilm,* 228–29.

29. This spectrum, according to the kit, went from "himmelblau" (sky blue) to "hellblaugrün" (light blue-green), "grün" (green), "hellviolett" (light purple), "intensivgrün" (intense green), and "erikafarben" (bluish purple) to "dunkel-grün" (dark green); lettering was to be in dark green and light yellow.

30. Rudolf Lange, "Das norddeutsche 'Schwarzwaldmädel.'"

31. The film's West German distributor, Rosemarie Kraemer of Union-Film, reputedly insisted that these make up at least 60 percent of the film; see Man-fred Barthel, *So war es wirklich,* 101.

32. Bobby Lüthge, "Remaking."

33. Fehrenbach, *Cinema in Democratizing Germany,* 152.

34. Quoted in Projektgruppe deutscher Heimatfilm, *Der deutsche Heimat-film,* 73.

35. The film's ostentatious wipes that separate individual scenes as much as they connect them further amplify this impression of an additive dramaturgy.

36. Joachim Storch, "Grün ist die Heide."

37. A contemporary review mentions the fact that these gags were particu-larly successful with the 350 refugee children who had been invited to the pre-miere. See G. Pf., "Auf der Leinwand."

38. Tom Gunning, "The Cinema of Attraction."

39. Rentschler, "Mountains and Modernity," 142.

40. See particularly Edward Dimendberg, *Film Noir and the Spaces of Modernity.*

41. See King, "Placing *Green Is the Heath.*"

42. The distributor for the 1932 version of *Grün ist die Heide* marketed an illustrated anthology of peasant novellas and hunting stories by Hermann Löns along with the film (and under the same title).

43. The quintessential example here would be *Mein Schatz ist aus Tirol* (1958), a *Nummernfilm* that tapped the market for Heimat tie-ins with the music industry and transported viewers from Tyrolean vineyards to South Sea beaches, sacrificing the unity of space for the unity of the musical spectacle.

44. A particularly good example of the latter occurs in *Wenn am Sonntagabend die Dorfmusik spielt.* Here we are treated to a composition by Rudolf Prack himself entitled "Meine Heimat ist die ganze Welt." Interestingly, the detachment of Heimat from a specific place (the heath, the Black Forest, the

Riesengebirge) results in its rearticulation with tropes of wandering, ostensibly the irreconcilable opposite of Heimat.

45. Riess, *Das gibt's nur einmal,* 226.

46. Massey, *Space, Place and Gender,* 170.

CHAPTER 4

Epigraph: W. G. Sebald, *On the Natural History of Destruction,* 13.

1. Göttler, "Westdeutscher Nachkriegsfilm," 197–98.

2. Schama, *Landscape and Memory,* 107.

3. Ibid.

4. "In a time of public euphoria," writes Karsten Witte, "this film indulges in liminal zones between city and country, Heimat and barren terrain." Witte, "Film im Nationalsozialismus," 131.

5. Enno Patalas, "Phantomkino."

6. On the role of the Heimat tradition for *Nachtschatten,* see dlw, "Grenzgänger, Grenzverletzer."

7. Besides Schilling, Werner Herzog played a central role in this return, most obviously with his remake of Murnau's famous film *Nosferatu, the Vampyre* (1979).

8. Majer O'Sickey, "Framing the *Unheimlich,*" 207.

9. Heinrich Böll, *Haus ohne Hüter,* 88; emphasis in original.

10. Alexander Mitscherlich and Margarete Mitscherlich, *The Inability to Mourn;* Wolfgang Benz, quoted in Alon Confino, "Traveling as a Culture of Remembrance," 93.

11. See Wolfdietrich Schnurre, *Rettung des deutschen Films;* Gunter Groll, *Magie des Films;* Arthur Maria Rabenalt, *Die Schnulze.*

12. Hembus, *Der deutsche Film kann gar nicht besser sein,* 133.

13. Schmieding, *Kunst oder Kasse.*

14. For a representative text in this vein from the 1970s, see Klaus Kreimeier, *Kino und Filmindustrie in der BRD.*

15. Heide Schlüpmann speaks of a wholesale "derealization" of the past in West German cinema during the 1950s (Schlüpmann, "Wir Wunderkinder").

16. Bliersbach, *So grün war die Heide,* 36.

17. Kreimeier, "Die Ökonomie der Gefühle," 24.

18. Frank Stern, "Film in the 1950s," 266.

19. Confino, "Traveling as a Culture of Remembrance," 94.

20. Theodor W. Adorno, "What Does Coming to Terms with the Past Mean."

21. Moeller, *War Stories,* 16.

22. Fehrenbach, *Cinema in Democratizing Germany;* Confino, "Traveling as a Culture of Remembrance"; Biess, "Survivors of Totalitarianism."

23. Alon Confino and Peter Fritzsche, "Introduction," in *The Work of Memory,* 14.

24. For a remarkably nuanced discussion, especially of the ways in which

recent history wound its way into the plots and character constellations of the *Heimatfilm*, see Rippey, Sundell, and Townley, "'Ein wunderbares heute,'" 144–46.

25. Hanna Schissler, ed., *The Miracle Years*, 235.

26. Apparently nervous about the title's generic implications, the distributor claims to have agreed to *Rosen blühen auf dem Heidegrab* only after being pressured by an "overwhelming" number of theater owners acting as proxy for "the wide base of the audience itself." Previous titles had been *Das Mädchen Dorothee* and *Das Lied der Heide*. See press kit, Stiftung deutsche Kinemathek (SdK), Berlin.

27. "Durchbruch zum stilechten deutschen Landschaftsfilm"; see press kit, SdK, Berlin.

28. Advertising copy further included tag lines such as "Ein Film der Heimat frei nach Hermann Löns" or "Eine Filmballade der Heimat—ein Gedicht nach dem Herzen von Löns."

29. This pretension could be further substantiated by reference to another intertext from the literary canon, not of Löns poems and *Heimatliteratur*, but of Goethe poems and "high" literature: *Rosen blühen auf dem Heidegrab* contains more than just an allusion to Goethe's *Heidenröslein* and the corresponding Schubert *Lied*. Thanks to Christopher Wickham for pointing out this striking analogy.

30. Press kit, SdK; emphasis in original.

31. Ibid.

32. J.-t., "Rosen blühen auf dem Heidegrab."

33. Schnurre, *Rettung des deutschen Films*, 9.

34. Fehrenbach, *Cinema in Democratizing Germany*, 156.

35. Ibid., 157.

36. Press kit, SdK, Berlin.

37. Indeed, it was already too realistic in Blachnitzky's film, which was censored by the Allied troops occupying the Rhineland in the wake of World War I. See *Mitteilungen des Reichskommissars für die besetzten rheinischen Gebiete Ausgegeben zu Koblenz*, no. 12 (15 December 1929), excerpted by Herbert Birett, http://www.unibw-muenchen.de/campus/Film/mitteil.htm.

38. On the relationship between cultural and generic verisimilitude, see Steve Neale, "Questions of Genre."

39. This is not to suggest that a war film would have been unacceptable to the public; on the contrary, the 1950s enjoyed a glut of war films that exculpated the soldiers of a "clean" Wehrmacht and indicted the high command for the "aberrations" of World War II.

40. Moeller, *War Stories*, 12.

41. HHK, "Rosen blühen auf dem Heidegrab."

42. In addition to the flashback and the story as it unfolds in the present, we are offered another mise-en-abîme of the rape story in a symbolic dance at a country fair.

43. Atina Grossmann, "A Question of Silence," 59.

44. Ibid., 49.

45. As late as 1965, Erich Kuby held that "everyone knows someone who has been raped or who knows someone in turn to whom this happened." Kuby, *Die Russen in Berlin, 1945*, quoted in Ingrid Schmidt-Harzbach, "Eine Woche im April," 28.

46. Elizabeth Heinemann, "The Hour of the Woman," 30.

47. Apparently, different translations of this book circulated in Germany during the early 1950s, among them one bearing the title *Frau, komm: Berlin 1945*, trans. Ursula Lynn (Berlin: Amsel, 1954). A 1952 translation by Werner Asendorf appeared under the original English title, *The Big Rape*, with the same publisher that had published the first English edition in 1951 (Rudl in Frankfurt).

48. Heinemann, "The Hour of the Woman," 21.

49. Ibid., 22.

50. Grossmann, "A Question of Silence." In particular, Grossman shows how different ideologemes concerning abortion, population politics, and race overlapped in these documents.

51. Helene Rahms, "Die bleiche Moorlilie."

52. See in particular the Anglo-American newsreel series *Welt im Film*, no. 5, "KZ," 15 June 1945. I am grateful to Ulrike Weckel for alerting me to these sources.

53. In compilation footage of exhumations at Hadamar, in particular, we witness workers disinterring a female corpse; the voice-over in *Todesmühlen* comments dryly, "That was a woman."

54. On the circulation of images of the Holocaust, see Habbo Knoch, *Die Tat als Bild*, and Cornelia Brink, *Ikonen der Vernichtung*.

55. Claudia Koonz, "Between Memory and Oblivion," 265.

56. On the notion of films as cultural events, see Anton Kaes, "German Cultural History and the Study of Film."

57. Göttler, "Westdeutscher Nachkriegsfilm," 182.

58. Norbert Grob, "Via Mala."

CHAPTER 5

Epigraph: Elisabeth Pfeil, *Der Flüchtling*, 11.

1. We should recall that Blachnitzky's original version of *Rosen blühen auf dem Heidegrab* framed the entire story as being occasioned by a couple's curiosity at the grave on the heath. Like Riefenstahl's *Das blaue Licht* before it and *Wenn die Heide blüht* (1960) after it, *Rosen blühen auf dem Heidegrab* foregrounds the urban visitor as the addressee of Heimat tradition.

2. In terms of economic growth, Germany led Western European economies and was surpassed only by Japan during the decade. GNP tripled between 1950 and 1960 and employment increased by 25 percent even as the labor market was forced to accommodate millions of refugees from the East. Axel Schildt and Arnold Sywottek, " 'Reconstruction' and 'Modernization.' "

3. The following discussion draws particularly on the work of Axel Schildt and Arnold Sywottek. They trace the restoration thesis to a generally leftist position that made it possible, both for contemporaries and for historians working in the 1970s, "to understand the gap between their expectations and the reality of developments after the collapse in 1945" (ibid., 414). See also Schildt and Sywottek, eds., *Modernisierung im Wiederaufbau*.

4. See Robert G. Moeller, *Protecting Motherhood*.

5. See Heide Fehrenbach, *Cinema in Democratizing Germany*.

6. Lutz Niethammer, " 'Normalization' in the West," 237.

7. Mitscherlich and Mitscherlich, *The Inability to Mourn*, 79.

8. Peter Blickle, *Heimat*, 7.

9. "What was mobility in the [American] musical freezes into hierarchy in the revue film; what was in motion rigidifies." Karsten Witte, "Visual Pleasure Inhibited," 244; Schlüpmann translates this diagnosis for the 1950s in "Wir Wunderkinder."

10. Göttler, "Westdeutscher Nachkriegsfilm," 173.

11. The introduction of the term *modernization* in discussions of the 1950s dates back to Ralf Dahrendorf, *Gesellschaft und Demokratie in Deutschland*. The most sustained work on the various aspects of modernization is undoubtedly Schildt and Sywottek's. However, cultural historians have also contributed significantly to our understanding of the different facets of modernization, especially in their focus on the Americanization of (youth) culture on both sides of the German border. See Kaspar Maase, *BRAVO Amerika*; Poiger, *Jazz, Rock, and Rebels*.

12. As has often been pointed out, the "inability to mourn" and the repressive force that enacted this rupture with the past found expression in the purposeful turn towards reconstruction and modernization now known as the *Wirtschaftswunder*. See Mitscherlich and Mitscherlich, *The Inability to Mourn*.

13. Bausinger, *Folk Culture in a World of Technology*, 39.

14. See Dietrich Hilger, "Die mobilisierte Gesellschaft"; also Schildt and Sywottek, " 'Reconstruction' and 'Modernization.' " Broadening this claim, Konrad Jarausch and Michael Geyer have recently advocated a paradigm of mobility and migration as one of the keys to rethinking twentieth-century German history. Jarausch and Geyer, *Shattered Past*, 197–220.

15. Schildt and Sywottek, " 'Reconstruction' and 'Modernization,' " 415.

16. Hilger, "Die mobilisierte Gesellschaft," 105.

17. Founded in 1927, Neue Heimat was union owned; it flourished during the 1950s and influenced architecture and urban planning through the 1970s until it collapsed amid scandals in the early 1980s.

18. Carter, *How German Is She?* especially chap. 2, "The Housewife as Consumer-Citizen."

19. Ibid., 68. Kristin Ross makes very similar observations about the modernization of the home in France during these years. See Ross, *Fast Cars, Clean Bodies*.

20. Kaspar Maase, "Freizeit," 212.

21. Christian Bongräber, "Hitparade des guten Geschmacks."

22. Anselm Doering-Manteuffel, "Die Kultur der 50er Jahre," 534.

23. Peter Ostermayr, manuscript for a speech on his eightieth birthday, POA, catalog no. 100020, 3.

24. Evaluations of the film ranged from "distinguished *Heimatfilm*" (*Kölner Rundschau*, 7 March 1959) to "synthetic *Heimatfilm*" (*Abendzeitung*, 6 November 1958) to "unimportant but—one has to admit—cleanly and appealingly made *Heimatfilm*. One for the heart" (*Hannoversche Allgemeine*, 16 Mai, 1959). This unquestioned rubricization of *Die Landärztin* as a *Heimatfilm* is particularly interesting in view of the fact that the distributor (Gloria) pushed the film as an *Arztfilm* (doctor film), another popular genre of the decade. Given the hybridity of the *Heimatfilm* as a genre, this presents no conflict in principle but reveals the dominance of the Heimat label in public and critical perception by 1958.

25. Only one in eighty citizens owned a car in 1950; by 1960 this figure had increased to one in twelve. The number of motorcycles and scooters peaked at 2.1 million around mid-decade. See Thomas Südbeck, "Motorisierung, Verkehrsentwicklung und Verkehrspolitik," 171.

26. Hannelore Brunhöber, "Wohnen," 201. See also Arnold Sywottek, "From Starvation to Excess?" 347.

27. Ross, *Fast Cars, Clean Bodies*, 21.

28. Hermann Glaser, *Kulturgeschichte der Bundesrepublik Deutschland*, vol. 2, 248.

29. Ibid., 23.

30. Confino, "Traveling as a Culture of Remembrance."

31. Ibid., 106.

32. For a contemporary topographical source, see Helmut Hahn, *Die Erholungsgebiete der Bundesrepublik*.

33. Hans-Joachim Knebel, *Soziologische Strukturwandlungen im modernen Tourismus*.

34. Hahn, *Die Erholungsgebiete der Bundesrepublik*.

35. The terms are Caren Kaplan's; see *Questions of Travel*, 58. An authoritative contemporary sociology of tourism is Knebel, *Soziologische Strukturwandlungen im modernen Tourismus*. For recent perspectives on the issue, see Eckhard Siepmann, ed., *Bikini*, and Südbeck, "Motorisierung, Verkehrsentwicklung und Verkehrspolitik." The standard sociological treatise on expellees, to which I return in chap. 6, is Helmut Schelsky, *Wandlungen der deutschen Familie*.

36. Undoubtedly, this has biographical reasons; Hans-Joachim Knebel, on whose work I am drawing here, was a student of Helmut Schelsky's.

37. Knebel, *Soziologische Strukturwandlungen im modernen Tourismus*, 56.

38. Südbeck, "Motorisierung, Verkehrsentwicklung und Verkehrspolitik."

39. Seeßlen, "Der Heimatfilm," 354.

40. Although the film's gender politics are hardly enlightened, one should note that its implicit critique of the villagers' reactionary misogyny is biting and effective. The open-mouthed silence with which the villagers "greet" the female doctor is sustained just long enough to let us experience their gender politics as

a profound humiliation of the protagonist, with whom we have been aligned from the start.

41. Ross, *Fast Cars, Clean Bodies,* 21–22; emphasis in original.

42. For a discussion of Rick Altman's approach to genre theory and history, from which I borrow these distinctions, see chap. 1.

43. An early exchange between Harcort and one of the locals, Dr. Erdmann, makes the warden's past explicit. Explaining his leniency towards a local poacher, Harcort notes that he has not been reinstalled in his position as civil servant and therefore "no longer has any say on the premises." When Erdmann tells him just to be patient, as if to suggest that the dust of the Nazi past will settle soon enough, Harcort complains, "Well, I certainly hope so. Right now, people are making it difficult to do your old job again." Later we learn that Harcort has just returned from detention as a POW. It seems remarkable that a film from 1960 would choose to set up its story in this way in 1950, only to retire the *Förster* altogether after his confession. The logics of guilt and acquittal played out in this film across the generational divide between Harcort and Rolf certainly merit a closer look. At the very least, their staging in such explicit terms suggests again that instead of simply claiming that the Nazi past is wholly absent from the cinema of the 1950s, we need to apply the categories of escapism and retreat in more nuanced ways..

44. "I'll always find some ship/That carries me off into the wide world/If I'm no longer happy at home/I'll head off to wherever I'm happy."

45. Rural audiences predictably had much greater qualms about the Heimat film's lack of authenticity and were clearly not the genre's intended audience. Willi Höfig quotes a 1951 survey in which *Schwarzwaldmädel,* one of the prototypes of the *Heimatfilm* of the 1950s, topped the audience ranking of then-current films; the only dip in the film's popularity was in the Schwarzwald itself. See Höfig, *Der deutsche Heimatfilm,* 74n414.

46. Hardt, "Der heimatlose Heimatfilm," 71.

47. Edgar Reitz, *Drehort Heimat,* 267.

48. Rentschler, *West German Film in the Course of Time,* 105.

49. Seeßlen, "Der Heimatfilm," 349.

50. Ross observes this motif in French films of the same years. Ross, *Fast Cars, Clean Bodies,* 29.

51. *Peter-Ostermayr-Express* 4, no. 12: 3 (POA, catalog no. W100614).

52. Ross, *Fast Cars, Clean Bodies,* 22–23.

53. Herf, *Reactionary Modernism,* 208.

54. According to Willi Höfig's statistics for the period 1947–1960 (*Der deutsche Heimatfilm,* 457). On Liebeneiner, see John Davidson, "Working for the Man, Whoever That May Be."

CHAPTER 6

Epigraph: Wolfgang Liebeneiner, "Machen künstlerische Filme den Staat ärmer?"

1. "The modernized remake of this film, which was first shot twenty years

ago, turned out to be a Heimat mixture of sentimentality, nobility, and love." Review in file on *Waldwinter* at Bundesarchiv/Filmarchiv, Berlin.

2. Quoted in press clipping from Bundesarchiv/Filmarchiv, Berlin, dated 1955 by hand.

3. Distributor's kit in Deutsches Filminstitut–DIF file on *Waldwinter*. Of all Germans fleeing west from the territories east of the Oder and Neisse rivers, 40 percent were Silesians, making this a particularly appealing demographic group for the marketers of Liebeneiner's film. See Theodor Schieder, *Die Vertreibung der deutschen Bevölkerung*, 51E.

4. The song lyrics encapsulate the impossibility of any return by displacing it to a utopian future, when it will snow red roses and rain green wine: "Adieu my little darling/But when will you return/But when will you return, my dearest love?/When it snows red roses and rains green wine/Adieu my darling, I leave you/Adieu my little darling."

5. Beginning in 1954, the Federal Ministry for Expellees (Bundesministerium für Vertriebene) published a series of volumes that document these stories, providing an unparalleled source for further historical research. The series, which includes Schieder's *Die Vertreibung der deutschen Bevölkerung*, was reissued in 1984; see Schieder, ed., *Dokumentation der Vertreibung*. An English-language version of the entire series followed the original 1958–60 German publication (Schieder, ed., *Documents on the Expulsion of the Germans from Eastern-Central-Europe*). For an in-depth account of the academic and political background of the study and its historiographical implications, see Moeller, *War Stories*, chap. 2, and an interview with historian Hans-Ulrich Wehler, "Die Debatte wirkt befreiend."

6. See Moeller, *War Stories*.

7. For the purposes of postwar representation, Martin's uniform has been stripped of any Nazi insignia, although it remains clearly legible as standard Wehrmacht issue.

8. K. Erik Franzen, ed., *Die Vertriebenen*, 280–81.

9. In 1950, expellees constituted 33 percent of the population of Schleswig-Holstein; other figures were lower, varying from roughly 5 percent in Rhineland-Palatinate to 27.2 percent in Lower Saxony. Ibid., 281. See also Hilger, "Die mobilisierte Gesellschaft," 105.

10. "Charta der deutschen Heimatvertriebenen, Stuttgart, 5. August 1950," available at http://www.bund-der-vertriebenen.de/derbdv/charta-dt.php3.

11. See Moeller, "Sinking Ships." These debates have recently resurfaced in a number of publications and in the popular media more generally. Moeller takes as his point of departure the recent publication of Günter Grass, *Im Krebsgang*. Other recent literary treatments of the topic include Walter Kempowski and Dirk Hempel, *Das Echolot*, and Suhrkamp's reissue of Arno Schmidt's *Die Umsiedler*. Both of the German public television stations addressed this topic in two highly publicized documentations, *Die große Flucht* (ZDF) and *Die Vertriebenen* (ARD). Both are available on video and were accompanied by copiously illustrated book publications; see Guido Knopp, *Die*

große Flucht, and Franzen, *Die Vertriebenen. Der Spiegel* published a special issue on the subject, "Die Flucht der Deutschen" (*Spiegel Spezial* 2 [2002]).

12. The credits for *Heimat, Deine Lieder* acknowledge the Bundesministerium für Vertriebene as the source for the proposed film, whose original title was "Städte in Schlesien."

13. Jürgen Trimborn, *Der deutsche Heimatfilm der fünfziger Jahre,* 116.

14. See especially *Kölner Zeitschrift für Soziologie* 3.2 (1951), reporting on the sociological congress of 1950, which was devoted to the topic of refugees. Also Pfeil, *Der Flüchtling;* Schelsky, *Wandlungen der deutschen Familie.*

15. Pfeil, *Der Flüchtling,* 213.

16. Ibid., 6, 13.

17. Cf. Schelsky, *Wandlungen der deutschen Familie,* 47.

18. Ibid., 50.

19. Pfeil, *Der Flüchtling,* 14.

20. Schelsky, *Wandlungen der deutschen Familie,* 50.

21. Ibid., 43.

22. The influential notion that the 1950s produced a "leveled-off middle-class society" was first formulated by Schelsky in the context of *Wandlungen der deutschen Familie.* Here he argued that the specific forms of upward and downward social mobility that characterized the sociopolitical landscape of the postwar decade had led "not only to an extraordinary increase in social mobility per se, [but also] to the development of a leveled-off, petit bourgeois/middle-class society which is neither proletarian nor bourgeois, and which is defined, therefore, by a loss of class tension and social hierarchies" (218). Schelsky's notion of the *nivellierte Mittelstandsgesellschaft* remained influential with sociologists for many years to come. For a recent critique of this paradigm, see Schildt and Sywottek, " 'Reconstruction' and 'Modernization.' "

23. Pfeil's study comes to similar conclusions; like Schelsky, she sees the increased importance of the role of women as decision makers within the family as a specific instance of a much broader development. Pfeil, *Der Flüchtling,* 79.

24. Schelsky, *Wandlungen der deutschen Familie,* 49. See also Schelsky, "Die Flüchtlingsfamilie," 163.

25. See Gilles Deleuze and Félix Guattari, *Nomadology.* For a useful critical overview of different concepts of mobility and their uses in postmodern theory, see John Durham Peters, "Exile, Nomadism, and Diaspora." Iain Chambers offers one of the more celebratory accounts of postmodern mobility in *Migrancy, Culture, Identity.* Caren Kaplan undertakes an extensive critique of some of the more troubling nomadological assumptions in *Questions of Travel.*

26. Clifford, *Routes,* 44.

27. Ibid., 43. Konrad Jarausch and Michael Geyer have recently advanced a similar argument for the particular case of Germany. Identifying migration as one of the central themes that ties together Germany's "shattered past," they emphasize that "twentieth-century Germany . . . ought not to be conceptualized as a bedrock of stability but rather considered as an 'unsettled society. . . . For many more Germans than is usually assumed, migration was a crucial part of

their individual or collective experiences. . . . Perhaps the German craving for a self-image of stability should itself be thought a response to a profound feeling of unsettlement." Jarausch and Geyer, *Shattered Past*, 219.

28. See Franzen, *Die Vertriebenen*, 212–21.

29. Indeed, West Germany (centered on the map) and Berlin (isolated behind the iron curtain in the prisoner-striped wasteland of the German Democratic Republic and Poland) are represented as agglomerations of airports, which provide so many points of entry to the territory.

30. See Franzen, *Die Vertriebenen*, 212, 215.

31. Literally "my people," the phrase can be taken to imply both that these people are of the same provenance as the baron and that they work for him.

32. See Rentschler, "Mountains and Modernity."

33. Lest this parallel escape any viewer, the baroness will later make it explicit: "Each one of them, after all, has brought a little piece of his Heimat along. The Bavarian Forest and the Riesengebirge are so similar that everyone almost feels at home already."

34. On the function of Heimat as "local metaphor," see Confino, *The Nation as Local Metaphor*.

35. The POW experience plays into the plot a number of times as both Gerstenberg and Martin refer to the hardships they endured. On the generalization of that experience as a foundational narrative for the Federal Republic, see Moeller, *War Stories*.

36. Seeßlen, "Der Heimatfilm," 350.

37. Ibid., 353.

38. Confino, *The Nation as Local Metaphor*, 112.

39. Press kit, Bundesarchiv/Filmarchiv, Berlin.

40. Moeller, *War Stories*, 137.

41. Ibid., 139.

42. Seeßlen, "Der Heimatfilm," 349.

43. Moeller, *War Stories*, 138.

44. Ibid., 139.

45. Barthel, *So war es wirklich*, 104.

46. I draw here on Willi Höfig's "quantitative" analysis of characteristic *Heimatfilm* elements in *Der deutsche Heimatfilm*.

47. Unlike *The Sound of Music*, Liebeneiner's films usually maintain diegetic continuity for the musical numbers, motivating them as part of a concert, a family activity, etc. In such cases, all singing and the instrumentation are given sources within the image, whereas a musical such as *The Sound of Music* will routinely orchestrate the song and dance numbers extradiegetically. I will return to an exception to this rule in my discussion of *Die Trapp-Familie in Amerika*.

48. For a total of exactly forty-three, according to Höfig, *Der deutsche Heimatfilm*, 185; viewers of *The Sound of Music* will recall the expansive aerial shots of this landscape that set the stage for Julie Andrews's opening number, "The Hills Are Alive with the Sound of Music."

49. I say "hyper-American" because many of these figures are played by German actors who overcompensate for their difficulty with the language by attempting to project every received cliché about America in their acting.

50. In Wise's film, we leave the family crossing the Alps into neutral Switzerland, a rewriting of biography and geography that outraged Maria von Trapp when she first saw the film.

51. Wolfgang Schwerbrock, "Der Siegeszug der Blockflöte." The phrase appears in English in the review.

52. Both its placement at the end of the film and the mise-en-scène identify this immigration scene as a quote from the first film.

53. This brief sequence of dissolves might profitably be read against the famous dissolve from *Der verlorene Sohn*. There, Trenker exploits a graphic match by dissolving from a towering Alpine setting to the Manhattan skyline in order to shift from Heimat to its modern American "other" (only to return, of course, to the former). Liebeneiner reverses the direction of the dissolve from Manhattan to the mountains; moreover, this series of cuts significantly contributes to the achievement of narrative closure *in* America even while foregrounding issues of emigration and cultural incongruity by returning us, ultimately, to the INS. On the function of America in *Der verlorene Sohn* see Rentschler, *The Ministry of Illusion*.

54. The performance of the final song is couched in a rhetoric of exchange: John D. Hammerfield (represented by the film as your average American millionaire) has helped the family members obtain their immigration papers. In return, Maria offers to sing for him and his Austrian wife. As they prepare for the final song, one of the Trapp children exclaims, "Pay by check and you earn trust, pay cash and you make friends!"—a line which he has picked up from a brochure titled "How to Become a Millionaire." Dr. Wasner agrees—"Fine, then let's pay cash"—though of course they end up paying in kind rather than in cash, substituting cultural exchange for economic currency.

55. The other direct address to the camera occurs when the family makes over its newly acquired Vermont barn into a Tyrolean farmhouse and accompanies this activity with a song (see the discussion in the following section).

56. Jameson, "Reification and Utopia in Mass Culture," 145.

57. In light of this explicit construction of the GI identity, an earlier shot of a towering black man holding a smiling and very white Trapp daughter becomes anchored as well in the historical cliché that it evokes.

58. Eric Rentschler, "How American Is It?"; see also Gerd Gemünden, *Framed Visions*.

59. Indeed, it seems noteworthy that the adaptation suppresses aspects of Maria von Trapp's memoir that would have complicated the family's sense of displacement by giving it historical specificity. In particular, von Trapp recounts a return trip to Salzburg in the summer of 1939, just before the outbreak of World War II, which leads her to make a distinction between Salzburg as her "home" and Heimat as a place where one can "*feel* at home"; accordingly, her return to Austria a year after the *Anschluß* teaches her that Salzburg can no

longer be Heimat, cementing her and her family's exile. See Maria Augusta von Trapp, *Die Trapp Familie,*157–58.

60. Bernhard Frankfurter, "Heile Welt und Untergang," 340.

61. Rentschler, "How American Is It?" 616.

62. Seeßlen, "Der Heimatfilm," 361–62.

63. In a sense, Maria's miraculous (and at the same time pragmatic) ability to see her family through marks her as a personification of the *Wirtschaftswunder* narrative. As her husband notes, "She manages everything. I don't know how she does it, but she manages everything."

64. Rentschler, "How American Is It?" 613.

65. See Kaspar Maase, *BRAVO Amerika.*

66. See Anne Friedberg, *Window Shopping;* Jane Gaines, "The Queen Christina Tie-Ups"; Charles Eckert, "The Carole Lombard in Macy's Window."

67. Laura Mulvey, "Visual Pleasure and Narrative Cinema," 19. Note however, that the salesman insists that sex appeal also works for men, where it means displaying your masculine charms. The reason this is not pursued is that one of the women insists that *"she* [i.e., Maria] wants to know."

68. See Pierre Bourdieu, *Distinction.*

69. Moreover, like many other films of this era, *Die Trapp-Familie in Amerika* contained songs which became *Schlager* in their own right, their lyrics reprinted in the program notes.

70. Maase, *BRAVO Amerika,* 14.

71. Ross, *Fast Cars, Clean Bodies,* 53.

72. This is Ross's reading of the discursive logic behind French car advertising during the 1950s. Ibid., 22.

73. Poiger, *Jazz, Rock, and Rebels,* 3; my emphasis.

74. Ibid., 225.

CHAPTER 7

1. Exceptions are Harry Blunk, "The Concept of 'Heimat-GDR' in DEFA Feature Films" and the chapter "Heimatfilm in der DDR: Annäherung an eine Fragestellung" in Projektgruppe deutscher Heimatfilm, *Der deutsche Heimatfilm,* 149–72. See also Elizabeth Boa and Rachel Palfreyman, *Heimat a German Dream,* 130–43. Leonie Naughton contributes a different twist on the topic by suggesting that the GDR itself has become a regained Heimat for the West since unification. See Naughton, *That Was the Wild East.* All of these contributions provide valuable insights on the topic but move too easily from films set in rural areas to the notion of Berlin as Heimat, thereby diluting the generic framework to the point where any connection to West German developments seems rather haphazard. By contrast, I hope to maintain the comparative focus in order to suggest points of contact and—perhaps unwitting, but often provocative— dialog between the two countries.

2. See especially Ralf Schenk and Christiane Mückenberger, *Das Zweite*

Leben der Filmstadt Babelsberg; Seán Allan and John Sandford, eds., *DEFA;* and Joshua Feinstein, *The Triumph of the Ordinary.*

3. See Eric Rentschler, "Film der achtziger Jahre" and "From New German Cinema to the Postwall Cinema of Consensus"; Hans-Joachim Neumann, *Der deutsche Film heute.*

4. Katie Trumpener's forthcoming book, *The Divided Screen,* promises to do so. For an approach that emphasizes the relations between DEFA and the international avant-garde, see Barton Byg, "DEFA and the Traditions of International Cinema."

5. Enno Patalas, "Die zerrissene Leinwand"; Peter Zimmermann, ed., *Der geteilte Himmel;* Filmarchiv Austria, ed., *Der geteilte Himmel.*

6. For numerous examples of such exchanges, see Ralf Schenk, "Mitten im kalten Krieg."

7. Byg, "DEFA and the Traditions of International Cinema," 23.

8. Ibid.

9. See Arnd Brauerkämper, "Collectivization and Memory."

10. Literally "over there," this term was habitually used as shorthand for the other part of Germany by citizens of the East and West alike.

11. Wolf completed this film as his final project for the Russian State Institute of Cinematography (VGIK) in Moscow.

12. "Günter Kochan's music creates a lighthearted, optimistic atmosphere and Werner Bergmann's camera has really captured colorful images of our Heimat. Together with the fresh play of the actors, music and image appeal strongly to the spectator's Heimat feeling." "Einmal ist keinmal."

13. Schenk, "Mitten im kalten Krieg," 115.

14. See, e.g., "Einmal ist keinmal"; ae, "Schöne Landschaft, Musik und Liebe"; Hermann Martin, "So märchenhaft und so modern."

15. In a somewhat willful interpretation, this comic effect might also be seen to suggest the considerably less funny limitation upon travel that was imposed by the GDR: before the train can reach its distant (Western) destination, it is forced back.

16. Wolf's film dovetails with the official valorization of folklore at the second party congress of the SED in 1952. Peter Hoff, *"Einmal ist keinmal."*

17. D.K., "Ein Film aus der Lausitz"; mtr, "Sorbische Ernte"; "52 Wochen sind ein Jahr"; Rainer Kerndl, "Das Jahr des alten Krestan."

18. See Hoff, *"Einmal ist keinmal."* Hoff's main reference for the definition of the genre and the categorization of *Einmal ist keinmal* within that genre is still Höfig's *Der deutsche Heimatfilm.*

19. Celia Applegate, *A Nation of Provincials,* 229.

20. E.g., Johannes R. Becher, *Schöne deutsche Heimat* or Uwe Berger, *Straße der Heimat.*

21. Sigrid Schwarz, "Die Liebe zur Heimat"; Günter Lange, *Heimat.*

22. Dieter Riesenberger, "Heimatgedanke und Heimatgeschichte in der DDR."

23. Some 4.3 million expellees resettled on GDR territory, amounting to 25

percent of the entire population. For a comparative discussion of the representation of expulsion in East and West German cinema, see Johannes von Moltke, "*Standort* Heimat."

24. Blunk, "The Concept of 'Heimat-GDR in DEFA Feature Films,'" 205.

25. Edeltanne literally fails to read his nephew's writing when he interprets a waltz that Peter has composed for Anna. The piece makes no musical sense whatsoever at the hands of Edeltanne's group, which he defends as "the last bastion of experienced musicians for the preservation of occidental tone"; only when Peter sits down at the piano to play his own composition are rhythm, melody, and coherence reestablished.

26. Schwarz, "Die Liebe zur Heimat."

27. Ibid., 75. The threat of a third world war becomes explicit in some of the films discussed later in this chapter, notably *Das verurteilte Dorf.*

28. G. Lange, *Heimat*, 67–69; Schwarz, "Die Liebe zur Heimat," 76–78; Otto Schröder, "Die bourgeoise Heimatideologie."

29. "Erfahrung Heimat," special issue, *Neue Deutsche Literatur* 32.10 (October 1984): 5.

30. Schwarz, "Die Liebe zur Heimat,"158, 109.

31. On the link between Heimat and the Marxist theory of labor, see G. Lange, *Heimat*, 84–90.

32. Günter Lange speaks in this sense of "the socialist Heimat as the future, desired perspective of class struggle, consciously adopted by the avant-garde of the proletariat." Ibid., 55.

33. Ibid., 29.

34. Hermann Martin, "52 Wochen sind ein Jahr."

35. Schenk, "Mitten im kalten Krieg," 112.

36. See the entry "Propaganda" in *Kleines politisches Wörterbuch*, 4th ed. (Berlin: J. H. W. Dietz, 1983), 778.

37. Rosemarie Rehahn, "Das große Filmepos."

38. Heinz Baumert, *Grundfragen der Filmdramaturgie*, 87–89.

39. Ibid., 85.

40. cz, "Ein Durchbruch im deutschen Filmschaffen"; W. Joho, "Ein beispielhafter Film," 3; Leo Menter, "Das verurteilte Dorf," 1–2; Lilly Becher, "Das Urteil wurde aufgehoben." See also Baumert, *Grundfragen der Filmdramaturgie.* Along with *Geheimakten Solvay*, *Das verurteilte Dorf* serves Baumert as an example of the third and highest stage in the development of DEFA films at the time of his writing.

41. d.w., "Das verurteilte Dorf."

42. Schenk, "Mitten im kalten Krieg," 74.

43. Rehahn, "Das große Filmepos."

44. Hermann Martin, "Die Hauptsache—Bärenweiler bleibt!"

45. L. Becher, "Das Urteil wurde aufgehoben."

46. Rehahn, "Das große Filmepos."

47. Moeller, *War Stories*, 3.

48. "Ein echtes Deutschland-Lied, das unsere Herzen leidenschaftlich

bewegt . . . ein einzigartiges vaterländisches Dokument." Rehahn, "Das große Filmepos."

49. In a reversal that suggests the volatility of this film's uncontained cold war politics, the slogan "Deutschland den Deutschen" has since been adopted by neo-Fascist groups whose xenophobia is no longer directed against American occupation troops, but largely against immigrant populations in a unified Germany.

50. Rehahn, "Das große Filmepos."

51. See one reviewer's claim that "the country becomes landscape, and the people that inhabit it cannot be separated from it." Menter, "Das verurteilte Dorf," 2.

52. L. Becher, "Das Urteil wurde aufgehoben."

53. Well into production, the working title for *Schlösser und Katen* was *Der Schein.* The motif of the *Schein* plays on a double entendre of the German word as both a note or document and as illusion or appearance. The document, it turns out, is a mere red herring, a motivating force for the action that is in itself completely insubstantial: in the end, the mayor will finally sum up what for Anton has been a long process of recognition: "Everything you believed was just an illusion [*Schein*]."

54. Significantly, the entire plot of the film is situated in Holzendorf; although the city is decidedly part of the diegesis, functioning alternatively as the dystopian site of *Landflucht* or the utopian place of modernity, the camera never leaves Holzendorf and its surroundings.

55. Kurt Barthel, who wrote the script for *Schlösser und Katen,* allegedly spent years studying life in the countryside.

56. Projektgruppe deutscher Heimatfilm, *Der deutsche Heimatfilm,* 157.

57. G. Lange, *Heimat,* 131–32.

58. Kurt Maetzig, *Filmarbeit.*

59. Hildegard Haase (LPG member in Dahlen), "Eine Genossenschaftsbäuerin schreibt"; Bergemann, "Als die Bauern heraustraten"; Wolfgang Heun (director of a *Maschinen-Traktoren-Station* [MTS] in Krüden), "Gedanken zu 'Schlösser und Katen.'"

60. Claudia Deltl, "Vorwärts und nicht vergessen." I have not been able to corroborate the existence of this label in any sources from the 1950s.

CHAPTER 8

Epigraphs: Anton Kaes, From Hitler to Heimat, 164; Edward Soja, Postmodern Geographies, 24.

1. Wolf Donner, "Das Idyll ist kaputt," 11.

2. Ibid.

3. On the relationship between the *Anti-Heimatfilm* and the *Volksstück,* see Rentschler, *West German Film in the Course of Time.*

4. Altman, *Film/Genre,* 208.

5. *Provinz-Film-Katalog,* Munich, 1981; quoted in Schacht, *Fluchtpunkt Provinz,* 227–28.

6. Rentschler, *West German Film in the Course of Time*, 122.

7. Ibid., 111.

8. Peter Harcourt, "The Sudden Wealth of the Poor People of Kombach," *Film Quarterly* (Fall 1980), quoted in ibid., 118.

9. On the critique of "everyday fascism" in *Jagdszenen*, see Schacht, *Fluchtpunkt Provinz*, 30–61.

10. Günter Pflaum, "Jagdszenen aus Niederbayern," *Jugend und Fernsehen* 4–5 (1969), quoted in ibid., 61.

11. Schacht, *Fluchtpunkt Provinz*, 215.

12. Ibid., 214.

13. Rentschler rightly points out a continued legacy of the *Anti-Heimatfilm* through the 1970s, which I also trace through more recent years in the epilogue. See Rentschler, *West German Film in the Course of Time*, 124.

14. One recent critic pitted it against *Schlösser und Katen*, claiming it as "a valuable corrective to Edgar Reitz's *Heimat*." Martin Brady, "Discussion with Kurt Maetzig," 80.

15. Massey, *Space, Place and Gender*, 170–71.

16. Reitz, *Drehort Heimat*, 132.

17. See http://reinder.rustema.nl/heimat/heimat.html; see also the *Heimat* link page http://home.t-online.de/home/th.hoenemann/heimat/heimlinks.htm.

18. Jim Hoberman, "Once in a Reich Time," reprinted in Miriam Hansen, "Dossier on *Heimat*," 9; Morley and Robbins, *Spaces of Identity*, 93.

19. Hoberman, "Once in a Reich Time," in Hansen, "Dossier on *Heimat*," 9; Gertrud Koch, "How Much Naiveté Can We Afford? The New *Heimat* Feeling," *Frauen und Film* 38 (May 1985), reprinted in Hansen, "Dossier on *Heimat*," 14, 16.

20. Hansen, "Dossier on *Heimat*," 3.

21. Michael Geisler, "*Heimat* and the German Left," 27–28.

22. Kaes, *From Hitler to Heimat*, 170.

23. Edgar Reitz, *Liebe zum Kino*, 141–43.

24. See Rachel Palfreyman, *Edgar Reitz's* Heimat.

25. Neale, "Questions of Genre," 160.

26. Heide Schlüpmann in "That's Why Our Mothers Were Such Nice Chicks" (discussion with Gertrud Koch, Heide Schlüpmann, and Klaus Kreimeier), reprinted in Hansen, "Dossier on *Heimat*," 19.

27. Bredow and Foltin, *Zwiespältige Zufluchten*.

28. Geisler, "*Heimat* and the German Left." The most exhaustive treatment of *Heimat* in the context of the Heimat tradition is Alon Confino, "Edgar Reitz's *Heimat* and German Nationhood."

29. Thomas Elsaesser, "The New German Cinema's Historical Imaginary," 281, 289.

30. See Saul Friedländer, *Reflections of Nazism*; Hansen, "Dossier on *Heimat*."

31. See Peter Baldwin, *Reworking the Past*. Rachel Palfreyman details the

importance of this context for Reitz's film in *Edgar Reitz's* Heimat. See also Eric Santner, "On the Difficulty of Saying 'We.'"

32. "That's Why Our Mothers Were Such Nice Chicks," in Hansen, "Dossier on *Heimat*," 18.

33. Jürgen Kocka, "Hitler sollte nicht durch Stalin und Pol Pot verdrängt werden," 141.

34. Eric Santner, *Stranded Objects*, 90.

35. Koch in "That's Why Our Mothers Were Such Nice Chicks," in Hansen, "Dossier on *Heimat*," 16.

36. Confino, "Edgar Reitz's *Heimat* and German Nationhood."

37. Ibid. Jim Hoberman makes a similar point in "Once in a Reich Time," in Hansen, "Dossier on *Heimat*," 9; Santner then repeatedly picks up Koch's notion of the fade-out (see, e.g., Santner, *Stranded Objects*, 92–93).

38. Confino, "Edgar Reitz's *Heimat* and German Nationhood." Unfortunately, Confino's own contribution stops short of the analysis he calls for. Discussing *Heimat* as a moment in (cultural) history, Confino fails to anchor his arguments in any sustained reading of the film as an aesthetic text involving specific generic patterns, formal constructions, and spectatorial dispositions. Instead, his reading relies, as many others have, more on Reitz's published essays and commentary than on his film.

39. Hoberman, "Once in a Reich Time," in Hansen, "Dossier on *Heimat*."

40. Thomas Elsaesser, "Heimat (Homeland)," *Monthly Film Bulletin* (February 1985), reprinted in Hansen, "Dossier on *Heimat*," 21.

41. Schlüpmann in "That's Why Our Mothers Were Such Nice Chicks," in Hansen, "Dossier on *Heimat*," 19.

42. Kaes, *From Hitler to Heimat*, 171.

43. Santner, *Stranded Objects*, 89.

44. See, e.g., Edgar Reitz, "Die Kamera ist keine Uhr: Über meine Erfahrung beim Erzählen von Geschichten aus der Geschichte," in *Liebe zum Kino*, 110.

45. Koch, "How Much Naiveté Can We Afford?" in Hansen, "Dossier on *Heimat*," 15.

46. Klaus Kreimeier remarks perceptively, but *en passant*, that *Heimat* "is certainly a product of the new sensibility towards the historicity of small spaces" (Kreimeier in "That's Why Our Mothers Were Such Nice Chicks," in Hansen, "Dossier on *Heimat*," 17). Kaes points out that "Reitz addresses the tension between time and place characteristic of regional narration by temporalizing space" (Kaes, *From Hitler to Heimat*, 177). This highly suggestive remark is amplified by Rachel Palfreyman's recent reading of *Heimat* for its various "chronotopes." Palfreyman breaks new ground in the analysis of space in *Heimat*, and my reading of the film consequently intersects in important ways with hers (Palfreyman, *Edgar Reitz's* Heimat).

47. Santner, *Stranded Objects*, 60.

48. Ibid., 78.

49. Ibid., quoting Jacques Derrida, "Plato's Pharmacy."

50. On the connection between Heimat and *Heimweh,* see Blickle, *Heimat,* 67–71.

51. Ibid., 7.

52. *Leaving Home* is the title of Edgar Reitz's follow-up series, *Die zweite Heimat,* for English-language distribution.

53. The notion of centrifugal space is developed by Edward Dimendberg in reference to the (cinematic) history of the autobahn and to the spaces of film noir in Dimendberg, "The Will to Motorization" and *Film Noir and the Spaces of Modernity.* I will return to his useful discussion later in this chapter.

54. David Morley, "Bounded Realms," 152.

55. Elsaesser, "Heimat (Homeland)," in Hansen, "Dossier on *Heimat,*" 23.

56. Reitz, *Liebe zum Kino,* 170–71. Interestingly, Reitz describes the pair Lucie/Eduard in terms of the commingling between inside and outside that my reading aims to track; viewing the rushes, he "can breathe again and the entire Hunsrück becomes bearable, because these are characters who signal that one can get back out and who simultaneously show me that one can be outside and yet here at the same time."

57. This motif has already been alluded to during the sequence showing Paul's entry into the village.

58. For a helpful discussion of viewer-character relations beyond the paradigm of identification, see Murray Smith, *Engaging Characters.*

59. Doreen Massey, "A Place Called Home," 8.

60. Edgar Reitz and Peter Steinbach, *Heimat,* shot 110.

61. For a related discussion, see Christopher Wickham, "Representation and Mediation in Edgar Reitz's *Heimat,*" 42.

62. Palfreyman, *Edgar Reitz's* Heimat, 156.

63. Morley, "Bounded Realms," 153.

64. Confino, "Edgar Reitz's *Heimat* and German Nationhood," 207.

65. Quoted in ibid., 190.

66. Elsaesser, "Heimat (Homeland)," in Hansen, "Dossier on *Heimat,*" 20. Besides *Deutschland bleiche Mutter,* Elsaesser lists Fassbinder's *Die Ehe der Maria Braun, Deutschland im Herbst,* and *Die bleierne Zeit.* On the allegorization of Germany as victim, see Eric Rentschler, "Remembering Not to Forget."

67. Elsaesser, "Heimat (Homeland)," in Hansen, "Dossier on *Heimat,*" 20.

68. This is Santner's reading of the film, and his most trenchant critique: "Mourning the destruction of Schabbach cannot replace or displace the *Trauerarbeit* created by Auschwitz. Or vice versa. The fatal error is to place these tasks in competition with one another, to imagine, as Reitz seems to, that *Heimat* must overcome *Holocaust.*" Santner, *Stranded Objects,* 101.

69. Confino, "Edgar Reitz's *Heimat* and German Nationhood," 191.

70. Ibid., 192.

71. Thomas McLaughlin, "Figurative Language," 83.

72. Ibid., 84.

73. "In the final analysis, the centripetal orientation of [Reitz's] gospel of a

new-found regionalism reveals a perennial and quintessentially German dichotomy: 'Heimat' and 'Deutschland' as seemingly irreconcilable antinomies." Dieter Saalmann, "Edgar Reitz's View of History," 12.

74. Hartmut Bitomsky, *Reichsautobahn*, quoted in Dimendberg, "The Will to Motorization," 104.

75. Ibid., 99.

76. The design of the autobahn actually favored curves for changing views. See ibid.

77. Ibid., 93.

78. Karsten Witte, "Of the Greatness of the Small People: The Rehabilitation of a Genre," reprinted in Hansen, "Dossier on *Heimat*," 8.

EPILOGUE

Epigraph: Salman Rushdie, *The Wizard of Oz*.

1. Williams, *The Country and the City*, 289.

2. Ibid., 248.

3. Ibid., 297.

4. Hobsbawm and Ranger, *The Invention of Tradition*, 1; cf. also Giddens's discussion of tradition in "Living in a Post-Traditional Society."

5. Hobsbawm and Ranger, *The Invention of Tradition*, 2. Celia Applegate also emphasizes both the "dubious antiquity" of *Heimat* and the fact that it "originated in a period of rapid social transformation," supplying a wealth of concrete historical evidence for both of these claims. Applegate, *A Nation of Provincials*, 10.

6. Hobsbawm and Ranger, *The Invention of Tradition*, 4.

7. Williams, *The Country and the City*, 1.

8. Ibid., 12.

9. Ibid., 289.

10. Ibid.

11. Bredow and Foltin, *Zwiespältige Zufluchten*, 24; see also Kirsten Belgum's study of *Die Gartenlaube*, which links the national imaginary of that magazine to the increased mobility of Germans in the nineteenth century; Belgum, *Popularizing the Nation*.

12. Peter Sloterdijk, "Der gesprengte Behälter."

13. Applegate, *A Nation of Provincials*, 15.

14. Bernhard Schlink, *Heimat als Utopie*, 23–24.

15. See, for example, the special edition of *Der Spiegel* "Sehnsucht nach Heimat" (*Spiegel Spezial* 6 [June 1999]); Thomas E. Schmidt, *Heimat*; Schlink, *Heimat als Utopie*; Martin Hecht, *Das Verschwinden der Heimat*.

16. Naughton, *That Was the Wild East*.

17. Ibid., 131–37.

18. Rentschler, "From New German Cinema to the Postwall Cinema of Consensus," 264.

19. Hake, *German National Cinema*, 179.

20. Rentschler, "From New German Cinema to the Postwall Cinema of Consensus," 263.

21. Lutz Koepnick, "Reframing the Past."

22. Andrew Higson, "The Heritage Film and British Cinema," 233.

23. This is to say nothing of the links to be found in heritage discourse outside of the cinema. An excellent overview by John Corner and Sylvia Harvey provides many suggestive leads for comparison. The relation of heritage and tourism, the emphasis on rural aspects of heritage, and the compensatory function of heritage in mediating tradition and modernity, in particular, speak directly to the uses of Heimat that I have discussed in this study. See John Corner and Sylvia Harvey, eds., *Enterprise and Heritage.*

24. Lutz Koepnick, " 'Amerika gibt's überhaupt nicht!' "

25. Ibid.

26. For close analysis of the scenes in question, see Johannes von Moltke, "Heimat and History."

27. Koepnick, "Reframing the Past," 51.

28. Kristin Kopp, "Exterritorialized Heritage in Caroline Link's *Nirgendwo in Afrika.*"

29. This is the term the film's official website uses in its synopsis: http://nirgendwoinafrika.de/flash.php.

30. Kopp, "Exterritorialized Heritage in Caroline Link's *Nirgendwo in Afrika*," 2.

31. *Cinema* 12 (2001), quoted at http://www.cyberkino.de/entertainment/kino/1110/111182.html.

32. Kopp, "Exterritorialized Heritage in Caroline Link's *Nirgendwo in Afrika*," 4.

33. Ibid., 13–20.

34. *Irgendwo in Deutschland* is the title of the second part of Stefanie Zweig's autobiographical narrative, which begins where Link's film leaves off.

35. For a detailed reading of Danquart's compelling *Heimatfilm*, see Moltke, "Heimat and History."

36. On the functions of nostalgia and its imaginary spaces in the culture of the Berlin Republic, see Julia Hell and Johannes von Moltke, "Unification Effects."

Bibliography

Adelt, Leonhard. "Filmkritik: Der Edelweißkönig." *Film-Kurier*, 6 September 1920.

Adorno, Theodor W. "What Does Coming to Terms with the Past Mean." In *Bitburg in Moral and Political Perspective*, ed. Geoffrey H. Hartmann, 114–29. Bloomington: Indiana University Press, 1986.

ae. "Schöne Landschaft, Musik und Liebe: Außenaufnahmen zu dem neuen DEFA-Film 'Einmal ist keinmal.'" *Der Morgen*, 24 October 1954.

Allan, Seán, and John Sandford, eds. *DEFA: East German Cinema, 1946–1992*. New York: Berghahn Books, 1999.

Altman, Rick. *Film/Genre*. London: BFI, 1999.

———. "A Semantic/Syntactic Approach to Film Genre." In *Film Genre Reader II*, ed. Barry Keith Grant. Austin: University of Texas Press, 1995.

Améry, Jean. "How Much Home Does a Person Need?" *At the Mind's Limits: Contemplations by a Survivor on Auschwitz and Its Realities*, 41–61. Bloomington: Indiana University Press, 1980.

Appadurai, Arjun. *Modernity at Large: Cultural Dimensions of Globalization*. Minneapolis: University of Minnesota Press, 1996.

Applegate, Celia. *A Nation of Provincials: The German Idea of Heimat*. Berkeley: University of California Press, 1990.

———. "The Question of Heimat in the Weimar Republic." *New Formations* 17 (1992): 64–74.

Ascheid, Antje. *Hitler's Heroines: Stardom and Womanhood in Nazi Cinema*. Philadelphia: Temple University Press, 2003.

Baldwin, Peter. *Reworking the Past: Hitler, the Holocaust, and the Historians' Debate*. Boston: Beacon Press, 1990.

Bartels, Adolf. "Heimatkunst." *Heimat: Blätter für Litteratur und Volkstum* 1.1 (1900): 10–19.

Barthel, Manfred. *So war es wirklich: Der deutsche Nachkriegsfilm*. Munich: Herbig, 1986.

Baumert, Heinz. *Grundfragen der Filmdramaturgie: Analysen von Drehbüchern der DEFA 1946–1953.* Heidenau: Mitteldeutsche Verlagsanstalt, 1956.

Bausinger, Hermann. *Folk Culture in a World of Technology.* Bloomington: Indiana University Press, 1990.

———. "Heimat und Identität." In *Heimat und Identität: Probleme regionaler Kultur,* ed. Konrad Köstlin and Hermann Bausinger. Neumünster: Wachholtz, 1980.

Becher, Johannes R. *Schöne deutsche Heimat.* Berlin: Aufbau-Verlag, 1952.

Becher, Lilly. "Das Urteil wurde aufgehoben." *Berliner Zeitung,* 17 February 1952.

Beck, Ulrich. *Risk Society: Towards a New Modernity.* London: Sage, 1992.

Beck, Ulrich, Anthony Giddens, and Scott Lash. *Reflexive Modernization: Politics, Tradition, and Aesthetics in the Modern Social Order.* Stanford: Stanford University Press, 1994.

Belgum, Kirsten. *Popularizing the Nation: Audience, Representation, and the Production of Identity in* Die Gartenlaube, *1853–1900.* Lincoln: University of Nebraska Press, 1998.

Bergemann. "Als die Bauern heraustraten: Zur Aufführung des zweiteiligen DEFA-Films 'Schlösser und Katen.' " *Freie Erde,* 14 March 1957.

Berger, Uwe. *Straße der Heimat: Gedichte.* Berlin: Aufbau-Verlag, 1955.

Berg-Ganschow, Uta. "Der Widerspenstigen Zähmung." *Frauen und Film* 35 (1984): 24–28.

Berman, Marshall. *All That Is Solid Melts into Air: The Experience of Modernity.* New York: Viking Penguin, 1988.

Biess, Frank. "Survivors of Totalitarianism: Returning POWs and the Reconstruction of Masculine Citizenship in West Germany, 1945–1955." In *The Miracle Years: A Cultural History of West Germany, 1949–1968,* ed. Hanna Schissler, 57–82. Princeton: Princeton University Press, 2001.

Birett, Herbert. *Das Filmangebot in Deutschland, 1895–1911.* Munich: Filmbuchverlag Winterberg, 1991.

Blickle, Peter. *Heimat: A Critical Theory of the German Idea of Homeland.* Rochester: Camden House, 2002.

Bliersbach, Gerhard. *So grün war die Heide.* Weinheim: Beltz, 1989.

Bloch, Ernst. *Das Prinzip Hoffnung.* 3 vols. Frankfurt: Suhrkamp, 1959.

Blunk, Harry. "The Concept of 'Heimat-GDR' in DEFA Feature Films." In *DEFA: East German Cinema, 1946–1992,* ed. Seán Allan and John Sandford, 204–21. New York: Berghahn Books, 1999.

Boa, Elizabeth, and Rachel Palfreyman. *Heimat, a German Dream: Regional Loyalties and National Identity in German Culture, 1890–1990.* Oxford: Oxford University Press, 2000.

Boehm, Max Hildebert. *Das eigenständige Volk: Volkstheoretische Grundlagen der Ethnopolitik und Geisteswissenschaften.* Göttingen: Vandenhoek & Ruprecht, 1932.

Böll, Heinrich. *Haus ohne Hüter.* Cologne: Kiepenheuer & Witsch, 1954.

Bolten, Jürgen. "Heimat im Aufwind: Anmerkungen zur Sozialgeschichte eines

Bedeutungswandels." In *Literatur und Provinz: Das Konzept "Heimat" in der neueren Literatur*, ed. Hans-Georg Pott, 23–38. Paderborn: Schöningh, 1989.

Bongräber, Christian. "Hitparade des guten Geschmacks: Wohnen, Kunst und Schönheitspflege in den 50er Jahren." In *Bikini: Die fünfziger Jahre: Kalter Krieg und Capri-Sonne*, ed. Eckhard Siepmann. Reinbek: Rowohlt, 1981.

Bourdieu, Pierre. *Distinction: A Social Critique of the Judgement of Taste*. Cambridge, Mass.: Harvard University Press, 1984.

Brady, Martin. "Discussion with Kurt Maetzig." In *DEFA: East German Cinema, 1946–1992*, ed. Seán Allan and John Sandford, 72–92. New York: Berghahn Books, 1999.

Brauerkämper, Arnd. "Collectivization and Memory: Views of the Past and the Transformation of Rural Society in the GDR from 1952 to the Early 1960s." *German Studies Review* 25.2 (2002): 213–25.

Bredow, Wilfried von, and Hans-Friedrich Foltin. *Zwiespältige Zufluchten: Zur Renaissance des Heimat-Gefühls*. Berlin: J. H. W. Dietz, 1981.

Brink, Cornelia. *Ikonen der Vernichtung: Öffentlicher Gebrauch von Fotografien aus nationalsozialistischen Konzentrationslagern nach 1945*. Berlin: Akademie-Verlag, 1998.

Bronfen, Elisabeth. *Heimweh: Illusionsspiele in Hollywood*. Berlin: Volk & Welt, 1999.

Brooks, Peter. *The Melodramatic Imagination: Balzac, Henry James, Melodrama, and the Mode of Excess*. New Haven: Yale University Press, 1976.

Brunhöber, Hannelore. "Wohnen." In *Die Bundesrepublik Deutschland: Geschichte in drei Bänden*, ed. Wolfgang Benz. Frankfurt: Fischer, 1983.

Bundeszentrale für politische Bildung, ed. *Heimat: Lehrpläne, Literatur, Filme*. Bonn: Bundeszentrale für politische Bildung, 1990.

Butry, Walter. *Münchner Porträts: Peter Ostermayr*. Munich: Olzog, 1957.

Byg, Barton. "DEFA and the Traditions of International Cinema." In *DEFA: East German Cinema, 1946–1992*, ed. Seán Allan and John Sandford, 22–41. New York: Berghahn Books, 1999.

Capito. "Zutaten: Grün ist die Heide." *Filmblätter*, 4 January 1952.

Caprio, Temby. "Women's Film Culture in the Federal Republic of Germany: Female Spectators, Politics, and Pleasure from the Fifties to the Nineties." Ph.D. diss., University of Chicago, 1999.

Carter, Erica. *How German Is She? Postwar West German Reconstruction and the Consuming Woman*. Ann Arbor: University of Michigan Press, 1997.

Chambers, Iain. *Migrancy, Culture, Identity*. London: Routledge, 1994.

Chiavacci, Vinzenz. *Ludwig Ganghofer: Ein Bild seines Lebens und Schaffens*. Stuttgart: Bonz, 1905.

Clifford, James. *Routes: Travel and Translation in the Late Twentieth Century*. Cambridge, Mass.: Harvard University Press, 1997.

Confino, Alon. "Edgar Reitz's *Heimat* and German Nationhood: Film, Memory, and Understandings of the Past." *German History* 16.2 (1998): 185–208.

———. *The Nation as Local Metaphor: Württemberg, Imperial Germany, and*

National Memory, 1871–1918. Chapel Hill: University of North Carolina Press, 1997.

———. "Traveling as a Culture of Remembrance: Traces of National Socialism in West Germany, 1945–1960." *History and Memory* 12.2 (2000): 92–121.

Confino, Alon, and Peter Fritzsche. *The Work of Memory: New Directions in the Study of German Society and Culture*. Urbana: University of Illinois Press, 2002.

Corner, John, and Sylvia Harvey, eds. *Enterprise and Heritage: Crosscurrents of National Culture*. London: Routledge, 1991.

Courtade, Francis, and Pierre Cadars. *Geschichte des Films im Dritten Reich*. Trans. Florian Hopf. Munich: Hanser, 1975.

cz. "Ein Durchbruch im deutschen Filmschaffen." *Forum* 5 (1952): 11–12.

Dahrendorf, Ralf. *Gesellschaft und Demokratie in Deutschland*. Munich: Piper, 1965.

Davidson, John. "Working for the Man, Whoever That May Be: The Vocation of Wolfgang Liebeneiner." In *Cultural History through a National Socialist Lens*, ed. Robert Reimer, 240–67. Rochester: Camden House, 2000.

Davidson, John, and Sabine Hake, eds. *German Cinema of the 1950s*. Providence: Berghahn Books, forthcoming.

Dear, Michael, and Steven Flusty, eds. *The Spaces of Postmodernity: Readings in Human Geography*. Oxford: Blackwell, 2002.

Deleuze, Gilles, and Félix Guattari. *Nomadology: The War Machine*. Trans. Brian Massumi. New York: Semiotext(e), 1986.

Deltl, Claudia. "Vorwärts und nicht vergessen." In *Der geteilte Himmel: Höhepunkte des DEFA-Kinos 1946–1992*, ed. Filmarchiv Austria. Vienna: Filmarchiv Austria, 2001.

Dimendberg, Edward. *Film Noir and the Spaces of Modernity*. Cambridge, Mass.: Harvard University Press, 2004.

———. "The Will to Motorization: Cinema, Highways, and Modernity." *October* 73 (1995): 91–137.

Dirlik, Alf. "The Global in the Local." In *Global/Local: Cultural Production and the Transnational Imaginary*, ed. Rob Wilson and Wimal Dissanayake, 21–45. Durham: Duke University Press, 1996.

D.K. "Ein Film aus der Lausitz." *Lausitzer Rundschau*, 2 December 1955.

dlw. "Grenzgänger, Grenzverletzer: Ein deutscher Filmemacher aus der Schweiz." *Neue Zürcher Zeitung*, 26 March 1987.

Doering-Manteuffel, Anselm. "Die Kultur der 50er Jahre im Spannungsfeld von 'Wiederaufbau' und 'Modernisierung.'" In *Modernisierung im Wiederaufbau: Die westdeutsche Gesellschaft der 50er Jahre*, ed. Axel Schildt and Arnold Sywottek. Bonn: J. H. W. Dietz, 1998.

Donner, Wolf. "Das Idyll ist kaputt: Der kritische Heimatfilm—eine neue Gattung." *Die Zeit*, 9 December 1972.

Durovicová, Natasa. "Some Thoughts at an Intersection of the Popular and the National." *The Velvet Light Trap* 34 (1994): 4–9.

d.w. "Das verurteilte Dorf." *Lausitzer Rundschau*, 30 March 1984.

Dyer, Richard, and Ginette Vincendeau. *Popular European Cinema*. London: Routledge, 1992.

Eckert, Charles. "The Carole Lombard in Macy's Window." In *Fabrications: Costume and the Female Body*, ed. Jane Gaines and Charlotte Herzog. New York: Routledge, 1990.

Editors. "Introduction." *The Velvet Light Trap* 34 (1994): 1–2.

"Einmal ist keinmal." *Neues Deutschland*, 31 March 1955.

Eleftheriotis, Dimitris. *Popular Cinemas of Europe: Studies of Texts, Contexts, and Frameworks*. New York: Continuum, 2001.

Elsaesser, Thomas. "Early German Cinema: A Second Life?" In *A Second Life: German Cinema's First Decades*, ed. Thomas Elsaesser and Michael Wedel. Amsterdam: Amsterdam University Press, 1996.

———. "Moderne und Modernisierung: Der deutsche Film der dreißiger Jahre." *Montage/AV* 3.2 (1994): 23–40.

———. *New German Cinema: A History*. New Brunswick: Rutgers University Press, 1989.

———. "The New German Cinema's Historical Imaginary." In *Framing the Past: The Historiography of German Cinema and Television*, ed. Bruce Murray and Christopher Wickham, 280–307. Carbondale: Southern Illinois University Press, 1992.

———. *Weimar Cinema and After: Germany's Historical Imaginary*. London: Routledge, 2000.

E.M. "Film-Ehe mit Ganghofer: Peter Ostermayr wurde 75." *Süddeutsche Zeitung*, 21 June 1957.

Fassbinder, Rainer Werner. *The Anarchy of the Imagination: Interviews, Essays, Notes*. Ed. Michael Töteberg and Leo A. Lensing, trans. Krishna Winston. Baltimore: Johns Hopkins University Press, 1992.

Fehrenbach, Heide. *Cinema in Democratizing Germany: Reconstructing National Identity after Hitler*. Chapel Hill: University of North Carolina Press, 1995.

Feinstein, Joshua. *The Triumph of the Ordinary: Depictions of Daily Life in the East German Cinema, 1949–1989*. Chapel Hill: University of North Carolina Press, 2002.

Filmarchiv Austria, ed. *Der geteilte Himmel: Höhepunkte des DEFA-Kinos 1946–1992*. Vienna: Filmarchiv Austria, 2001.

Frankfurter, Bernhard. "Heile Welt und Untergang: Heimat/film als Subkultur." In *Der Sprung im Spiegel: Filmisches Wahrnehmen zwischen Fiktion und Wirklichkeit*, ed. Christa Blümlinger, 335–42. Vienna: Sonderzahl, 1990.

Franzen, K. Erik, ed. *Die Vertriebenen: Hitlers letzte Opfer*. Berlin: Propyläen, 2001.

Freisburger, Walter. *Theater im Film: Eine Untersuchung über die Grundzüge und Wandlungen in den Beziehungen zwischen Theater und Film*. Emsdetten: Lechte, 1936.

Freud, Sigmund. "The Uncanny." *Complete Pyschological Works: Standard Edition*. Vol. 17, 219–52. London: Hogarth Press, 1955.

Friedberg, Anne. *Window Shopping: Cinema and the Postmodern.* Berkeley: University of California Press, 1993.

Friedländer, Saul. *Reflections of Nazism: An Essay on Kitsch and Death.* New York: Harper & Row, 1984.

Gaines, Jane. "The Queen Christina Tie-Ups: Convergence of Show Window and Screen." *Quarterly Review of Film and Video* 11.1 (1990): 35–60.

Ganghofer, Ludwig. *Edelweißkönig: Hochlandsroman.* Stuttgart: Th. Knaur Nachf., n.d.

———. *Gewitter im Mai.* Munich: Droemersche Verlagsanstalt, n.d.

———. *Der Jäger von Fall: Hochlandsroman.* Stuttgart: Th. Knaur Nachf., n.d.

———. *Lebenslauf eines Optimisten.* Stuttgart: Bonz, 1912.

———. *Das Schweigen im Walde.* Berlin: G. Grote'sche Verlagsbuchhandlung, 1930.

Geisler, Michael. "*Heimat* and the German Left: The Anamnesis of a Trauma." *New German Critique* 36 (1985): 25–66.

Gemünden, Gerd. *Framed Visions: Popular Culture, Americanization, and the Contemporary German and Austrian Imagination.* Ann Arbor: University of Michigan Press, 1998.

Giddens, Anthony. *The Consequences of Modernity.* Stanford: Stanford University Press, 1990.

———. "Living in a Post-Traditional Society." In Ulrich Beck, Anthony Giddens, and Scott Lash, *Reflexive Modernization: Politics, Tradition, and Aesthetics in the Modern Social Order.* Stanford: Stanford University Press, 1994.

Glaser, Hermann. *Kulturgeschichte der Bundesrepublik Deutschland.* Vol. 2, *Zwischen Grundgesetz und großer Koalition.* Frankfurt: Fischer, 1990.

Göttler, Fritz. "Westdeutscher Nachkriegsfilm: Land der Väter." In *Geschichte des deutschen Films,* ed. Wolfgang Jacobsen, Anton Kaes, and Hans Helmut Prinzler. Stuttgart: Metzler, 1993.

Grass, Günter. *Im Krebsgang: Eine Novelle.* Göttingen: Steidl, 2002.

Gregor, Ulrich, and Enno Patalas. *Geschichte des Films.* Munich: Bertelsmann, 1973.

Grob, Norbert. "Via Mala." In *Das Jahr 1945,* ed. Hans Helmut Prinzler and Michael Althen. Berlin: Stiftung deutsche Kinemathek, 1990.

Groll, Gunter. *Magie des Films: Kritische Notizen über Film, Zeit und Welt.* Munich: Süddeutscher Verlag, 1953.

Grossmann, Atina. "A Question of Silence: The Rape of German Women by Occupation Soldiers." *October* 72 (1995): 42–63.

"Grün ist die Heide." *Evangelischer Film-Beobachter* 411 (1951).

Gunning, Tom. "Before Documentary: Early Nonfiction Film and the 'View' Aesthetic." In *Uncharted Territory: Essays on Early Nonfiction Film,* ed. Daan Hertogs and Nico de Klerk. Amsterdam: Nederlands Film Museum, 1997.

———. "The Cinema of Attraction: Early Film, Its Spectator, and the Avant-Garde." *Wide Angle* 8.3–4 (1986): 63–70.

Haase, Hildegard. "Eine Genossenschaftsbäuerin schreibt." *Leipziger Volkszeitung,* 13 March 1957.

Hahn, Helmut. *Die Erholungsgebiete der Bundesrepublik: Erläuterungen zu einer Karte der Fremdenverkehrsorte in der Deutschen Bundesrepublik.* Bonn: F. Dümmler, 1958.

Hake, Sabine. *German National Cinema.* London: Routledge, 2002.

———. *Popular Cinema of the Third Reich.* Austin: University of Texas Press, 2001.

Hansen, Miriam. "Dossier on *Heimat.*" *New German Critique* 36 (1985): 3–24.

Hardt, Claus. "Der heimatlose Heimatfilm." *Die Literatur* 11 (1952). Reprinted in *Nicht mehr fliehen: Das Kino des Ära Adenauer,* ed. Ulrich Kurowski and Thomas Brandlmeier, vol. 1, 70–72. 3 vols. Munich: Münchner Filmzentrum, 1981.

Harvey, David. *The Condition of Postmodernity: An Enquiry into the Origins of Cultural Change.* Cambridge, Mass.: Blackwell, 1990.

Haß, Ulrike. *Militante Pastorale: Zur Literatur der antimodernen Bewegungen im frühen 20. Jahrhundert.* Munich: Fink, 1993.

———. "Vom 'Aufstand der Landschaft gegen Berlin.'" In *Literatur der Weimarer Republik 1918–1933,* ed. Bernhard Weyergraf, 340–70. Munich: dtv, 1995.

Hecht, Martin. *Das Verschwinden der Heimat: Zur Gefühlslage der Nation.* Leipzig: Reclam, 2000.

Heidegger, Martin. "Creative Landscape: Why Do We Stay in the Provinces?" In *The Weimar Republic Sourcebook,* ed. Anton Kaes, Martin Jay, and Edward Dimendberg, 426–28. Berkeley: University of California Press, 1994.

"Die Heimatfilm-Welle rollt wieder." *Konkret* (15 November 1973): 18–19.

Heinemann, Elizabeth. "The Hour of the Woman: Memories of Germany's 'Crisis Years' and West German National Identity." In *The Miracle Years: A Cultural History of West Germany, 1949–1968,* ed. Hanna Schissler, 21–56. Princeton: Princeton University Press, 2001.

Hell, Julia, and Johannes von Moltke. "Unification Effects: Imaginary Landscapes of the Berlin Republic." *Germanic Review,* 80.1 (2005): 74–95.

Hembus, Joe. *Der deutsche Film kann gar nicht besser sein.* Munich: Rogner & Bernhard, 1981.

Herf, Jeffrey. *Reactionary Modernism: Technology, Culture, and Politics in Weimar and the Third Reich.* Cambridge: Cambridge University Press, 1984.

Heun, Wolfgang. "Gedanken zu 'Schlösser und Katen': Leser schreiben über einen Film." *Junge Welt,* 21 February 1957.

"Die heutige Berliner Uraufführung." *Film-Kurier,* 2 August 1927.

HHK. "Rosen blühen auf dem Heidegrab." *Münchner Merkur,* 30 March 1953.

Higson, Andrew. "The Heritage Film and British Cinema." *Dissolving Views: Key Writing on British Cinema,* 232–57. London: Cassell, 1996.

Hilger, Dietrich. "Die mobilisierte Gesellschaft." In *Die zweite Republik: 25 Jahre Bundesrepublik Deutschland: Eine Bilanz,* ed. Richard Löwenthal and Hans-Peter Schwarz. Stuttgart: Seewald Verlag, 1974.

Hobsbawm, Eric, and Terence Ranger. *The Invention of Tradition*. Cambridge: Cambridge University Press, 1992.

Hoff, Peter. "*Einmal ist keinmal:* Auf der Suche nach dem verlorenen Land der Kindheit." *Beiträge zur Film- und Fernsehwissenschaft* 31.39 (1990): 6–14.

Höfig, Willi. *Der deutsche Heimatfilm 1947–1960*. Stuttgart: Enke, 1973.

Horak, Jan-Christopher, ed. *Berge, Licht und Traum: Dr. Arnold Fanck und der deutsche Bergfilm*. Munich: Münchner Stadtmuseum, 1997.

Jacobs, Thomas. "Der Bergfilm als Heimatfilm: Überlegungen zu einem Filmgenre." *Augen-Blick* 5 (1988): 19–30.

Jameson, Fredric. "Reification and Utopia in Mass Culture." *Social Text* 1 (1979): 130–48.

———. *Signatures of the Visible*. London: Routledge, 1990.

Jarausch, Konrad, and Michael Geyer. *Shattered Past: Reconstructing German Histories*. Princeton: Princeton University Press, 2003.

Joho, W. "Ein beispielhafter Film." *Sonntag* 8 (1952).

J.-t. "Rosen blühen auf dem Heidegrab." *Film-Dienst* 2308 (1953).

Kaes, Anton. *From Hitler to Heimat: The Return of History as Film*. Cambridge, Mass.: Harvard University Press, 1989.

———. "German Cultural History and the Study of Film: Ten Theses and a Postscript." *New German Critique* 65 (1995): 47–58.

Kalbus, Oskar. *Vom Werden deutscher Filmkunst*. Altona: Cigaretten-Bilderanstalt, 1935.

Kaplan, Caren. *Questions of Travel: Postmodern Discourses of Displacement*. Durham: Duke University Press, 1996.

Kempowski, Walter, and Dirk Hempel. *Das Echolot: Fuga furiosa—ein kollektives Tagebuch, Winter 1945*. Munich: A. Knaus, 1999.

Kerndl, Rainer. "Das Jahr des alten Krestan: Ein neuer DEFA-Film nach dem Roman '52 Wochen sind ein Jahr.'" *Junge Welt*, 22 November 1955.

King, Alisdair. "Placing *Green Is the Heath* (1951): Spatial Politics and Emergent West German Identity." In *Light Motives: German Popular Film in Perspective*, ed. Randall Halle and Margaret McCarthy, 130–47. Detroit: Wayne State University Press, 2003.

Klueting, Edeltraud, ed. *Antimodernismus und Reform: Zur Geschichte der deutschen Heimatbewegung*. Darmstadt: Wissenschaftliche Buchgesellschaft, 1991.

Knebel, Hans-Joachim. *Soziologische Strukturwandlungen im modernen Tourismus*. Stuttgart: Enke, 1960.

Knoch, Habbo. *Die Tat als Bild: Fotografien des Holocaust in der deutschen Erinnerungskultur*. Hamburg: Hamburger Edition, 2001.

Knopp, Guido. *Die große Flucht: Das Schicksal der Vertriebenen*. Munich: Econ, 2001.

Koch, Gertrud. "Wir tanzen in den Urlaub: Musikfilm als Betriebsausflug." *Filme* 3 (1980): 24–29.

Kochenrath, Hans-Peter. "Kontinuität im deutschen Film." In *Film und*

Gesellschaft in Deutschland: Dokumente und Materialien, ed. Wilfried von Bredow and Rolf Zurek, 401–7. Hamburg: Hoffmann und Campe, 1975.

Kocka, Jürgen. "Hitler sollte nicht durch Stalin und Pol Pot verdrängt werden: Über Versuche deutscher Historiker, die Ungeheuerlichkeit von NS-Verbrechen zu relativieren." In *"Historikerstreit": Die Dokumentation der Kontroverse um die Einzigartigkeit der nationalsozialistischen Judenvernichtung,* ed. Rudolf Augstein. Munich: Piper, 1987.

Koepnick, Lutz. "'Amerika gibt's überhaupt nicht!' Notes on the German Heritage Film." In *German Pop Culture: How American Is It?* ed. Agnes Müller, 191–208. Ann Arbor: University of Michigan Press, 2004.

———. "Reframing the Past: Heritage Cinema and the Holocaust in the 1990s." *New German Critique* 87 (2002): 47–82.

Koonz, Claudia. "Between Memory and Oblivion: Concentration Camps in German Memory." In *Commemorations: The Politics of National Identity,* ed. John R. Gillis. Princeton: Princeton University Press, 1994.

Kopp, Kristin. "Exterritorialized Heritage in Caroline Link's *Nirgendwo in Afrika.*" *New German Critique* 87 (2002): 1–27.

Koshar, Rudy. "The Antinomies of *Heimat*: Homeland, History, Nazism." In *Heimat, Nation, Fatherland: The German Sense of Belonging,* ed. Jost Hermand and James D. Steakley, 113–36. New York: P. Lang, 1996.

Kraatz, Karl. *Deutscher Film Katalog, 1930–1945: Ufa, Tobis, Bavaria.* Frankfurt: Transit-Film, n.d.

Kracauer, Siegfried. *From Caligari to Hitler: A Psychological History of the German Film.* Ed. Leonardo Quaresima. Rev. and exp. ed. Princeton: Princeton University Press, 2004.

Kreimeier, Klaus. *Kino und Filmindustrie in der BRD: Ideologieproduktion und Klassenwirklichkeit nach 1945.* Kronberg: Scriptor, 1973.

———. "Die Ökonomie der Gefühle: Aspekte des westdeutschen Nachkriegsfilms." In *Zwischen Gestern und Morgen: Westdeutscher Nachkriegsfilm 1946–1962,* ed. Hilmar Hoffmann and Walter Schobert, 8–28. Frankfurt: Deutsches Filmmuseum, 1989.

Krüger, Kai. "Im Kino darf wieder geweint werden: Ein Obstbaumhändler macht mit alten Heimatfilmen ein Millionengeschäft." *Die Zeit,* 16 February 1973.

Kurowski, Ulrich. "1945–1960: Eine kleine (west-)deutsche Filmgeschichte." *epd Film* 7 (1985): 22–26.

Kurowski, Ulrich, and Sylvia Wolf. *Das Münchner Film- und Kinobuch.* Ebersberg: Achteinhalb, 1988.

Lange, Günter. *Heimat: Realität und Aufgabe: Zur marxistischen Auffassung des Heimatbegriffs.* Berlin: Akademie-Verlag, 1973.

Lange, Rudolf. "Das norddeutsche 'Schwarzwaldmädel': Der Farbfilm 'Grün ist die Heide' im Palast-Theater uraufgeführt." *Hannoversche Allgemeine,* 15 November 1951.

Liebeneiner, Wolfgang. "Filmindustrie und Filmkunst sind zweierlei!" *Film-Telegramm* 40 (1961): 3–4.

———. "Machen künstlerische Filme den Staat ärmer? Gute Filme müssen Deutschland in der Welt vertreten." *Kölnische Rundschau,* 3 August 1952.

Lienhard, Friedrich. "Heimatkunst?" *Das litterarische Echo* 2.20 (1899–1900): 1394–98.

———. "Los von Berlin?" In *Die Berliner Moderne, 1885–1914,* ed. Jürgen Schutte and Peter Sprengel, 220–24. Stuttgart: Reclam, 1987.

———. *Wasgaufahrten: Ein Zeitbuch.* Stuttgart: Greiner & Pfeiffer, 1912.

Lienhard, Fritz. *Die Vorherrschaft Berlins: Literarische Anregungen.* Leipzig: Georg Heinrich Meyer Heimatverlag, 1900.

Lowry, Stephen. "Ideology and Excess in Nazi Melodrama: *The Golden City.*" *New German Critique* 74 (1998): 125–50.

Lüthge, Bobby. "Remaking." *Filmblätter* 51–52 (1951): 1065–66.

Maase, Kaspar. *BRAVO Amerika: Erkundungen zur Jugendkultur der Bundesrepublik in den fünfziger Jahren.* Hamburg: Junius, 1992.

———. "Freizeit." In *Die Bundesrepublik Deutschland: Geschichte in drei Bänden,* ed. Wolfgang Benz, vol. 3, 345–83. Frankfurt: Fischer, 1983.

Maetzig, Kurt. *Filmarbeit: Gespräche, Reden, Schriften.* Berlin: Henschel, 1987.

Majer O'Sickey, Ingeborg. "Framing the *Unheimlich: Heimatfilm* and Bambi." In *Gender and Germanness: Cultural Productions of Nation,* ed. Patricia Herminghouse and Magda Mueller. Providence: Berghahn Books, 1997.

Marker, Chris. "Adieu au cinéma allemand?" *Positif* 12 (1954).

Martin, Hermann. "Die Hauptsache—Bärenweiler bleibt! Zur Uraufführung des jüngsten DEFA-Films *Das verurteilte Dorf.*" *BZ am Abend,* 20 February 1952.

———. "So märchenhaft und so modern: 'Einmal ist keinmal'—ein heiterer, musikalischer Farbfilm der DEFA." *BZ am Abend,* 28 March 1955.

———. "52 Wochen sind eine Jahr: Ein DEFA-Film nach dem gleichnamigen Roman von Nationalpreisträger Jurij Brezan." *BZ am Abend,* 21 November 1955.

Massey, Doreen. "A Place Called Home." *New Formations* 17 (1992): 3–15.

———. *Space, Place and Gender.* Cambridge: Polity, 1994.

McLaughlin, Thomas. "Figurative Language." In *Critical Terms for Literary Study,* ed. Frank Lentricchia and Thomas McLaughlin. Chicago: University of Chicago Press, 1990.

Menter, Leo. "Das verurteilte Dorf." *Neue Filmwelt,* 1952–53.

Mettenleiter, Peter. *Destruktion der Heimatdichtung: Typologische Untersuchungen zu Gotthelf, Auerbach, Ganghofer.* Tübingen: Tübinger Vereinigung für Volkskunde, 1974.

Meyer, Jochen, ed. *Berlin/Provinz: Literarische Kontroversen um 1930.* Marbach: Deutsche Schillergesellschaft, 1985.

Mitscherlich, Alexander, and Margarete Mitscherlich. *The Inability to Mourn: Principles of Collective Behavior.* Trans. Beverly Placzek. New York: Grove, 1975.

Moeller, Robert G. *Protecting Motherhood: Women and the Family in the Politics of Postwar West Germany.* Berkeley: University of California Press, 1993.

———. "Sinking Ships, the Lost Heimat, and Broken Taboos: Günter Grass and the Politics of Memory in Contemporary Germany." *Contemporary European History* 12.2 (2003): 147–81.

———. *War Stories: The Search for a Usable Past in the Federal Republic of Germany.* Berkeley: University of California Press, 2001.

Moltke, Johannes von. "Evergreens: The Heimat Genre." In *The German Cinema Book,* ed. Tim Bergfelder, Erica Carter, and Deniz Göktürk, 18–28. London: BFI, 2002.

———. "Heimat and History: *Viehjud Levi.*" *New German Critique* 87 (2002): 83–105.

———. "*Standort* Heimat: Tracking Refugee Images from DEFA to the *Heimatfilm.*" In *German Cinema of the 1950s,* ed. John Davidson and Sabine Hake. Providence: Berghahn Books, forthcoming.

———. "Trapped in America: The Americanization of the *Trapp-Familie.*" *German Studies Review* 19.3 (1996): 455–78.

Moltke, Johannes von, and Hans J. Wulff. "Trümmer-Diva: Hilde Knef." In *Idole des deutschen Films,* ed. Thomas Koebner, 304–17. Munich: Text + Kritik, 1997.

Morley, David. "Bounded Realms: Household, Family, Community, and Nation." In *Home, Exile, Homeland: Film, Media, and the Politics of Place,* ed. Hamid Naficy, 151–68. London: Routledge, 1999.

———. *Home Territories: Media, Mobility, and Identity.* London: Routledge, 2000.

Morley, David, and Kevin Robbins. *Spaces of Identity: Global Media, Electronic Landscapes, and Cultural Boundaries.* London: Routledge, 1995.

mtr. "Sorbische Ernte." *Die Frau von heute,* 16 December 1952.

Mulvey, Laura. "Visual Pleasure and Narrative Cinema." *Visual and Other Pleasures.* Bloomington: Indiana University Press, 1989.

Naficy, Hamid, ed. *Home, Exile, Homeland: Film, Media, and the Politics of Place.* London: Routledge, 1999.

Naughton, Leonie. *That Was the Wild East: Film Culture, Unification, and the "New" Germany.* Ann Arbor: University of Michigan Press, 2002.

Neale, Stephen. *Genre.* London: BFI, 1980.

———. *Genre and Hollywood.* London: Routledge, 2000.

———. "Questions of Genre." *Screen* 31.1 (1990): 44–66.

Neumann, Hans-Joachim. *Der deutsche Film heute.* Frankfurt: Ullstein, 1986.

Niethammer, Lutz. " 'Normalization' in the West: Traces of Memory Leading Back into the 1950s." In *The Miracle Years: A Cultural History of West Germany, 1949–1968,* ed. Hanna Schissler, 237–65. Princeton: Princeton University Press, 2001.

Nipperdey, Thomas. "Probleme der Modernisierung in Deutschland." *Nachdenken über die deutsche Geschichte: Essays,* 44–59. Munich: Beck, 1986.

Oly. "Grün ist die Heide." *Film-Kurier,* 10 December 1932.

Ostermayr, Peter. "Bessere Autoren, bessere Filme." *Film-Kurier,* 13 July 1962.

Palfreyman, Rachel. *Edgar Reitz's Heimat: Histories, Traditions, Fictions.* Oxford: P. Lang, 2000.

Patalas, Enno. "Phantomkino: *Nachtschatten* von Niklaus Schilling." *Süddeutsche Zeitung,* 28 November 1972.

———. "Die zerrissene Leinwand: Zweimal Kino deutsch, 1945 bis heute." *Die Zeit,* 18 October 1999.

Peters, John Durham. "Exile, Nomadism, and Diaspora: The Stakes of Mobility in the Western Canon." In *Home, Exile, Homeland: Film, Media, and the Politics of Place,* ed. Hamid Naficy, 17–41. London: Routledge, 1999.

Petri, Rolf. "Deutsche Heimat 1850–1950." *Comparativ: Leipziger Beiträge zur Universalgeschichte und vergleichenden Gesellschaftsforschung* 11.1 (2001): 77–127.

Pf., G. "Auf der Leinwand: Grün ist die Heide." *Der Tagesspiegel,* 20 December 1951.

Pfeil, Elisabeth. *Der Flüchtling: Gestalt einer Zeitenwende.* Hamburg: H. von Hugo, 1948.

Pflaum, Hans Günther. "Auf der Suche nach Heimat." In *Film in der BRD,* ed. Heinz Müller. Berlin: Henschel, 1990.

Poiger, Uta. *Jazz, Rock, and Rebels: Cold War Politics and American Culture in a Divided Germany.* Berkeley: University of California Press, 2000.

Projektgruppe deutscher Heimatfilm. *Der deutsche Heimatfilm—Bildwelten und Weltbilder: Bilder, Texte, Analysen zu 70 Jahren deutscher Filmgeschichte.* Tübingen: Tübinger Vereinigung für Volkskunde, 1989.

Rabenalt, Arthur Maria. *Die Schnulze: Capriccios über ein sämiges Thema.* Munich: Kreisselmeier, 1959.

Rahms, Helene. "Die bleiche Moorlilie: Rosen blühen auf dem Heidegrab." *Frankfurter Allgemeine Zeitung,* 2 February 1953.

Rapp, Christian. *Höhenrausch: Der deutsche Bergfilm.* Vienna: Sonderzahl, 1997.

Rehahn, Rosemarie. "Das große Filmepos vom nationalen Widerstand: Der neue realistische Film der DEFA *Das verurteilte Dorf* mit großem Erfolg uraufgeführt." *Neues Deutschland,* 17 February 1952.

Reitz, Edgar. *Drehort Heimat: Arbeitsnotizen und Zukunftsentwürfe.* Frankfurt: Verlag der Autoren, 1993.

———. *Liebe zum Kino.* Cologne: Verlag Köln, 1983.

Reitz, Edgar, and Peter Steinbach. *Heimat: Eine deutsche Chronik.* Nördlingen: Grenco, 1984.

Rentschler, Eric. "Film der achtziger Jahre: Endzeitspiele und Zeitgeistszenarien." In *Geschichte des deutschen Films,* ed. Wolfgang Jacobsen, Anton Kaes, and Hans Helmut Prinzler, 283–322. Stuttgart: Metzler, 1993.

———. "From New German Cinema to the Postwall Cinema of Consensus." In *Cinema and Nation,* ed. Mette Hjort and Scott MacKenzie, 260–77. London: Routledge, 2000.

———. "How American Is It? The U.S. as Image and Imaginary in German Film." *German Quarterly* 57.4 (1984): 603–20.

———. *The Ministry of Illusion: Nazi Cinema and Its Afterlife.* Cambridge, Mass.: Harvard University Press, 1996.

———. "Mountains and Modernity: Relocating the *Bergfilm*." *New German Critique* 51 (1990): 137–61.

———. "Remembering Not to Forget: A Retrospective Reading of Kluge's *Brutality in Stone*." *New German Critique* 49 (1990): 23–41.

———. *West German Film in the Course of Time: Reflections on the Twenty Years since Oberhausen*. Bedford Hills: Redgrave, 1984.

———, ed. *West German Filmmakers on Film: Visions and Voices*. New York: Holmes & Meier, 1988.

Riesenberger, Dieter. "Heimatgedanke und Heimatgeschichte in der DDR." In *Antimodernismus und Reform: Zur Geschichte der deutschen Heimatbewegung*, ed. Edeltraud Klueting, 320–43. Darmstadt: Wissenschaftliche Buchgesellschaft, 1991.

Riess, Curt. *Das gibt's nur einmal: Das Buch des deutschen Films nach 1945*. Hamburg: Nannen, 1958.

Rippey, Ted, Melissa Sundell, and Suzanne Townley. "'Ein wunderbares Heute': The Evolution and Functionalization of 'Heimat' in West German Heimat Films of the 1950s." In *Heimat, Nation, Fatherland: The German Sense of Belonging*, ed. Jost Hermand and James D. Steakley, 137–59. New York: P. Lang, 1996.

Ross, Kristin. *Fast Cars, Clean Bodies: Decolonization and the Reordering of French Culture*. Cambridge, Mass.: MIT Press, 1995.

Rossbacher, Karlheinz. *Heimatkunstbewegung und Heimatroman: Zu einer Literatursoziologie der Jahrhundertwende*. Stuttgart: Klett, 1975.

Rushdie, Salman. *The Wizard of Oz*. London: BFI, 1992.

Saalmann, Dieter. "Edgar Reitz's View of History: The New Religion of Regionalism and the Concept of Heimat." *Germanic Notes* 19.1–2 (1988): 8–14.

Santner, Eric. "On the Difficulty of Saying 'We': The Historians' Debate and Edgar Reitz's *Heimat*." In *Framing the Past: The Historiography of German Cinema and Television*, ed. Bruce Murray and Christopher Wickham, 261–79. Carbondale: Southern Illinois University Press, 1992.

———. *Stranded Objects: Mourning, Memory, and Film in Postwar Germany*. Ithaca: Cornell University Press, 1989.

Schacht, Daniel Alexander. *Fluchtpunkt Provinz: Der neue Heimatfilm zwischen 1968 und 1972*. Münster: MAkS, 1991.

Schama, Simon. *Landscape and Memory*. New York: A. A. Knopf, 1995.

Schelsky, Helmut. "Die Flüchtlingsfamilie." *Kölner Zeitschrift für Soziologie* 3.2 (1951): 159–77.

———. *Wandlungen der deutschen Familie in der Gegenwart: Darstellung und Deutung einer empirisch-soziologischen Tatbestandsaufnahme*. Dortmund: Ardey, 1953.

Schenk, Ralf. "Mitten im kalten Krieg: 1950 bis 1960." In *Das Zweite Leben der Filmstadt Babelsberg: DEFA-Spielfilme, 1946–1992*, ed. Ralf Schenk and Christiane Mückenberger. Berlin: Henschel, 1994.

Schenk, Ralf, and Christiane Mückenberger. *Das Zweite Leben der Filmstadt Babelsberg: DEFA-Spielfilme, 1946–1992*. Berlin: Henschel, 1994.

Schieder, Theodor, ed. *Documents on the Expulsion of the Germans from Eastern-Central-Europe.* Bonn: Bundesministerium für Vertriebene, 1958–60.

————, ed. *Dokumentation der Vertreibung der Deutschen aus Ost-Mitteleuropa: Gesamtausgabe in 8 Bänden.* Reissue. Munich: dtv, 1984.

————. *Die Vertreibung der deutschen Bevölkerung aus den Gebieten östlich der Oder-Neisse.* Bonn: Bundesministerium für Vertriebene, 1954.

Schildt, Axel, and Arnold Sywottek, eds. *Modernisierung im Wiederaufbau: Die westdeutsche Gesellschaft der 50er Jahre.* Bonn: J. H. W. Dietz, 1998.

————. "'Reconstruction' and 'Modernization': West German Social History during the 1950s." In *West Germany under Construction: Politics, Society, and Culture in the Adenauer Era,* ed. Robert G. Moeller. Ann Arbor: University of Michigan Press, 1997.

Schissler, Hanna, ed. *The Miracle Years: A Cultural History of West Germany, 1949–1968.* Princeton: Princeton University Press, 2001.

Schlink, Bernhard. *Heimat als Utopie.* Frankfurt: Suhrkamp, 2000.

Schlüpmann, Heide. "Wir Wunderkinder: Tradition und Regression im bundesdeutschen Film der fünfziger Jahre." *Frauen und Film* 35 (1983): 4–11.

Schmidt, Arno. *Die Umsiedler.* Frankfurt: Suhrkamp, 2002.

Schmidt, Thomas E. *Heimat: Leichtigkeit und Last des Herkommens.* Berlin: Aufbau-Verlag, 1999.

Schmidt-Harzbach, Ingrid. "Eine Woche im April: Vergewaltigung als Massenschicksal." In *BeFreier und Befreite: Krieg, Vergewaltigungen, Kinder,* ed. Helke Sander and Barbara Johr, 21–45. Munich: Kunstmann, 1992.

Schmieding, Walter. *Kunst oder Kasse: Der Ärger mit dem deutschen Film.* Hamburg: Rütten & Löning, 1961.

Schneider, Tassilo. "Genre and Ideology in the Popular German Cinema 1950–1972." Ph.D. diss., University of Southern California, 1994.

Schnurre, Wolfdietrich. *Rettung des deutschen Films: Eine Streitschrift.* Stuttgart: DVA, 1952.

Schröder, Otto. "Die bourgeoise Heimatideologie: Bestandteil imperialistischer Massenverführung." In *Der Bürger und seine Heimatstadt,* ed. Akademie für Staats- und Rechtswissenschaft der DDR, 87–91. Berlin: Staatsverlag der DDR, 1979.

Schulte-Sasse, Linda. *Entertaining the Third Reich: Illusions of Wholeness in Nazi Cinema.* Durham: Duke University Press, 1996.

Schwarz, Sigrid. "Die Liebe zur Heimat." Ph.D. diss., Humboldt Universität, 1957.

Schwerbrock, Wolfgang. "Der Siegeszug der Blockflöte: Zu dem Film *Die Trapp-Familie.*" *Frankfurter Allgemeine Zeitung,* 3 January 1957.

Schwerte, Hans. "Ganghofers Gesundung." In *Studien zur Trivialliteratur,* ed. Heinz Otto Burger, 154–208. Frankfurt: Vittorio Klostermann, 1976.

Sebald, W. G. *On the Natural History of Destruction: With Essays on Alfred Andersch, Jean Améry and Peter Weiss.* Trans. Anthea Bell. London: Hamish Hamilton, 2003.

Seeßlen, Georg. "Durch die Heimat und so weiter: Heimatfilme, Schlagerfilme und Ferienfilme der fünfziger Jahre." In *Zwischen Gestern und Morgen:*

Westdeutscher Nachkriegsfilm 1946–1962, ed. Hilmar Hoffmann and Walter Schobert, 136–61. Frankfurt: Deutsches Filmmuseum, 1989.

———. "Der Heimatfilm: Zur Mythologie eines Genres." In *Der Sprung im Spiegel: Filmisches Wahrnehmen zwischen Fiktion und Wirklichkeit,* ed. Christa Blümlinger, 343–62. Vienna: Sonderzahl, 1990.

———. *Volks Tümlichkeit.* Greiz: Weisser Stein, 1993.

Seeßlen, Georg, and Bernt Kling. *Unterhaltung: Lexikon zur populären Kultur.* 2 vols. Reinbek: Rowohlt, 1977.

Seidl, Claudius. *Der deutsche Film der fünfziger Jahre.* Munich: Heyne, 1987.

Shandley, Robert R. *Rubble Films: German Cinema in the Shadow of the Third Reich.* Philadelphia: Temple University Press, 2001.

Sibley, David. *Geographies of Exclusion: Society and Difference in the West.* London: Routledge, 1995.

Siepmann, Eckhard, ed. *Bikini: Die fünfziger Jahre: Kalter Krieg und Capri-Sonne.* Reinbek: Rowohlt, 1981.

Simmel, Georg. "The Alpine Journey." *Simmel on Culture: Selected Writings.* Ed. David Frisby and Mike Featherstone. London: Sage, 1997.

Sinjen, Marlen. "Der Vater des Heimatfilms." *Bild-Zeitung,* 16 July 1957.

Sirk, Douglas. *Sirk on Sirk: Conversations with Jon Halliday.* London: Faber & Faber, 1997.

Sloterdijk, Peter. "Der gesprengte Behälter: Notiz über die Krise des Heimatbegriffs in der globalisierten Welt." *Spiegel Spezial* 6 (1999): 24–29.

Smith, Murray. *Engaging Characters: Fiction, Emotion, and the Cinema.* Oxford: Oxford University Press, 1995.

Soja, Edward W. *Postmodern Geographies: The Reassertion of Space in Critical Social Theory.* London: Verso, 1989.

Sontag, Susan. "Fascinating Fascism." *Under the Sign of Saturn,* 71–105. New York: Vintage, 1981.

Spickernagel, Wilhelm. "Der Kinematograph im Dienste der Heimatkunst." *Hannoverland: Parteilose Zeitschrift für die Pflege der Heimatkunde und des Heimatschutzes unserer niedersächsischen Heimat* 6 (1912): 234.

Spranger, Eduard. *Der Bildungswert der Heimatkunde.* Stuttgart: Reclam, 1952.

Stapel, Wilhelm. "The Intellectual and His People." In *The Weimar Republic Sourcebook,* ed. Anton Kaes, Martin Jay, and Edward Dimendberg, 423–25. Berkeley: University of California Press, 1994.

Stavenhagen, Kurt. *Heimat als Lebenssinn.* Göttingen: Vandenhoeck & Ruprecht, 1948.

Steiner, Gertraud. "Von der Heimatdichtung zum Heimatfilm." In *Heimat: Auf der Suche nach der verlorenen Identität,* ed. Joachim Riedl, 80–85. Vienna: Brandstätter, 1995.

Stern, Frank. "Film in the 1950s: Passing Images of Guilt and Responsibility." In *The Miracle Years: A Cultural History of West Germany, 1949–1968,* ed. Hanna Schissler, 266–80. Princeton: Princeton University Press, 2001.

Stern, Fritz Richard. *The Politics of Cultural Despair: A Study in the Rise of the Germanic Ideology.* Berkeley: University of California Press, 1974.

Storch, Joachim. "Grün ist die Heide." *Frankfurter Allgemeine Zeitung,* 15 September 1980.

Südbeck, Thomas. "Motorisierung, Verkehrsentwicklung und Verkehrspolitik in Westdeutschland in den 50er Jahren." In *Modernisierung im Wiederaufbau: Die westdeutsche Gesellschaft der 50er Jahre,* ed. Arnold Sywottek, 170–87. Bonn: J. H. W. Dietz, 1998.

Sywottek, Arnold. "From Starvation to Excess? Trends in Consumer Society from the 1940s to the 1970s." In *The Miracle Years: A Cultural History of West Germany, 1949–1968,* ed. Hanna Schissler, 341–58. Princeton: Princeton University Press, 2001.

Tönnies, Ferdinand. *Gemeinschaft und Gesellschaft: Grundbegriffe der reinen Soziologie.* Darmstadt: Wissenschaftliche Buchgesellschaft, 1972.

Trapp, Maria Augusta von. *Die Trapp Familie: Vom Kloster zum Welterfolg.* Vienna: Fink, 1957.

Travers, Martin. *Critics of Modernity: The Literature of the Conservative Revolution in Germany, 1890–1933.* New York: P. Lang, 2001.

Trimborn, Jürgen. *Der deutsche Heimatfilm der fünfziger Jahre: Motive, Symbole und Handlungsmuster.* Cologne: Teiresias, 1998.

Trimmel, Gerald. *Heimkehr: Strategien eines nationalsozialistischen Films.* Vienna: Werner Eichbauer Verlag, 1998.

Truffaut, François. "A Certain Tendency in the French Cinema." In *Movies and Methods: An Anthology,* ed. Bill Nichols, 224–37. Berkeley: University of California Press, 1976.

Trumpener, Katie. *The Divided Screen: The Cinemas of Postwar Germany.* Princeton: Princeton University Press, forthcoming.

Urry, John. *Consuming Places.* London: Routledge, 1995.

Wächtler, Fritz. *Deutsches Volk, deutsche Heimat.* 4 vols. Munich: Deutscher Volksverlag, 1935.

Wehler, Hans-Ulrich. "Die Debatte wirkt befreiend." *Spiegel Spezial* 2 (2000): 19–21.

Welch, David. *Propaganda and the German Cinema, 1933–1945.* London: I. B. Tauris, 2001.

"Wer kennt den 'Ostmärkischen Heimatfilm.'" *Film-Kurier,* 20 October 1926.

Westermann, Bärbel. *Nationale Identität im Spielfilm der fünfziger Jahre.* Frankfurt: P. Lang, 1990.

Wickham, Christopher. "Representation and Mediation in Edgar Reitz's *Heimat.*" *German Quarterly* 64.1 (1991): 35–45.

Williams, Raymond. *The Country and the City.* Oxford: Oxford University Press, 1973.

———. *Keywords: A Vocabulary of Culture and Society.* New York: Oxford University Press, 1985.

Witte, Karsten. "Film im Nationalsozialismus: Blendung und Überblendung." In *Geschichte des deutschen Films,* ed. Wolfgang Jacobsen, Anton Kaes, and Hans Helmut Prinzler, 119–70. Stuttgart: Metzler, 1993.

————. "Visual Pleasure Inhibited: Aspects of the German Revue Film." *New German Critique* 24–25 (1983): 238–63.

Wolfram, Manfred K. "Film in the Federal Republic of Germany." In *Contemporary Germany: Politics and Culture,* ed. Charles Burton Burdick, Hans Adolf Jacobsen, and Winfried Kudszus. Boulder: Westview Press, 1984.

Zimmermann, Peter, ed. *Der geteilte Himmel: Arbeit, Alltag und Geschichte im ost- und westdeutschen Film.* Constance: UVK-Medien, 2000.

"Zum Tode Peter Ostermayrs." *Süddeutsche Zeitung,* 10 May 1967.

"52 Wochen sind ein Jahr: Ein packender Film aus der schönen deutschen Heimat." *Baustoffe des Friedens: Betriebszeitung des VEB Zement- und Betonwerke Rüdersdorf,* 8 December 1955.

Index